Gay Rights, Military Wrongs

D0076743

GARLAND REFERENCE LIBRARY OF SOCIAL SCIENCE
VOLUME 1049

Gay Rights, Military Wrongs
Political Perspectives on Lesbians and Gays in the Military

Edited by
Craig A. Rimmerman

Garland Publishing, Inc.
New York and London
1996

Copyright © 1996 by Craig A. Rimmerman
All rights reserved

Library of Congress Cataloging-in-Publication Data

Gay rights, military wrongs : political perspectives on lesbians and gays in the
    military / edited by Craig A. Rimmerman.
            p.   cm. — (Garland reference library of social science ; v. 1049)
    Includes bibliographical references and index.
    ISBN 0-8153-2086-8 (hardcover)(alk. paper)—
    ISBN 0-8153-2580-0 (paperback)
        1. United States—Armed Forces—Gays.   2. United States—Military
policy.   3. United States—Politics and government—1993–
I. Rimmerman, Craig A.   II. Series.
UB418.G38G35   1996
355'.008'664—dc20   96-20929
                                                                            CIP

Cover design by Heather Parke, Neuwirth Associates, New York.

Printed on acid-free, 250-year-life paper
Manufactured in the United States of America

To my lesbian, gay, and bisexual students

Contents

Part III: Policy Implications

Contributors

Michelle M. Benecke is a former Captain and Battery Commander in the United States Army who has counseled gay servicemembers and veterans on their legal rights for the past four years. She has written and spoken extensively on the military's policy toward lesbians, gay men, and bisexuals. She became an authority on how the military's gay ban disproportionately affects all women, regardless of sexual orientation, via her article "Military Women in Nontraditional Job Fields" (*Harvard Women's Law Journal*). She has made numerous public appearances, including testimony before Congressional committees and Department of Defense advisory groups. She was a consultant to the Campaign for Military Service on military and legal issues during the Campaign's recent effort to lift the ban. She is a National Board member of the Gay, Lesbian, and Bisexual Alumni/ae Committee of the Harvard Law School Association, Co-Chair of the Military Law Committee for the National Lesbian and Gay Law Association, and a 1994 Irving R. Kaufman Public Service Fellowship recipient. Her law degree is from Harvard Law School and her B.A. from the University of Virginia.

David Ari Bianco has an M.A. in history from Stanford University. He teaches gay and lesbian history and politics at the Institute of Gay and Lesbian Education in West Hollywood, California.

Francine D'Amico is Assistant Professor of Political Science at Hobart and William Smith Colleges in Geneva, New York, and Visiting Research Fellow with the project on race/gender/sexuality/class and the military in the Peace Studies Program at Cornell University. She and Peter Beckman are coeditors of two anthologies on gender and international relations, *Women, Gender, and World Politics: Perspectives, Policies, and Prospects* (Berbin & Garvey, 1994) and *Women in World Politics: An Introduction* (Berbin & Garvey, 1995). She is an officer of the Feminist Theory and Gender Studies Section of the International Studies Association, and she obtained her Ph.D. from Cornell University's Department of Government in 1989.

Kirstin S. Dodge has written several law journal articles concerning lesbian and gay rights. In addition to the article that was updated for this volume, Ms. Dodge has explored the negative impacts of military exclusion policies on American society and democracy as a whole in "Countenancing Corruption: A Civic Republican Case Against Judicial Deference to the Military" in the *Yale Journal of Law and Feminism*. Her article "'Bashing Back': Gay and Lesbian Street Patrols and the Criminal Justice System" appeared in *Law and Inequality: A Journal of Theory and Practice*. Ms. Dodge recently created and taught a seminar on Women and the Law, including lesbian rights, to law students and practitioners at the University of Bern, Switzerland. She currently practices employment law in Seattle, Washington, and specializes in bringing lawsuits challenging sex, race, and disability discrimination in the workplace. Ms. Dodge received her law degree from Harvard Law School and her B.A. from Yale University.

Mary Fainsod Katzenstein is Associate Professor of Government, Political Science Department, Cornell University. She is the author/co-author of two books on preferential policies and ethnic politics in India. Her most recent book, co-edited with Carol Meuller, is *Women's Movements of the United States and Western Europe* (Temple, 1987). She is completing a book on feminism in the U.S. military and American Catholic Church tentatively titled *Liberating the Mainstream*.

Gary L. Lehring is an Assistant Professor of Government at Smith College in Northampton, Massachusetts, where he teaches courses in political theory, American politics, and gender and politics. He is author of *Officially Gay: Politics and the Public Construction of Sexuality* (Temple University Press) and a number of articles on lesbian and gay politics.

C. Dixon Osburn worked at the Campaign for Military Service as one of its leading policy/legal analysts. He has counseled servicemembers on their rights under the Reagan policy, the interim policy, and the new Clinton policy. He is Co-Chair of the Military Law Committee for the National Lesbian and Gay Law Association and Co-Chair of the Legal Committee for the Military Freedom Project. Osburn's policy experience includes analysis of current research on sexuality and choice and the military's policy on racial segregation. He worked for the Clinton/Gore transition team's Government Operations cluster and has done extensive research into domestic policy issues. While at Georgetown Graduate School of Business, he created and led seminars on sexual orientation in the workplace. He received both his J.D. and M.B.A. from Georgetown University and his A.B. from Stanford University.

Richard Pacelle is Assistant Professor of Political Science at the University of Missouri-St. Louis. He did his graduate work at Ohio State University. He is the author of *Transformation of the Supreme Court's Agenda: From the New Deal to the Reagan Administration* (Westview, 1991). He has also done work on political litigation and the use of the courts by politically disadvantaged groups. Professor Pacelle's current research is concerned with the notion of issue evolution in the Supreme Court. In that context, he has examined the evolution of First Amendment and abortion rights doctrine.

David M. Rayside is Professor of Political Science and Vice-Principal of University College at the University of Toronto, with an activist as well as an academic interest in gay/lesbian issues. Since the late 1980s, he has published on such topics as anti-discrimination legislation in Ontario, public opinion and gay rights, homophobia in Britain, and AIDS politics in Canada. The article in this volume is part of a book-length manuscript on the entry of gays and lesbians into mainstream politics in Britain, Canada, and the United States to be published by Cornell University Press.

Craig A. Rimmerman is Associate Professor of Political Science at Hobart and William Smith Colleges. He teaches courses in American politics, environmental and urban policy, democratic theory, and gay and lesbian politics. He spent the 1992-93 academic year as an American Political Science Association congressional fellow in the Washington, D.C., offices of Senator Tom Daschle (D-South Dakota) and Rep. Barbara Kennelly (D-Connecticut). Rimmerman is the author of *Presidency by Plebiscite: The Reagan-Bush Era in Institutional Perspective* (Westview, 1993) and a number of articles. He is currently working on a book that examines the relationship between democracy, participation, community service, and the New Citizenship in American politics.

Clyde Wilcox is an Associate Professor of Government at Georgetown University. His research interests include religion and politics. His most recent books are *God at the Grassroots: The Christian Right in the 1994 Elections* (Rowman & Littlefield); *Second Coming: The Christian Right in Virginia Republican Politics* (Johns Hopkins); and *Onward Christian Soldiers: The Christian Right in American Politics* (Westview). He also writes on gender politics (he is co-editor of *The Year of the Woman: Myths and Realities*) and on campaign finance (he is co-author of *Serious Money: Fundraising and Contributing in Presidential Nomination Campaigns* (Cambridge).

Robin M. Wolpert received her Ph.D. in political science at the University of Chicago in 1995. She is currently Assistant Professor of Government and International Studies at the University of South Carolina. Her research interests lie in the field of judicial politics and public law. Her dissertation, "Reframing the Countermajoritarian Problem: Accountability, Representation, and Judicial Review," focuses on whether and under what conditions the Supreme Court is an accountable and representative institution. Her publications include "Opinion-Holding and Public Attitudes Toward Controversial Supreme Court Nominees," with James Gimpel, *Political Research Quarterly* (Spring 1996), and "Rationalizing Support and Opposition to Supreme Court Nominations: The Role of Credentials," with James Gimpel, *Polity* (Fall 1995).

Preface

Margarethe Cammermeyer

Experiencing prejudice is shocking, painful, negating, and eye opening. What is subtle and silenced by discreetness can become a battle cry to mobilize for action. Never in my wildest imagination had I thought I would end up challenging a military policy. I had spent a lifetime in uniform, believing in democracy, in freedom and justice for all. With four words my world was turned upside down and my belief system challenged. In response to questioning in a top secret investigation, I said, "I am a lesbian." Those words triggered the military to initiate discharge procedures against me based on military policy barring homosexuals from serving in the military.

The shock of being declared disruptive to the military after having served for 23 years, including a hellacious 14 months in Viet Nam, was personally devastating. Learning about one's own self is hard enough; accepting being different, and dealing with disclosure to children, family, and friends is like stepping on quicksand and not knowing if you will sink or be supported. To be discarded by the government which I had defended, physically and emotionally, was devastating. And, of course, thinking I was the only one who had made this journey was still more lonely and frightening. It was many months later I found out that I was not alone.

The military has a tragic history of discrimination. No organization justifies discrimination as readily as the military. The rationale for this discrimination is based on the presumption that to not discriminate will reduce the efficiency of the military and impair its ability to perform its mission. This "collective military wisdom" has historically perpetuated discriminating against its membership based on gender, creed, race, ability, physical characteristics, and sexual orientation. Contrary to the "collective military wisdom," the policies which support such discrimination have an uncanny way of changing as the social/cultural climate or the needs of the military change.

Women who had for years been denied career tracks in the military saw changes in policy such that there are now women as general officers, fighter pilots, and, in general, few opportunities denied them based on gender. Likewise, non-white males are now afforded equal opportunity to advance in an integrated military, because the policy of segregation has changed. In neither case has the military been unable to meet its military mission or become less efficient. The military has matured and become more reflective of the greater society by changing its former policies of discrimination based on gender and race.

The foremost bastion of sacred turf in the military and in society has been around the issues of human sexuality, sexual harassment, bonding, sexual conduct and misconduct, and homosexuality. We've seen examples of politicians involved in sexual harassment and misconduct. We've seen examples of military misconduct with Tailhook. We have not heard from or about the thousands of women harassed and physically molested through misconduct of servicemembers. The military's policy surrounding human sexuality and sexual conduct is totally out of sync with today's reality in terms of sexual conduct and misconduct.

Today's youth have a totally different tolerance for sexual conduct and human sexuality than the adult youth of the 1960s. At the same time, the youth of today will and do not tolerate the type of sexual harassment which was supposed to be flattering to women 30 years ago. Catcalls, fanny pinching, unsolicited touching, and being whistled at are not acceptable social behaviors by anyone today.

Until recently, even the word "homosexuality" was not spoken. Issues related to homosexuality, as well as the policy banning homosexuals from serving in the military, were not part of the social consciousness. The ban against homosexuals serving in the military has been an ongoing and evolving change in military policy. The surveillance and scrutiny, the witch hunts, the lesbian baiting, the physical abuse, the imprisonment of gays and lesbians—this has been a hidden secret of military service. From 1980 to 1990 nearly 17,000 servicemembers were discharged from the military because of homosexuality. They were discharged not for misconduct, but merely because they were or were presumed to be homosexual. Servicemembers such as James Woodward, Mariam ben Shalom, Leonard Matlovich and Perry Watkins challenged their discharges. Some cases were won and others lost, but ultimately the policy changed. However, the ban persisted, and the mere statement of "homosexual orientation" remained sufficient to cause discharge from the military.

By the late 1980s and early 1990s, there was a resurgence of challenges to discharges because of homosexual status. Joe Steffan, Tracy Thorn, Tom Paniccia, Justin Elise, Keith Meinhold, Pam Mindt, and Margarethe Cammermeyer, among others, fought to remain in the military. Several of these servicemembers were successful and remain or were reinstated into the military. These cases have also acted as the impetus for public and governmental dialogue on the status of lesbians and gays serving in the military.

During the presidential campaign of 1992, candidate Bill Clinton pledged to repeal the ban. Instead, political pressure, fundamental resistance, and advice of biased military generals persuaded President Clinton to accept a "Don't Ask, Don't Tell, Don't Pursue" policy, which was codified into law in 1993. The new law is being challenged through the courts on constitutional grounds. There is no reprieve at this point, and more lives are in jeopardy, but the struggle for equal protection will continue.

The profound tragedy is that this book needed to be written to make explicit the prejudice and discrimination that continue to exist in the military around the issue of sexual orientation. The persistence of stereotyping and nurturing prejudice and discarding the contributions of servicemembers willing to serve and die for America is America's shame. This book provides the background and rationale (or lack thereof) to explain the political, social, judicial, and personal ramifications of the "Don't Ask, Don't Tell" law.

The frustration is, of course, that those who read it are those who have a vested interest in the issue because they are somehow affected by the policy. They may also be trying to understand the historical underpinnings of the policy. The sadness is that the very people who need to move beyond their own prejudice will not profit from the words herein.

As you read the pages of this book, I hope you can put a face, a life to the existence of servicemembers who are experiencing the prejudice. There is no logic to explain irrational policy, there is no justification for denying humanity, there is no liberty when anyone is denied theirs, and there is no free America until everyone is free.

In Appreciation,
Colonel Margarethe Cammermeyer AN, Ph.D., ARNP

Acknowledgments

This book would not have been completed without the support of many different people. First, and foremost, I thank my contributors who worked so hard and diligently to complete their respective essays in a relatively short period of time. I couldn't have asked for a more dedicated and supportive group of colleagues with whom to work.

Thank you to Hazel Dayton Gunn, as well, for her superb work in preparing this manuscript in its necessary camera ready form. I am fortunate to have had Hazel's talent and expertise devoted to this manuscript. When I became frustrated or worried that I would never make the necessary deadlines, Hazel offered words of encouragement, support, and general good cheer.

There would have been no book were it not for the encouragement and dedication of Garland Publishing editor Claudia Hirsch. I am privileged to have worked with such a talented editor. I know that this book is a much better volume as a result of Claudia's many thoughtful suggestions throughout the writing and editorial process. Claudia represents the perfect combination of toughness, seriousness of purpose, and genuine support that I associate with the very best editors.

I am indebted to Anne Sanow, whose copyediting efforts have improved the overall quality of this book. Garland editor Phyllis Korper entered the production process at a crucial stage and helped massage the edited manuscript into final form. Chuck Bartelt, Garland's Director of Computer Resources, patiently provided technical assistance to guide the production process.

Ken Sherrill read the entire manuscript carefully and made a number of useful suggestions to all of the contributors. I know that the book is much improved as a result of Ken's thoughtful and perceptive comments. I am honored to have had this edited volume reviewed by someone who has demonstrated a record of scholarly excellence in American politics and the politics of sexual minorities.

Mary Newcombe was most helpful in sending me an array of legal documents pertaining to the Cammermeyer case. Thank you to Mary and others in the legal profession who are working daily to challenge laws that discriminate against lesbians and gays who wish to serve openly in the military. And I am grateful to David Ari Bianco for contributing the title of the book.

Thank you, as well, to the Hobart and William Smith Colleges research committee, which was generous enough to support this book's completion with a 1994-95 research grant. I appreciate the faith that my faculty colleagues serving on the research committee had in this project.

Finally, there are a number of colleagues who have supported me in so many ways since I arrived at Hobart and William Smith Colleges roughly ten years ago. Many of these colleagues have reminded me by example of the integral connection between quality teaching and scholarship. Thank you to Peter Beckman, Mary Caponegro, Manisha Desai, Richard Dillon, Alan Frishman, Robert Gross, Chris Gunn, Steven Lee, Derek Linton, Judith McKinney, Scott McKinney, Dunbar Moodie, Ilene Nicholas, David Ost, Eric Patterson, Lee Quinby, and Deborah Tall.

I gratefully acknowledge permission from West Publishing Company to reprint Judge Thomas Zilly's decision in the Cammermeyer v. Aspin case. Mary Fainsod Katzenstein's essay is a revised version of an article published earlier in the Spring 1993 issue of *Minerva*. Michelle M. Benecke and Kirstin S. Dodge's chapter is a revised version of "Military Women in Nontraditional Job Fields: Casualties of the Armed Forces' War on Homosexuals," originally published in Volume 12 of *The Harvard Women's Law Journal* (1990). I gratefully acknowledge, as well, permission from the RAND National Defense Research Institute to reprint tables 4 and 5 in Francine D'Amico's essay. These tables were originally published in RAND's *Sexual Orientation and US Military Personnel Policy: Options and Assessment* (1993).

I dedicate this book to my lesbian, gay, and bisexual students. I often tell my students that it is much easier for lesbian, gay, and bisexual students to "come out" now, than it was for those of us grappling with issues of sexuality as college undergraduates in the mid to late 1970s. But I realize that it is still not easy now. I admire the courage and commitment of so many young people at Hobart and William Smith Colleges and other college campuses who reveal such inner strength by identifying themselves as lesbian, gay, or bisexual. If anything, I hope that the existence of this book serves as enthusiastic support and encouragement for these individual and collective acts of courage, solidarity, and resistance.

Introduction

Craig A. Rimmerman

In the fall of 1991, then-presidential candidate Bill Clinton was asked at a Harvard University forum whether he would issue an executive order to rescind the ban on lesbians and gays in the military. Clinton responded "Yes," and explained further: "I think people who are gay should be expected to work, and should be given the opportunity to serve the country." He continued with this pledge as a presidential candidate and as President-elect. It is that promise which serves as the basis for this book.

The military ban and Clinton's attempt to overturn it raise a number of compelling questions. Why was there such furious and sustained opposition to Clinton's original promise? What are the sources of this opposition? To what extent was Clinton's promise due to changing cultural factors regarding lesbians and gays in the larger society? Why did Congress toughen Clinton's compromise proposal? What are the broader implications of how this issue was resolved for the lesbian and gay movement? What specific strategies should the movement pursue in light of how the military ban issue was resolved by the President and Congress? How have other nations addressed lesbian and gay participation in the armed forces? What can the United States learn from their experiences?

The debate over the military ban also raises an interesting set of questions rooted in race and gender concerns. What parallels might be drawn between the experiences of African Americans and lesbians and gay men in the military in both contemporary and historical context? Have the experiences of lesbians in the military been different from those of gay men? Are there any similarities in the ways that heterosexual military women have been treated when compared to the experiences of lesbians and gay men? The essays in this volume will collectively address all of the above questions.

In doing so, this book places the recent debate over lesbians and gays in its appropriate historical, theoretical, political, and policy context. The central focus, however, is on the forces that led to the Clinton compromise proposal and the consequences of the compromise in its first year of policy implementation. The Clinton compromise policy would have ended the long time military practice of questioning recruits or those seeking security clearances about their sexual orientation. In addition, all investigations designed to interrogate unsubstantiated reports of homosexuality would also have been eliminated. However, the Clinton proposal still permitted the military to investigate private disclosures of an individual's sexual orientation with the possibility that individual could be discharged.[1]

For the lesbian and gay movement, the Clinton compromise was a shattering disappointment. For students of American politics, however, the way that the issue was resolved raises interesting questions regarding how a developing social movement interacts with established political institutions such as the Presidency, the Congress, and the judicial system as it pursues its goals. With the election of a "friend" in the White House, movement members expected progress to be made in three areas—the military ban, AIDS, and a lesbian and gay civil rights bill. The movement clearly viewed Clinton's election as an opportunity for progress in achieving greater equality for lesbians and gays.

The authors in this volume have much to say about the broader implications of Clinton's failed attempt to overturn the military ban. Clinton himself has responded with anger on various occasions when he has been criticized by the press, the public, and fellow politicians for being too eager to compromise without fighting for principle. He does deserve some credit for raising a difficult political issue and attempting to overturn the ban. However, by failing to explain to the American people that the military ban is rooted in bigotry and prejudice, and thus needs to be abolished, Clinton failed to assume his important leadership and educative role.

The Clinton compromise prompted furious debate in the lesbian and gay community over whether progress had really been made. Some argued that the compromise represented a step forward, however small. Margarethe Cammermeyer, for one, believes that it "showed a new realization that gays and lesbians really were in the military, and that their silent presence was not a problem and did not undermine the mission." Cammermeyer points out, as well, that the Clinton plan would enable gradual and incremental change within the broad policy itself, thus ultimately leading to an elimination of the ban.[2]

Others were outraged that a President who appeared to be so committed to eliminating the ban through executive order would be so eager to compromise without fighting for his original goal as a matter of principle. To think that this is all the lesbian and gay community achieved after many months of public debate and discussion of the issue is a serious disappointment. This disappointment is reflected in the view that Bill Clinton sacrificed a golden opportunity to extend the civil rights of lesbians and gays by adhering to his original promise. Furthermore, as one student of lesbian and gay politics told me, Clinton's unwillingness to fight for a principled civil rights position on this issue has made it much more difficult for future Presidents to support an outright elimination of the ban.

Of course, many members of Congress certainly deserve considerable blame for their reaction to Clinton's original promise, as well as for their response to Clinton's compromise proposal. His proposal had been carefully negotiated to secure the approval of the Joint Chiefs of Staff, who had previously steadfastly opposed outright elimination of the ban. Unfortunately, in response to the efforts of the Senate and House Armed Services Committee,

Congress approved legislation that prohibited open lesbians and gays from serving in the military. A crucial difference between the Clinton compromise proposal and the tougher congressional law is that the Clinton proposal would have been issued with a Defense Department Directive, whereas Congress actually passed tough legislation designed to prevent open lesbians and gays from serving. If this policy is to be altered in the future, Congress will have to hold hearings on specific legislation, and take a formal vote. After many months of national debate, discussion, and compromise, it is no longer possible for a President of the United States to issue an executive order to overturn the ban. In addition, the way that the "Don't Ask, Don't Tell, Don't Pursue" compromise has been implemented over the first year of its existence suggests that the final policy adopted by Congress has been an abysmal short term failure from the vantage point of lesbians and gays. Military officials continue to violate the basic elements of the new policy. There is little evidence that the situation for lesbians and gays in the military will improve in the foreseeable future.

Perhaps to better understand how lesbians and gays are the targets of discrimination in the United States military, we need to examine the military policies of other countries. For example, we might ask this question: why is it that the United States is the only NATO country, except Britain, that has not recognized the right of lesbian women and gay men to serve openly in the military? We know that lesbians and gays have lost their lives, have been wounded, and have served with dignity and honor on behalf of the United States for years. But as a country we seemingly cannot accept the idea of open lesbians and gays serving in the United States military. To be sure, open integration challenges conservative interpretations of masculinity that are understandably associated with the military, interpretations that women have had to resist and challenge for years. This notion of masculinity, which is inextricably linked with the construction of heterosexuality, is associated with the military's vision of what it means to be a good soldier. Perhaps this is why the Joint Chiefs of Staff, led by Colin Powell, fought to thwart President Clinton's original goal to overturn the ban. From Clinton's vantage point, it was too much to ask that he would challenge the defense and military establishment, given his own lack of popularity with the military as well as the fact that he secured only 43 percent of the popular vote in the 1992 presidential election. Not surprisingly, then, Clinton caved in to forces that reflect the primacy and dominance of heterosexuality within both the military and the larger society.

In the end, opponents of overturning the ban recognize that the acceptance of lesbians and gays in the military could well lead to expanded civil rights in other areas of society. The religious right and conservative forces in Congress and the military want to prevent the extension of basic civil rights to all lesbians and gays at all cost. It is precisely the importance of achieving basic civil rights that makes overturning the ban so important, given that this policy is sanctioned by the highest levels of government. As we will see in the essays that follow, the failure to achieve this goal makes the short term resolution of the issue all the more disappointing.

THE POLICY CONTEXT

The first section of the book explores the broad policy context for understanding the military ban and President Clinton's attempt to overturn it. All three chapters in this section explore the ways in which race and gender intersect with sexuality in both contemporary and historical context as reflected in the military's attempts to prevent lesbians and gays from serving openly. This section embraces the notion that the real question emanating from this debate is not whether lesbians and gays will serve, but what the military's policy should be for those who do serve.

Francine D'Amico's essay examines the importance of studying race and gender for gaining a better understanding of the military ban in contemporary context. Her analysis explores how the U.S. military's gay/lesbian exclusion policy is both raced and gendered. The very fact that African Americans and women can now serve suggests that there has been progress over time in combatting military discrimination. This point is important because it indicates that it is possible for the military to embrace change within its ranks (albeit incremental change generally imposed by outside forces, such as the President or the legal system). Her chapter also offers a comparative analysis of the military ban by examining how other NATO countries have dealt with lesbians and gays who wish to serve openly. The goal is to draw lessons from other countries' policies and practices so that we might better understand the limitations of the military ban in the United States.

Race has intersected with the debate over Clinton's promise in other ways as well. One frequent strategy of those opposed to the ban was to compare it to racial segregation in the military. The ban's supporters, including General Colin Powell, rejected this comparison by arguing that the two situations were incomparable. Powell's claim appeared to carry the day, at least in mainstream public discourse. David Ari Bianco's essay compares the debate over military racial integration in the late 1940s and the recent debate over lesbians and gays, and finds striking similarities in the rhetoric and argumentation of those who supported the status quo. Bianco delineates 16 specific lines of argument employed by those opposed to a more inclusive armed forces in both cases, and discusses the broader implications of those claims. His essay is an important contribution because it provides compelling empirical evidence that can be used to reject the argument of those ban supporters who refused to acknowledge the historical parallels across the two debates.

The treatment of women in the United States military is at the core of Michelle Benecke and Kirstin Dodge's essay. Originally published in 1990, this essay has been revised to take into account the recent debate over the military ban. Its conclusions are still relevant for understanding the causes of lesbian baiting in the military and its prevalence in nontraditional military jobs. To Benecke and Dodge, lesbian baiting in the form of calling or threatening to call women lesbians was a central consequence of the pre-Clinton era policy. They broaden their analysis to conclude that the military ban has been used in the past to justify campaigns of sexual harassment against women who hold nontraditional jobs. In the way that the policy is applied, it confines and controls women's presence and behavior in the military. Their chapter places the policy against servicewomen in historical context and outlines the ways in which women who are suspected of being lesbians have been and are currently being investigated. Benecke and Dodge also document the specific consequences of daily military harassment and investigations in the lives of servicewomen who are suspected of being lesbians. Their conclusion includes an array of important reforms that would improve the daily lives of women.

POLICY ANALYSIS

Section two of the book offers a more detailed policy analysis. The goal of this section is to examine the roles that various institutional actors—the President, Congress, and the judicial system—have played in affecting the resolution of the military ban. The first two essays in this section take a presidential perspective, by examining the consequences of the Clinton administration's efforts for public policy and public opinion. The essays by Clyde Wilcox, Robin Wolpert, and myself raise an array of issues pertaining to the Clinton promise and the resulting national debate. These issues are necessary for framing the discussion developed in the remainder of the book.

"Promise Unfulfilled" examines the circumstances surrounding candidate Bill Clinton's promise to overturn the ban on lesbians and gays in the military. In doing so, it explores the nature of the opposition to Clinton's initial promise, and offers possible explanations for why there has been so much opposition to overturning the ban. The essay concludes by suggesting that a central issue growing out of this debate is whether lesbians, gays, and bisexuals can now live open and honest lives out of the closet, free from harassment and discrimination. In the short term, the answer appears to be "no."

This negative conclusion does not necessarily mean that the consequences of Bill Clinton's efforts to overturn the ban have had exclusively negative consequences from the vantage point of lesbians and gays. Clyde Wilcox and Robin Wolpert conclude, for example, that Clinton's leadership on the issue has had positive consequences for public opinion. As Wilcox and Wolpert point out, this is a significant contribution. Using data from the 1993 National Election Survey (NES) Pilot survey, they begin by describing opinion on gays and lesbians, and on their role in the military.Their essay concludes by exploring the impact of those attitudes on support for Clinton in 1993, a year after the public controversy.

David Rayside offers a thorough analysis of the congressional response to Clinton's proposal in the essay which introduces this section. As Rayside's essay suggests, one explanation for congressional opposition to the original Clinton promise to overturn the ban lies in the power of antigay forces. Rayside's analysis is important because it underscores the potential impact of the religious right in American politics. The overall fragmentation of Congress, which is reflected in the decline of party loyalty in the electorate and party organization, means that groups like the religious right fill an important vacuum and thus have the potential to be more influential vis-à-vis congressional members. This development is particularly American, as the Right is not as well organized in countries such as Canada and England. As a result, legislators in those countries do not feel the kind of electoral pressure from radical right organizations that is felt by their counterparts in the United States. Rayside concludes by discussing the implications of his institutional analysis for the lesbian and gay movement. The upshot of Rayside's analysis is that if the lesbian and gay movement hopes to be successful in the future, it will need to do a better job of lobbying members of Congress than it did during the military debate, and build coalitions among other groups committed to civil rights.

If the President and Congress have been unreceptive to extending basic civil rights to lesbians and gays in the military and in the larger society, perhaps the movement should turn to the courts. This is the issue that Richard Pacelle explores in his essay. Pacelle's analysis identifies some of the pitfalls faced by activist organizations who rely on the courts to affect political and social change. One notable limitation is the inability of the judicial system to construct coherent public policy. In addition, victories in the courts often energize opponents, who then work to block those gains through other venues. We may well see this latter development as the lower courts rule favorably on plaintiffs in individual cases where the military ban has been challenged. Pacelle also recognizes, however, that "the courts can be useful as a triggering mechanism to provide momentum for a nascent social movement or to remove lingering obstacles." This was the case for the Legal Defense Fund of the National Association for the Advancement of Colored Persons (NAACP) in the Brown v. Board of Education decision (1954) and for women's rights groups in Roe v. Wade (1973). Indeed, activists for lesbian and gay rights have followed similar litigation strategies, but have been much less successful than the Legal Defense Fund and women's rights groups. But in the end, Pacelle concludes somewhat optimistically that there may be hope as states continue to pass repressive measures that "directly or indirectly restrict gay rights or seek to limit the ability of lesbian and gay individuals to use civil right laws as other victims of discrimination." His optimism lies in the recognition that these overly restrictive laws actually open a policy window for legal change, by creating a more favorable climate rooted in changing public opinion in favor of extending basic civil rights to lesbians and gays. However, this strategy is an incremental one, meaning that any lasting change will take considerable time.

POLICY IMPLICATIONS
Section three builds on the analysis of the previous two sections by discussing broad policy implications and lessons learned from the debate over the military ban. What are the implications of the recent debate and policy revision for the lesbian and gay movement? What strategy or strategies should the movement pursue in order to achieve basic civil rights for lesbians and gays in all sectors

of society? This section addresses these compelling questions from a number of perspectives.

One possible strategy available to the lesbian and gay movement is the use of political theater. As Mary Katzenstein points out in her essay, the movement recognized that "the media's capacity to dramatize both the ordinary and unusual" by covering dramatic political theater has the potential to affect policy change. Katzenstein contrasts the media spectacle that prefaced the controversy over the homosexual ban with the media spectacle that preceded the reversal of the legislation barring women from combat pilot positions, and concludes that the feminist movement was able to achieve particular policy results through the use of political theater much more readily than the lesbian and gay movement. The lesson for the lesbian and gay movement is that if protest is to inspire immediate policy change, then a particular kind of media dramatized political protest is necessary. Such media coverage must elicit support from the public as well as public policy decisionmakers for major policy reform. As it pertains to the military ban, the only kind of media coverage that will successfully galvanize policy change is coverage that emphasizes death in combat. Because the lesbian and gay movement was unable to obtain that kind of coverage during the recent debate, it failed to create the conditions necessary for short-term policy change. Katzenstein concludes by suggesting that if the movement and the media had been able to convey that gays and lesbians had served and died in combat, the military's policy in 1993 might have been quite different. In light of Katzenstein's analysis, we are left with this important question: Why did the lesbian and gay movement fail to recognize that its strategy for overturning the ban was fundamentally flawed from the outset? Perhaps it is due to an integration movement strategy. Can a strategy be successful if it embraces military integration without challenging the heterosexist values that underlie both the military and the larger society? And what are the empirical criteria for success?

C. Dixon Osburn and Michelle M. Benecke, co-Executive Directors of Servicemembers Legal Defense Network, answer these questions in their exhaustive study of how the Don't Ask, Don't Tell, Don't Pursue policy has been enforced in its first year. Their study is an invaluable contribution because it is the first empirical study conducted evaluating the new policy. Given the policy's first-year implementation, they conclude that the military's new policy on lesbians and gays should be renamed "Ask, Pursue, and Harass." The Servicemembers Legal Defense Network found that numerous military officials conduct witch hunts, condone harassment of lesbian and gay servicemembers, and continue to ask questions about sexual orientation. These actions are all in direct violation of Don't Ask, Don't Tell, Don't Pursue, which promised to stop all of these activities. At the same time, however, Osburn and Benecke identify some good news during the first-year implementation of the new policy. They find that "in cases where courts have allowed lesbian and gay servicemembers to serve openly, there have been no problems." For example, both Petty Officer Keith Meinhold, who won his legal case before the Ninth Circuit Court of Appeals in 1994, and Colonel Margarethe Cammermeyer, who won her court case in June 1994, received strong support from their colleagues when they returned to their respective units. In fact, their return had a positive impact on their unit's order, discipline, and morale. This development suggests that the problem with the implementation of the new policy lies not with the troops, but with those in the military hierarchy, who continue to harass those individuals suspected of being lesbian or gay.

Gary Lehring's chapter examines the implications of the recent public debate for the future of the lesbian and gay movement. His analysis points to the importance of articulating a shared agenda and linking the concerns of the lesbian and gay movement with other oppressed groups. To Lehring, the movement must do a much better job in building coalitions if meaningful policy change is to occur. He criticizes movement leaders for failing to recognize that broad societal changes must occur if we are to challenge "cultural practices that posit straight white men as the standard bearers of culture and mark everyone else as decidedly 'other.'" Perhaps the failure to wage a successful mobilization effort to overturn the ban will force movement leaders to rethink their individual and collective political strategies. The political and social movement literature suggests that other movements have learned much about organizing for political and social change in the face of defeat. For this to occur, however, movement leaders must recognize that the Clinton and congressional compromise policy is a defeat if the criteria for movement success is extending basic civil rights to all lesbians and gays.

It is fitting that the book ends with Thomas Zilly's June 1994 opinion and a legal brief filed by the government in the Margarethe Cammermeyer case. Unlike the government's brief, Zilly's opinion suggests that it is possible for reasonable people in positions of power to recognize that the military ban of open lesbians and gays is rooted in bigotry and prejudice. Indeed, responding to the pre-Clinton era policy, Zilly concludes that "Colonel Cammermeyer was discharged from the National Guard pursuant to a governmental policy that is based solely on prejudice." Zilly points out, as well, that Margarethe Cammermeyer had performed her duties as an officer and Army Nurse with care and professionalism. For the hundreds of lesbians and gay men who have served in silence through the years, as well as for those courageous few who have risked their careers by openly declaring their sexuality, Zilly's opinion in the Cammermeyer case can only be an inspiration.

As the essays in this volume illustrate, lesbians and gay men who serve in the military deserve to be evaluated based on their overall performances. It is indeed a shame that the new Don't Ask, Don't Tell, Don't Pursue policy is grounded in the kind of bigoted assumptions about lesbians and gays that have been at the core of the military's thinking throughout this century. Bill Clinton's apparent eagerness to compromise, without exercising decisive leadership and fighting on behalf of his original promise, suggests that this President deserves much of the criticism leveled by lesbian and gay groups as well as others concerned with basic civil rights for all Americans both inside and outside the military. In the end, one can only hope that the recent furor over Clinton's promise to end the ban on lesbians and gays will lead over the long term to a greater acceptance of lesbians and gays in the larger society, an acceptance that ultimately means increased tolerance as well as an extension of basic civil rights—values which are the hallmark of a dignified and humane society. We must recognize, as well, that this acceptance is only a first and crucial step in the challenging and unending process of restructuring the larger society's views of sexuality.

NOTES

1. Cammermeyer, Margarethe with Chris Fisher, *Serving in Silence* (New York: Viking, 1994), 300.
2. Cammermeyer, 300-01.

PART I

The Policy Context

CHAPTER 1

Race-ing and Gendering the Military Closet

Francine D'Amico

The U.S. military's lesbian/gay exclusion policy is built on intersecting ideas about sexuality, race, and gender.[1] The exclusion policy embodies a particular array of race and gender relations and encourages violence against sexual minorities—and, by extension, against any group constructed as "Other" or "undesirable." It provides sexual harassers with a tool for sexual extortion, and it has been applied disproportionately against women in the U.S. armed forces.

In its newest incarnation as "Don't Ask, Don't Tell, Don't Pursue," the military lesbian/gay exclusion policy institutionalizes rather than eliminates the military closet. Lesbians and gay men in the military are asked to remain silent and invisible, to hide their "othered" identities, so that the military can bolster its androcentric, heterocentric image. Their ability to remain closeted is constrained by the predominant society's ideas about sexual behavior of people of color and of people gendered "masculine" and "feminine." That is, the military closet comes in "White" and "Colored," "His" and "Hers" versions, and the Don't Ask, Don't Tell policy is used to police the race and gender lines in the U.S. armed forces. This chapter explores the construction of the military closet through an examination of: 1) the context of the policy debate; 2) the comparative studies used to inform that debate, including the personnel practices of other state militaries and the past integration experiences of the U.S. military; and 3) the raced and gendered conceptualization of human sexuality prevalent in contemporary U.S. society.

Fundamentally, the debate over lesbians and gay men in the military is about the politics of identity and practices of inclusion/exclusion. Who am I? Who are "we"? Gender identity, racial/ethnic identity, sexual identity, and civilian/military identity are dimensions of these questions. Conflicts emerge in the intersection of our multiple identities and the politics of drawing boundaries between "us" and "them." State institutions, such as the legislature, the courts, and the military, officially draw and redraw these boundaries through acts of law, case decisions, and personnel policies. These (re)drawings are political; that is, they are based on the power of the state to determine who belongs and the price of belonging, as well as to coerce or punish, or to issue benefits—that is, to dictate "who gets what, when, and how" in terms of the distribution of resources in a society.[2]

In 1992, the U.S. military's personnel policy regarding sexuality came under intense public scrutiny, and efforts were made to draw lessons from the practices and policies of other state militaries and from analogous experiences in U.S. society. In its search for such lessons, the U.S. government commissioned analyses by the RAND corporation and the U.S. General Accounting Office (GAO). These studies are important because they were intended for use as scholarly and nonpartisan justification for either maintaining or ending the U.S. military's lesbian/gay exclusion policy. Although they provided important information for the policy debate, the RAND and GAO studies neglected the raced and gendered construction of the U.S. military lesbian/gay exclusion policy.

Students of comparative politics know that we must be very careful about what we seek to compare. We must identify the assumptions underlying our comparisons and the models we measure against, and we must acknowledge the distortions across cultures, communities, and time created by the degree of abstraction necessary to make generalized comparisons. In examining the RAND and GAO analyses, I began to wonder about the politics of comparative analysis of research on military personnel policies. Where ought the United States look for lessons on this issue?

The experiences of foreign state militaries which have ended policies of exclusion (such as Canada, Australia, Israel, and the Netherlands) show that policy change is possible, that the circumstances under which such change occurs vary, and that inclusion policies and their implementation differ widely. The U.S. military's own history of ending racial segregation and opening to include women in first auxiliary and then regular military service illustrates both resistance to change in military culture/identity and the possibility for such change. The U.S. domestic analogies of ending sexuality-based exclusion policies among fire and police personnel show that this is not a case of the military going first in changing social attitudes and behaviors in the United States.[3]

THE U.S. POLICY DEBATE

On the campaign trail and in his campaign text, *Putting People First*, U.S. presidential candidate Bill Clinton outlined his plan to create a more democratic and representative government. Among other things, he pledged to end the exclusion of lesbians and gay men from military service.[4] On 29 January 1993, President Clinton began action to fulfill this pledge. He sent a memorandum to the Secretary of Defense telling him to draft an executive order "to end discrimination on the basis of sexual orientation in determining who may serve in the Armed Forces."[5] The announcement met with tremendous opposition from the military as well as much of the Congress and the general public, and the issue dominated the media, cutting Clinton's post-inauguration "honeymoon" short.

For the next six months, members of the administration met with the Joint Chiefs of Staff and congressional representatives, trying to design a policy that would keep Clinton's promise without alienating key military and political leaders. During this time, the lesbian/gay exclusion policy was "suspended": recruiters were not supposed to ask about sexuality or sexual identity, and pending discharge proceedings were postponed, leaving many service personnel in a quandary—they were unable to resign and leave the service if charges were pending, yet they were being passed over for promotion and could not be deployed with their units outside the continental United States. Meanwhile, investigations of suspected lesbian/gay personnel by the Army Criminal Investigative Command (CIC), the Naval Investigative Service (NIS), and the Air Force Office of Special Investigations (OSI) continued, targeting people who had made public statements about their sexuality.[6]

Finally, on 19 July 1993, Clinton announced the new "compromise" policy Don't Ask, Don't Tell, Don't Pursue, which would allow lesbians and gay men to serve so long as they did so quietly and discreetly—rather than "openly and avowedly," as supporters of a continued ban phrased it—and did not engage in any prohibited conduct. After much debate and revision, Congress incorporated the new policy into the Defense Authorization Act of 1994, which Clinton signed on 30 November 1993.[7] The Act took effect at the beginning of the fiscal year; in the interim, preliminary regulations were issued by the Department of Defense on 22 December 1993, with the finalized rules coming into effect on 28 February 1994.[8] In March 1995, a federal court held the Don't Ask, Don't Tell policy unconstitutional; the Justice Department announced that it would appeal the case.[9] House Speaker Newt Gingrich (R-GA), who had earlier called for the new Republican majority in Congress to reinstate the lesbian/gay exclusion rule, appeared to drop the issue.[10]

The lesbian/gay exclusion policy has a long history in the U.S. military. Soldiers in the Continental Army were "drummed out of the service" for engaging in same-sex relations, according to researcher Randy Shilts, and during the 1860s, could be rejected from enlistment or removed from the ranks for "(h)abitual or confirmed intemperance, or solitary vice," according to the *Manual of Instruction for Military Surgeons*.[11] The first explicit policy to sanction "assault with intent to commit sodomy" was codified in the *Articles of War* of 1916, which took effect 1 March 1917. The behavior or conduct of the soldiers, not their sexual identity per se, was the grounds for court-martial and, usually, imprisonment and subsequent dishonorable discharge. At the end of World War I, Article 93 of the *Articles of War* (4 June 1920) established consensual sodomy as a dischargeable offense. Efforts to purge gay men from the ranks included the Navy's infamous "gay dragnet" at Newport, Rhode Island, in 1919-20.[12]

In 1942, the regulations were revised to reflect the then-current interpretation of homosexuality as a psychological illness rather than a criminal offense.[13] Recruits or draftees with "homosexual tendencies" were deemed unsuitable for service and were not enlisted or were discharged if already in service, unless they were considered "treatable," in which case they underwent "rehabilitation" and were retained for service. The language of the 1942-43 regulations blurred the distinction between identity and conduct and allowed greater command discretion to determine whether soldiers identified as gay would be retained or discharged. Some gay soldiers were given honorable discharges; many were given general or "bad conduct" discharges.[14]

At the end of World War II, the diverse policies of the different services were replaced by the *Uniform Code of Military Justice (UCMJ)*. Article 125 of the *UCMJ* prohibits sodomy, defined as anal or oral penetration, whether consensual or coerced and whether same-sex or opposite-sex, and does not exempt married couples. Under Article 125, the maximum penalty for sodomy with a consenting adult is five years at hard labor, forfeiture of pay and allowances, and dishonorable discharge. Article 134 of the *UCMJ*, also known as the "General Article," sanctions assault with the intent to commit sodomy, indecent assault, and indecent acts, and prohibits all conduct "to the prejudice of good order and discipline in the armed forces."[15] The maximum penalty is the same for each of these offenses as for sodomy, except in the case of assault with intent, which has a maximum of ten rather than five years confinement.

On 16 January 1981, W. Graham Claytor Jr., a Carter appointee in the Department of Defense, issued a directive to "fine-tune" the policy. The directive was supposed to make the policy uniform across all branches of the service, eliminating command discretion on the issue. While this ended the practice of giving dishonorable discharges when no violations of the UCMJ were alleged, it also made exceptions to the rule and retention of some individuals impossible. Department of Defense Directive 1332.14, section H.1 reads as follows:

> Homosexuality is incompatible with military service. The presence in the military environment of persons who engage in homosexual conduct or who, by their statements, demonstrate a propensity to engage in homosexual conduct, seriously impairs the accomplishment of the military mission. The presence of such members adversely affects the ability of the Military Services to maintain discipline, good order, and morale; to foster mutual trust and confidence among service members; to insure the integrity of the system of rank and command; to facilitate assignment and worldwide deployment of service members who frequently must live and work under close conditions affording minimal privacy; to recruit and retain members of the Military Services; to maintain public acceptability of military service; and to prevent breaches of security.[16]

Under this directive, which took effect 28 January 1982, one need no longer *engage* in same-sex acts to be discharged; one need only *be* lesbian/gay (that is, identify or be identified as lesbian/gay), and thus have a "*propensity* to or *intent* to engage in" same-sex acts, to be discharged. Directive 1332.30, issued

12 February 1986, amended the "Separation of Regular Commissioned Officers for Cause" to include the same language for officers which 1332.14 applied to enlisted personnel.[17]

Between 1980 and 1990, a total of 16,919 people—an average of 1,500 per year—were discharged under the lesbian/gay exclusion policy, according to statistics provided to the GAO by the Department of Defense.[18] Between 1991 and 1994, another 2,936 were discharged, bringing the total number of people discharged since 1980 to almost 20,000.[19] Since 1990, the *number* of personnel discharged annually has fallen below 1,000 and has decreased each subsequent year, according to information recently released by the Pentagon, but the *proportion* of people discharged relative to the total number of people serving has remained fairly constant since 1980.[20]

Individuals discharged from the services, such as Keith Meinhold and Margarethe Cammermeyer, and organized interest groups in the United States, such as Gay, Lesbian, and Bisexual Veterans of America and the American Civil Liberties Union, have worked to change this exclusion policy for many years.[21] Efforts to challenge the ban were sometimes successful at lower levels of the federal court system, but the Supreme Court generally did not review such cases.[22] This implied that these "political matters" should be left to the legislature and the Executive to decide, and that the Court would defer to the military on personnel issues, which fell under the Cold War's "national security" blanket.[23] Until Clinton's administration, neither Congress nor the President had taken the initiative on this issue. Only a handful of members of Congress, most notably Gerry Studds (D-CA), Barney Frank (D-MA), and Patricia Schroeder (D-CO), had pursued the issue prior to Clinton's campaign.[24]

The United States is not the first country to have an explicit policy banning lesbians and gay men from military service, nor is it the first to consider revising or rescinding that ban. Many state militaries exclude lesbians and gay men; several have lifted bans; others have no policy regarding the sexuality or sexual identity of service members. Two decades ago, the Netherlands became the first country to eliminate a formal policy of lesbian/gay exclusion from military service. Exclusion policies were also dropped or amended in Germany in 1969, Sweden in 1976, Ireland in 1977, Denmark in 1978, Norway in 1979, Spain in 1985, and Portugal in 1989.[25] Some militaries allow lesbians and gay men to serve but apply restrictions, as is true in Belgium, France, and the Republic of Korea. Most recently, exclusion policies have been dropped in both Canada (27 October 1992) and Australia (23 November 1992). Israel "clarified" its policy in mid-1993, removing restrictions and special requirements directed at lesbians and gay men.

At the behest of Congress and the Pentagon, respectively, the U.S. General Accounting Office (GAO) and the RAND Corporation undertook comparative studies to examine the policies and practices of other countries with regard to the sexuality of military personnel. These studies helped to inform the unfolding debate and to frame the resultant compromise policy regarding lesbians and gay men in the U.S. armed forces.

Both the RAND and the GAO researchers faced practical limits on their research efforts, including time, limited access to information, the sensitivity of the topic and a tendency toward obfuscation, and the gap between stated policy and actual practice. Despite these constraints, both the GAO studies and the RAND report made a significant contribution to the policy process. The GAO studies documented the gender bias of the exclusion policy, while the RAND report examined the hardest issues (privacy, cohesion, HIV/AIDS) and offered a pragmatic program of action for ending the exclusion policy. While these studies acknowledged the gendered impact of the lesbian/gay exclusion policy, neither RAND nor the GAO examined the raced and gendered construction of the policy, making fundamental change both less likely and less possible.

THE GAO REPORTS

The General Accounting Office has released three documents regarding the U.S. military's lesbian/gay exclusion policy. The first two, *DOD's Policy on Homosexuality* and a supplement titled *Statistics Related to DOD's Policy on Homosexuality*, were released in June 1992. The study and supplement were prepared at the request of congressional representatives John Conyers, Jr. (D-MI), Gerry Studds (D-CA), and Ted Weiss (D-NY). A third report, *Homosexuals in the Military: Policies and Practices of Foreign Countries*, was released in June 1993. This report was prepared at the request of Senator John Warner (R-VA).

In the 1992 *Policy* report, the GAO briefly compared the United States' exclusion policy with personnel policies "of 17 other nations, predominantly U.S. allies and North Atlantic Treaty Organization countries," and focused on the policies of Canada and the United Kingdom.[26] The chart the GAO provided in Appendix II of the *Policy* report is reproduced in Table 1. Since the report was issued in 1992, both Canada and Australia (which was not included in the initial GAO report) have rescinded their bans on lesbian and gay service personnel. Among its allies, the United States is clearly in the minority on this issue.

Subsequently, in June 1993, the GAO released the *Foreign Countries* document, its more extensive comparative study of state military personnel practices regarding sexuality. For this study, the GAO selected twenty-nine states with active armed forces numbering 50,000 or more in 1991. Six of the seventeen states in the 1992 study—Austria, Denmark, Finland, Luxembourg, New Zealand, and Norway—were omitted from the 1993 comparative report by this quantitative criterion. Of these, only New Zealand has an exclusion policy.

Representatives of four of the states approached by the GAO researchers declined to participate in the 1993 *Foreign Countries* study. Of the twenty-five respondents, eleven reported they permit lesbians and gay men to serve, and eleven reported they prohibit lesbians and gay men from serving.

Table 1
GAO *Policy* 1992—Appendix II: Other Nations' Policies Regarding Homosexuals in the Military

Country	Specifically Exclude	Allow	Country	Specifically Exclude	Allow
Austria		X	Luxembourg		X
Belgium[a]		X	New Zealand	X	
Canada		X	Norway		X
Denmark		X	Portugal	X	
Finland[a]		X	Spain		X
France[a]		X	Sweden		X
Germany[a]		X	United Kingdom[b]	X	
Italy		X	United States[b]	X	
Japan		X			

Source: Reproduced verbatim from United States General Accounting Office (US GAO), *Defense Force Management: DOD's Policy on Homosexuality* (US GAO/NSIAD-92-98, June 1992) Appendix II: 54. Of the states listed above by the GAO, Austria, Finland, Japan, New Zealand, and Sweden are not NATO members.

[a] Although these countries allow homosexuals to serve in their armed forces, they place certain restrictions on homosexuals. These restrictions include (1) limiting their access to confidential documents; (2) excluding them from certain tasks, such as officer and recruit training; (3) excluding them from leadership roles; and (4) relieving them from duty if the behavior becomes disturbing to other service members.

[b] These countries specifically ask during the recruiting process if the individual has homosexual tendencies in an effort to prevent homosexuals from entering.

Table 2
Policies Concerning Military Service of Homosexuals in Foreign Countries

Country	Size of active force	Primary source of personnel	Policy allows homosexuals to serve[a]	Applicable laws, regulations, policies, and/or restrictions
Australia	68,000	All-volunteer	Yes	Military policy changed in Nov. 1992.
Belgium	85,000	Both[b]	Yes	No specific law/military reg.
Brazil	297,000	Both	No	No specific law/military reg.
Canada	78,000	All-volunteer	Yes	Prohibition lifted in October 1992.
Chile	92,000	Both	No	Civilian law applies.
Colombia	134,000	Both	No	Military code applies.
France	453,000	Both	Yes	No specific law/military reg.
Germany	476,000	Conscript Volunteer	Yes No	Civilian laws changed in 1969.
Greece	159,000	Conscript	No	Military reg. applies.
Hungary	87,000	Both	No	No specific law/military reg. Restrictions apply to volunteers.
Israel	141,000	Conscript	Yes	Military regulation on restrictions revoked in May 1993.
Italy	361,000	Conscript	No	Codified into law in 1985.
Japan	246,000	All-volunteer	[c]	No specific law/military reg.

Peru	105,000	Conscript	No	No specific law/military reg. on acceptance. Military code applies regarding discharge.
Poland	305,000	Conscript	d	No specific law/military reg.
Portugal	62,000	Both	Yes	Military laws modified in 1989.
Republic of Korea	600,000	Conscript	Yes	Military law applies.
Romania	201,000	Conscript	No	Civilian law applies.
South Africa	72,000	Both	d	No specific law/military reg.
Spain	257,000	Both	Yes	Civilian laws revised in 1985.
Sweden	53,000	Conscript	Yes	Civilian law/military policy.
The Netherlands	92,000	Both	Yes	No specific law/military reg. Military law revised in 1974.
Turkey	579,000	Conscript	No	Military law applies.
United Kingdom	300,000	All-volunteer	No	Military law applies.
Venezuela	75,000	Both	No	Military law applies.

Source: U.S. Government Accounting Office (GAO), *Homosexuals in the Military: Policies and Practices of Foreign Countries* (Washington, D.C.: U.S. GAO, GAO/NSIAD-93-215, June, 1993).

Note: Appendix II provides additional information concerning these military policies.
[a]When no specific law or regulation applies, the countries' officials informed us of the policy.
[b]The Belgian military is currently transitioning to an all-volunteer force.
[c]Japanese officials indicated the issue is handled on a case-by-case basis.
[d]Officials did not provide detailed information to enable us to make this determination.

Three—Japan, Poland, and South Africa—reported that they have no regulations regarding the sexual identity of military personnel.[27]

Cynthia Enloe has described the North Atlantic Treaty Organization (NATO) as a "lesson machine" regarding the integration and role of women in the armed forces, arguing that NATO member states observe one another's "experiments" with personnel policies and take their cues from these.[28] Thirteen of the states the GAO included in the 1992 *Policy* study are NATO members; nine of these allowed lesbians and gay men to serve when the GAO published its study in 1992. Two NATO members—Denmark and Luxembourg—are excluded from the GAO's 1993 *Foreign Countries* report because of the small size of their militaries; the 1993 report does not note that both allow lesbians and gay men to serve. Those in the United States who support the ban might not want the United States to take lessons from NATO on this issue: altogether, ten of the sixteen NATO member states either do not exclude lesbians and gay men from military service or have no policy regarding the sexuality of military personnel.

The 1992 *Policy* report included non-NATO Austria, Finland, and Japan, all of which permit lesbians and gay men to serve, and omitted NATO members Greece and Turkey, which exclude lesbians and gay men. The 1993 *Foreign Countries* report added NATO members Greece and Turkey and included four different European non-NATO member states: Sweden, Hungary, Romania, and Poland; of these, only Sweden allows lesbians and gay men to serve. With all of these substitutions, it is not surprising that the 1993 GAO *Foreign Countries* study presented an *equal* number of states on each side of this issue, as illustrated in Table 3. Perhaps this balanced finding was supposed to be unbiased and nonpartisan, as the GAO's mandate requires? Yet this *appearance* of balance can be interpreted (and perhaps was intended) to signify the acceptability of either policy option.

Perceptions of cultural affinity (North American/Western European) and political, diplomatic, and military connections seem to have also been implicit selection criteria in the overview portion of the 1992 GAO *Policy* study. These seem to have been discarded in the overview of the 1993 *Foreign Countries* study, as it included five Latin American states (Brazil, Chile, Colombia, Peru, Venezuela) as well as three states in Asia/Oceania (Japan, Republic of Korea, Australia), one in the Middle East (Israel), and one in Africa (South Africa). Indeed, one wonders why *any* Third World or Eastern European states were included, since the United States is unlikely to pattern its military personnel practices after any of these countries—until one considers that without these states, few would have lined up on the side of then-current U.S. policy. This might have suggested that the United States lagged behind its European counterparts in guaranteeing the human rights of its citizens.

While the 1993 GAO *Foreign Countries* report provided an overview on the personnel policies of twenty-five state militaries, it also presented focused case studies on four state militaries: Canada, Germany, Israel, and Sweden. Here, the GAO acknowledged that its selection criteria included the "cultural

Table 3
State Military Personnel Policies on Sexual Orientation

Exclusion	Inclusion	No Policy
Brazil	Australia	Japan
Chile	Belgium	Poland
Colombia	Canada	South Africa
Greece	France	
Hungary	Germany (conscript)	
Italy	Israel	
Peru	Netherlands	
Romania	Portugal	
Turkey	ROKorea	
United Kingdom	Spain	
Venezuela	Sweden	

Source: Adapted from United States General Accounting Office, *Homosexuals in the Military: Policies and Practices of Foreign Countries* (Washington, DC: GAO, GAO/NSIAD-93-215, June 1993), Table 1:5.

heritage" or "western cultural values" of the states, as well as the military's "recent combat or deployment experience" in regional conflicts, U.N. peacekeeping, and/or the Persian Gulf coalition force. Cultural homo- or heterogeneity and "a range of attitudes concerning homosexuality" were also among the explicit case study selection criteria.[29] Clearly, the "cultural affinity" criterion can be challenged, particularly with regard to the racial/ethnic composition of the communities being compared here.

On reading the 1993 *Foreign Countries* report, I wondered why the GAO examined only states with militaries of 50,000 or more and why the GAO included *only* twenty-nine states with militaries this size in 1991, since the International Institute for Strategic Studies identified *seventy* militaries of this size in 1992.[30] As a comparativist, I am sensitive to the need to compare like things, but on one level, there is clearly no analog, foreign or domestic, for the U.S. military either in terms of number of personnel and level of expenditure or mission, force structure, and deployment history; therefore, the GAO's 50,000 mark seemed arbitrary, and twenty-nine of seventy cases seemed an inadequate comparison. The unification of the Germanies and the divisions of the USSR, Yugoslavia, and Czechoslovakia might explain some of the difference in the scope of the GAO's data, but what of the rest?

Four states declined to participate in the GAO's 1993 *Foreign Countries* study. Perhaps other countries with large militaries were excluded because information about their military personnel policies was unavailable to the GAO researchers. Or perhaps the GAO was worried that the United States might line up on this issue with many of its recent enemies, such as Iraq, Iran, and Vietnam, or with states the United States has condemned as violators of human rights, such as China, North Korea, and Myanmar/Burma, and with other "less developed" countries such as Ethiopia, Pakistan, and the Philippines.

The time lapse between the issue date of the *Policy* study in June 1992 and the comparative *Foreign Countries* study in June 1993 suggests that the politics of comparative analysis have come into play in response to the opposition that developed to the proposed policy change. This opposition was part of a more general conservative backlash against efforts to guarantee lesbian and gay rights, reflected in antigay/lesbian ballot initiatives on the ballot in several states in 1992 and in the results of the 1994 interim elections. Indeed, as noted above, the second GAO report was requested by Senator John Warner (R-VA), who is a member of the Senate Armed Services Committee and former Secretary of the Navy; Warner has been one of the most vociferous opponents to ending the ban.[31] Senators Warner and Sam Nunn (D-GA) were among those who toured the Norfolk Naval Base in Virginia on 10 May 1993 to demonstrate the "lack of privacy" on shipboard—and therefore vulnerability of straight military personnel—sensationalized in the AP photo and satirized in several editorial cartoons.

Some conclusions can be drawn from even the small sample of state militaries the GAO study covered. First, the size of the armed forces has little apparent relationship to policies on sexuality. Larger state militaries both include and exclude lesbians and gay men, as do smaller state militaries. This leaves me wondering, again, why the size of the military was deemed so important by the GAO.

Second, policies of exclusion or inclusion are unrelated to how the military gets people to serve (also called the "method of personnel procurement"). Some states which conscript soldiers exclude lesbians and gay men; others draft citizens regardless of their sexual identity. Some states which have volunteer forces prohibit lesbians and gay men from serving; others permit them to volunteer. States which use both conscripts and volunteers may or may not include lesbians and gay men in their ranks. One state, Germany, conscripts all males regardless of sexuality but does not allow gays to volunteer for service in the "professional" force. Here, an exploration of the politics of military personnel procurement (ability to conscript versus need to seek volunteers) and perceived military requirements in terms of number of personnel needed would have been useful. The GAO did not provide this in its analysis.

THE RAND REPORT

In April 1993, the RAND Corporation's National Defense Research Institute issued its report *Sexual Orientation and U.S. Military Personnel Policy: Options and Assessment* to military and administration officials. The report was commissioned by the Department of Defense and was made available to the public in August 1993, just two months after the GAO *Foreign Countries* report was released. The RAND report examines medical research on sexuality and military personnel policies regarding sexuality in seven countries.

Like the 1993 GAO *Foreign Countries* report, the RAND *Sexual Orientation* study looked in depth at Canada, Germany, and Israel, but also considered France, the Netherlands, Norway, and the United Kingdom (rather than Sweden, as the GAO had). Of these, only the U.K. excludes lesbians and gay men from military service.[32] RAND's selection criteria included states with a range of policies on sexuality among service personnel and recent military engagement or peacekeeping deployment in which troops had been deployed away from the home country, with no limit on force size considered (Tables 4 and 5). The RAND report acknowledged the difficulty of cross-national comparisons and factors such as time restrictions and lack of information, which limited the scope of its study.

Examining the selection criteria for the comparative analyses undertaken by the GAO and RAND suggests that a central question for both groups of researchers was: to whom ought the United States look for "lessons" regarding sexuality and military personnel policies? The GAO and RAND have slightly different responses and different final recommendations. Because of its "nonpartisan" mandate, the GAO reports make no explicit policy recommendation. The RAND study recommends a policy of "no policy." RAND says only one policy option is "logically and internally consistent" as well as consistent with the findings of its research and with the criteria of

Table 4
Selected National and Military Statistics

	CAN	FRA	GER	ISR	NET	NOR	UK	USA
Size (1000 km^2)	9976	547	357	21	42	324	244	9159
population (millions)	27	57	81	5	15	4	58	256
GNP (billions of US$)	517	874	164	46	222	74	858	5678
% of GNP on military	2%	4%	2%	10%	4%	5%	5%	5%
Active military (thousands)	87	453	476	141	101	33	300	2030
% women	11%	4%	few[a]	???[b]	2%	2%	6%	12%
% conscripts	zero	50%	43%	78%	45%	70%	zero	zero
months conscription[c]	N/A	10	12	36[d]	12	12	N/A	N/A
Warfighting in past 20 years	no	yes	no	yes	no	no	yes	yes
Force projection deployment	no	yes	no	no	no	no	yes	yes
Peacekeeping deployment	yes	yes	no	no	yes	yes	yes	yes

Source: RAND, *Sexual Orientation and U.S. Military Personnel Policy: Options and Assessment* (Monterey, CA: National Defense Research Institute, MR-323-OSD, 1993) 70.

[a]Women do not serve in Germany except in medical or musical jobs.

[b]Israeli authorities would not release this information. However, Israel has universal conscription to active duty and women must serve two years.

[c]This is the minimum tour of duty. Conscripts volunteering for special services (e.g., for some countries the navy or for others deployment abroad) may have longer terms of service. Israel and Norway have reserve service obligations beyond the period of active duty.

[d]The tabled figure is for males. Israel also drafts females, who serve for 24 months.

Table 5

Civilian Laws Regarding Homosexuality

	CAN	FRA	GER	ISR	NET	NOR	UK	USA
Legal status for homosexual partnerships	no	no	no	no	no	yes	no	no[a]
Economic benefits for nonmarried couples	no	some	some	no	yes	yes	no	varies[b]
Nondiscrimination in employment	no	yes	no	no	yes	yes	no	varies[c]
Decriminalization of homosexual behavior	yes	yes	yes	yes	yes	yes	yes	27 states

Source: RAND, *Sexual Orientation and U.S. Military Personnel Policy: Options and Assessment* (Monterey, CA: National Defense Research Institute, MR-323-OSD, 1993) 72.

[a]While some cities "recognize" partnerships, legal status must be conferred by state or federal law.
[b]Some cities provide economic benefits; no states do.
[c]Some cities and some states have nondiscrimination laws.

President Clinton's directive of 29 January 1993 to the Secretary of Defense. That policy is that "sexual orientation" is "not germane" to military service suitability.[33] This policy option would privatize or dismantle the military closet for lesbian and gay service personnel, depending upon the extent to which the *UCMJ* is revised and the policy is implemented. The RAND report recommends that the standard of professional conduct be "neutral" with regard to sexuality, that Article 125 of the *UCMJ* be rescinded, and that relevant portions of the *Manual of Courts Martial* (*MCM*) be revised so that only nonconsenting sexual activity, sex acts with a minor, or acts committed on duty, on base, or in violation of antifraternization regulations be penalized.[34]

The RAND study was not the first time that a group of researchers had reached the conclusion that the sexual identity of service personnel is not relevant to military service or job performance. Previous studies of sexuality and U.S. military service were the Crittenden report (1957), the PERSEREC/Sarbin-Karols study (1988), and the PERSEREC/McDaniel study (1989). None of these studies found evidence to confirm the exclusion policy rationale that homosexuality was incompatible with service in the armed forces. The Crittenden report found that gay men posed no great national security risk in terms of susceptibility to extortion.[35] The PERSEREC/Sarbin-Karols report concluded that homosexuality was as unrelated to military job performance, as was right- or left-handedness.[36] The PERSEREC/McDaniel study found that in terms of background characteristics prior to entering military service, gay men were "as good or better than the average heterosexual" in terms of suitability for positions of trust—that is, gay men did not appear to be a national security risk.[37]

But the RAND report was unique in that it was the first time the research was ordered by *politically accountable* members of the executive branch rather than by *politically insulated* members of the military services. And the RAND report was made available to the public almost immediately, while the Crittenden report was buried for 32 years (completed in 1957 and released by federal court order in 1989) and the PERSEREC/Sarbin-Karols report was tied up by the Pentagon for almost a year (completed in December 1988, and released October 1989 under congressional pressure). The second PERSEREC report (McDaniel) was never submitted to DOD, so its release was not delayed.

The RAND study also tackles what the Department of Defense said the GAO and PERSEREC reports failed to consider: the impact of the end of the ban on "combat effectiveness and unit cohesion."[38] Unlike the GAO reports, the RAND researchers spoke to not only top government officials but also rank-and-file military members, and RAND was careful to point out the degree to which the cases it examined were comparable (or not) to the U.S. military. Significantly, RAND looked to NATO for lessons; the only non-NATO case study in its report was Israel.

LOOKING FOR LESSONS: POLICIES OF OTHER STATE MILITARIES

What lessons should we draw from the policies and practices of other states' militaries? There seem to be at least three points that merit attention. First, a policy of "no policy" does not mean that lesbians and gay men are free to serve. Second, an explicit policy of inclusion does not mean that there are no problems with implementation or that bias, discrimination, and violence against lesbians and gay men will be eliminated; that is, there may be a greater or lesser gap between policy and practice. Third, the experiences of states which have changed from policies of exclusion to policies of inclusion are varied, but also demonstrate some similarities. Typically, policy change has been instigated from outside the armed forces by discharged individuals, supportive interest groups, and/or political representatives, and has followed changes in civilian law and medical practice. Policy change has also generally met resistance both within and outside the military, and has sometimes been staged through a series of interim measures gradually reducing restrictions on lesbian/gay personnel. The cases of Cuba, South Africa, Canada, Australia, Israel, and the Netherlands illustrate these points.

Neither the GAO reports nor the RAND study provide detailed information on personnel practices in the militaries of non-European, non-Western militaries such as Cuba. Government officials I interviewed in Cuba in 1984 stated that the Cuban military had no policy on lesbians and gay men in military service because there were no lesbians or gay men in Cuba. One official said homosexuality was a symptom of the "sickness of capitalist society" and did not, therefore, exist in Cuba.[39] Researchers Lourdes Arguelles and B. Ruby Rich report that the "puritanism" and homophobia of the Cuban revolution have abated somewhat, but they discuss civilian policy and practice rather than military personnel policy.[40] Lesbian/gay rights activists in Cuba have only recently begun organizing, and their focus has been on releasing jailed lesbians and gay men and decriminalizing consensual same-sex relations rather than on military personnel policy.[41] The universal conscription law is supposed to apply to all able-bodied Cuban men. Thus, Cuba's policy of "no policy" does not mean lesbians and gay men are free to serve.

The same was true in apartheid South Africa: the 1993 GAO *Foreign Countries* report states that there were "no written laws, regulations, or policies regarding the service of homosexuals" in the South African Defence Force.[42] Randy Shilts has said that in practice, the South African military under apartheid excluded lesbians and gay men.[43] Information on the personnel policies of the postapartheid military in South Africa focuses on the "representativeness" of the composition of the forces and is silent on the sexuality of personnel.

What of states that have shifted from policies of exclusion to policies of inclusion? The Canadian experience with ending a policy of lesbian/gay exclusion bears much similarity to the process of policy change in the United States, and thus merits special scrutiny. Canada's ban, in effect since World War II, was comparable to the U.S. ban. Military recruits were discharged if they acknowledged homosexuality and were subject to investigation by a

Special Investigative Unit (SIU), sometimes assisted by the Royal Canadian Mounted Police (RCMP).[44] The purge campaigns against lesbians and gays in the military, civil service, and police were part of the progressive criminalization of homosexuality in Canadian society in the 1940s and 1950s, and, as in the United States, the basis of the purges was the alleged security risk posed by lesbians/gays in the anti-Communist Cold War context.[45] Ultimately, the courts ruled the ban illegal. The change came as a result of litigation brought by military personnel discharged under the exclusion regulation.

In 1982, Canada adopted a new Constitution which took effect in 1985. The Constitution contains a Charter of Rights and Freedoms, which in Section 15 prohibits discrimination on the basis of sex and race/ethnicity. While sexuality or sexual identity was not specified, the Charter contains a clause similar to the 9th Amendment to the U.S. Constitution, which states that citizens have rights not enumerated explicitly in the document.

Once the new Canadian Constitution took effect, many ex-servicemembers ousted because of their sexual identity used Section 15 of the Charter to bring court challenges against the lesbian/gay exclusion policy. These Charter challenges, together with political pressure on Parliament from lesbian/gay rights supporters, forced the military to suspend application of the policy pending review. Under this suspension (which lasted about three and a half years) the SIU investigations continued, but lesbians and gay men identified in investigations were not discharged. Instead, their careers were stalled or frozen: promotions and advancements stopped, and they were often relieved of their duties or reassigned to obscure positions—what might be described as a kind of internal exile. In the meantime, the military conducted an internal review which led to the Charter Task Force Report, issued in September 1986. This report attempted to justify maintenance of the exclusion policy, demonstrating the recalcitrance of the defense hierarchy on this issue.[46]

One Charter challenge was the case of Michelle Douglas. Douglas was part of the SIU team until their suspicions focused on her in a McCarthyesque twist. She was badgered by her former colleagues until she signed a voluntary resignation. Then she got angry and filed a Charter challenge—not for reinstatement, but for compensation to cover her legal costs, lost salary, and lost security clearance. She also petitioned for an end to the exclusion policy.

As Douglas put together her case, an external review (much like the PERSEREC studies in the United States) was conducted in August 1990. This review led to a report which recommended an end to investigations and the disbanding of the SIU. On top of this report, Douglas seemed likely to win her Charter challenge, so military leaders reportedly asked the Minister of Defense to drop the exclusion policy. The Cabinet (dominated by the Conservative Party) refused. The Douglas case went to court, and the government conceded that the policy was unconstitutional and agreed to the court's order for its abolition. The result was that the elected politicians could effectively throw up their hands and blame the decision on the court, thereby absolving themselves of responsibility for what many believed would be an unpopular policy change.

The impending end of the ban produced the same kinds of concern over privacy in living quarters and violence against lesbians and gay men, and generated much recalcitrance as is current in the United States. In the end, in October 1993, the ban was lifted. The Canadian armed forces have thus far reported no change in patterns of recruitment or retention, and no relevant incidents of violence as a result of the policy change. While this issue was one of the rallying cries of the Conservatives, their loss in the recent election suggests that the public outrage they predicted has failed to materialize. Despite the end of the ban, discrimination against lesbians/gays persists in both informal and formal practices, such as denial of spousal benefits to lesbian/gay partners of military members and denial of travel support to military personnel to visit a same-sex partner.[47]

Australia also recently ended its ban, though no information on this is included in the RAND report and very little is said in the 1993 GAO *Foreign Countries* report. In practice, the ban was part of military personnel policy since World War I, but was not inscribed in the military code until 1986. In 1990, a female sergeant in the Army Reserves challenged her discharge under the lesbian/gay exclusion policy through an appeal to the Equal Opportunity Commission. The policy change was resisted by the Defense Minister and service chiefs, but enacted by the Cabinet on the EOC's recommendation on 23 November 1992.[48]

Both the RAND study and the 1993 GAO *Foreign Countries* report provide detailed information on the personnel policy of Israel. RAND included Israel as one of its comparative case studies because Israel was in the process of changing its policy, and because of "an opinion expressed by some in the U.S. military that the Israeli Defense Force is most comparable to [the U.S.'s]" due to Israel's "extensive recent warfighting experience."[49] RAND noted that there are significant differences between the U.S. and Israeli militaries in terms of size, service conditions, and cultural context.

The Israeli Knesset decriminalized sodomy under civil law in 1988 and amended civil labor law "to prohibit discrimination against homosexuals in the workplace" in 1992.[50] Although the Israeli military code prohibits sexual activity on bases and fraternization between officers and subordinates, there are no explicit regulations about same-sex activity. Conscripts are not asked about sexual identity as a matter of policy or routine, and there is no provision of automatic discharge for being lesbian/gay. However, between 1983 and 1993, soldiers identified as gay were required to submit to mandatory psychological evaluation to determine their "mental fortitude and maturity," and were subjected to intense investigation to determine whether their "sexual inclination" might constitute a security hazard.[51] For example, Professor Uzi Even, Chair of the Chemistry Department at Tel Aviv University, had his security clearance canceled and was stripped of his rank when an investigation in 1983 revealed he was in a gay relationship.[52]

In February 1993, these practices came under scrutiny by a subcommittee of the Knesset seeking to establish "homosexual equality before the law."[53]

According to the GAO, these legislative hearings prompted the military to review its policy and to rescind the requirements for psychological testing and special security clearances. The GAO report states that the Israeli Defense Force (IDF) "clarified" its policy on sexuality on 18 May 1993; RAND dates the announcement as 11 June 1993.[54] Despite official statements of the suspension of this policy, many gay Israeli soldiers believe they would be denied security clearances and/or promotions, so they continue to conceal their sexual identity; the Israeli military closet is thus "privatized" rather than institutionalized.

Among NATO member countries, the Dutch example is often cited by those who support an end to the lesbian/gay ban in the U.S. military. The Netherlands ended its lesbian/gay exclusion policy in 1974, nearly two decades ago.[55] The time elapsed since the policy change distinguishes the Netherlands from the Canadian, Australian, and Israeli cases, and provides more of a track record to evaluate in terms of the costs and effects of policy implementation.

Between 1911 and 1971, the age of consent for opposite-sex sexual relations in the Netherlands was 16, while the age of consent for same-sex sexual relations was 21. Lesbians and gay men were excluded from military service during these years. In 1972, the Dutch legislature decriminalized same-sex relations. The RAND study reports that "concomitant with the abolition of the civilian law, pressure was applied on the military to admit homosexuals," and the Minister of Defense changed the policy in 1974 so that homosexuality did not automatically disqualify someone from service. Instead, homosexuality was to be viewed as a medical rather than a moral factor in the evaluation of the recruit, and would not by itself disqualify a recruit from service. In 1986, the Minister of Defense declared that homosexuality would no longer be considered in the evaluation of recruits. In 1991, the Dutch parliament revised all of its antidiscrimination laws to state that discrimination on the basis of sexual identity was prohibited.[56]

For military personnel in the Netherlands, it is now a sanctionable offense to discriminate physically or verbally against another servicemember because of sexuality. Sanctions can include court-martial and prison if physical assault is involved. This is called a "zero tolerance" policy. Information brochures about careers in the Dutch armed forces include an explanation of the zero tolerance policy, and programs for all recruits are part of the training process. In addition, the armed forces funds runs an advocacy/support organization (funded and staffed with volunteers) and a hotline for lesbians and gay men in the service based on a peer counseling concept.[57]

Researchers Marion Andersen-Boers and Jan van der Meulen argue that the policy change in the Netherlands needs to be understood in the context of an overall process of "civilianization" of the Dutch military, reflected in the phrase "as civil as possible, as military as necessary," which gained currency in the 1960s and culminated in the abolition of conscription on 1 January 1988.[58] While the policy regarding lesbians and gay men in military service has changed, many lesbians and gay men remain closeted, as they see on balance more risk than benefit to disclosure.[59]

According to RAND, the Dutch report no change in recruitment, retention, or performance of its armed forces before and after the policy was implemented. The RAND report, however, was not enthusiastic about the Dutch model because, the RAND researchers argued, the type of "tolerance education" practiced by the Dutch might provoke strong reactions and hostility among U.S. servicemembers. Reflecting the RAND report's concerns, training materials issued by the U.S. Department of Defense to announce the Don't Ask, Don't Tell policy, indicated that officers were to clarify that the purposes of the briefing sessions were informational and factual, and not sensitivity training, a forum for debate, or a "gripe session."[60]

Should the U.S. military take its lessons from countries such as Canada, Australia, Israel, and the Netherlands? Critics such as Tom Bethell decry the Dutch example of a "feminized" military: "The Dutch army's pigtailed, earringed battalions do not inspire confidence, and the European Community's failure to muster a fighting force against the Serbs should come as no surprise."[61] In a 1993 journal article, John Luddy offers a similar critique of state militaries which do not exclude lesbians and gay men.[62] This calls to mind the work of Brian Mitchell in his book *Weak Link*, in which he argues that women are undermining the U.S. armed forces esprit d'corps and fighting capability.[63] The language of the protests by Bethell, Luddy, and others and its parallel with Mitchell's thesis illustrate the gendered construction and impact of the lesbian/gay ban. Close examination of the constructions of sexuality also reveal the extent to which the ban is raced in both its formulation and its implementation.

MAKING CONNECTIONS: RACE, GENDER, AND LESBIAN/GAY EXCLUSION

Military personnel exclusion policies have at least two functions. First, they control access to military service, excluding groups deemed "unfit" for service. Second, they control the *behavior* of individuals in the service, providing a mechanism for the removal of "misfits." These labels—the "unfit" and the "misfits"—lead me to ask what it is these people are being measured against: who doesn't fit, and what don't they fit?

Perhaps the notion of the "exclusivity" of military service is part of its appeal. Perhaps there is a parallel to be drawn between membership in the military and membership in a fraternity or particular religious congregation; that parallel concerns the notion of being chosen, of being special ("the few, the proud, the Marines"), a notion which can be self-affirming and self-empowering, but which can also require the simultaneous devaluation of those who are not members, who are outsiders or the "Other." There seems to me to be an intimate connection between constructions of gender, race, and sexuality underlying the U.S. lesbian/gay exclusion policy. In this section, I will try to sketch these connections.

What of the U.S. military's own experiences with race desegregation and sex integration? RAND dismissed women's integration into the U.S. armed forces as an inappropriate analogy:

Our review of the military's experience with integrating blacks and women shows that racial integration is the more applicable analogy: women are still largely excluded from combat and, therefore, in a very fundamental way, are treated as a special class.[64]

While the RAND researchers note that restrictions on women in combat aircraft were under review, they argue that the "remaining restrictions with regard to combat set women apart from men," and that if the purpose of the policy review "is to fully end discrimination on the basis of sexual orientation," then the sex analogy works less well than the race analogy.[65] It is always suspicious when someone says that the experiences of women "don't count." Aren't some of the people excluded by or discharged because of the ban on women? And aren't there many ways in which the sex and sexuality integration analogies "fit," as well as the race analogy? Aren't all women—straight or lesbian—misfits/unfit for the same reason as gay men? And why focus on combat exclusion?

The RAND report argues that the experience of racial desegregation in the armed forces shows how the military can and has adapted to changing social circumstances. This is the military's success story. The report points out that racial integration was opposed by whites with vehement hostility and rhetoric similar to what is currently being directed against lesbian/gay integration. Physical violence against blacks was predicted, as it is now against gays. Much of the focus, then as now, related to housing facilities and privacy. Public opinion in general was, then as now, opposed to the policy change, and service personnel were even more opposed to the policy change than were nonmilitary people. The report concludes that the experience of racial integration illustrates that such changes take time, that public opinion can shift on such issues, and that workplace integration "does not automatically translate into social integration."[66]

The race and sexuality analogies, of course, are not a perfect fit, the RAND researchers admit. Racial integration was "spurred in part by critical *man*power needs" (emphasis added) and by the recognition on the part of some military leaders that "operational effectiveness was impaired by continued segregation."[67] The need for manpower (that is, personnel) is not applicable in this time of downsizing the military, though the operational question may come into play when one considers how all the personnel formerly engaged in investigation and litigation to ferret out lesbians/gays may be reassigned or removed. Of course, allowing resignations or early retirement of those opposed to serving with lesbians/gays, as Senator Sam Nunn (D-GA) proposed, could help with the downsizing. The DOD proposal to segregate lesbians and gay men from straights if the services are forced to accept them would create an operational nightmare.

There is another difference between the race and sexuality analogies: prima facie, racial exclusion would seem more easily accomplished than lesbian/gay exclusion, because sexuality would seem to be camouflaged more readily than race; although many straights believe they can identify lesbians and gay men by how they talk and act, lesbians and gay men are, in fact, a largely *invisible* minority group—unless they choose to be otherwise (whether simply "out" or "flaming queens"). Here, there seems more parallel between race and sex integration than between race and sexuality integration. However, this contrast between race and sexuality rests on the notion of racial classification as rooted in fundamental biological and superficially identifiable distinctions—distinctions which, try as they might, the Nazis were unable to make clearly enough to differentiate the "Aryan race" from the Jews, and which confounded white supremacists who sought to figure percentages of racial heritage for enforcing Jim Crow segregation. Clearly, lesbians and gay men already serve despite the witch hunts and "gay dragnets," so rather than talk about integration perhaps we should talk about *recognition, tolerance,* and *accommodation.*

Many African Americans are angered by the use of the race analogy, though the RAND report does not say so.[68] Some argue that their blackness is something over which they have no control, while they believe lesbians and gay men "choose" their "lifestyles." Let's think about this, aside from the research conducted on the issue which the RAND report summarizes. Why would someone choose to be part of a minority group which is despised, baited, verbally and physically abused, denied job opportunities, and generally seen as morally perverse? Why would someone choose to be lesbian or gay, knowing that such a "choice" brings social censure and shame to one's family and to oneself? This may be why so many who believe they are or may be lesbian or gay live celibate lives or seek conversion to heterosexuality through straight relationships or marriage, or through careers which will confirm their masculinity/femininity, such as military service for men.[69]

There are similarities in the social constructions of blackness and of gayness which I think make the analogy useful in ways the RAND researchers did not mention. These parallels have to do with perceptions of sexuality. As many of the authors in Toni Morrison's anthology *Race-ing Justice* point out, African Americans, both male and female, have been cast as sexually promiscuous and/or as sexual predators by white society.[70] Many of the arguments for keeping lesbians and gay men out of the military today are also cast in these terms. In the early 1900s, Blacks were blamed for the spread of venereal diseases such as syphilis and gonorrhea, just as gay men were blamed for AIDS (the so-called "gay plague") in the early 1980s. There is an interesting interface here: Blacks are also sometimes blamed for AIDS—Haitians and Ugandans especially, at different times in the past few years.

Similarly, Blacks and lesbians/gays (including lesbians and gays of color) have been the targets of violence because of their difference from the white/heterosexual majority population. For African Americans, this violence existed during three centuries of slavery and another century of de jure segregation with the sanction of authorities; with de facto segregation and physical and structural violence against African Americans a continuing reality, as the much publicized case of the beating of Rodney King by members of the Los Angeles Police Department illustrates. The argument that ending segregation in the military would lead to violence against Blacks ignored the reality of violence to which Blacks were already subjected. Similarly, the worry over violence against lesbians and gay men if the ban ends ignores current documented instances of violence perpetrated by members of the armed forces against both military personnel and civilians thought to be gay or lesbian, as in the case of Allen Schindler Jr.[71]

So why did the RAND researchers dismiss the sex integration analogy? The report makes the case for the race analogy in terms of the rhetoric directed against both minority groups. Consider the language in this statement by Lieutenant Colonel John H. Woodyard (US Army-Retired):

I worry not that soldiers will make love. I worry about the inevitable results of lovemaking—jealousy, spite, rivalry, favoritism, and diverted loyalties. These emotions can erode military discipline, and, thus, military effectiveness.

There is a danger that peer relationships will suffer also. Rivalry for that pretty corporal in the second platoon could damage the cohesiveness of the first platoon. Unit cohesiveness is vital. It relates to saving lives, and we should not trifle with it.[72]

If we remove the gendered term "pretty" from the second paragraph, we might wonder whether the Lieutenant Colonel was talking about women in the 1970s or lesbians/gays in the 1990s.

Other parallels between the experience of sex integration and proposed sexuality integration include the issues of housing and privacy, and the cost of conversion of living space for the "outsiders" or "Other." These same objections were raised against racial desegregation. In the case of sex integration, public opinion was more positive than it has been with regard to sexuality integration, but even here the connections are apparent. Many who objected to women's integration in the armed forces after World War II argued that the only women who would be interested in military service as a career were whores (unfits) or lesbians (misfits). These perceptions of women in the military still exist in some quarters.

The opinions of male service members about women's integration in 1948 were mixed; some favored full integration, while others opposed it. Congress conducted extensive hearings after 1945 to determine the extent and nature of women's participation in the U.S. military. Some argued that without an opportunity (or duty) to serve as full members of the military, women could never be full citizens. The perceived connection between military service and citizenship was also offered as a rationale for allowing African American men to serve and for ending troop segregation.

Ultimately, women's service was "regularized" but marginalized; women's numbers were limited to 2 percent of force total from 1948 to 1967. Too many women, it was thought, would ruin morale and discipline and impede the deployability of the troops, and thus the ability of the armed forces to fulfill its mission. This same rationale was offered by the Reagan administration when it announced a review of the Carter administration's policy of expanding women's numbers and roles in the armed forces in the early 1980s.

It is interesting to note that in the case of sexuality integration, both civilian and military women are more tolerant or accepting of the proposed change than are either civilian or military men, with military men most vehemently opposed.[73] Why are women more comfortable than men with the idea of ending the ban? Perhaps they feel less threatened at the thought of dealing with unwanted sexual advances and being "ogled," because they have experienced such treatment already—from men. Perhaps the construction of the feminine gender as more intimate and caring makes same-sex intimacy less threatening to women's gender identity than it is to men's.

Why was women's combat exclusion an automatic dismissal of the analogy of women's integration? For one thing, women are not considered to be "real" soldiers if they don't fight (never mind that in reality they have fought and died and been prisoners of war). More importantly, in terms of the construction of gender, combat is apparently perceived as the true test of manhood (just as birthing is apparently perceived as the fulfillment of womanhood). Congress has now rescinded sections 6015 and 8549 of the *U.S. Code* which excluded women from combat vessels and aircraft, so perhaps RAND should reconsider its dismissal of the sex integration analogy.[74]

Perhaps the real question the RAND researchers (and the Pentagon) were interested in is, "will gays be allowed in combat?" Supporters of the ban raise the specter of AIDS at this juncture. Currently, all recruits are routinely tested upon entering the service; recruits who test HIV positive are not accepted.[75] All other military personnel are tested either at their annual physicals or in connection with other medical procedures. The military automatically discharged anyone who tested positive during much of the 1980s, because anyone who had AIDS had to be gay, they reasoned.

The policy changed in the late 1980s, and service personnel who test positive are now retained but may only be deployed in the continental United States. They are given medical retirements when they become too ill to work.[76] According to the Pentagon, 1,214 service personnel were HIV positive as of December 1994. Recently, congressional representative Robert K. Dornan (R-CA), proposed that all HIV positive servicemembers should be discharged on the grounds that retaining people not available to serve worldwide impaired military readiness; his proposal received little open support from top military officials.[77]

DISCHARGE RATES AND THE CONSTRUCTION OF SEXUALITY

In the analysis presented in the RAND report, women are nearly invisible. There are almost no data on lesbians included, but this seems a fault in the data bases and surveys RAND consulted, rather than of RAND's own efforts.[78] Only two of the five U.S.-based studies of sexuality RAND examined included women in the sample, and foreign officials provided little or no information on lesbians in their state militaries. For example, RAND interviewers of French officials said that "all interviewees stated that they had no knowledge of lesbians in the military," and found that lesbianism was not mentioned "in any written materials" on the French military's policy.[79]

This tendency to focus on gay men and military exclusion suggests that we need to look at what Cynthia Enloe has called "militarized masculinity" to understand opposition to ending the ban.[80] Steven Zeeland sees the lesbian/gay exclusion policy as rooted in gendered constructions of sexuality and militarized constructions of gender, of military masculinity:

> The discriminatory regulation serves the men in the Pentagon as a weapon to be used against military queers who, in becoming visible, are perceived to undermine cherished gender stereotypes considered necessary for the maintenance of authority. How can the American fighting man, aggressive and predatory, be expected to stand naked in the shower before a man *known to penetrate other men*—without that macho soldier being made to *feel like a woman*? (emphasis original)[81]

The gender lines of military service were also described by a graduate of West Point who experienced the hazing of plebe year as gendered terrorism.[82] Herbert Richardson highlighted the intersection of gender and sexuality in his argument that the military's lesbian/gay exclusion policy is grounded in "gender fundamentalism," and that "the Tailhook pattern of military hostility towards women is SYSTEMATICALLY LINKED to the military's hostility to homosexuals" (emphasis original).[83] RAND's analysis neglects this intersection.

Significantly, RAND offered no explanation of the fact that the exclusion policy has a disproportionate effect on women, although RAND includes this information in a reference note, citing the GAO *Policy* report.[84] Over the decade of 1980 to 1990, women service personnel were three times as likely to be discharged under this policy than were men, and eight times more likely to be discharged under this policy than were men if they happened to be Marines.[85] While the gender bias of the application of the policy remains nearly invisible in the RAND report, it is well documented by the GAO. However, the GAO neglected to consider how the intersections of gender and race play out in the application of the policy.

To be sure, more men than women are discharged under the ban in terms of raw numbers. Data supplied by the Department of Defense to the GAO show that over the ten year period from 1980 to 1990, 13,022 men and 3,897 women were separated under the ban. However, since many more men than women serve, a disproportionate number of women are discharged under the exclusion rule, as is illustrated in Tables 6 and 7.

For example, in 1990, there were 1,806,146 men in the four services, but only 223,154 women; women comprised 11 percent of the total force. In that year, 733 men and 199 women were discharged under the exclusion rule; women comprised 21.4 percent of these discharges. In other words, for 1990, one in every 2,464 men was discharged, while one in every 1,121 women was discharged. As the numbers and proportion of women serving increased over

Table 6
DOD Discharges by Race, Gender, and Rank

Homosexual discharges

Fiscal Year	Involuntary discharges[a]	Homosexual discharges	Race White	Race Black	Race Other	Gender Male	Gender Female	Rank Enlisted	Rank Officer
1980	87,771	1,754	1,517	186	51	1,390	364	1,738	16
1981	96,004	1,817	1,542	225	50	1,466	351	1,789	28
1982	108,584	1,998	1,686	252	60	1,563	435	1,974	24
1983	108,697	1,815	1,512	247	56	1,376	439	1,800	15
1984	106,470	1,822	1,517	239	66	1,353	469	1,801	21
1985	87,777	1,660	1,386	210	64	1,256	404	1,647	13
1986	89,409	1,644	1,327	253	64	1,272	372	1,619	25
1987	83,047	1,380	1,129	192	59	1,068	312	1,356	24
1988	82,050	1,100	902	152	46	820	280	1,073	27
1989	77,149	997	820	130	47	725	272	975	22
1990	69,967	932	787	118	27	733	199	920	12
Total	996,925	16,919	14,125	2,204	590	13,022	3,897	16,692	227
Average	90,630	1,538	1,284	200	54	1,184	354	1,517	21

Source: U.S. Government Accounting Office (GAO), *Defense Force Management: Statistics Related to DOD's Policy on Homosexuality* (GAO/NSIAD-92-98, June 1992) 31.

[a]Discharges for failure to meet minimum behavioral/performance criteria.

Table 7

Composition of DOD Discharges by Race, Gender, and Rank (figures in percentages)

Fiscal Year	Homosexual discharges	Homosexual discharges							
		Race			Gender		Rank		
		White	Black	Other	Male	Female	Enlisted	Officer	
1980	2.0	86.5	10.6	2.9	79.2	20.8	99.1	0.9	
1981	1.9	84.9	12.4	2.8	80.7	19.3	98.5	1.5	
1982	1.8	84.4	12.6	3.0	78.2	21.8	98.8	1.2	
1983	1.7	83.3	13.6	3.1	75.8	24.2	99.2	0.8	
1984	1.7	83.3	13.1	3.6	74.3	25.7	98.8	1.2	
1985	1.9	83.5	12.7	3.9	75.7	24.3	99.2	0.8	
1986	1.8	80.7	15.4	3.9	77.4	22.6	98.5	1.5	
1987	1.7	81.8	13.9	4.3	77.4	22.6	98.3	1.7	
1988	1.3	82.0	13.8	4.2	74.5	25.5	97.5	2.5	
1989	1.3	82.2	13.0	4.7	72.7	27.3	97.8	2.2	
1990	1.3	84.4	12.7	2.9	78.6	21.4	98.7	1.3	
Average	1.7	83.5	13.0	3.5	77.0	23.0	98.7	1.3	

Source: U.S. Government Accounting Office (GAO), *Defense Force Management: Statistics Related to DOD's Policy on Homosexuality* (GAO/NSIAD-92-98, June 1992) 31.

the ten-year period GAO reviewed, the proportion of women discharged under the policy fluctuated, peaking in the two-year period after President Reagan announced that the services should "hold the line" on the recruitment of women until their impact on "readiness" could be more fully assessed.

From the GAO data, I have calculated the discharge rates for men and women relative to their presence in the armed forces overall and in each of the four service branches. For 1990, the discharge rates for men and women DOD-wide were .04 percent and .09 percent, respectively. Across the branches, the average discharge rates for men and women over the ten-year period from 1980-1990 differed substantially, as illustrated in Table 8. These data raise several questions. For example, do more lesbians choose to enlist in the Marine Corps, or is the Marine Corps simply the most zealous service in terms of implementing the lesbian/gay exclusion policy against women? The Marine Corps has the smallest proportion of women serving of the four services. In 1990, women comprised 13.9 percent of Air Force personnel, 11.4 percent of Army personnel, 10 percent of Navy personnel, and 4.7 percent of Marine Corps personnel; by 1995, women comprised 16 percent of the Air Force, 13.4 percent of the Army, 12.2 percent of the Navy, and still only 4.6 percent of the Marines.[86] One could speculate that perhaps the small numbers and proportion of women Marines distort the discharge data, but the GAO does not attempt to answer this question.

Over that same ten-year period, 98.7 percent of the discharges were of enlisted personnel, with officers accounting for only 1.3 percent of such discharges. Altogether, 16,692 enlisted servicemembers were discharged, and only 227 officers. The discharge rates relative to presence in the force are lower for officers than for enlisted personnel; using the average numbers of discharges and numbers of officers and enlisted personnel in service from 1980-1990, the rates are .01 percent and .08 percent, respectively. For each of the services, the discharge rate for officers was below .01 percent on average for the 1980-1990 period GAO studied. Randy Shilts attributes this to the fact that officers can resign and avoid administrative hearings.[87] For the three-year period reviewed in the PERSEREC/Sarbin-Karols report (1985, 1986, and 1987), the discharge rates for male and female officers were approximately the same in the Navy, but female officers were twice as likely to be discharged from the Army and the Air Force as were male officers on these grounds. Marine Corps data on male/female officer discharges are negligible.[88]

The GAO emphasized in its analysis that the rate of discharge for homosexuality relative to the rate of representation in the armed services was most disproportionate for white women over the ten-year period of 1980-1990. But the GAO did not point out that the discharge rate was also significantly disproportionate for women of color other than African American women. African American women and white men were discharged at rates roughly proportionate to their presence, and African American men and other men of color were discharged at rates far below their presence in the ranks DOD-wide.[89]

Table 8

Discharges for Homosexuality Relative to Representation in Military, by Sex and by Service

	Men	Women
Air Force	.04%	.12%
Army	.04%	.17%
Navy	.13%	.24%
Marine Corps	.04%	.31%

Source: Calculated from data presented in United States General Accounting Office (US GAO), *Defense Force Management: Statistics Related to DOD's Policy on Homosexuality* (Washington, DC: US GAO, GAO/NSIAD-92-98S, June 1992).

Rates of discharge for homosexuality relative to rates of representation by race as well as by sex also differed across the individual service branches over the period GAO examined. In each of the four services, white women were discharged well above their rate of representation in the ranks. In the Army, the pattern followed that of the overall DOD, except that white men were discharged at rates *below* their presence in the ranks, as were African American men and other men of color. In the Air Force, African American women and other women of color were discharged proportionately to their representation, and, as in the Army, all men were discharged at rates below their representation. In the Navy, white men, African American men and women, and other women of color were discharged at rates proportionate to their representation; other men of color were discharged at a rate below their presence. In the Marine Corps, white women were discharged at roughly eight times their rate of representation; African American women and other women of color were discharged at twice their rates of representation; white men and African American men were discharged at rates at or only slightly below their rates of representation, and other men of color were discharged at one-half times their rate of representation.[90]

How do we explain these patterns in the discharge rates? If we examine social constructions of sexuality, we find that they are both raced and gendered. It may be that for the African American gay soldier, the myth of Black male hypersexuality may create a presumption of straightness which may make his closet easier to construct.[91] That is, he may be presumed to be straight because he is Black. The sexuality of the White soldier may be less certain in our social mythology; perhaps his heterosexuality must be proven rather than being assumed. His closet may therefore be more difficult to construct.

Ethnographic interviews of male soldiers and sailors indicate that presumptions about male sexuality are also based upon the individual's branch of service and the genderedness of his occupation.[92] Interservice rivalry and higher rates of discharge on grounds of sexuality in some services—for example, Navy versus Marines—foster these perceptions. The serviceman in caretaking or otherwise "feminized" professions—such as medical corpsman or chaplain's assistant, and especially those in positions of subordination rather than command—is suspect, and may be presumed to be gay. His closet may be transparent. Choosing more "masculine" jobs in the military police, special operations, or combat arms may help a gay soldier mask his sexual identity.

Tracy Timmons argues that the differential discharge rates for men and women and across the services correlate to the services' respective requirements for male-identified (gendered masculine) behaviors as well as to the presence of women in nontraditional military jobs.[93] Mary Ann Humphrey argues that the exclusion rule is used to keep women in their place and to keep them available to bolster the morale of male service personnel.[94] Many military women see the exclusion rule as a way for their supervisors and colleagues to extort sexual compliance, a tool in the arsenal of sexual harassment.[95]

Because there are no "nice girls" in the military, the sexuality of all military women is suspect: they are seen as either whores or lesbians.[96] It may be that because of raced and gendered perceptions of Black female sexuality, the African American female soldier is interpreted more often as whore rather than as lesbian, as sexually available (as slave women were available), while the White female soldier, because presumed less "sexed" or libidinous on the basis of race (the "lady" of Victorian chasteness), gets scrutinized as lesbian.[97]

Researchers Michelle Benecke and Kirstin Dodge offer a different view of the way the military interprets Black female sexuality. They argue that African American women and other women of color are scrutinized more closely than are white women by promotion review boards who want military women to be "appropriately feminine" (not too girly, not too butch), and that "when women of color seek each other out and spend time together, their smaller numbers may open them to special scrutiny and thus to greater dangers of investigation" under the lesbian/gay exclusion policy.[98] The case of the U.S.S. Norton Sound, in which every African American woman crew member was "identified" as lesbian, offers evidence of this.[99]

The race/gender/sexuality interface may vary across occupations for women as it does for men. Women in nontraditional occupations and in "unfeminine" positions of command/control may be most suspect of homosexuality or most heterosexualized: either "she's so 'butch' she's as good as a man" or "she slept her way to the top."[100] These women challenge traditional gender identity and confound the androcentric construction of military identity: if you're me (soldier), who am I? For example, consider the witch hunt against women drill instructors at Parris Island, South Carolina. Because Marine basic training is considered so intense as to be a "military mindfuck," the women drill instructors and military police at Parris Island confounded and reversed the gendered construction of soldiers. The same holds true for women aboard nonhospital Navy ships. Randy Shilts reports special scrutiny of women who play on all-female sports teams.[101]

One of the most common strategies for coping with exclusion, heterosexism, and homophobia is "passing" as heterosexual, either in seemingly monogamous straight relationships or through heteropromiscuity.[102] How credible are the different variants of the passing strategy when race and gender are considered? For men, passing in heterosexual couples may not be enough, because of a generalized presumption of military macho promiscuity; this may be especially true for African American men.[103] For White women, passing as part of a heterosexual couple may be enough, while for African American women, assumptions about Black female sexuality may deny the credibility of this strategy for closeting.

As the Cold War framework unravels, the constructions of race/gender/ sexuality underlying that framework are exposed and may be challenged. Benecke and Dodge argue that the lesbian/gay exclusion policy "controls and confines women's presence and behavior in the military," and note that increased hostility toward lesbians and gay men "was part and parcel of the 1950s McCarthyism."[104] For example, the RAND report notes that the

Eisenhower administration issued Executive Order 10450 in 1953 which made "sexual perversion" grounds for dismissal from federal employment.[105]

The military has used other aspects of women's sexuality (beyond straight/ bisexual/lesbian) to police the gender line. In the past, women were discharged for pregnancy, marriage, and heteropromiscuity as well as for lesbianism. Using women's sexuality to police the gender line has taken on a new twist since the Gulf War: one partner of a dual-career couple (usually the woman) and single parents (again, disproportionately women) will not be deployed overseas with their units during military emergencies.

The new Don't Ask, Don't Tell policy has significant implications for women because of what I call "gender culture." The dominant feminine gender culture permits a variety of same-sex touching which is prohibited in the dominant masculine gender culture. For men, permissible same-sex touching involves hand-shaking and back-slapping (both having an undercurrent of competition and violence/dominance, for example, the "firm" handshake) and, in athletic contexts, butt-smacking and group-hugging. Feminine gender culture same-sex touching, such as hugging, cheek-kissing, and walking arm-in-arm, tends to be gentle and affectionate. Michelle Benecke of the National Women's Law Center reports that cheek-kissing has been construed as a dischargeable offense under Don't Ask, Don't Tell because the offensive "conduct" occurred "in public and in uniform."[106]

The type of same-sex touching and conversation permitted in the dominant gender cultures may be quite different from that permitted in minority gender cultures. Both physical contact and language may be more or less intimate. For example, Latina women from Caribbean countries often walk hand-in-hand or arm-across-shoulders; African American women sometimes address one another as "girl" or "girlfriend," with reference to friendship rather than to sexuality. The Don't Ask, Don't Tell policy's conduct rule presents a rigidity of gender culture interpretation ill-suited for our multicultural society.

POLICY PROPOSALS AND REVISIONS

In the congressional hearings about Clinton's plan to issue an executive order ending lesbian/gay military exclusion, Senators and representatives offered two alternatives to the "radical" or "extreme" policy of a complete end to the lesbian/gay exclusion: accept lesbians and gay men for military service, but either segregate them from straights or silence them—that is, forbid lesbians and gay men from discussing or revealing their sexuality.

I call the first policy option—homo/heterosexual segregation—the "*Plessy v. Ferguson* reprise." This proposal called for "separate but equal" accommodations and deployment groups for straights and lesbians/gays. Of course, separate accommodations for males and females would have to have been maintained, which would have resulted in four militaries: straight men, gay men, straight women, lesbian women. Of course, the question of what to do with bisexuals and transsexuals was not addressed. The proposal would have been laughable if those making it were not in a position to make it official policy.

The second option proposed what I call the "ostrich approach": let lesbians and gay men in, but don't let them "out"—that is, end the ban on lesbian/gay personnel, but make them keep their sexual identity a secret for the good of morale, national security, good order, and discipline. Include lesbians and gay men, but don't condone their "lifestyle choice." (Former Senator Barry Goldwater invokes this ostrich image in his critique of the Don't Ask, Don't Tell compromise.[107]) This policy alternative allowed Congress to approve inclusion grudgingly, based on a narrow civil rights argument, but avoided further discussion, controversy, and cost (both political and financial) of determining, for example, whether lesbian/gay couples and partners are entitled to dependent benefits or joint posting, housing, and leave consideration.

President Clinton's Don't Ask, Don't Tell, Don't Pursue policy embodies a variant of the ostrich approach.[108] Under this compromise policy, the military may discharge members "who engage in homosexual conduct, which is defined as a homosexual act, a statement that the member is homosexual or bisexual, or a marriage or attempted marriage to someone of the same gender" (sic).[109] This compromise allows lesbians and gay men a space in the military—an institutionalized closet—but no voice.

Both former Senator Goldwater and former Assistant Secretary of Defense Lawrence Korb opposed the compromise policy. In his assessment that "there's no valid reason for keeping the ban on gays" and that it's time "to pull the curtains on this charade of policy," Goldwater wrote, "You don't need to be 'straight' to fight and die for your country. You just need to shoot straight."[110] Korb wrote that the sentence given to Air Force Lt. Joann Newark and the PERSEREC/Sarbin-Karols report convinced him that "the nation and the military would be best served by dropping the ban entirely."[111]

The U.S. policy review process has borne a striking similarity to the Canadian experience. Opponents of the new compromise policy hoped that, like the Douglas case in Canada, the Meinhold case in the United States might be the vehicle through which the lesbian/gay exclusion policy would be completely ended. On 8 October 1993, a federal district court ruled that the exclusion policy was unconstitutional discrimination and ordered the reinstatement of Meinhold in the Navy. The U.S. Court of Appeals upheld the ruling of the district court in August 1994, and Meinhold reports that his coworkers have been "supportive and professional" since his reinstatement.[112]

While the policy change was announced in 1993, implementation was delayed. Perhaps the Clinton administration hoped that the delay would allow the Supreme Court to step in and decide the case "above the political fray," thus saving the administration from further political damage on this issue. It seemed unlikely that the Court would decide to hear the case, given the Court's past performance. But even if the Court had granted certiorari, the current composition of the Bench and the Court's decision in *Bowers v. Hardwick* suggested that no "right of privacy" or "equal protection" argument would persuade the conservative majority of the Court to end the ban.[113]

Since Meinhold won reinstatement, six other servicemembers have challenged the new compromise policy in a collective suit. Five of the six plaintiffs disclosed their sexual identity for the first time in the suit, and the sixth filed under a pseudonym. As a result, the Brooklyn federal district court ruled Don't Ask, Don't Tell unconstitutional; the Clinton administration has said it will appeal the decision.[114] Whether the Supreme Court will grant certiorari remains to be seen.

Since its founding but especially since the 1970s, the question of the nature of military culture and the military institution has been the focus of inquiry: is the military to be representative of the larger society, or is it an elite or exclusive club? Candidate Clinton promised a more representative government "that better reflect[ed] this country's population."[115] Before his retirement, Joint Chiefs of Staff Chair Colin Powell maintained (as is stated in DOD directive 1332.14 section H.1/1982) that homosexuality "is incompatible with military service because the presence of homosexuals is prejudicial to the good order and discipline of the armed forces." He is partly right: the "good order and discipline" of the military *as currently constructed* is predicated on a masculinist credo built on the depersonalization and homogenization of recruits. Part of this process requires their defeminization and masculinization.

The military's job is, indeed, to "make a man" out of its recruits. How does it attempt to accomplish this? First, military training seeks to systematically destroy or control all of the characteristics which comprise individual personality. The ability to choose freely must be denied in order to ensure that orders will be obeyed instantly and unconditionally. All forms of personal expression are obliterated as the recruit enters military training: heads are shorn, civilian clothing shed, identical uniforms donned. Every aspect of the recruit's life is scheduled and controlled: working, sleeping, eating, and relaxing.

The presence of people of color, of gay or bisexual men, and of straight, lesbian, or bisexual women in a predominantly and officially white, heterocentric, androcentric military culture makes military training's process of depersonalization and homogenization impossible: their very presence says "I'm different, I'm a person with feelings, desires, history, origin, and color, with body parts different from yours." Perhaps the depersonalization *is* necessary to create "universal soldiers" who will be able to dehumanize an enemy and kill without question.[116] But as citizens of the United States, we must ask ourselves if we want such soldiers to represent us in our armed forces. Is this the *only* way to make soldiers? Must boot camp instructors rely on the fears and hatreds of racism, misogyny, and homophobia?

Without the foundation of hate and fear of those who are different, what is there to create military unity, esprit de corps, morale, and discipline? If the military's job is to protect and defend the citizens of the United States, then the military must demonstrate respect for all U.S. citizens in its own policies. Perhaps recruit training could make an appeal to patriotism based on diversity or "nationalisms" (*E Pluribus unum*, as is attempted in *One Nation, Many*

Voices, the new curriculum guide for New York State) rather than to racism, sexism, and heterosexism? If the military's mission is not only to fight and win the nation's wars but also to police the "New World Order," to promote democracy, and to protect human rights, it cannot systematically deny the rights of any group in our society. Perhaps we should base military training on a new loyalty, internationalism, given the U.S. military's recent tasks to help refugees (most of whom are women, according to the United Nations High Commission on Refugees), to feed starving Somalians, and to assist noncombatants in the former Yugoslavia. For these tasks, our soldiers must be the most compassionate, the most tolerant, the most enlightened of our citizens.

The Don't Ask, Don't Tell policy legitimizes discrimination and violence against "Others" and institutionalizes the military closet on a foundation of ideas about race and gender that further divides rather than unites us and that poorly serves the evolving mission of the U.S. armed forces in the post-Cold War era. While the Don't Ask, Don't Tell policy may have been the best compromise possible in the then-current political context, the next steps must be taken through political organization and litigation to realize first RAND's sexuality-neutral "not germane" standard and eventually to adopt a more positive policy like that of the Netherlands.

NOTES

I wish to acknowledge my indebtedness to Nicole LaViolette and Karin Fierke for their assistance with research on Canada and the Netherlands, and to Judith Reppy and Mary Fainsod Katzenstein at Cornell University, and the Ford Foundation for their interest in and support for this project. Earlier versions of this chapter were presented at the "Workshop on Women in the Military," 12-14 November 1993, in Ithaca, N.Y., sponsored by the Peace Studies Program at Cornell University and the Ford Foundation, and at the 35th Annual Conference of the International Studies Association, 29 March 1994, in Washington, D.C. I thank participants at those meetings and the editor of this volume, Craig Rimmerman, for their thoughtful comments and suggestions.

1. I have adapted my title from that of the anthology edited by Toni Morrison, *Race-ing Justice, En-Gendering Power: Essays on Anita Hill, Clarence Thomas, and the Construction of Social Reality* (NY: Pantheon, 1992).

I must begin by problematizing the language used in this chapter. I reject both the terms "sexual preference" and "sexual orientation" to describe human sexuality. The first, as many have noted, suggests "choice"; the second, though currently preferred by most, suggests a leaning toward or "tendency," and possibly training or "indoctrination." Neither describes the full range of human sexuality as natural and immutable. I therefore employ the terms "sexuality" or "sexual identity" in discussing human sexuality, except when quoting from sources which employ other terms.

Joining Nicole LaViolette and Sandra Whitworth, I must also problematize the use of the phrase "lesbians and gay men." I recognize that these terms are Eurocentric and dualistic, that human sexuality and sexual behavior vary along a continuum (as Kinsey argued long ago), and that many people throughout the world do not self-identify with these labels. The phrase "sexual minorities" has been offered as an alternative but has not gained wide currency, so I will employ "lesbians and gay men" to describe a wide range of sexual behaviors and identities, including those of bisexuals, transsexuals, and transvestites. See LaViolette and Whitworth, "No Safe Haven: Sexuality as a Universal Human Right and Gay and Lesbian Activism in International Politics," *Millennium: Journal of International Studies* 23:3 (1994) 563-88.

I define "race" as a political and subjective category rather than a biological certainty, and elide race and ethnicity to describe the division between those whom a society privileges and those whom it identifies as "different" or "Other" based on racial/ethnic heritage, nationality, or "color."

Similarly, I define "gender" as the political construction of roles, space, and place, and of expected behaviors, from those whom a society designates as "masculine" and "feminine," in contrast to biological "sex," which distinguishes "male" from "female." Unfortunately, the terms "gender" and "sex" are used interchangeably by some, as though gender were merely a polite way to say sex. For example, the GAO refers to the "gender" rather than "sex" of military personnel in its data, and RAND describes "same-gender relations" rather than "same-sex relations" in its study. A problem with the confusion of these terms is that recent psychological research suggests that same-sex couples tend to be similarly gendered, whereas earlier studies argued that people sought differently-gendered partners in same-sex relationships (the butch-femme argument). My goal is to examine the intersection of gender, race, and sexuality.

2. Harold Lasswell, *Politics: Who Gets What, When, How* (New York: McGraw-Hill, 1936).

3. The GAO and RAND looked not only to the policies of other state militaries but also to the "domestic analogies" of police and fire departments in major U.S. cities. The GAO studied personnel practices of departments in New York, Seattle, San Francisco, and Washington, D.C. RAND examined departments in New York, Seattle, Chicago, Houston, Los Angeles, and San Diego.

4. Bill Clinton, with Albert Gore Jr., *Putting People First: How We Can All Change America* (NY: Times Books, 1992), 64.

5. Quoted in RAND, *Sexual Orientation and U.S. Military Personnel Policy: Options and Assessment* (Santa Monica, CA: RAND National Defense Research Institute, MR-323-OSD, April 1993), xvii.

6. As in the cases of Marine Sgt. Justin C. Elzie, Navy Lt. Tracy Thorne, and Navy Lt. j.g. R. Dirk Selland. See, for example, José Zuniga, *Soldier of the Year* (NY: Pocket, 1994).

7. Congressional Quarterly, *Congressional Quarterly Almanac, 103d Congress, 1st Session, 1993* (hereafter *1993 CQ Almanac*) 49: 461.

8. See "Gays May Be Returned to Active Duty," *Los Angeles Times*, reprinted in *Binghamton Press and Sun-Bulletin* (8 January 1994): 3A.

9. Eric Schmitt, "First Hearing in Court Test on Gay Rules," *New York Times* (14 March 1995): All; Eric Schmitt, "Judge Overturns Pentagon Policy on Homosexuals," *New York Times* (31 March 1995): A1, A24; "Banning Gay Soldiers by Trickery," *New York Times* (1 April 1995): OpEd 18; Pat Towell, "Federal Judge Strikes Down 'Don't Ask, Don't Tell,'" *CQ Weekly Report* 53:13 (1 April 1995): 957.

10. Katharine Q. Seelye, "Gingrich Seems to Back Off on Step Against Gay Policy," *New York Times* (5 April 1995): A23; Pat Towell, "Gingrich Retreats From Calling For Tougher Policy on Gays," *CQ Weekly Report* 53:14 (8 April 1995): 1036; "Republican Showing in Election Renews Gay Rights Debate," *Washington Post* (25 November 1994): A33.

11. See Randy Shilts, *Conduct Unbecoming: Gays & Lesbians in the U.S. Military, Vietnam to the Persian Gulf* (NY: St. Martin's, 1993), 7-12, and David F. Burrelli, "The Debate on Homosexuals in the Military," in *Gays and Lesbians in the Military: Issues, Concerns, and Contrasts*, eds. Wilbur J. Scott and Sandra Carson Stanley (Hawthorne, NY: Aldine de Gruyter, 1994), 18.

12. The Newport investigation and trials are detailed in Lawrence R. Murphy, *Perverts by official Order: The Campaign Against Homosexuals by the United States Navy* (NY: Haworth/Harrington Park, 1988).

13. See Allan Bérubé, *Coming Out Under Fire: The History of Gay Men and Women in World War Two* (NY: Plume, 1991), 8-33.

14. For a summary of the history of the U.S. exclusion policy, see Shilts, *Conduct Unbecoming*, 1-18; Burrelli in *Gays and Lesbians in the Military*, eds. Scott and Carson Stanley (1994), 17-31; and RAND *Sexual Orientation*, 3-10.

15. Quoted in Theodore R. Sarbin and Kenneth E. Karols, "Nonconforming Sexual Orientations and Military Suitability," PERS-TR-89-002 (Defense Personnel Security Research and Education Center, December 1988) [hereafter PERSEREC/Sarbin-Karols], reproduced verbatim in *Gays in Uniform: The Pentagon's Secret Reports*, ed. Kate Dyer (Boston, MA: Alyson, 1990), 56-61, 68; also quoted in Burrelli in *Gays and Lesbians in the Military*, eds. Scott and Carson Stanley (1994), 18.

16. Shilts, *Conduct Unbecoming*, 378-79.

17. United States General Accounting Office (US GAO), *Defense Force Management: DOD's Policy on Homosexuality* (Washington, DC: US GAO/NSIAD-92-98, June 1992) [hereafter GAO Policy], 11.

18. United States General Accounting Office (US GAO), *Defense Force Management: Statistics Related to DOD's Policy on Homosexuality* (Washington, D.C.: US GAO, GAO/NSIAD-92-98S, June 1992) [hereafter GAO Statistics], 31.

19. In 1991, 949; in 1992, 708; in 1993, 682; in 1994, 597, according to Defense Department data in Eric Schmitt, "New Rules on Gay Soldiers: A Year Later, No Clear Results," *New York Times* (13 March 1995): A1, A16.

20. See C. Dixon Osburn and Michelle M. Benecke, "Conduct Unbecoming Continues: The First Year Under 'Don't Ask, Don't Tell, Don't Pursue,'" Servicemembers Legal Defense Network, 28 February 1995. See also John Gallagher, "One Year Later" and "Some Things Never Change," *Advocate* 655 (17 May 1994): 39-45, 46-47, and Hanna Rosin, "The Fallacy of 'Don't Ask, Don't Tell': The Ban Plays On," *New Republic* 210:18 (2 May 1994): 11-13. Rosin reports 708 people were discharged in FY 1992 and that 773 were discharged in FY 1993 "including eight months in which the new policy was in effect . . ." but cites no source for the data.

21. See Keith Meinhold, "The Navy vs. Me," *New York Times* (16 December 1993): OpEd A29, and "Pentagon's Policy Has to End," *Los Angeles Times*, reprinted in *Finger Lakes Times* (Geneva, NY) (17 April 1995): OpEd 9; re: Meinhold, see also: Katrina M. Dewey, "Conduct Unconstitutional," *California Lawyer* 84 (July 1993):

36-40, 84. See also Margarethe Cammermeyer with Chris Fisher, *Serving in Silence* (NY: Viking, 1994).

22. Many of these cases are summarized in RAND *Sexual Orientation* Chapter 11: 332-67, and GAO *Policy* 46-53. See also Donald N. Bergsoff and David W. Ogden, "APA *Amicus Curiae* Briefs Furthering Lesbian and Gay Male Civil Rights," *American Psychologist* 46:9 (September 1991): 950-56. There are monographs published on several cases: see, for example, Mike Hippler, *Matlovich: The Good Soldier* (Boston: Alyson, 1989); Joseph Steffan, *Honor Bound: A Gay American Fights for the Right to Serve His Country* (NY: Villard, 1992); and Jim Holobaugh with Keith Hale, *Torn Allegiances: The Story of a Gay (ROTC) Cadet* (Boston: Alyson, 1993). In her defense of the exclusion policy, Melissa Wells-Petry identifies twelve cases "that reached substantive challenges" to the policy: see *EXCLUSION: Homosexuals and the Right to Serve* (Washington, DC: Regnery, 1993), 8, 192-3.

23. The pattern of federal courts' deference to the military (and to Congress) on personnel issues is reflected in such cases as *Rostker v. Goldberg* 453 US 57 (1981), which upheld the all-male draft; *Dillard v. Brown* 652 F.2d 316 (3d Cit. 1981), which upheld military exclusion of single parents; *Goldman v. Weinberger* 475 US 503 (1985), which upheld the military prohibition against wearing yarmulke; and *Brown v. Glines* 444 US 348 (1980), which upheld the military's prohibition against service members circulating a petition addressed to Congress. See Wells-Petry *EXCLUSION* 28. Exceptions to the pattern include *Crawford v. Cushman* 531 F.2d 1114 (2d Cit. 1976), in which the courts would not allow the military to continue to discharge women for pregnancy, and *Owens v. Brown* (DC) 455 FSupp 291 (27 July 1978), in which Judge John Sirica ruled that the Navy must open nonhospital/noncombat ships to women.

24. Mary Fainsod Katzenstein reports that Schroeder, Paul Tsongas (D-MA), Howard Metzenbaum (D-OH), and Barbara Boxer (D-CA) introduced legislative initiatives to overturn the lesbian/gay exclusion. See her article, "The Spectacle as Political Resistance: Feminist and Gay/Lesbian Politics in the Military," *Minerva: Quarterly Report on Women in the Military* XI:1 (Spring 1993): 1-16.

25. United States General Accounting Office (US GAO), *Homosexuals in the Military: Policies and Practices of Foreign Countries* (Washington, D.C.: US GAO, GAO/NSAID-93-215, June 1993) [hereafter *GAO Foreign Countries*] 5, 19-26; RAND *Sexual Orientation* 65-104. Shilts reports that exclusion policies were dropped in Norway in 1977, Sweden in 1980, Spain in 1984, and France in 1985 (*Conduct Unbecoming*, 578-80). The discrepancies might be attributed to differences between the data of passage of a policy change and its subsequent implementation or to a staged process of policy change.

26. GAO *Policy*, 40.

27. GAO *Foreign Countries*, 22-23.

28. Cynthia Enloe, "NATO: The Lesson Machine," in *Loaded Questions: Women in the Military*, ed. Wendy Chapkis (Amsterdam/Washington, D.C.: Transnational Institute, 1981), 65-72.

29. GAO *Foreign Countries*, 1-2.

30. International Institute for Strategic Studies (IISS), *The Military Balance 1993-1994* (London: Brassey's, 1994), 224-28; data are for 1992.

31. See *1993 CQ Almanac*, 458.

32. British common law prohibiting same-sex relations did not apply to women; see Gwyn Harries-Jenkins and Christopher Dandeker, "Sexual Orientation and Military Service: The British Case," in *Gays and Lesbians in the Military*, eds. Scott and Carson Stanley (1994), 192-93.

33. RAND *Sexual Orientation*, 1-3.

34. See RAND *Sexual Orientation*, 332-67, and Appendix C.

35. The text of the Crittenden report, or "Report of the Board Appointed to Prepare and Submit Recommendations to the Secretary of the Navy for the Revision of Policies, Procedures, and Directives Dealing with Homosexuals" chaired by Captain S. H. Crittenden Jr., is found in E. Lawrence Gibson, *Get Off My Ship: Ensign Berg v. The U.S. Navy* (NY: Avon, 1978), Appendix E.

36. PERSEREC/Sarbin-Karols 33, reprinted in Dyer, *Gays in Uniform*, 39.

37. Michael A. McDaniel, "Preservice Adjustment of Homosexual and Heterosexual Military Accessions: Implications for Security Clearance Suitability," PERS-TR-89-004 (Monterey, CA: Defense Personnel Security Research and Education Center/PERSEREC, January 1989), iii, reprinted in Dyer, *Gays in Uniform*. The report refers only to gay men.

38. RAND *Sexual Orientation*, xxii.

39. Statements made anonymously during a "Cara al Pueblo Internacional," (international press conference/townmeeting), Habana, Cuba, July 1984.

40. Lourdes Arguelles and B. Ruby Rich, "Homosexuality, Homophobia, and Revolution: Notes Toward an Understanding of the Cuban Lesbian and Gay Male Experience," in *Hidden From History: Reclaiming the Gay and Lesbian Past*, eds. Martin Bauml Duberman, Martha Vicinus, and George Chauncey Jr. (Canada: New American Library Books, 1986), 441-55, revised from *Signs* (Summer 1984).

41. Jessica Mates, "For Cuba's Gays and Lesbians, Change is in the Wind," *Gay Community News* 20:1/2 (June 1994), 23.

42. GAO *Foreign Countries*, 23.

43. Shilts *Conduct Unbecoming*, 580.

44. See Rosemary E. Park, "Opening the Canadian Forces to Gays and Lesbians: An Inevitable Decision But Improbable Reconfiguration," in *Gays and Lesbians in the Military*, eds. Scott and Carson Stanley (1994), 165-80. Canadian MP Svend Robinson and his assistant Nicole LaViolette provided a wealth of information on Canada's recision; see E. Kaye Fulton, "Gay and Proud," *Maclean's* 107:20 (16 May 1994), 36-39, re: Robinson's work on this and other lesbian/gay rights issues.

45. Gary Kinsman, "'Character Weaknesses' and 'Fruit Machines': Toward an Analysis of the Anti-Homosexual Security Campaign in the Canadian Civil Service," *Labour/Le Trevail* 35 (Spring 1995): 133-61; see also Kinsman, *The Regulation of Desire: Sexuality in Canada* (Montreal: Black Rose, 1987).

46. "Charter Task Force Final Report" (September 1986), Part 4.

47. Gary Kinsman, Professor of Sociology and Anthropology, Laurentian University, Sudbury, Ontario, Canada, in a letter to the author dated 2 October 1995.

48. See "Lesbians in Australian Military Test Limits of Change," *Minerva's Bulletin Board* (Spring 1993): 4-5; GAO Foreign Countries, 19.

49. RAND *Sexual Orientation*, 66.

50. GAO *Foreign Countries*, 40.

51. RAND does not provide information on lesbian Israeli soldiers. See RAND *Sexual Orientation*, 85-90; GAO *Foreign Countries*, 40-41.

52. See Clyde Haberman, "Homosexuals in Israeli Army: No Official Discrimination, But Keep It Secret," *New York Times* (21 February 1993): 14. Researcher Rueven Gal argues that Even's case was "the exception, not the rule," and that the "integration of homosexuals occurred with little opposition." See his essay, "Gays in the Military: Policy and Practice in the Israeli Defense Forces," in *Gays and Lesbians in the Military*, eds. Scott and Carson Stanley (1994), 186-87.

53. GAO *Foreign Countries*, 40.

54. GAO *Foreign Countries*, 41; RAND *Sexual Orientation*, 87.

55. See Marion Andersen-Boers and Jan Van Der Meulen, "Homosexuality and the Armed Forces in the Netherlands," in *Gays and Lesbians in the Military*, eds. Scott and Carson Stanley (1994), 205-16.

56. RAND *Sexual Orientation*, 90-91.

57. Directie Voorlichting, Ministerie van Defensie, Stichting Homosexualiteit en Krijgsmacht, "Homosexualiteit en Defensie" (Den Haag, Nederland, 1992) and Maatschappelijke Raad voor de Krijgsmacht, "The Government's Position on Homosexuality and the Armed Forces" (n.d., unpublished ms.; available from Directie Voorlichting, Ministerie van Defensie, Den Haag, Nederland).

58. Andersen-Boers and Van der Meulen in *Gays and Lesbians in the Military*, eds. Scott and Carson Stanley (1994), 214-15.

59. See David R. Segal, Paul A. Gade, and Edgar M. Johnson, "Homosexuals in Western Armed Forces (U.K., Germany, Belgium, Denmark, the Netherlands)," *Society* 31:1 (November/December 1993): 37-42, and Eric Konigsberg, "Gays in Arms," *Washington Monthly* 24:11 (November 1992): 10-13.

60. "DOD Policy on Homosexual Conduct," official briefing materials issued to officers responsible for implementing the new policy with instructions that all personnel be made aware of the policy change within a specified time from the effective date of the policy change.

61. Tom Bethell, "A Good Army Doesn't Have Room for Gays," *Times-Post News Service*, reprinted in *Binghamton Press & Sun-Bulletin* (29 November 1992): 1E, 4E.

62. John Luddy, "Make War, Not Love: The Pentagon's Ban is Wise and Just," *Policy Review* 64 (Spring 1993): 68-71; see also an editorial piece by Lt. Gen. Bernard E. Trainor (Marine-Retired) and Col. Eric L. Chase (Marine Reserve), "Keep Gays Out," *New York Times* (29 March 1993): A15.

63. Brian Mitchell, *Weak Link: The Feminization of the American Military* (Washington, D.C.: Regnery, 1989).

64. RAND *Sexual Orientation*, 20; see also 158-59.

65. RAND *Sexual Orientation*, 159.

66. RAND *Sexual Orientation*, 22.

67. RAND *Sexual Orientation*, 20, 21-22.

68. See John Sibley Butler, "Homosexuals and the Military Establishment," *Society* 31:1 (November/December 1993): 13-21, and Henry Louis Gates Jr., "Blacklash?" *New Yorker* (17 May 1993): 42-44. Like General Colin Powell, Butler rejects the effort to use the Black experience as a comparative metaphor; Gates problematizes it. See also, "Blacks Reject Gay Rights Fight as Equal to Their Own," *New York Times* (28 June 1993): A1+, and David W. Dunlap, "Leaders of Gay Blacks Emphasize Local Issues," *New York Times* (20 February 1995): A13.

69. Shilts documents these attempts at "passing" in *Conduct Unbecoming* (1993); see also Mary Ann Humphrey, *My Country, My Right to Serve: Experiences of Gay Men and Women in the Military, World War II to the Present* (New York: Harper Collins, 1990); Clinton W. Anderson and H. Ron Smith, "Stigma and Honor: Gay, Lesbian, and Bisexual People in the U.S. Military," in *Homosexual Issues in the Workplace*, ed. Louis Diamant (Washington, D.C.: Taylor & Francis, 1993), 65-89; and Roy Cain, "Stigma Management and Gay Identity Development," *Social Work* 36 (January 1991): 67-73.

70. See essays by Nell Irvin Painter, "Hill, Thomas, and Racial Stereotype," and Paula Giddings, "The Last Taboo," in *Race-ing Justice, En-Gendering Power*, ed. Morrison (1992), 200-14 and 441-70.

71. Shilts *Conduct Unbecoming*, 359-60, 721; Jesse Green, "What the Navy Taught Allen Schindler's Mother," *New York Times Magazine* (12 September 1993): 58-63; see also Gary David Comstock, *Violence Against Lesbians and Gay Men* (New York: Columbia, 1991), and Gregory M. Herek and Kevin T. Berrill, *Hate Crimes: Confronting Violence Against Lesbians and Gay Men* (Newbury Park: Sage, 1992). Schindler's accused killer, Terry M. Helvey, was convicted.

72. Woodyard, "Women Soldiers: A View from the Field," *Army* 28:2 (February 1978): 23-25.

73. RAND *Sexual Orientation*, Chapter 6-7.

74. Donald H. Horner Jr., and Michael T. Anderson weigh the similarities and differences in "Integration of Homosexuals into the Armed Forces: Racial and Gender Integration as a Point of Departure," in *Gays and Lesbians in the Military*, eds. Scott and Carson Stanley (1994), Chapter 17: 247-60.

75. A federal court upheld the exclusion of HIV positive applicants in Doe v. Garrett 903 F.2d 1455 (1990); see Wells-Petry *EXCLUSION* 5, 191 note 9.

76. Shilts *Conduct Unbecoming*, 543-75.

77. Eric Schmitt, "Measure Seeks to Bar HIV Positive Troops," *New York Times* (18 May 1995): A3.

78. For example, data on "female-female sexual contact" was collected in surveys but not reported in Kinsey et al. research summaries that RAND consulted (*Sexual Orientation* 45, 49, 58, 63), in part because the summaries were concerned with AIDS transmission, which was perceived as an exclusively gay male disease at the time. However, reliance on data drawn from surveys of Playboy subscribers and male prison inmates which RAND researchers consulted are unlikely to reveal much about lesbians.

79. RAND *Sexual Orientation*, 82; similar statements appear in the discussions of Dutch (94) and Norwegian military policy (98).

80. See Cynthia Enloe, *The Morning After: Sexual Politics at the End of the Cold War* (Berkeley: University of California Press, 1993), and *Bananas, Beaches, & Bases: Making Feminist Sense of International Politics* (Berkeley: University of California Press, 1990).

81. Steven Zeeland, *Barracks Buddies and Soldier Lovers: Dialogues with Gay Young Men in the U.S. Military* (New York: Harrington Park/Haworth, 1993) 15.

82. Captain Carol Barkalow, with Andrea Raab, *In the Men's House* (New York: Berkley/Simon & Schuster, 1990) 26.

83. Herbert Richardson, "On Homosexuals in the Military: A Question of Professionalization," in *The Christian Argument for Gays and Lesbians in the Military: Essays by Mainline Church Leaders*, ed. John J. Carey (Lewiston: Edwin Mellen University Press, 1993), 32.

84. RAND *Sexual Orientation*, 49, fn. 12.

85. Humphrey *My Country, My Right*, xxv.

86. Figures are for fiscal year 1990. GAO Statistics, 10-16. Figures for 1995 are from the Defense Manpower Data Center as of 30 September 1995.

87. Shilts *Conduct Unbecoming*, 104, 154, 164, 222, 280.

88. PERSEREC/Sarbin-Karols (December 1988) Appendix B: B-4, reprinted in Dyer *Gays in Uniform*, 84.

89. GAO *Statistics*, Table III.24: 47. The DOD data GAO reported constructed three racial categories: White, Black, and "Other."

90. GAO *Statistics*, Tables III.4, III.9, III.14, III.19: 36-37, 39-40, 42, 44-45.

91. See Irvin Painter and Giddings in *Race-ing Justice, En-Gendering Power*, ed. Morrison (1992) 200-14, 441-70.

92. See Steven Zeeland, *Sailors and Sexual Identity: Crossing the Line Between "Straight" and "Gay" in the U.S. Navy* (New York: Harrington Park/Haworth, 1995); Zeeland *Barracks Buddies* (1993), and Bérubé *Coming Out* (1990).

93. Tracy Timmons, "'We're Looking for a Few Good Men': The Impact of Gender Stereotypes on Women in the Military," *Minerva* X:2 (Summer 1992): 20-29.

94. Humphrey *My Country, My Right*, xxv.

95. See Winni S. Webber, (pseudonym), *Lesbians in the Military Speak Out* (Northboro, MA: Madwoman Press, 1993); Michelle M. Benecke and Kirstin S. Dodge, "Military Women in Nontraditional Job Fields: Casualties of the Armed Forces' War on Homosexuals," *Harvard Women's Law Journal* 13 (1990): 215-50; Benecke and Dodge, "Lesbian Baiting as Sexual Harassment: Women in the Military," in *Homophobia: How We All Pay the Price*, ed. Warren J. Blumenfeld (Boston: Beacon, 1992), 167-76.

96. See Barkalow *Men's House* (1990), and Webber *Lesbians in the Military*, 3-4, 22-23, 48-49, 54.

97. Jacqui Alexander examines this construction in her essay, "Redrafting Morality: The Postcolonial State and the Sexual Offenses Bill of Trinidad and Tobago," in *Third World Women and the Politics of Feminism*, eds. Chandra Talpade Mohanty, Ann Russo, and Lourdes Torres (Bloomington: University of Indiana Press, 1991), 133-152.

98. Benecke and Dodge "Military Women" (1990), 243-44.

99. Shilts *Conduct Unbecoming*, 336-39, 341-64.

100. Benecke and Dodge "Military Women" (1990) 215-250; Benecke and Dodge "Lesbian Baiting" in *Homophobia*, ed. Blumenfeld (1992), 167-76; Webber *Lesbians in the Military*, 99.

101. Shilts *Conduct Unbecoming*, 493-95, 556-58, 596-97, 626-31, 651-54, and 695 re: Parris Island; 317, 356, 388, 418, 560, 636-37, 653 re: sports teams.

102. See, for example, the discussion of coping strategies in Anderson and Smith, "Stigma and Honor," in *Homosexual Issues*, ed. Diamant (1993), 76-79, and Eric Schmitt, "In Fear, Gay Soldiers Marry for Camouflage," *New York Times* (12 July 1993): A7, A10.

103. R. W. Connell examines the connections between gender and sexuality and "the variety of masculinities in a range of class and ethnic contexts" in "A Very Straight Gay: Masculinity, Homosexual Experience, and the Dynamics of Gender," *American Sociological Review* 57 (December 1992): 735-51.

104. Benecke & Dodge "Military Women" (1990), 217-18.

105. RAND *Sexual Orientation*, 6.

106. See her chapter in this volume.

107. Barry M. Goldwater, "The Gay Ban: Just Plain Un-American," *Washington Post* (10 June 1993): A23.

108. Senator Sam Nunn (D-GA) reportedly proposed the Don't Ask, Don't Tell formula. See Pat Towell, "Nunn Offers a Compromise," *CQ Weekly Report* 51 (15 May 1993): 1240.

109. "Pentagon to Seek Gay Policy Delay," *New York Times* (13 October 1993): A19.

110. Goldwater, "The Gay Ban," A23.

111. Newark's sentence was five years at hard labor and dishonorable discharge for consensual same-sex acts; Lawrence Korb, "Evolving Perspectives on the Military's Policy on Homosexuals: A Personal Note," in *Gays and Lesbians in the Military*, eds. Scott and Carson Stanley (1994), 219-29.

112. Keith Meinhold, "Pentagon's Policy Has to End," Special to *Los Angeles Times*, reprinted in *Finger Lakes Times* (Geneva, NY) (17 April 1995): OpEd 9. This responds to an earlier article, "Gay Sailor's Colleagues Remain Upset," *New York Times* (5 April 1993): A18, C10.

113. *Bowers v. Hardwick* 478 US 186 (1986). The military's response to the constitutional challenges brought by many discharged servicemembers has been that there "is no right to serve" and that the military must discriminate in the interest of national security. This argument is detailed in Wells-Petry, *EXCLUSION* (1993).

114. Malcolm Gladwell, "Suit Challenges New Policy on Gays in the Military," *Washington Post* (14 March 1995): A8. See also Eric Schmitt, "Judge Overturns Pentagon Policy on Homosexuals," *New York Times* (31 March 1995): A1, A24.

115. Clinton *People First*, 171.

116. See Sam Keen, *Faces of the Enemy: Reflections of the Hostile Imagination* (San Francisco, CA: Harper & Row, 1986).

CHAPTER 2

Echoes of Prejudice:
The Debates Over Race and Sexuality in the Armed Forces

David Ari Bianco

INTRODUCTION

During the debate over President Bill Clinton's campaign promise to sign an Executive Order ending the military's ban on lesbians and gays, many writers and political actors on both sides evoked the experience of military racial integration. Those opposed to the ban suggested that military homophobia was just another incarnation of military racism, and that by ending discrimination on the basis of sexual orientation, Clinton would be acting in the spirit of Harry S. Truman when he ordered an end to discrimination on the basis of race (an order which eventually led to desegregation of the military). For example, an editorial in the *Atlanta Constitution* declared: "Truman's decision [to end segregation] strengthened the military and contributed to making America a more tolerant society. Mr. Clinton can do the same."[1] Similarly, African American columnist Robert C. Maynard wrote, "When Bill Clinton becomes president, he is pledged to end an injustice no less real than the racial injustice President Truman ended 44 years ago."[2]

Those in favor of the ban, however, noted vast differences between the categories of race and sexual orientation, and even bristled at the very comparison. The most noteworthy resister of any such comparison was General Colin L. Powell, then Chairman of the Joint Chiefs of Staff, whose open opposition to overturning the ban probably had more influence in the final outcome than that of any other single individual. In a letter to Congresswoman Patricia Schroeder, Powell wrote:

> I can assure you I need no reminders concerning the history of African Americans in the defense of their Nation and the tribulations they faced. I am a part of that history. Skin color is a benign, nonbehavioral characteristic. Sexual orientation is perhaps the most profound of human behavioral characteristics. Comparison of the two is a convenient but invalid argument.[3]

Other writers were less polite. A non-African American scholar suggested that "to lump blacks with homosexuals is an affront to most African Americans."[4] But despite the impassioned rhetoric, few participants in the debate based their arguments on a thorough comparison of the late 1940s argument over African Americans in the military with the current debate over lesbians and gays. This chapter will show that whether or not race is precisely parallel to sexual orientation, military racism and military homophobia are strikingly similar. By systematically comparing 16 arguments currently made against allowing gays in the military to similar arguments made opposing military racial integration, I will show that the defense of the military's current ban on lesbians and gays in uniform is absolutely based on the same prejudice that kept African Americans segregated 45 years ago.

RACE VS. SEXUAL ORIENTATION

In the fall of 1992, when it appeared that Clinton was likely to end the ban on gays in the military, many conservatives and military leaders argued that race and sexual orientation are not comparable categories. Their basic line of argument was that homosexuality is a chosen behavior, whereas race is involuntary and nonbehavioral. For example, Charles R. Jackson, Executive Vice President of the Non Commissioned Officers Association (NCOA), testified before the Republican Study Committee on Homosexuals in the Armed Forces in December 1992 that

> the recruitment and retention of homosexuals in the U.S. Armed Forces is not a situation analogous to the full integration of African Americans into military service. That action corrected a racial inequity based on an inert, benign characteristic, skin color. Homosexuality is a behavioral characteristic. Recruiting and retention of homosexuals would force upon others tolerance of a lifestyle many consider abnormal and totally unacceptable.[5]

Robert H. Knight, Director of Cultural Studies for the Family Research Council, similarly asserted that "Race is an immutable characteristic (such as skin color), while active homosexuality concerns behavior. . . . You cannot hide or change your skin color, but you can choose to act or not on your inclinations."[6]

These arguments rest upon questionable assumptions. First of all, many researchers and activists would question the dismissal of homosexuality as nonbenign and changeable. Although science has not proven that lesbians and gays are born that way, it has not proven that they are not, either. Also, the ban on lesbians and gays as codified and enforced before "Don't Ask, Don't Tell" *did* evict soldiers and sailors on the basis of sexual orientation and not behavior (and apparently some lesbians and gays are still discharged with no evidence of same-sex behavior). Before it was dropped as part of President Clinton's so-called compromise in the summer of 1993, Question 36d on the Enlistment/Reenlistment Document of the Armed Forces of the United States asked: "Are you a homosexual or a bisexual? ('Homosexual' is defined as: sexual desire or behavior directed at a person(s) of one's own sex. 'Bisexual' is defined as: a person sexually responsive to both sexes.)" Based on that policy, an officer such as Dusty Pruitt, who accepted the label "lesbian" during a newspaper interview, could be discharged even absent any evidence that she had engaged in any homosexual conduct.[7]

There are, however, other legitimate differences between the categories of race and sexual orientation. Before military racial integration, there were few "closet blacks" posing as whites and serving among white troops. But there are thousands of closeted gays currently serving, most of whom to some extent maintain a charade of being heterosexual. Also, there are no segregated units of lesbians and gays as there were of African Americans during the Civil War and the two world wars. These differences, however, are logistical, and it is fair to say that for the purposes of studying military policy, race and sexual orientation are comparable categories.

RACISM VS. HOMOPHOBIA

The most important question, however, is not whether race is similar to sexual orientation, but whether racism is similar to homophobia. In the case of conservative politicians and military leaders' objections to allowing African Americans and lesbians and gays to serve, racism and homophobia have been strikingly similar. Dr. Robert Cabaj of the American Psychiatric Association wrote that the Defense Department policy is "based completely on prejudice, bias, and discrimination. The nearly identical statements were made years ago to exclude and segregate blacks in the armed services." Dr. Cabaj called both exclusionary arguments "blaming the victim"; prejudice he described as occurring when "the discriminated population is blamed for the position in which the discriminating majority places it."[8] As Congressman Barney Frank put it,

It is unfortunately the same thing that led to racial discrimination. . .
Saying we can't have gay people in the military because heterosexuals
won't like them, regardless of how they behave, is like saying we can't
have black people around because white people won't like them. That
was wrong, and this is wrong.[9]

The arguments used to keep African Americans segregated are so similar to those that barred lesbians and gays in the early 1990s that a gay newspaper, the *Washington Blade*, argued that the history of the military's exclusion of African Americans "seems to be serving as a blueprint for the military on how to dissuade the government from allowing gays to serve openly in the ranks."[10]

The 16 major arguments used by the military and conservatives to keep gays out of the military in the face of the threat of a Clinton executive order[11] can be divided into four major assertions: that lesbians and gays are not fit to serve, that heterosexuals and homosexuals cannot serve together effectively, that nondiscrimination would violate the rights of heterosexuals, and that lifting the ban would impair the military mission. None of these assertions and arguments were new, as each of them was raised in a similar form during the debate over military racial integration.

Gays and Lesbians Are Not Fit to Serve
Crime

Several of the arguments against homosexuals in uniform are rooted in basic prejudice—the belief that in some objective way lesbians and gays are inferior to heterosexuals and thus make poor soldiers. For example, the belief that gay men in particular have uncontrollable sexual appetites that frequently lead to seduction and rape often entered the military debate. The defenders of the military's ban on lesbians and gays frequently raised the specter of homosexual rapists and pedophiles endangering young soldiers and sailors. In interviewing military authorities casually and formally, one military researcher repeatedly came across what she called "the stereotypical view that homosexuals somehow have an uncontrollable sex drive that demands constant satisfaction." As an example, she cited Norman Schwarzkopf's testimony that he knew of "instances where heterosexuals have been solicited to commit homosexual acts, and even more traumatic emotionally, physically coerced to engage in such acts."[12] Similarly, a retired businessman wrote in the *Wall Street Journal* of his experience soon after World War II on a Navy ship which had five "aggressive homosexuals" who stroked his leg at night and exposed themselves to him. "All homosexuals aren't rapists," he wrote. "But in this closed male society, with its enforced communal living, unchecked homosexual appetites wrought havoc."[13] Such comments suggested that gays should be kept out of the military because of their propensity for rape.

Southern conservatives made a similar argument in 1948, suggesting that the higher rate of rape and other crimes among African Americans was a danger to the military. Georgia Senator Richard Russell presented an amendment before the Senate that would guarantee enlistees the option of serving with members of their own race. In defense of his amendment, one of Russell's arguments was that allowing integration "will increase the rate of crime committed by servicemen."[14] He also pointed to the rates of incidence of several crimes (including rape and sodomy) among the African American population as opposed to the white population: "As to the crime of rape the ratio was 13 times as great among the Negro troops per hundred thousand as it was in the case of the white troops. . . . In the crime of sodomy the rate was 2 1/2 times as great."[15] Hence in both debates discrimination was defended as a means of protecting the in-group from rape. This is undoubtedly an effective scare tactic. Many straight men have a strong revulsion to the very suggestion of being raped by another man—a revulsion that is even stronger for many to the suggestion of being raped by an African American man. By appealing to this fear, those who support discrimination can tap into deep anxieties among white, straight men. A convenient way of excluding an unwanted group is to maintain that they pose a physical threat, and any discrimination is simply self-defense. The next argument is, in fact, a variation of this approach.

Disease

One major way of defending the policy banning gays has been to point to the higher prevalence of sexually transmitted diseases, particularly AIDS, among gay men. A publication by the conservative Family Research Council put the argument this way:

> The AIDS risk is very real, since two-thirds of all current AIDS cases involved transmission through homosexual activity, according to the Centers for Disease Control. Homosexuals also account for a disproportionate number of cases of sexually transmitted diseases, such as syphilis, gonorrhea, genital warts, hepatitis A, hepatitis B and also diseases associated with anal intercourse, such as the parasites collectively referred to as "gay bowel syndrome." According to the American Medical Association, homosexual youths are 23 times more likely to contract a sexually-transmitted disease than are heterosexuals.[16]

Similarly, Kevin Tebedo, a cofounder of "Colorado for Family Values," argued against gays in the military by stating that "There is no question that the homosexual community, particularly males, are (sic) very diseased."[17] One colonel testified that according to his research, "It has been proven in the scientific literature that homosexuals are not able-bodied."[18] He argued that if the policy were to change, "At the very least homosexuals would have to be specially identified to ensure their blood not be used as a protection to other soldiers."[19]

The military has some experience with segregated blood. During World War II the Red Cross—with no scientific justification—maintained racially segregated blood banks at the demand of the armed forces.[20] Disease rates were also mentioned by Senator Russell in his campaign to keep the military segregated. Russell declared:

> The incidence of syphilis, gonorrhea, chancre, and all other venereal diseases is appallingly higher among the members of the Negro race than among the members of the white race. . . . The incidence of tuberculosis . . . is almost unbelievable; and of course tuberculosis is a highly communicable disease. . . . I submit that it is unfair to vote to compel a boy from North Dakota or any other State to serve against his will in an unsegregated unit where the chances for his innocently acquiring this dread disease of syphilis is 19 times greater than it would be if he were permitted to serve only with members of his own race.[21]

Senator Russell's comments highlight the deep roots that antigay prejudice has in military history. If syphilis is a sexually transmitted disease, how is that boy from North Dakota going to contract it "innocently" by serving alongside African Americans?

As is quite common in the debate over sexual orientation in the military, lesbians are usually ignored in the argument over rates of disease. Partly because lesbians have a much lower rate of AIDS and other sexually transmitted diseases than gay and even straight men, and partly because of general lesbian invisibility, when Tebedo and other opponents of inclusion bring up disease rates, they only discuss gay men.

The fact that fear of the spread of disease is raised in both debates is interesting for two reasons. First, as mentioned above, the argument implies that sex between gay soldiers and straight male soldiers (or African American and white soldiers) is inevitable; these diseases don't spread through sharing ammunition. Second, the ridiculous insistence on separate blood banks for African Americans and lesbians and gays plays on fears of straight, white soldiers somehow assuming characteristics of the out-group by incorporating "black blood" or "gay blood" into their bodies. Blood taboos are among the most primordial responses people have.

Performance

Some of those who opposed gays in the military suggested that gays, as a class, were not up to the demands of serving in uniform for reasons other than crime or disease. Colonel Jim Schwenk, director of the Defense Department's Policy Division, explained to a representative of the General Accounting Office that

> it is a perception that soldiers are suppose [sic] to be tough. People tend to look at homosexuals as being somewhat weak and nonaggressive individuals. Good performers, but weak in statu[r]e. This perception is also embedded in the minds of those who made the policy.[22]

That perception has also been apparent in the ranks. One squad leader from the 82nd Airborne reportedly said "Whatever the army makes right on gays, it won't be right for the grunt. . . . If a dude has a flaw, he'll fold."[23] Such enlisted men see homosexuality as a "flaw" that would keep gay soldiers from performing. Colonel Ray presented a similar argument, writing,

> As for adjustment within the demanding confines of military service, the sociology literature indicates that homosexuals generally need support groups in order to function and that absent a supportive environment most will fail.[24]

These arguments assume lesbians and gays are somehow inherently inferior individuals less fit to be soldiers.

There is certainly no lack of parallels in the history of the military's racist policies. According to one historian of African Americans in the military,

> Basically, the military traditionalists—that is, most senior officials and commanders of the armed forces and their allies in Congress—took the position that black servicemen were difficult to train and undependable in battle.[25]

Similarly, the chairman of the General Board of the Navy wrote in 1942 that the Navy was composed of whites because "those in control have believed and experience has demonstrated that the white man is more adaptable and more efficient in the various conditions which are involved in the making of an effective man-of-war."[26] African Americans were kept out of the Navy for many years, in part because military officials believed they were less capable soldiers and sailors than whites were. This argument works well only among those who already hold strong prejudices against the given group. People who are prepared to see African Americans or gays as equal in nonmilitary life are unlikely to accept arguments that they make poor soldiers and sailors. But undoubtedly a majority of Americans in the early 1990s still had some doubts about the abilities of lesbians and gay men, just as in the late 1940s most Americans were not prepared to accept theories of equality of ability among the races.

Homosexuals and Heterosexuals Cannot Serve Together Effectively
Morale
Perhaps no argument has been more frequently cited to oppose lesbians and gays in the military than the notion that the presence of openly homosexual soldiers would harm morale and thereby diminish combat effectiveness. Decorated Vietnam veteran David H. Hackworth explained this idea as follows:

> To survive in a killing field, a warrior has to believe he's invincible, that he's wearing golden armor; that he can buck 1,000-to-1 odds and live. To think that way, he has to be macho. Fairly or unfairly, gays threaten that macho. When it goes, the warrior starts thinking, "Maybe I won't make it." And from that moment, the unit goes to hell.[27]

In Hackworth's view, openly gay soldiers puncture the military illusion of masculine invincibility, causing soldiers to fight less effectively. Charles Jackson of the Non Commissioned Officers Association argued that any major change in policy can lead to a disruption of morale, with dire consequences:

> Morale in the armed forces is a fragile asset. It can be instantly destroyed even by those acting with the best intentions. History has proven that the degradation of morale quickly leads to the erosion of discipline, diminished performance, poor retention, readiness reduction and recruiting difficulties. NCOA submits . . . that any change in current policy will most assuredly have identical results.[28]

The perceived danger of gays in the military to morale is so great that Hackworth put it this starkly: "I cannot think of a better way to destroy fighting spirit and gut U.S. combat effectiveness."[29]

Another commentator, 44 years earlier, sounded a nearly identical warning: "One of the surest ways to break down the morale of the Army and to destroy its efficiency" is to integrate the races, wrote *New York Times* military editor

Hanson W. Baldwin in August 1948.[30] Assertions that integration would hurt morale were ubiquitous in the debate over African Americans in the military. For example, the pre-World War II Army staff argued against integration because segregation had "proved satisfactory over a long period of time. To change would destroy morale and impair preparations for national defense."[31] Also, before the General Board of the Navy in 1942, Lt. General Thomas Holcomb, USMC, argued:

In an infantry battalion is the very last place they [blacks] would be put. There is no branch of the service that requires more character and a higher degree of morale than the infantry.[32]

The majority report of a Navy Secretary's committee to study integration used the morale argument when it claimed:

The close and intimate conditions of life aboard ship, the necessity for the highest possible degree of unity and esprit-de-corps; the requirement of morale—all these demand that nothing be done which may adversely affect the situation. Past experience has shown irrefutably that the enlistment of Negroes (other than for mess attendants) leads to disruptive and undermining conditions.[33]

Omar Bradley made a similar argument in his testimony before the Fahy Committee, which was set up by Truman's Executive Order to end discrimination in the military. Bradley testified:

In addition, such as system of complete integration might seriously affect morale and thus affect battle efficiency. I consider that a unit has high morale when the men have confidence in themselves, confidence in their fellow-members of their unit, and confidence in their leaders. If we try to force integration on the Army before the country is ready to accept these customs, we may have difficulty attaining high morale along the lines I mentioned.[34]

In both the 1940s and 1990s cases, the morale argument is basically an accommodation to prejudice. Rather than recognizing the attitudes of current soldiers and sailors as the problem, those attitudes are assumed to be permanent, and are accommodated—even to the detriment of around 10 percent of the population at large. This attitude, in both cases, was backwards. As one military researcher wrote,

Of course, even if (the) DOD's position were valid, and a unit's cohesion, order, and discipline were adversely affected by the presence of homosexuals, one must still ask, "Whose fault is that? The homosexual's? Or the ones who will not accept them?" When blacks and women were integrated into military service, was it their fault when the white or male majority did not accept them? Did we blame them for the color of their skin or gender? Clearly not. Instead, we asked people to change—if not their attitudes, at least their overt behavior.[35]

Recruitment and Retention

The ability "to recruit and retain members of the armed forces" was one of the justifications for the ban on lesbians and gays listed in the Defense Department policy on homosexuality that Clinton initially sought to overturn. Supporters of the ban often raised the specter of a depleted military force and weakened recruitment efforts if those who join or remain in the military were forced to associate with people known to be lesbian or gay. As Schwarzkopf put it,

> The impact on the Army's public image would also endanger recruitment and retention, by causing potential servicemembers to hesitate to enlist, making parents of potential servicemembers reluctant to recommend or approve the enlistment of their sons and daughters in an organization in which they would be forced to live and work with known homosexuals, and causing members of the Army to hesitate to reenlist.[36]

One four-star general told the *Washington Times* in November, 1992, that "It would be a wrenching change. . . . We're not ready for it. Good people will leave the military in droves over this."[37] Similarly, Hackworth wrote in *Newsweek* that "Hundreds of marine and army grunts and leaders have told me that if the ban is lifted, they're walking."[38]

In a parallel fashion, the threat of white desertion from the military was raised by proponents of segregation in the 1940s. For example, Captain F.E.M. Whiting, U.S.N., testified before the General Board of the Navy as follows:

> The minute the negro is introduced into general service . . . the high type of man that we have been getting for the last twenty years will go elsewhere and we will get the type of man who will lie in bed with a negro.[39]

Again we see here the overlap between military racism and military homophobia—Captain Whiting could have written "share a latrine with a negro" or appealed to a racial stereotype like "shine shoes with a negro" but instead chose to imply that the kind of whites who would serve with African Americans would be of questionable sexuality as well. Whiting then quoted from a letter from Texas Congressman W. R. Poage, in which he declared that Southerners have been dependable volunteers for the military until now, but

> if they be forced to serve with Negroes, they will cease to volunteer; and when drafted, they will not serve with that enthusiasm and high

morale that has always characterized the soldiers and sailors of the southern states.[40]

In the same vein, Bradley testified that "a lot of those people that we now get to enlist and reenlist from the southern states might drop out on us in case you had a completely integrated unit."[41] Again, this argument accommodates prejudice rather than face it. The armed forces should examine what it can do to make sure its men and women in uniform are able to work with diverse people, and to make sure hesitant recruits' myths about working with minorities are debunked. Simply keeping people out cannot be the answer to fears of reduced voluntary enlistments.

Command

Another official rationale for excluding lesbians and gays was "to ensure the integrity of the system of rank and command."[42] General C.E. Mundy, Commandant of the Marine Corps, put the argument in terms of "role models." He wrote:

Would you (or most American families) want your son or daughter to have as his or her role model a person who has a homosexual lifestyle, and who, in most cases, is involved in homosexual *conduct?*[43]

Schwarzkopf was more direct. He wrote:

If homosexuals were allowed to serve, military leaders, known to be homosexual, would be unable to effectively command or lead his/her soldiers because of a loss of respect and trust in his/her abilities.[44]

White opponents to integration put forth the identical argument in the 1940s. Major General Henry H. Arnold, Chief of the Air Corps, explained in 1940 that pilots had to be white because otherwise "this would result in having Negro officers serving over white enlisted men. This would create an impossible social problem."[45] Omar Bradley opined similarly before the Fahy committee in 1949:

In a completely integrated unit where you'd have white soldiers, particularly from the southern states, serving under Negro noncommissioned officers or officers. . . . I think you would have a problem definitely.[46]

Of course, the military was able to get over its nervousness about African American commanders, even to the point where just 40 years later the highest ranking officer in the U.S. military was an African American, Colin Powell. In the military, an order is an order, and all soldiers and sailors are used to taking orders from people they do not like. But refusing to obey a superior officer has court martial as its consequence, and few soldiers would likely risk being tried for their prejudice, whether it be racism or homophobia.

Discipline

Another reason some said soldiers of different sexual orientations could not serve together smoothly is because such an arrangement would harm discipline and good order. As General Powell put it, "It is just my judgment and the judgment of the chiefs that homosexual behavior is inconsistent with maintaining good order and discipline."[47] Another variant of this argument was that straight soldiers would not come to the aid of wounded gay soldiers out of fear of AIDS or discomfort of homosexuality. Army Major Edward Proskie told the *Washington Post* in November 1992 that "in the event soldiers are wounded and blood is spilled, if that person is suspected of being infected with AIDS, there could be some apprehension in responding to his aid."[48] Hackworth argued that the key element of good military discipline is trust, and straight soldiers just won't trust gay soldiers to come to their aid.[49]

Opponents of allowing African Americans into general service in the Navy also raised the specter of discipline problems. The Chairman of the General Board of the Navy wrote:

How many white men would choose, of their own accord, that their closest associates in sleeping quarters, at mess, and in a gun's crew should be of another race? How many would accept such conditions, if required to do so, without resentment and just as a matter of course? The General Board believes that the answer is "few, if any," and further believes that if the issue were forced, there would be a lowering of contentment, teamwork, and discipline in the service.[50]

A letter from the Secretary of the Navy to the Lt. Gov. of New York in 1940 suggested the discipline problem would be especially acute if nonwhites were given supervisory responsibility. They then would be unable to maintain discipline among white subordinates, he wrote, with a resulting loss in teamwork, harmony, and efficiency.[51]

In both cases, those who argue that discipline will be compromised if the rules are changed assume that such occasions occur in a vacuum. Rather, as has happened over and over since racial integration, when people know and work with members of groups they are unfamiliar with, their prejudices lessen, and they are able to come to an ability to work with people different from them. Allowing gays to serve openly may incite some prejudice among straight soldiers initially, but openly working with lesbians and gay men on a regular basis cannot but bring those soldiers to at least a grudging respect for their compatriots, which should help them perform in the emergency situations raised by Proskie and Hackworth.

Violence

Some of those opposed to allowing lesbians and gays to serve suggested that openly gay soldiers would encounter violence from antigay soldiers. An officer at Kings Bay Naval Submarine Base in southeast Georgia said, "They shouldn't be allowed in. . . . They're gonna get hurt. There's gonna be a lot of slipping in the showers."[52] Colonel Schwenk told the GAO that "there are isolated cases that show that homosexuals do not fit in the units with heterosexuals. There are incidents of brawls among heterosexuals and homosexuals that have been documented."[53] Senate Armed Services Committee Chairman Sam Nunn said on CBS' Face the Nation shortly after Clinton's election that "violence against homosexuals [is] one thing that has to be considered. If you did it overnight, I'd fear for the lives of the people in the military themselves."[54]

Such patronizing attitudes have precedent in the racial debate. Navy Secretary Frank Knox raised the danger of violence against African Americans when he stated he was convinced that "it is no kindness to Negroes to thrust them upon men of the white race."[55] General Eisenhower went so far as to suggest that if the Army allowed soldiers of different races to live and socialize together, it ran the risk of riots and racial disturbances.[56] In actuality, the military is quite effective at controlling and punishing unwanted conduct on the part of its enlisted men. Comments like those of Schwenk, Nunn, and Knox appear to be paternalistic warnings for the protection of lesbians, gays, and African Americans. But on another level they are veiled threats—a warning to stay out of our club or get hurt.

Nondiscrimination would Violate the Rights of Heterosexuals
Privacy
Whether or not gays are fit to be soldiers, and whether or not they can do their jobs alongside heterosexual soldiers, some supporters of the ban suggested that allowing lesbians and gays to serve would violate the rights of current soldiers. Supporters of the ban were particularly sensitive to the notion that allowing gays in uniform would violate heterosexual rights to privacy in sleeping, showering, and using the latrines. General Powell maintained that it would be difficult for people of different sexual orientations to "share the most private facilities together, the bedroom, the barracks, latrines, the showers."[57] One sailor said the privacy concern might be enough to convince her to leave the military: "We have to live in close dormitories and take showers with 50 women, and I don't want some woman leering at me."[58] Another opponent of admitting gays put it this way: "As a rule, soldiers don't like taking showers with the kind of guys who like taking showers with soldiers."[59]

Opponents of racial integration also argued that the intimacy of military life meant integration would be unworkable. Secretary Knox told President Roosevelt that "men live in such intimacy aboard ship that we simply can't enlist Negroes above the rank of messman."[60] Once again, some of the more inflammatory comments about African Americans in the military have a hint of homoeroticism in them—that soldiers of both races would "sleep together." Georgia Congressman Stephen Pace wrote the Secretary of the Navy in 1946 to complain that "white boys are being forced to sleep with these negroes."[61] Congressman Powell of Michigan, referring to an African American colleague of his, said in Congress:

> Do we not fight better, more courageously, more tenaciously, when we fight with those we like? The gentleman may not like me. Should we have a law which will force him to sleep in my bed, in my room with me, to eat with me, if he does not like me nor my ways?[62]

These comments about soldiers sleeping together (along with Senator Russell's citation of statistics showing African Americans as more likely to carry syphilis and be convicted of sodomy) underscore the fact that military racism and military homophobia are two sides of the same coin.

Freedom of Association
Another variation of the privacy argument is that allowing lesbians and gays into the military would violate heterosexuals' right to choose not to associate with homosexuals. As one Christian leader put it,

> We think lifting the ban would violate the civil rights of members of the Armed Forces, forcing them to live in conditions of close proximity with men attracted to other men, and women attracted to other women.[63]

Eugene Gomulka, a military chaplain took an even more extreme position:

> In this period of history when militant homosexuals not only reveal their liaisons and lifestyles, but actively and articulately promote the homosexual relationship as a morally acceptable alternative to marriage, legislation which would require the military to accept homosexuals would do much more to violate the rights of heterosexual personnel than it would to promote the rights of homosexuals.[64]

Much of the 1940s debate in Congress over racial integration also focused on the freedom of association of the majority. Senator Russell's amendment would have allowed soldiers to choose to serve only with members of their own race. In defending his amendment, Russell said:

> It merely proposes to guarantee any individual citizen brought into the services the right to serve in a military unit composed of members of his own race where such individual makes an affirmative declaration of his desire to do so. . . . I submit, Mr. President, that if there is any one fundamental and sacred right inherent in every individual in a free state it is the right of choosing the type of people with whom we will associate in our daily lives.[65]

Six weeks later, Congressman Ed Gossett from Texas declared, "Insofar as the armed services go, the whites—not the Negroes—have been the victims of discrimination."[66] But Americans abandon their freedom of association the moment they enlist. The chaos that would result from allowing them to retain it is unimaginable. Soldiers could insist on being stationed with certain other soldiers, and sailors could refuse to serve on a ship with anyone they don't want to spend time with. The argument that expanding the military to include African Americans, lesbians, or gays would violate the majority's civil rights are based on a "civil right" that does not exist for Americans in uniform.

Lifting the Ban would Impair the Military Mission
Efficiency
Many of those opposed to allowing lesbians and gays to serve openly have asserted that to do so would harm the overall performance and effectiveness of the military. For example, one naval officer told a newspaper reporter, "Unfortunately, I think it would affect overall performance. . . . There are a lot of people in the military who come from the old school, who just couldn't accept it."[67] Syndicated columnist Stephen Chapman wrote:

> The armed forces, unlike other institutions of government, are not expected to place personal rights above all. They have always been allowed (particularly when there was a draft) to put military effectiveness above individual needs. To introduce openly gay men and women without serious regard for the consequences is to put what is desirable above what is vital.[68]

Hackworth, in urging a "go slow" approach to the Defense Department's ban on gays in uniform, emphasized the centrality of military effectiveness in evaluating what kind of change is appropriate. He wrote:

> Can gays and straights train and fight together without a drop in combat effectiveness? Instead of assuming that they can or can't why not ask open-minded generals and sergeants, civilian psychiatrists and sociologists and gay leaders to investigate the matter openly for the first time? If I am wrong and the answer is yes, there is no problem. If, as I suspect, the answer is no, then we should consider which units gays can and should serve in.[69]

Similar arguments were made against allowing African Americans to serve alongside whites. Even as late as 1972, one former Korean War commander insisted integration harmed military efficiency. Lt. General Edward M. Almond wrote, "I do not agree that integration improves military efficiency; I believe that it weakens it."[70] He followed up that comment with outright racism (despite his denial) which in its arrogance and self-righteousness echoes the comments of men like Chapman and Hackworth:

There is no question in my mind of the inherent difference in races. This is not racism—it is common sense and understanding. Those who ignore these differences merely interfere with the combat effectiveness of battle units.[71]

Another example of this line of argument is Hoffman's argument before Congress:

"In my humble judgment, forcing our drafted men, where they are of different races, have different ways of life, to live together day and night, where each irritates the other, is not conducive to an effective military force."[72]

Of course, words like "efficiency" and "effectiveness" are difficult to measure quantitatively. Just like the argument about morale, using these words is an accommodation to the racism or homophobia already present in the armed forces. Moreover, the American military already recognizes that there are some things more important than efficiency—the army might be more efficient if all soldiers followed the same religion or no religion at all, but the services accommodate quite a number of religions nonetheless.

Public Acceptance
Those against admitting lesbians and gays to the services also warned that such a move would harm the U.S. military's public acceptance and image, both at home and worldwide. General Schwarzkopf argued: "Because of the prevailing aversion to homosexuals in our society, the Army would suffer in esteem if known homosexuals were allowed to serve."[73] A conservative columnist drew a more extreme picture:

To a considerable extent, the federal government derives its legitimacy and its public acceptance from the Department of Defense, and no President can afford to oppose it. . . . The Dutch army's pigtailed, earringed battalions do not inspire confidence.[74]

Jackson suggested that lesbians and gays should be banned from uniform because homosexuality is not accepted or even "legal"[75] in many of the places gay soldiers would serve:

Permitting homosexuals to serve in a military capacity would place the services in a position to micromanage a force where worldwide deployability requirements of its members may be questionable. Therefore, NCOA suggests to the committee that prior to any change in current policy, efforts must be redirected to making homosexual conduct legal in all states and foreign countries before imposing tolerance of it on members of the armed forces.[76]

Similarly, the 1940s saw arguments that the public's racism would exclude African Americans from full participation in military affairs. For example, one historian of military integration described the attitude of Army Chief of Staff General Omar Bradley immediately after Truman's executive order as follows: "[As] emphasizing that the Army could not afford to differ greatly in customs, traditions, and prejudices from the general population."[77] The question of worldwide deployment also came up in the racial context; for example, before the General Board of the Navy. One admiral testified that "there are a great many places in the world where [African Americans] could *not* be used."[78] In truth, however, the military does not allow enemy nations or even allies to veto which troops can enter their country. Jews fought in the Persian Gulf War, for example, even in countries like Saudi Arabia whose leaders would have preferred otherwise. To suggest that the military must accommodate a view that is inherently discriminatory just because other countries or even some segments of our country hold that view is to suggest that the military cannot be a pioneer. Military racial integration took place a few years before the American civil rights struggle was at the forefront of the nation's agenda, and allowing lesbian and gay soldiers to serve does not have to await the passage of a federal gay and lesbian civil rights bill.

SOCIAL EXPERIMENTATION

The first twelve arguments described in this paper are the major substantive reasons that were put forth by opponents of ending the military's ban on lesbians and gays. The final four arguments are really more like rationalizations. They tended to be brought up when the bigotry of the ban is pointed to, in an attempt to assert the military's right to maintain its current rules. One of these rationalizations is that the military is not the place for social experiments. Jackson stated on behalf of the Non Commissioned Officers Association that "the use of the armed forces for the purpose of social experimentation will only serve to disrupt and degrade the institution recognized as the very best in the world." Likewise, a Family Research Council position paper declared that "No social experiment is worth risking the lives of our nation's fighting men." This approach belittled the very problem of soldiers and sailors being expelled on the basis of sexual orientation and loyal Americans being denied equal access to serve their country without fair justification. Instead, those who called ending the ban a "social experiment" suggest that a Clinton executive order would be nothing but a pet project of gay activists aiming to force their agenda on the rest of the country.

Military racial integration was called a "social experiment" as well, yet few today would deny that transition's profound significance in America's maturation. Before World War II, an Army colonel declared that the Army would not integrate because "Experiments to meet the wishes and demands of the champions of every race and creed for the solution of their problems are a danger to efficiency, discipline and morale and would result in ultimate defeat."[79] Similarly, Bradley told the Associated Press:

The Army is not about to make any social reforms. The Army will put men of different races in different companies. It will change that policy when the nation as a whole changes it.[80]

The phrase "social experiment" is an interesting one, because the military as a whole is an experiment in creating a model society for a given purpose, and military leaders are continually making adjustments to that experiment in everything from housing to food to uniforms. If the opponents of integration were opposed to any social experimentation in the military, the army wouldn't have changed at all since the Revolutionary War.

Timing

Another defense of the policy ban supporters turned to when confronted with the weakness of their argument was that the timing is bad. "Even if discrimination is wrong," they seemed to say, "the military can't afford to risk changes now that [insert crisis here]." The three main crises pointed to in 1992-93 were the end of the Cold War, the subsequent cutbacks in military force, and sexual harassment issues such as those brought up by the Tailhook scandal. One major told the *Washington Post* that the debate over lesbians and gays in uniform has become another thorn to a military already trying to cope with cutbacks as well as race and sex divisions. "There's been so much change going on in the service already. I believe the system is overburdened as it is."[81] An article in the *San Francisco Examiner* stated that:

Many inside the military think their institution has suffered too many hits in recent years. The institution already faces fundamental changes and cutbacks since the Cold War has ended, they say, and more change now will be hard to accept.[82]

Knight pointed out that the military was already having problems with heterosexual harassment as well as with pregnant soldiers returning from the Gulf War and asked, "If illicit heterosexual relations are already a problem, why create an additional problem by accepting active homosexuals?"[83] These comments were generally vapid, as they ignore the merits of the debate over allowing lesbians and gays to serve openly in favor of indefinite postponements.

When Truman decided that the time for military integration had come in 1948, his move also met with objections about timing—in that case that the beginning of the Cold War was the worst possible time for such dramatic change. Congressman Overton Brooks of Louisiana declared in Congress that

In these times of major crises throughout the world it is a mistake to try to provide social reforms for the armed services. . . . The result may be to injure them at a time when the world looks to us for strength and courage.[84]

Similarly, Bradley testified before the Fahy Committee that he was "afraid that the time hasn't arrived that we can do it and maintain efficiency during this critical time in our international relations."[85]

Military Uniqueness

Another rationalization ban supporters turned to when cornered is the uniqueness of the military. Even if banning openly lesbian and gay soldiers were a form of prejudice, the uniqueness of the military requires that it be made an exception to the principle of not discriminating on the basis of sexual orientation, they said. Congressman William Dannemeyer declared in December 1992:

> The military is quite simply, unique by definition. What is important in society may not be important in the military and vice versa. The military need only be concerned with winning this nation's wars—nothing more.[86]

Chaplain Gomulka wrote that "In the unique, intensely close environment of the military, homosexual conduct can threaten the lives, including the physical (e.g., AIDS) and psychological well-being of others."[87] Hackworth also declared the Army to be exempt from the rules the rest of us live by in the following tongue-in-cheek manner:

> In the ranks, young men from working class and "moral majority" families will tell you that U.S. Army or Marine Corps combat units don't operate like 8-to-5 institutions such as the Chevrolet dealer, the Post Office or most of the United States Air Force.[88]

White opponents of integration also objected that the military can't be held to the same civil rights standards as other institutions. For example, Bradley told the Fahy Committee:

> Neither is integration in a military unit as simple as integration in public gatherings or places of work during the day. The big problems arise after work or training hours, in living quarters and social gatherings.[89]

Again, the argument for uniqueness offers no insight into whether integration is moral or valid, but rather insists that standards applied to the rest of society cannot be applied to the military. Of course, in the case of sexual orientation, few of those who insisted that the military is unique would agree to then support nondiscrimination laws for nonmilitary settings.

Red Herrings

When all else failed, opponents of allowing lesbians and gays to serve openly predicted that a change in policy would inevitably lead to dire consequences that must be considered before any change is made. These purported consequences, which are really only red herrings, range from the plausible to the ridiculous. One professor of military sociology suggested that an end to discrimination on the basis of sexual orientation would force the military to consider "promotion quotas" for gays and lesbians.[90] Colonel Schwenk told the GAO that gays and lesbians shouldn't be allowed in the military because of the substantial cost of accommodating them. By his logic:

> If homosexuals were allowed to serve in the military, to eliminate embarrassment and unwanted sexual advances, DOD would have to make changes in the living arrangements. This of course, would cost the government money. No one knows exactly [how] much, but it would be an added cost.[91]

A Family Research Council publication warned that a likely effect of a change in policy would be military suppliers being pressured into carrying homosexual pornography alongside *Playboy* and *Hustler*.[92] A policy analyst for the Council told the *Washington Times* that:

> We have a special concern for military families. [Mr. Clinton] seems to be suggesting that special housing might be arranged [for homosexual couples]. He may try to give them the equivalent of married housing and survivors' benefits.[93]

Jackson testified that his organization believes that a change in the policy could eventually lead to "such problems as homosexual/lesbian marriages, housing assignment policies, separate living quarters, homosexual clubs and service centers. . . ."[94]

The "red herring" strategy was often used as a scare tactic by opponents of racial integration. The most frequent form of such a strategy was raising the specter of "miscegenation" and marriage between the races (not unlike the perceived threat of marriage between two men or two women). Before World War II the Chairman of the Navy General Board wrote:

> The Navy Department is accused of discriminating against the negro by refusing to permit the enlistment of negroes, in the Navy, in other than messman ratings. If such is discrimination, it is but part and parcel of similar discrimination throughout the United States. . . . The reasons for discrimination, in the United States, are rather generally that:
> (a) the white man will not accept the negro in a position of authority over him;
> (b) the white man considers that he is of a superior race and will not admit the negro as an equal; and
> (c) the white man refuses to admit the negro to intimate family relationships leading to marriage.

These concepts may not be truly democratic, but it is doubted if the most ardent lovers of democracy will dispute them, particularly in regard to intermarriage.[95]

Congressman Hoffman made a similar suggestion—that allowing both races to serve equally would lead to race-mixing—on the House floor:

> But, the ultimate objective of most of these people that advocate this sort of legislation is amalgamation of the races, and in that I do not believe, because I think the Lord tried to do a fairly good job, and I do not believe that these modern agitators . . . know any more about how the people should be colored or live than did the Lord.[96]

General Eisenhower provides an interesting parallel with the fear about "homosexual clubs and service centers" with his comment about the dangers of integration: "Objection involved primarily the social side of the soldier's life. It was argued that through integration we would get into all kinds of difficulty in staging soldier's dances and other social events."[97] These kinds of arguments are really just scare tactics. Because the notions of interracial mixing and gay marriage are particularly anathema to large segments of the population, opponents of nondiscrimination rules in each case have tried to prove that an end to discrimination will eventually lead to marriage.

CONCLUSION

The military is a conservative institution, so it resists change of any kind. Also, the military is an elite institution, so it systematically categorizes many Americans as "other" and excludes them. When groups like African Americans or lesbians and gays have tried to break into the club, the military falls back on a series of arguments designed to resist their entry. Argument for argument, the debate over the inclusion of African Americans and gays has revolved around the same rhetoric, and, more importantly, the same ways of thinking.

Of course, saying that all the arguments are the same is not sufficient justification to change the policy. The specifics of ban supporters' arguments are certainly open to challenge on their own merits, without resort to racial analogies. But for supporters of both the old ban and the Don't Ask, Don't Tell reworking of it, knowing that opponents of racial integration were thinking in similar ways should be enough to at least give them pause, if not make them reconsider whether their arguments are based on bigotry and not logic. And for those who support allowing lesbian and gay soldiers to serve openly, seeing the stark parallels in the rhetoric of the opposition should provide renewed hope that today's prejudice will also be overcome.

In the end, the military structure is based on total obedience and absolute discipline in following orders. After the commanders in the Korean War realized they needed to integrate to effectively fight the war, they ordered integration, and integration was carried out. While Bill Clinton did not find the courage to stand up for nondiscrimination in the military, it is entirely possible that the courts will do it for him. When that happens, the military will undoubtedly adjust. As one Air Force colonel who opposed open gays and lesbians in the military put it:

> It's the military tradition. We resist it, and then we do it. We did it with integration, and now we're doing it with women. It's the same as the other things. We'll find a way.[98]

NOTES

1. Quoted in "Lifting Gay Military Ban Hits Emotional Chord." *Los Angeles Times* (19 November 1992).

2. Maynard, Robert C. "One Day, Arguments Against Gays in the Military will Seem Quaint, Outdated." *Ft. Lauderdale Sun Sentinel* (17 November 1992).

3. Letter, Gen. Colin L. Powell to The Honorable Patricia Schroeder, 8 May 1992.

4. Moskos, Charles. "Why Banning Homosexuals Still Makes Sense." *Navy Times* (30 March 1992): 27.

5. Jackson, Charles R., statement before the Republican Study Committee on Homosexuals in the Armed Forces, December 9, 1992.

6. Knight, Robert H. "Should the Military's Ban on Homosexuals Be Lifted?" *Insight* No. 9 (November 1992): 5. Published by the Family Research Council.

7. Rubenstein, William B. "Challenging the Military's Antilesbian and Antigay Policy." *Law and Sexuality* 1:239 (1991): 257.

8. Cabaj, Dr. Robert Paul, M.D. Letter to Irene A. Robertson, Assignment Manager, Defense Force Management Issues, United States General Accounting Office.

9. Graves, Amy. "Barney Frank Grills Colin Powell on Military Gay Ban." *Philadelphia Gay News* (21 February 1991).

10. Keen, Lisa. "Military History: Blueprint for Bias." *Washington Blade* (11 December 1992): 11.

11. One other argument, that lesbians and gays are a security risk, fell into disfavor by the military leadership by 1991, when Pentagon studies showed gays are not a security risk and both General Powell and Secretary Cheney dismissed the danger of blackmail against gay and lesbian soldiers.

12. Longenecker, Vickie S., Lt. Col., U.S. Army. "Facts or Fear from the Foxhole: An Individual Study Project." USAWC Military Studies Program Paper. 15 April 1992, p. 19.

13. McCrane, Kevin M. "Gays in the Military? A Cautionary Tale." *Wall Street Journal* (2 December 1992): A10.

14. Russell, Richard. Remarks in Senate, Congressional Record June 8, 1948, p. 7361.

15. Ibid., 7362.

16. Knight, 2. In this section, two of his three sources are from the early 1980s, before the AIDS epidemic caused major behavioral changes among gay men.

17. Quoted in "Lifting Gay Military Ban Hits Emotional Chord." *Los Angeles Times* (19 November 1992).

18. Ray, Col. Ronald D., USMCR. Testimony before the Republican Research Committee, U.S. House of Representatives, December 9, 1992, p. 5.

19. Ibid., 4.

20. MacGregor, Morris J. Jr. *Integration of the Armed Forces 1940-1965.* Washington, DC: Center of Military History, United States Army, 1981, 36.

21. Russell, Richard. Remarks in Senate Congressional Record, June 8, 1948, p. 7361-2.

22. Appendix to "Homosexuals in the Military," Testimony of Congressman William E. Dannemeyer (R-CA), December 9, 1992.

23. Hackworth, David H. "The Key Issue Is Trust: Clinton Should Review the Gay Question." *Newsweek* (23 November 1992): 27.

24. Ray, 4.

25. MacGregor, 610.

26. Memorandum G.B. NO. 420 (Serial No. 201) from Chairman of General Board to Secretary of the Navy. Subject: Enlistment of men of colored race in other than messman branch.

27. Hackworth, "Key Issue."

28. Jackson statement.

29. Hackworth, David, "The Case for a Military Gay Ban: My Combat Experience Tells Me It's the Only Sensible Policy." *The Washington Post* (28 June 1992): C-5, Outlook.

30. "Striking Parallels." *Washington Blade* (20 November 1992): 14.

31. MacGregor, 18.

32. Hearings before the General Board of the Navy, 23 January 1942.

33. Majority report, committee appointed by Secretary of Navy, 24 December 1941.

34. Fahy Committee testimony, Gen. Omar Bradley, p. 71-2.

35. Longenecker, 25.

36. Longenecker, 22.

37. Moss, J. Jennings. "Clinton Vows to Allow Gays in Military." *Washington Times* (12 November 1992).

38. Hackworth, "Key Issue."

39. Hearings before the General Board of the Navy, 23 January 1942.

40. Ibid.

41. Fahy Committee testimony, Gen. Omar Bradley, p. 78.

42. See Appendix B.

43. Mundy, Gen. C. E. jr., "Proposed CMC Comments on the DOD Policy Regarding Homosexuality," 21 July 1992. Emphasis in original.

44. Longenecker, 23.

45. MacGregor, 27.

46. Fahy Committee testimony, Gen Omar Bradley, p. 74.

47. Graves.

48. Hall, Charles W., "Area Servicemen Split on Lifting Ban on Gays." *Washington Post* (21 November 1992): A10.

49. Hackworth, "Key Issue."

50. Memorandum G.B. No. 420.

51. MacGregor, 59.

52. Williams, Mike and Davis, Jingle. "Gays in Uniform Will Face Resistance, Troops Say." *Atlanta Journal/Atlanta Constitution* (13 November 1992): A5.

53. Appendix to Dannemeyer testimony.

54. "Striking Parallels." *Washington Blade* (20 November 1992): 16.

55. MacGregor, 60.

56. MacGregor, 227.

57. Graves.

58. Williams and Davis.

59. Bethell, Tom. "A Good Army Doesn't Have Room for Gays." *Los Angeles Times* (19 November 1992).

60. MacGregor, 60.

61. Ibid., 169.

62. Congressional Record, House. June 15, 1948, p. 8392.

63. Comments of Jack Clayton, representative of Christian Legal Defense and Education Foundation. Quoted in Stepanek, Marcia and Johnson, Christopher R., "Baptists, Military Team Up to Keep Gays Out." *San Francisco Examiner* (2 December 1992): A19.

64. Gomulka, Eugene T., Deputy Chaplain, USMC. "Position Paper on the DOD Policy on Homosexuality," 20 June 1992.

65. Congressional Record, Senate. June 8, 1948, p. 7355-6.

66. Congressional Record Appendix. July 27, 1948, p. A4645.

67. Williams and Davis, A1.

68. Chapman, Stephen. "Clinton's Military Experiment." *Washington Times* (17 November 1992).

69. Hackworth, "Key Issue."

70. MacGregor, 440.

71. Ibid., 441.

72. Congressional Record, House. June 17, 1948, p. 8694.

73. Longenecker, 22.

74. Bethell.

75. Jackson equates sodomy with homosexuality. In actuality, many sodomy laws (including that of the Universal Code of Military Justice) apply equally to heterosexual and homosexual acts. Also, a person can be a homosexual and not violate any sodomy laws.

76. Jackson statement.

77. MacGregor, 317.

78. Hearings before the General Board of the Navy, 23 January 1942. Emphasis in original.

79. MacGregor, 23.
80. "Army Segregation to Go, Says Truman." *New York Times* (29 July 1948): 12.
81. Hall, A10.
82. Stepanek, Marcia. "Fear Over Gay Rights Grips Military." *San Francisco Examiner* (22 November 1992).
83. Knight, p. 5.
84. Congressional Record, Appendix. July 27, 1948, p. A4650.
85. Fahy Committee testimony, Gen. Omar Bradley, p. 77.
86. "Homosexuals in the Military." Testimony of Congressman William E. Dannemeyer (R-CA) before a Republican Research Committee Hearing. December 9, 1992.
87. Gomulka, 6.
88. Hackworth, "Key Issue."
89. Fahy Committee testimony, Gen. Omar Bradley, p. 68.
90. Moss, A10.
91. Appendix to "Homosexuals in the Military," Testimony of Congressman William E. Dannemeyer, December 9, 1992.
92. Knight, Robert H. and Garcia, Daniel S. "How Lifting the Military Homosexual Ban May Affect Families." Family Research Council "In Focus."
93. Price, Joyce. "Gay Ban Backed in Ranks." *Washington Times* (18 November 1992): A8.
94. Jackson statement.
95. Memorandum G.B. No. 420.
96. Congressional Record, House. June 15, 1948, p. 8394.
97. MacGregor, 227.
98. Hall, A10.

CHAPTER 3

Military Women:
Casualties of the Armed Forces' War on Lesbians and Gay Men

Michelle M. Benecke
Kirstin S. Dodge

Military men, from the bottom ranks to the top, don't want women in their midst and the most expedient way to get rid of women—whether they be Gay women or married heterosexuals with children—is to pin them with the label "Lesbian."[1]

Where sexism and homophobia meet, you get a viciousness the likes of which you have never seen.[2]

Women's involvement in the Gulf War and highly publicized court battles challenging the exclusion of women by the Citadel and Virginia Military Institute have focused renewed attention on the acceptance and integration of women in the U.S. armed forces. In the wake of these actions, servicewomen's advocates have revived their efforts to remedy the negative effect of the services' remaining combat exclusion policies on women's assignment opportunities and promotion potential. Advocates recognize that the exclusion of women from combat roles prevents women from gaining experience that is a de facto prerequisite for advancement to senior ranks and policymaking positions.[3]

While combat exclusion policies are an obvious obstacle to equal treatment of women servicemembers, perhaps a more insidious bar is the prevalence of informal barriers that prevent full recognition of women's contributions in job fields already open to them.[4] This chapter will examine one such informal barrier: the institutionalized sexual harassment of military women through "lesbian baiting"—the practice of pressuring and harassing women through calling, or threatening to call them, lesbians.

Lesbian baiting gains its legitimacy and power through the Department of Defense (DOD) policy banning service by known homosexuals,[5] and from the codification of this policy into law.[6] This chapter argues that the policy is used to justify campaigns of sexual harassment against women and that, in its application, the policy controls and confines women's presence and behavior in the military.

This chapter is an updated version of a paper originally published in the *Harvard Women's Law Journal*[7] prior to the national debate on lifting the military ban and the resulting policy known as "Don't Ask, Don't Tell, Don't Pursue." Although not a significant improvement, this policy did promise to end witch hunts, harassment, and questions about servicemembers' sexual orientation. It was hoped that these few promises would help to protect military women from the practice of lesbian baiting. That has not, by and large, been the result. Witch hunts have continued in the first two years of the policy, and antigay harassment has actually skyrocketed.[8] The rate of homosexual discharges has, in fact, increased,[9] and women continue to be disproportionately targeted.[10] The new policy has done little to discourage retaliatory investigations against women who report sexual assault or harassment. Unfortunately, the dynamic described in this chapter remains as alive and pernicious as ever.

There is one significant difference, however. Women who are targeted by lesbian baiting harassment now have an outside advocate, the Servicemembers Legal Defense Network,[11] to help them stop witch hunts and shift the focus of investigations back onto perpetrators of sexual harassment, instead of on women complainants' private lives. Lesbian baiting and other abuses should not occur, however, and servicemembers should not have to rely on outside intervention to stop them.

The first part of this chapter provides a brief history of the military's use of its antigay policies against servicewomen. Next, we detail the type of investigations conducted against women alleged to be lesbians. Personal stories of servicewomen are then used to illustrate the criminal and administrative procedures and sanctions that women face when targeted for investigation.

Later in the chapter we discuss a prominent sociological study that suggests that a modern theory of gender identity formation may account for servicemen's hostility to servicewomen. It also explores the reasons why such hostility is manifested in sexual exploitation and lesbian baiting. We document the practical consequences of lesbian baiting in the daily lives of servicewomen. Finally, we offer recommendations for change.

A HISTORY OF ABUSE

[T]he status of women in the military remains marginal, subject to changes in perceptions of necessity and propriety that have less to do with the rights and obligations of citizens than with political and demographic constraints on "manpower."[12]

The military's use of its policies against homosexuality to harass women is not a new phenomenon. From the first entry of women into specialties other than nursing through the Women's Auxiliaries of World War II,[13] purges have occurred in a pattern which seems to be linked to women's entry into nontraditional job fields, personnel gluts which provide a rationale for decreasing the numbers of women in the military, and the social and political climate of the time.

While women in the Women's Auxiliaries were subject to lesbian baiting,[14] official sanctions against women for alleged lesbian activity during World War II appear to have been limited to an occasional discharge.[15] Low discharge rates were probably due to the policies of the Women's Auxiliaries themselves. For example, the Women's Army Auxiliary Corps' (WAAC) wartime lectures, written in 1943, spoke highly of friendships between women and downplayed the differences between lesbians and "normal" women.[16] Although the WAAC prohibited sexual relationships between servicewomen, its lectures warned officers that "bringing an unjust or unprovable charge against a woman in this regard will be severely reprimanded."[17]

By the early 1950s, the virulent anticommunist and antihomosexual sentiments of McCarthyism had taken hold of the political and social world. Senator Joseph McCarthy and his colleagues charged, among other things, that "'homosexuals and other sex perverts. . .' threatened the moral welfare of the nation."[18] This increased hostility toward gay people is reflected in the military discharge rates for homosexuality, which doubled between the late 1940s and early 1950s, with women detected at higher rates than men.[19] At the same time, civilian women who had been mobilized for the war effort were encouraged to return to their traditional homemaking roles to make jobs available for returning male war veterans. As these shifts occurred, the women's military auxiliaries became one of the few places in society where women could pursue independent careers.[20]

The belief that military women were particularly prone to lesbianism is apparent in the investigation and training procedures advocated by the services for ferreting out lesbians. A 1952 speech given to Navy Auxiliary (WAVE) recruits combined the topics of maintenance of femininity and avoidance of homosexuality,[21] suggesting the degree to which suspicions of lesbianism were tied to popular stereotypes that lesbians were unfeminine in appearance and actions. Officers reminded recruits that they were "supplementing and complementing" the men, not competing with them, and urged them to "be sure that we retain as much of our basic femininity as possible."[22]

The investigative tactics used by the military in the 1950s foreshadowed modern investigations of women suspected of lesbianism. In the Air Force, investigators urged women "to spy on the other girls and to list girls who [were] friends and who *might* be engaging in homosexual relations. . . ."[23] According to one Air Force woman under investigation, those accused of lesbian activities were informed of their rights, but "in such a way that you [were] sure if you [did not answer questions] the consequences [would] be little short of fatal."[24] Women who refused to sign discharge papers or requested military trials to fight charges were involuntarily discharged through administrative procedures.[25]

In the late 1970s, the military services began enlisting more women to make up for a decline in the number of new male recruits,[26] and in 1979 proposed legislation to eliminate restrictions on women serving in combat jobs.[27] At the same time, lesbians and gay men in the military began to challenge the government's right to discharge them for homosexuality.[28] By the end of the decade, this challenge appeared to have achieved some success when both the Navy and the Air Force suggested, for the first time, that discharge of homosexual servicemembers was discretionary, rather than mandatory.[29]

In 1980, with the economy in recession and unemployment rates high, the services were able to recruit more men.[30] Predictably, regulations and procedures discriminating against all women, as well as those against lesbians and gay men, began to be enforced vigorously once again. In 1981 the Army capped the number of new female recruits.[31] The DOD reversed its position on homosexual servicemembers as well, and changed its policies to mandate discharge of gay and lesbian personnel.[32] As men became available to fill recruiting quotas, field commanders who had resisted having women in their units challenged women's continued presence in nontraditional areas.[33]

It appears that this combination of factors resulted in women becoming a special target for discharge. The 1980s were characterized by a wave of investigations and discharges for alleged lesbian activities.[34] The most infamous investigation occurred from 1986-1988 at the Marine Corps Recruit Training Depot at Parris Island, South Carolina, where almost half of the post's 246 women were questioned about alleged lesbian activities.[35] Sixty-five women eventually left the Marine Corps as a direct result of the investigation.[36] Three women were jailed on criminal convictions for homosexual activity.[37]

In the early 1990s, Air Force and Navy women saw an expansion of positions available to them. Fueled by women's participation in the Gulf War and increasing acceptance of women in nontraditional occupations, Congress repealed the statute excluding women from combat aviation.[38] The Navy and Air Force followed suit by repealing their own aviation exclusion policies. The Navy's top officer, Admiral Kelso, further opened positions on all surface ships to women in direct response to Tailhook and personnel shortfalls in certain specialties caused by the impact of the personnel drawdown on the Navy's ship-to-shore rotation policy.[39] Meanwhile, the Army and Marine Corps retained their policies excluding women from direct ground combat positions. Opportunities for Army women actually decreased as the few field artillery positions previously available to them were closed and no new positions were opened.

The issue of lesbians and gay men in the military burst on the national scene in 1993, when military leaders faced pressures on a number of personnel issues. The services were still reeling from Tailhook, and from additional revelations of mistreatment of military women by their male coworkers and superiors.[40] At the same time, the House Armed Services Subcommittee staff, under the direction of then-Chairman Ronald Dellums (D-CA), had embarked on a tour of major military bases to interview personnel about complaints of racial tension and discrimination in promotions and assignments. Further, the drawdown required military leaders to reorganize force structures and reallocate missions accordingly, and led to forced retirements and career insecurity in the ranks.

Many veteran observers believe that this combination of factors relieved pressure from the Joint Chiefs of Staff and other senior military leaders to respond in a fair manner to President Clinton's proposal to lift the ban.[41] One retired Army Colonel summarized, "This isn't about 'homosexual conduct.' The Joint Chiefs viewed the gay issue as yet another 'problem' and just didn't want to deal with it."[42] Despite the new assignment policies and official efforts to stem sexual harassment, others see a direct link between sexism and military leaders' opposition to lifting the ban. For example, one officer related opinions expressed by his colleagues that "If someone has to go [as the result of downsizing], it ought to be the women and the gays."[43]

Thus, the historically parallel developments in exclusionary policies based on gender and sexual orientation began to diverge in the early 1990s. Officially, Navy and Air Force women could serve in nearly every position[44] (with the notable exception of submarines in the Navy), and the services had implemented new policies designed to crack down on sexual harassment.

Yet official policies have done little to actually change the hostile climate experienced by many military women. Women in the Navy have especially experienced a backlash by some male colleagues, who blame them for the negative fallout resulting from Tailhook and other sexual harassment scandals. One Navy officer summed up her male colleagues' view on the lessons of Tailhook: "I don't think many men in the Navy see Tailhook as being something bad. They just got caught. And now women are perceived as a threat to their careers."[45] The accuracy of this officer's perception was unfortunately confirmed by a recent television report in which a Navy man blamed "women on ships" for the latest scandal, an incident in which a male Chief Petty Officer repeatedly groped a lower-ranking woman in front of twenty other sailors, none of whom stopped him.[46] Women in the other services report similar attitudes on the part of many coworkers and superior officers.

The outcome of the debate over gays in the military and the continued practice of singling out women for investigation should not be surprising given this environment, especially in combination with career insecurities felt by many servicemen because of the drawdown. In this climate, the antigay policy provides a means to circumvent official policies and regulations opening jobs to women and forbidding harassment. Quite simply, it creates a situation where women may be routed out of the services by a mere accusation of lesbianism, regardless of their service record and despite policies and regulatory safeguards intended to encourage fair treatment of women and gays.

THE INVESTIGATIONS
While the DOD policy on homosexuality does not distinguish between male and female servicemembers, women are investigated and discharged at rates far higher than their male counterparts.[47] The different investigative methods used to target women and men may account for this disparity. Men are most often investigated on a case-by-case basis, with efforts made to usher servicemen out of the service as quickly as possible.[48] In contrast, women are more likely to be targeted and discharged as the result of mass investigations,[49] aptly referred to as "witch-hunts."[50]

Witch-hunts are often initiated by military authorities on the basis of rumors started by male servicemembers against women who refuse sexual advances.[51] Such rumors are ready weapons of retaliation, involving little risk to those who start them. The most frequent targets of witch-hunts are competent, assertive, and athletic women[52]—i.e., women whose service records are above reproach, leaving no other vulnerability. Witch-hunts flourish when women under investigation are coerced into naming other military women who are rumored to be lesbians.[53]

The 1988 investigation of women sailors on the USS Grapple is a classic example of a witch-hunt. The USS Grapple investigation began when a male crew member started rumors about the close friendship between a woman who rebuffed his sexual advances and another sailor, Petty Officer Mary Beth Harrison.[54] The rumors were followed by an incident in which this male sailor, in front of the ship's crew and at least one of its officers, shouted profanities and accusations that the women were lesbians. On a subsequent deployment, flyers bearing the sign "no dykes" appeared around the ship.[55]

A woman who files complaints about such harassment often finds that her chain of command either is unresponsive or responds by initiating an investigation against the woman herself, incorrectly presuming that only lesbians are lesbian baited.[56] The experience of the women on the USS Grapple was no exception. Harrison's superiors actually advised her not to file a complaint[57] and appeared to have dropped the matter, until, in November 1988, she and three other women were questioned by the Naval Criminal Investigative Service (NCIS) about alleged homosexual activities.[58] Like many women targeted in witch-hunts,[59] the accused sailors were outstanding performers in nontraditional job assignments.[60] According to Harrison, the fairness of these proceedings was dubious. "We were not asked if we were gay—we were automatically presumed guilty."[61]

Many women who have been investigated in witch-hunts have reported that they were subjected to lengthy and harsh interrogations.[62] Investigative techniques used during the USS Grapple witch-hunt fit this pattern. Harrison's requests for an attorney were denied until after she had endured two and a half hours of intense questioning during her initial interrogation, and another woman was interrogated for six hours without a break.[63]

One of the most common tactics used by investigators is to pressure women to name others who might be gay in order to save themselves.[64] During the USS Grapple investigation, NCIS agents told the sailors they would be "protected" if they turned the other women in, that the others had already confessed to being lesbians, and that the NCIS had obtained "conclusive evidence" of their guilt.[65]

More recent investigations have been disturbingly similar. In September 1994, for example, Army Private First Class Jane Wain[66] was accosted by drunken soldiers in her barracks hallway, forced down a Tailhook-like gauntlet, and threatened with rape. Within hours of reporting the incident, Wain became the subject of an aggressive campaign to label her as a lesbian and pin her with trumped-up charges of "lesbian conduct." Her commander did nothing to discipline the men who attacked Wain, instead starting a witch-hunt against her and the other women military police officers at her base.

Like Harrison of the USS Grapple, Wain faced harsh interrogation tactics. Wain endured nearly two hours of continuous yelling and threats by the investigating officer, sometimes delivered only an inch from her face, during her initial interrogation. Her repeated requests for an attorney went unheeded.

Wain's command subsequently pressured her to accuse fifteen other military women as lesbians, in exchange for leniency. When she refused, the command tried to court-martial and imprison Wain based on the trumped-up charges. A military judge eventually dismissed the charges for lack of evidence, but Wain's ordeal did not end there. Instead, her command then tried to railroad Wain out of the Army through administrative separation proceedings based on the same false accusations.[67]

CRIMINAL AND ADMINISTRATIVE SANCTIONS

The Uniform Code of Military Justice (the armed forces' criminal code) criminalizes many sexual activities between consenting adults. Although the code applies to heterosexuals and homosexuals alike, in practice only servicemembers accused of same-sex activities face criminal investigation and prosecution. Military personnel accused of sex or touching with someone of the same gender typically have been charged with sodomy (oral or anal sex), "conduct unbecoming an officer and gentleman," and indecent acts with another.[68]

Conviction by general court-martial, analogous to a civilian criminal trial, carries harsh consequences. Servicemembers convicted for consensual, adult sodomy face up to fifteen years in prison for each incident, demotion, a dishonorable discharge, and total forfeiture of pay and allowances. Those convicted for indecent acts or "conduct unbecoming" face similar results, with the exception of a five-year maximum sentence per incident.

Military members may also face administrative discharge boards for engaging in homosexual acts, attempting to engage in homosexual acts, or making a verbal or nonverbal statement to the effect that they are gay.[69]

Homosexual acts are defined broadly under current policy to include many forms of touching, not only sex. A homosexual act means:

(a) Any bodily contact, actively undertaken or passively permitted, between members of the same sex for the purpose of satisfying sexual desires; and (b) Any bodily contact that a reasonable person would understand to demonstrate a propensity or intent to engage in an act described in subparagraph (a).[70]

The regulations specifically define "handholding or kissing, in most circumstances" as homosexual acts.[71]

This problematic definition especially lends itself to abuse of servicewomen by encouraging contentions that a sisterly kiss or a companionable hug constitute a homosexual act.[72] Marine Lance Corporal Elena Martinez, for example, was accused of homosexual acts in April 1994 after a coworker observed her giving a woman friend a peck on the cheek as they said goodbye after a social engagement. Martinez was ultimately discharged, despite her protestations that she is heterosexual and that the kiss was platonic.[73]

Allegations of consensual homosexual acts are more likely to be handled through administrative discharge proceedings than by court-martial. However, investigators often use the threat of a court-martial and imprisonment to pressure women either to leave the service "voluntarily" or to submit to administrative discharge proceedings. Due in part to the susceptibility of discharge boards to abuses of authority, bias, and to procedural errors made by inexperienced board members, many women opt to leave the service rather than fight for their careers.[74]

The following incidents illustrate the military's criminal and administrative discharge proceedings. These have not been changed by the current military policy, and problems faced by the women in these examples remain widespread.

Criminal Trials: The General Court-Martial
In July 1988, twenty-three-year-old Corporal Barbara Baum, a military policewoman, was convicted by a general court-martial of sodomy, seven counts of indecency, and conspiracy to obstruct justice.[75] Baum was sentenced to one year in jail, demotion to private, and a dishonorable discharge.[76]

The charges against Baum arose from information provided to investigators by Baum's former lover, Lance Corporal Diana Maldonado, in exchange for a grant of testimonial immunity. The brief affair between Baum and Maldonado was discovered by Maldonado's spurned boyfriend in October 1986 when he kicked in the door of their motel room and found them in bed together.[77]

At first, military officials took no action against Baum. Instead, over one year later, they recalled Baum for questioning and pressured her to provide information to agents conducting an investigation of alleged lesbian activities among female drill instructors at Parris Island.[78] Baum's refusal to cooperate with investigators contributed to the military prosecutor's decision to try her case by general court-martial, even though it involved only consensual allegations.[79] This decision sent a strong message to other Marines to cooperate in the investigation.[80]

Explicit questioning of Maldonado at Baum's trial provided sufficient evidence to prove the necessary elements of the sodomy offense.[81] Maldonado also admitted to "passionate kissing and fondling of genitalia" between her and Baum at Baum's residence,[82] and gave uncorroborated testimony that Baum had told her of Baum's other physical contact with women during a game of "truth or dare" at a party in May 1986.[83] This testimony was found sufficient to convict Baum under the ambiguous wording of UCMJ Article 134, Indecent Acts with Another.[84]

In June 1988, three weeks after her imprisonment, Baum succumbed to agents' promises of clemency and an upgraded discharge if she cooperated in the ongoing investigation of women Marines. During fourteen hours of questioning,[85] she gave investigators the names of over 77 women she suspected to be homosexual or to have engaged in homosexual activities.[86] Baum served 226 days of her one-year sentence before being released from the military prison[87] at Quantico Marine Corps Base in Quantico, Virginia.

On February 15, 1990, a military appeals court overturned Baum's conviction, ruling that two jury members in Baum's trial had extrajudicial knowledge of the evidence and an interest in the outcome of the case, and that the military trial judge had allowed uncorroborated testimony.[88] The appeals court did not rule on arguments that it is unconstitutional to prosecute and punish homosexuals selectively for sodomy while heterosexuals are not punished for the same actions.[89] Baum opted to leave the Marine Corps despite her victory on appeal, perceiving no way to salvage her career.

Administrative Discharge Proceedings

One of the women implicated by Baum was Captain Judy Meade, a twelve-year military police veteran stationed at Camp Lejeune, North Carolina. Meade's case exemplifies how investigative proceedings and bias on the part of administrative board members may combine to deny women charged during witchhunts the opportunity for a fair hearing.

The NCIS originally investigated Meade for homosexual activities based on Baum's statement that a civilian lesbian had told her that she and Meade had a sexual relationship.[90] When an investigation failed to substantiate this allegation,[91] Meade was charged instead with "conduct unbecoming an officer," based primarily on her friendship with the civilian lesbian.[92] In February 1989, the five colonels on Meade's Board of Inquiry found her guilty by a preponderance of the evidence,[93] and recommended to her commander that she be given an other than honorable discharge from the Marine Corps.[94] On appeal, the Board of Inquiry's recommendation was reversed for insufficient evidence.[95] Many familiar with military policy believe that the publicity generated by Meade's case may have influenced the Board of Review's decision.[96]

Following the relaxed evidentiary rules that govern discharge boards,[97] the panel that heard Meade's case was permitted to consider hearsay and circumstantial evidence. None of Meade's accusers were present, despite her request that they appear.[98] Instead, Meade's board reviewed statements from three individuals who had been promised clemency or immunity for providing information about other women Marines.[99]

In addition to procedural abuses, the fairness of administrative board proceedings is more questionable in lesbian-related cases than in other separation hearings, because of the widespread acceptance by military men of stereotypes about women in the military and about lesbians. During her hearing, Meade was asked why her "antenna did not go up" that other military women might be homosexuals because they "looked like homosexuals."[100] Board members indicated that she should know that women who play softball are lesbians because of "how aggressive these women are," and seemed to imply that she exercised poor judgment by not avoiding them.[101]

For servicewomen who choose to fight lesbian-related allegations, the process is costly. Meade spent over $16,000 in attorney's fees over the course of her year-long investigation in an attempt to clear her name and salvage her career.[102] Although Jane Wain (whose story appears in the previous section) obtained a volunteer attorney, her family's nonlegal expenses in seeking a fair review of her case exceeded over $8,000.[103]

The effect of an investigation on a woman's career and professional credibility can be devastating.[104] Regardless of the board's findings and recommendations, the fact that an investigation was conducted is annotated in servicemembers' permanent records.[105] Ultimately, Meade was twice passed over for promotion after winning her board and, as a result, was forced to leave the Marine Corps. Wain was likewise refused promotion and is now attempting to overcome this setback—a tough task in today's highly competitive force.

In her 1989 testimony before a Defense Advisory Committee on Women in the Services (DACOWITS) panel, Meade appealed to them to scrutinize administrative proceedings before more good women opt to leave military service rather than face unfair discharge boards.[106] Her warning bears repeating today.

ANALYSIS

[T]hose of us who actively pursue our goals and seek the challenges of the most demanding assignments are perceived as threats by our male counterparts. Displaying those qualities most valued in male sailors—conviction, aggressiveness, and strength—earns us ridicule and scorn.[107]

I thank God every day that I'm a male Marine in this male Marine Corps. . . . If a woman Marine is a little too friendly, she's a slut. If she doesn't smile at all, she's a dyke. I personally believe that a woman Marine in the normal course of a day confronts more stress and more bull-shit than a male Marine would in twenty years.[108]

Why does the phenomenon of lesbian baiting occur in the military? What might be done to protect servicewomen from such abuses in the future? The following analysis explores the existence of sexism in the military and presents a theory of gender identity formation which helps to account for the hostility to women in nontraditional fields. This section ends with an analysis of the sexual nature of the expression of this hostility.

Sexism in the Military

Lesbian baiting and resistance to the integration of women in the military might be explained through a variety of theories. For instance, harassment in the application of policies might be the result of general homophobia and sexism on the part of individual commanders. Commanders have a great deal of discretion in the application of military policies and are the individuals who make decisions about whether to investigate, tolerate, or squelch rumors of lesbian activity. Homophobia and sexism may influence commanders' perceptions of whether a rumor constitutes credible evidence for investigation, and which of the servicemembers interviewed at informal stages of investigation are credible.

Another explanation may be found in the fact that maintenance of formal segregation protects the common economic and status interests of military men. When women are excluded from certain positions, the rewards associated with such fields are reserved for men.[109] The secondary effects of formal exclusion carry over into areas where women do serve, because lack of combat training or experience may impede women's advancement to upper echelons of power, prestige, and pay even in military fields populated by women.[110] As Representative Patricia Schroeder described the situation, "[T]he services need women, lure them in and advertise for them. DOD is trying to get all the services of women with none of the credit given to them."[111]

These proposals may help explain some harassment suffered by women in the services, but they do not account for the fact that in areas such as finance, personnel, and medical specialties servicewomen are accepted with little more harassment than women in similar civilian positions. Evidence suggests that it is the nontraditional nature of women's service in certain military positions which triggers lesbian baiting and harassment. The constant in the witchhunt scenarios described above is that the women involved all served in nontraditional occupations or at nontraditional job sites.[112] It is these women who bear the brunt of harassment in the form of lesbian baiting.

Gender Identity: Theory and Practice

A woman's army to defend the United States of America. Think of the humiliation. What has become of the manhood of America, that we have to call on our women to do what has ever been the duty of men? —Mr. Somers, U.S. Representative to New York, during debate to approve establishment of the Women's Army Auxiliary Corps, March 1942.[113]

War is man's work. [The idea of women in combat] tramples the male ego. When you get right down to it, you have to protect the manliness of war. —General Barrows, former Marine Corps Commandant, 1982.[114]

Recent works by sociologists which incorporate psychoanalytic insights into gender role theory[115] indicate that male gender identity formation and maintenance may cause the phenomenon of lesbian baiting of women in traditionally male specialties. The entry of women into nontraditional job fields makes it difficult for men to maintain masculinity in traditional terms.[116] Retired Air Force Major General Jeanne Holm describes the military as a "cult of masculinity."[117] Many servicemen may have internalized the idea that the military is "a man's world, not fit for women"[118] to the point that "integration of women is likely to require . . . their complete redefinition of themselves as 'men.'"[119] Calling servicewomen lesbians is one way for servicemen to maintain their sense of masculinity when traditional gender distinctions based on job field begin to break down.

According to one theorist, because most children in our society were raised by women, both boys and girls are originally woman-identified.[120] This becomes problematic for male children who, to grow into their socially prescribed gender role, must struggle to put their earliest gender identifications behind them. Masculinity becomes defined "negatively, as that which is not feminine."[121]

> Much of what we see as masculinity is . . . the effect . . . of struggling not to be seen by oneself or others as having feminine attributes, physical or psychologic. One must maintain one's distance from women or be irreparably infected with femininity.[122]

During this process, boys assuage feelings of loss associated with giving up their earliest attachments through "an unconscious rejection and denigration of femininity."[123] Sociologist Christine Williams argues that it is precisely "[t]his contempt for femininity [which is] institutionalized in military policy."[124]

While the process of separation and identification is completed primarily in early childhood, many men retain "a kind of perpetual insecurity" around gender identity.[125] This results in the need to demonstrate their masculinity to themselves and others. Being able to do a "man's job" is one way of proving one's masculinity. If a woman can perform the same job, however, the job loses its usefulness as a proving ground for masculinity.[126]

The military capitalizes on young men's insecurities during basic training. Recruiters promise to "make a man" of new recruits through the tasks demanded in training, and drill instructors label recruits "ladies" or "girls" until they prove themselves deserving enough to be called "men."[127] A male recruit who has internalized the military's message may feel his masculinity threatened by seeing women accomplish the same tasks that are supposedly proof of his manhood.[128] The military both promotes and relies on the maintenance of these dynamics to such an extent that during the period that basic training in the Army was integrated by gender, officials feared they would have trouble recruiting young men if it looked like military service "has become something a 'girl can do.'"[129]

The contempt for women and femininity described by theorists[130] is expressed and encouraged in the military in many ways, including the derogatory use of "girls" and "ladies" as labels of inferiority, the covering of some work areas and lounges with nude pinups and *Playboy* insignias,[131] the practice of marching while singing sexist cadences, and the tolerance of male units whose members whistle, catcall, and bark at women they pass while running in formation.[132] Women Marines are called "BAMs" or "Bammies," which stands for "Broad-Assed Marines,"[133] while women paratroopers in the Army are referred to as "BAPs." Linda Grant De Pauw, an expert on women in the military, argues that underlying such behavior is a "folk wisdom tradition" that "'male bonding,' assumed to be essential for combat performance, is built most efficiently by drawing on sexual insecurities in adolescent males and encouraging them to bond on a 'gang rape' model—proving that they are men and one of the group by verbally attacking and demeaning females."[134] One way to avoid challenges to servicemen's masculinity is to prohibit the entry of women into certain job categories.[135] Combat exclusion policies serve this purpose by protecting the last proving grounds of masculinity.

When job categories are integrated, other means are needed to "separate . . . the 'men' from the 'girls.'"[136] Special uniform and conduct requirements for women serve this purpose by emphasizing servicewomen's "otherness," an example of what sociologist Rosabeth Moss Kantor calls "boundary heightening."[137] This model helps to explain why the Marine Corps, which is viewed by many as the most traditionally masculine service, takes the most care to emphasize the femininity of its women. It is the only branch which requires female recruits to wear makeup and take classes on hair care, poise, and etiquette.[138]

The Marine Corps is not alone in reinforcing gender differences through the use of uniform and conduct requirements. The Army designed a special hat for its women drill instructors rather than provide them with the traditional "smokey bear" hats of their male colleagues (and the potent aura of authority which accompanies them). In all the services, women's dress uniforms are cut to cling rather than for comfort or function,[139] making it difficult for women to display excellent "military bearing."[140] Officers and noncommissioned officers often address this problem by having their uniforms tailor-made, but junior enlisted women, with lower pay and fewer resources, must make do with the confining, revealing uniforms issued to them.[141]

The discretion of commanders plays a large role in applying gender-specific conduct policies to ensure that servicewomen are clearly delineated from servicemen. The former commander of Parris Island, for example, issued orders "prohibiting women from riding motorcycles on post [or] wearing blue jeans off duty while on the island."[142] Women drill instructors were required to wear the skirt version of their uniform and allowed to wear their uniform slacks only at temperatures below freezing, a rare condition in South Carolina.[143]

Another way to avoid demasculinization when a woman does a man's job is to make her *not* a woman. Women who perform men's jobs are "classed as deviants,"[144] "man-women,"[145] and lesbians. Generic stereotypes of lesbians as big, aggressive, tough women with short hair give force to such classifications, especially because such traits are often prerequisites for success in nontraditional job fields. For example, although women need only pin long hair to collar length rather than cut it, most women in units that train outdoors for long periods with no access to basic comforts such as running water, or women who work around dangerous machinery, wear their hair short for convenience and safety. Also, women in leadership positions depend on an assertive style to maintain authority. These qualities make them likely targets of harassment and investigation for homosexuality[146] in fields where many men may already be predisposed to categorizing women as "dykes."[147]

Sexual Harassment

Men see [lesbian baiting] as a real good way to stop women dead in their tracks. Women will either backtrack from their assertiveness or comply sexually.[148]

A disturbing constant in the picture of harassment is the frequency with which lesbian baiting is triggered by a servicewoman's refusal of sexual advances. For example, one officer interviewed by the authors told of sexual advances made by a male peer toward her and two colleagues. All three made it clear that they were not interested in pursuing a sexual relationship. Soon after, they learned that the spurned officer was suggesting to other men in the unit that the three were lesbians and were engaging in sexual acts together.[149] In some respects, this follows the typical pattern of sexual harassment.[150] The difference in the military is the degree of pressure which can be brought to bear against a woman not only by her superiors[151] but by her peers, and in the case of a woman officer or noncommissioned officer, by her subordinates. The legitimization of lesbian baiting arms all men with a tool for sexual harassment, because any time a woman is called a "dyke" her reputation, her career, and even her liberty are on the line.[152]

While not all servicemen seek to extort sexual compliance from their female peers through such methods, those who do are extremely dangerous to servicewomen. A common maxim in the military is that a woman must be three times as good as a man to be recognized, and absolutely above reproach. Given the small size of the community in a particular specialty and branch, a single allegation can haunt a woman from assignment to assignment throughout her career.

Recourse for women faced with lesbian baiting or sexual harassment is limited.[153] A woman who reports abuse is likely to be "labeled as . . . not being a team player,"[154] an extremely degrading pronouncement in the military.[155] As Harrison of the USS Grapple protested, "[t]hose times when I did move to make official reports I met hostility and reluctance to believe that incidents like these could happen aboard such a fine vessel."[156] In addition, because of the military's antigay policy, a woman who reports lesbian baiting harassment risks focusing increased scrutiny upon herself, which may lead to full-blown investigation.[157] As a result, many women are reluctant to report incidents, and many accede to sexual demands.[158]

Social Dynamics of Sexual Accessibility

Andrea Dworkin argues that sexual intercourse is a crucial means by which men prove their masculinity to themselves and to other men.[159] Considered from the perspective of the gender identity theory explored above, it appears that sexual access to women servicemembers may help compensate men for the breakdown of gender boundaries in nontraditional job fields by providing an alternative means of proving masculinity.

Dworkin argues that in a system in which the male is defined as dominant/active and the female as submissive/passive,[160] penile/vaginal sexual intercourse represents "[m]asculinity in action."[161] "The woman is acted on; the man acts and through action expresses sexual power, the power of masculinity. . . . In the male system, sex is the penis, the penis is sexual power, its use in fucking is manhood."[162]

Sexual intercourse, then, can be a means of "boundary heightening," of clarifying the distinction between male and female. In nontraditional job fields, this may be one of the few remaining ways to do so. But for sexual intercourse to serve its masculinizing function, women must be sexually accessible to men.[163]

Women who choose to make themselves inaccessible to men face harassment in the most innocent of circumstances:

"Lesbian tendencies" may be seen in behavior that seems perfectly conventional—even puritanical—to civilian women. We see Mrs. Reagan on the evening news hug and kiss friends she greets. Born-again Christians speak approvingly of chastity for unmarried women. Yet military women, tired of fighting off sexual advances from the only available men, who choose instead to spend their free time with women friends, drinking Diet Coke and playing board games, find themselves branded as "Lezzies."[164]

This sexual accessibility analysis appears to apply to the Parris Island investigation, and may help to explain why investigations of drill instructors have taken place repeatedly at the installation.[165] At Parris Island, Marine Corps policy segregates women recruits into their own units with women drill instructors[166] and strictly separates male and female recruits during basic training.[167] Servicemen on Parris Island find a host of psychological and social messages in this arrangement: they see a group of women sexually inaccessible to themselves or other men, grouped together under the instruction of assertive, competent female drill instructors who have sole access to the female recruits. The mixture is a potential powder keg of sexism, homophobia, and gender identity conflict to men who may be insecure in their masculinity.[168]

CONFINEMENT AND CONTROL OF WOMEN'S BEHAVIOR

The practical consequences of lesbian baiting to women in the military are extreme. Servicewomen in nontraditional job fields expend an enormous amount of energy seeking to walk the fine line between effective competence and nonthreatening femininity; they must be feminine enough to reduce harassment, but must avoid the danger of being considered inferior or incompetent by virtue of this femininity. Because of the threat of harassment against women who associate together in groups, servicewomen cannot even turn to each other for relief and support in the face of this daily challenge.

Women quickly learn the restrictions on their behavior. This education often takes place through informal means, such as listening to their male peers speculating about other women.

> [T]o put it delicately, the talk is directed to determining the answer to the question "does she or doesn't she?" At first those set on categorizing the woman have nothing at all to go on but their first impressions of her appearance; but that is enough. "Is she or isn't she too pretty to be queer?" Does she wear makeup, have short hair, prefer flat shoes to heels? Has she gone to bed yet with anyone we know?[169]

In an attempt to counter such speculation, many women adjust their appearance and behavior.[170] Williams noted a "hyperfemininity" in many of the women Marines she studied which resulted from their efforts to counteract assumptions that they were all lesbians.[171]

The need to cultivate one's femininity is in direct conflict with the need to avoid supervisors' tendency to perceive feminine women as incompetent or inferior to men.[172] Women in nontraditional job fields are newcomers to a system which was created by men for men. Thus, when women are evaluated by superiors, it is "on the men's terms rather than on their own terms or even on 'human,' androgynous terms. . . ."[173] Women complain that evaluative categories such as "forcefulness" are often euphemisms for "masculinity."[174] A supervisor who perceives any sign of femininity, or even femaleness, as signs of weakness or inferiority will not consider women "up to snuff."[175] The result is poor performance evaluations for the servicewomen under such leadership.

The balancing act in which servicewomen must engage is crucial not only to the reduction of the threat of harassment in their daily lives, but also to their advancement within the military. When promotion boards are given servicemembers' files and evaluations, "the first thing they see when they open a file is a photograph."[176] To those who have served on such boards and to those who observe patterns of promotion, it is clear that women must be attractive and "feminine" looking to succeed in the military. If a woman is too pretty, however, evaluators will not take her seriously. A woman must look athletic, but not too "jockish," to avoid the suspicion that she may be a lesbian.[177]

Women of color are especially hard hit by the underlying dynamics of the military system.[178] Promotion boards are likely to be composed of white men whose perceptions are often filtered by racism as well as sexism. Because of this, the records of women of color on their way up the ranks will tend to be scrutinized more closely than those of white women and with greater skepticism.[179] This may in part explain why women of color are underrepresented in the officers corps[180] and why women of color above the grade of 03 (analogous to midlevel management positions) are almost nonexistent.[181] In addition, when women of color seek each other out and spend time together, their smaller numbers may open them to special scrutiny, and thus to greater danger of investigation.[182]

Rather than turning to each other for support, solidarity, and assistance in learning successfully to negotiate a path through the stresses of their daily lives, servicewomen are forced to remain largely isolated from one another because of the tendency of women in groups to trigger lesbian baiting harassment and investigations.[183] "Guilt by association" makes women especially shun lesbians or women who fit the traditional stereotypes.[184] The damage resulting from "the consequent emotional isolation for military women, especially when they are in a small minority, as aboard a ship, can scarcely be overstated."[185]

RECOMMENDATIONS

The harmful effects of lesbian baiting harassment described in this chapter could be eliminated or greatly reduced through action by the Executive Branch, including the Department of Defense, Congress, or the federal courts. Efforts should target reform of training methods that aggravate servicemen's gender insecurities and elimination of other official and unofficial support for the harassment of women. This would include abolishing the law that bars known lesbians and gay men from military service. In the meantime, limits in the current policy designed to end witchhunts, asking about sexual orientation, and harassment must be fully implemented and enforced.

A concerted long-term effort is necessary to lessen the gender identity insecurities of servicemen that contribute to the social environment in which harassment flourishes. Change of military procedures that denigrate women would be an important first step. For instance, drill instructors should be trained in alternative methods of motivating recruits.[186] Recruitment campaigns should avoid playing on men's insecurities about their masculinity.[187] They could instead emphasize military service as a means of transition from adolescence to responsible adulthood, and proud performance of civic duty for both men and women. Demeaning catcalls and barking and the use of insulting epithets should be strictly punished, just as racial epithets are now. While some progress has been made in this area in the aftermath of the Tailhook scandal, far more needs to be done.

Simultaneously, the services should recruit more women, given that most of the exclusion policies traditionally cited as the rationale for artificially capping the number of women have now been abandoned.[188] The effect of tokenism, the current condition for military women, in fueling harassment is well documented.[189] The more women are integrated into the armed forces, the less remarkable their presence will be, and the more men will see them and treat them as colleagues, rather than abstract stereotypes.[190]

In the meantime, the attitudes of senior leaders are of utmost importance regarding the climate of the services for women.[191] A clear message must be sent that lesbian baiting is a tool of sexual harassment and that such harassment of women is unacceptable. At the minimum, commanders and senior noncommissioned leaders should, in the context of existing sexual harassment programs, be given training and instructions on the potential misuse of allegations of lesbian conduct as a tool of sexual harassment.[192]

Senior leaders must also take seriously the few limits contained in the Don't Ask, Don't Tell, Don't Pursue policy, and make it clear they expect subordinates to comply with them. This effort must start at the top. A significant first step would be for the Commander-in-Chief to inform the Secretary of Defense that he expects abuses of the policy, including its retaliatory use against women, to stop. Whether or not this occurs, the Secretary of Defense should issue official guidance to the field (such as a letter of instruction) communicating the serious intent of the policy to stop witchhunts, asking, and harassment. This would be in line with steps usually taken to implement new personnel policies, but which neither civilian or military leaders have yet taken concerning this policy.

The Secretary of Defense and the services should go further and provide more adequate information and training on the policy than has yet been conducted. In particular, there is a critical need to clarify and reinforce the provisions designed to stop witchhunts. Two in particular have been widely misunderstood or ignored by commanders in the field.[193] First, it should be made clear that the requirement to have "credible information" before starting an investigation[194] does not include *any* information, especially if it seems spurious or retaliatory. Allegations lodged against a woman after she reports sexual harassment or assault should automatically be suspect and should not constitute credible information to begin an investigation against her. Instead, they should be treated as incidents of sexual harassment.

Second, commanders must limit the scope of investigations to the instant allegations.[195] Commanders should be strongly reminded that they may not use one allegation against a servicemember—even if credible—as an excuse to start a fishing expedition to dig up additional allegations against her or her associates, or to identify others who might be lesbians. Although not the only step that needs to be taken, these provisions would, in fact, help to reduce witchhunts, if they were enforced.

Commanders should also be instructed, in the strongest terms, to desist from questioning servicemembers about their sexual orientation. "Don't ask" means just that—don't ask. There is no excuse for violating this unambiguous requirement.

Finally, as we have seen, stopping antigay harassment is doubly important to women. To this end, troops as well as leaders need clear guidance and instructions. Although the current policy forbids "harassment against any servicemember for any reason,"[196] harassment has skyrocketed since the current policy was announced (except, ironically, in units where gays are serving openly pending discharge or federal court proceedings, where harassment has become almost nonexistent).[197] This trend is due, in part, to pressure many servicemembers now feel to "prove" they are not gay.[198] One way to do so is to make antigay remarks in the company of coworkers or to directly harass those perceived to be gay.[199] Servicemen can also prove they are not gay, however, by making sexual advances toward women or by joining in sexual harassment of women. In this vicious circle, women who refuse the men's sexual advances then become suspect as lesbians and suffer the consequences of lesbian baiting. Leaders need to set a climate that discourages, not incites, this dynamic. Further, troops need to know that such behavior, both sexual harassment of women and harassment based on perceived sexual orientation, is unacceptable and will be punished.

Ultimately, however, military culture changes when commanders perceive that their careers are at stake. Quite simply, those commanders who witchhunt, ask about sexual orientation, or tolerate harassment of any kind must be held accountable by their superiors. Only then will commanders be wary of pressing unwarranted investigations against women.

Congress could also take steps to remedy lesbian baiting and the disproportionate impact of the policy on women. Congressional hearings into investigative techniques and procedural abuses could serve to make clear to military leaders that harassment of women in the guise of enforcing official policy is not acceptable. In the current Congress, however, hearings might well create further harm by provoking renewed efforts to reduce women's participation in the armed forces, or to codify an even more draconian policy against lesbians and gay men. Even in this climate, however, individual senators and representatives can take actions to stem abuses against their constituents. When pursued with vigor, Congressional inquiries have proven effective in forcing an end to specific command violations.

However, since in the end analysis it is the DOD policy against lesbians and gay men in the services that gives force to the harassment of women through lesbian baiting, it may be impossible to eradicate harassment as long as the policy exists. Elimination of the military's policy would be the fastest, most effective way to eliminate the extreme consequences of lesbian baiting harassment.

Congress, of course, has the power to abolish the statute codifying the current policy. This outcome is not likely in the near future, however, given the recent political bloodletting that resulted in the codification of the policy. This step has effectively tied the President's hands, preventing him from ending the policy via an Executive Order. Thus, at the present time, the courts are the only realistic avenue available to seek repeal of the statute and its resulting DOD policy.

Legal challenges to the DOD policy itself have been largely unsuccessful.[200] Court decisions in the last few years, however, have produced more mixed results, including several favorable to gays and lesbians, allowing the military plaintiffs to continue serving.[201] Furthermore, lesbian and gay servicemembers have been much more successful in obtaining preliminary injunctions, allowing them to serve pending the outcome of their litigation challenging the policy.[202] The presence of these officially acknowledged lesbians and gay men and their uniformly favorable impact on their units further undermines the government's rationale that openly gay servicemembers would detract from unit morale and cohesion and thereby impair military readiness and effectiveness. It is expected that cases challenging the current regulations that are now in the federal appeals courts will reach the Supreme Court within one or two years.[203]

The courts remain, however, an imperfect solution to the problems engendered by the policy. The few favorable court decisions have thus far been decided on narrow grounds and have been limited in the scope of their application. Moreover, many courts have adopted a position of great deference to the military.[204] These courts assume the validity of the government's contention that the policy is necessary to maintain morale and cohesion and, therefore, uphold the constitutionality of the policy based on the lowest level of constitutional scrutiny.[205] The military's policy is assumed to be valid as long as the classification and discharge of homosexuals "rationally furthers some legitimate, articulated state purpose."[206] The military's stated purpose for the policy includes the need to preserve "the armed forces' high standards of morale, good order, discipline and unit cohesion that are the essence of military capability."[207]

Yet despite the overwhelming evidence that contradicts the military's purported rationale,[208] courts have yet to require the military to produce concrete arguments and facts to support its position that discharge of lesbian and gay servicemembers rationally furthers these stated ends. Instead, courts have, by and large, accepted the military's arguments that

> the Army should not be required by this court to assume the risk . . . that accepting admitted homosexuals into the armed forces might imperil morale, discipline, and the effectiveness of our fighting forces. . . . We . . . should not undertake to order such a risky change with possible consequences we cannot safely evaluate. [209]

In contrast to the nebulous potential risks of doing away with the antigay policy, the widescale harassment and sexual exploitation of women servicemembers which result from the policy's application are a concrete and immediate threat to stated military interests. The readiness of the armed forces to defend the nation as well as economic interests are damaged as resources are spent training women who are then discharged for allegedly violating the policy, or who leave because they are tired of being harassed. The climate of suspicion and fear fostered by the policy does little to build unit cohesion among those who remain, or bridge divides between men and women in the service.

As the military budget is reduced in the future and an expected recruiting shortfall takes its toll,[210] such concerns will become even more important.[211] However, women are not likely to stay in the military until the conditions of harassment which face women and cause them to leave are significantly improved. While changes in policy following the Tailhook scandal have made some progress in reducing overtly harassing behaviors, they have not solved the problem and certainly have not eliminated the hostile climate faced by many women.

Force morale also suffers when women experience stress and isolation due to the harassment resulting from the policy's application. Discipline and good order can hardly be said to be maintained in a system that encourages the harassment of many of its key players. The policy and its application effectively condone the harassment and rape of servicewomen. They encourage a kind of wanton preying on women which is met not by swift and sure punishment for the wrongdoer, but all too frequently with the complicity of superiors. The mutual trust necessary for high morale in a unit is unlikely to be fostered by such an environment.

The military's fears of a breakdown in unit cohesion,[212] although not supported by the facts, could be adequately addressed by the enforcement of existing policies and regulations forbidding fraternization, abuse of authority, and sexual harassment. The latter regulations in particular could be used to address the concerns, however ill-founded, of servicemembers afraid of being harassed in the showers or barracks. Although many individual servicemembers may not be accustomed to working with openly gay or lesbian colleagues, neither are they used to close contact with people of various racial, ethnic, and economic identities when they enter the military. According to the military's own experts, unit cohesion is not disrupted by differences among a unit's members; unit cohesion is impaired when individuals do not make the unit—as an entity—the paramount priority.[213] Such a concern is, on its face, not peculiar to sexual orientation as a characteristic or gay sexual orientation in particular. All of the evidence shows, in fact, that known lesbian and gay servicemembers are strongly motivated to "become a part of the team" and, because they have experienced exclusion in the general population, are more likely than heterosexuals to conform to the military regimen.[214] The good experience of those lesbians and gay men who are serving openly—despite the services' attempts to discharge them—strongly support this position.[215]

Leadership environments which encourage teamwork and strictly forbid and punish harassment have largely overcome the difficulties associated with racial integration of the military[216] and, where applied with commitment, have speeded sexual integration. Likewise, with good leadership, any transitional problems associated with official acknowledgment of lesbian and gay servicemembers could be overcome with minimal effort, especially since gay men and lesbians are already present and performing well.

When the concrete harm being done by the policy is weighed against the vague potential risk of harm if the policy is repealed—a position unsupported by the facts—it seems reasonable at the very least to demand that the government articulate more clearly the military's assessment of its grounds for retention of the policy.

In the meantime, public scrutiny, in conjunction with proactive efforts by political allies, will play the major role in influencing DOD policymaking and enforcement. Activists in the field point to media attention as an important factor in the Marine Corps and Navy decisions to reverse board recommendations of discharge for Judy Meade and Mary Beth Harrison.[217] Legal and political intervention, coupled with the threat of adverse publicity, saved the career of Jane Wain.[218] The military seems to want to avoid calling attention to its policies and investigative procedures,[219] and it is precisely for this reason that such scrutiny is appropriate and necessary. Policies and procedures which cannot be clearly justified and defended have no place in an institution whose role is to defend a democratic society.

Military leaders must take seriously the harassment of women, accepting responsibility for their role—and acknowledging the role of the gay ban—in helping to create, support, and further such harassment. Harassment is an unjust return to the dedicated women who serve their country in some of the military's toughest, most demanding jobs. If policymakers are not willing to recognize this out of a sense of fairness and human decency, then they should at least do so in the interest of developing an effective fighting force. Until measures preventing lesbian baiting are implemented and existing measures against other forms of sexual harassment are supported and enforced by military commanders at all levels, on a consistent basis, women will continue to suffer harassment and will continue to leave the services. Those who push women out deprive the military and the nation of their training and skill. As a result, both the military as an institution and the defense of the nation suffer.

NOTES

The authors are especially grateful to Kirk Childress, a Glaefke Fellow at Servicemembers Legal Defense Network (SLDN), and to C. Dixon Osburn, Patricia Gormley, Georgia Sadler, Jean Podrasky, and Mary Ester for their assistance.

1. Lisa M. Keen, "'Lesbian' Label Often Used to Route Women from Military," *Washington Blade* (March 10, 1989): 3, col. 2 (paraphrasing the views of women she interviewed).

2. Attorney Sandra Lowe, Lambda Legal Defense and Education Fund, speaking about gays and lesbians in the military at *Inside/Outside*, Gay and Lesbian Studies Center at Yale Conference, Yale University (October 28, 1989).

3. See, e.g., Patricia Schroeder, U.S. Representative, Interview on *Face the Nation* (CBS television broadcast, January 15, 1990); Christine L. Williams, *Gender Differences at Work: Women and Men in Nontraditional Occupations* (Berkeley: University of California Press, 1989), 9.

4. See discussion of the impact of the informal barriers in the "Confinement and Control of Women's Behavior" section later in this chapter.

5. Department of Defense Directive 1332.30 (Officer Separations) (hereinafter DoDD 1332.30); Department of Defense Directive Directive 1332.14 (Enlisted Separations) (hereinafter DoDD 1332.14).

6. 10 U.S.C. ¶654, *Policy Concerning Homosexuality in the Armed Forces* (1994).

7. Michelle Benecke and Kirstin Dodge, "Military Women in Nontraditional Fields: Casualties of the Armed Forces' War on Homosexuals." *Harvard Women's Law Journal* 215 (1990).

8. See C. Dixon Osburn and Michelle M. Benecke, *Conduct Unbecoming Continues: The First Year Under "Don't Ask, Don't Tell, Don't Pursue"* (Chapter 9 in this volume). Copies of this report may also be obtained through Servicemembers Legal Defense Network, P.O. Box 53013, Washington, D.C. 20009.

9. According to DoD figures, the rate of discharges under the new policy increased to .05 percent of the military in fiscal year 1995. From 1991 to 1994, the rate of discharges remained constant at .04 percent of the force. Neff Hudson, "More Gays Were Discharged in '95 than any Year Since '91," *Navy Times* (January 29, 1996): 8.

10. A Government Accounting Office study conducted during the previous policy found that the discharge rate for Air Force, Army, and Navy women was three times higher than men; women in the Marine Corps were discharged at a rate six times greater than male marines. *Defense Force Management: DOD's Policy on Homosexuality*, 1992 (hereinafter "First GAO Report"). More recent data compiled by Servicemembers Legal Defense Network confirms this trend, with over 30% of their active caseload being women, while women represent only approximately 13% of military personnel. For more information on the policy's disproportionate impact on women, see Judith Stiehm, Comment, "Managing the Military's Homosexual Exclusion Policy: Text and Subtext" 46 *U. Miami L. Rev.* 685 (1992).

11. Servicemembers Legal Defense Network (SLDN) is a private legal aid and watchdog organization in Washington, D.C. that was formed in October 1993 to assist servicemembers harmed under the current policy and to hold military and political leaders accountable. In the interest of full disclosure, one of the coauthors, Michelle Benecke, codirects SLDN with her colleague C. Dixon Osburn.

12. Mary Ann Tetreault, "Gender Belief Systems and the Integration of Women in the U.S. Military." *Minerva* (Spring 1988): 44.

13. The Women's Auxiliary was designed to provide replacements for men who were needed for combat duties overseas. See Allan Berube & John D'Emilio, "The Military and Lesbians During the McCarthy Years." *9 Signs: J. Women in Culture & Society* 4 (1984): 759-75, reprinted in Estelle B. Freedman, Barbara C. Gelm, Susan I. Jameson & Kathleen M. Weston, eds. *The Lesbian Issue: Essays from Signs* 280-81 (1985). For a detailed discussion of the events of this period, see generally John D'Emilio, *Sexual Politics, Sexual Communities* (1983), 40-46.

14. Rumors of lesbianism in the Women's Auxiliaries were so widespread and harassment was so severe that the Federal Bureau of Investigation launched an investigation to determine whether rumors were the result of an enemy plot to undermine morale. Investigators traced the source of the rumors to American servicemen. See Williams, 31.

15. See Berube & D'Emilio, 282.

16. Ibid., 281.

17. Ibid.

18. Ibid., quoting Senate Committee on Expenditures in Executive Departments, "Employment of Homosexuals and Other Sex Perverts in Government" (1950).

19. Ibid., 280.

20. Ibid., 280.

21. Ibid., 287.

22. Ibid., 287.

23. Letter from an unnamed Women's Air Force member to American Civil Liberties Union (1951), reprinted in Berube & D'Emilio, 291.

24. Ibid.

25. Ibid., 292; see also *id.* 293-94. See the "Administrative Discharge Proceedings" header in the "Criminal and Administrative Sanctions" section (later in this chapter) for an explanation of administrative discharge proceedings.

26. This decline is attributable to the move to an all volunteer force in the 1970s. Williams, 48-49.

27. Ibid., 54-55. The proposal was defeated.

28. See Rhonda Rivera, "Sexual Orientation Law," 11 *U. Dayton L. Rev.* 2, 288 (1986).

29. See *Vicki R. Champagne v. James R. Schlesinger*, 506 F.2d 979 (7th Cir. 1974); *Vernon E. Berg v. W. Graham Claytor*, 436 F. Supp. 76 (D.D.C. 1977), vacated, 591 F.2d 8-19 (D.C. Cir. 1978); *Leonard P. Matlovich v. Secretary of the Air Force*, 414 F. Supp. 690 (D.D.C. 1976), vacated, 591 F.2d 852 (D.C. Cir. 1978).

30. See Williams, 56.

31. Williams, 55.

32. Rivera, 291, 296-97. See also the "Criminal and Administrative Sanctions" section later in this chapter.

33. See Williams, 56.

34. These included the following: the investigation of women on the USS Norton Sound in 1980, which resulted in the discharge of eight women sailors; investigations on the hospital ship Sanctuary and on the USS Dixon; the Army's ouster of eight female military police officers from the United States Military Academy at West Point in 1986; the 1988 investigation of thirty women, including every African American woman, on board the destroyer-tender USS Yellowstone, which resulted in the discharge of eight women; and, the 1988 investigation of five of the thirteen female crewmembers on board the USS Grapple. Lisa M. Keen, "Women Are Separated From Military at a Higher Rate," *Washington Blade* (March 3, 1989): 7. Testimony of Mary Beth Harrison, Defense Advisory Committee on Women in the Services (DACOWITS) 1988 Spring Conference (April 16-20, 1988), at 8, on file at the *Harvard Women's Law Journal* (hereinafter Harrison Testimony); Interview with Vicki Almquist, Women's Equity Action League, in Washington, D.C. (November 10, 1989); telephone interview with Kate Dyer, then-legislative Assistant to U.S. Representative Gerry Studds (February 13, 1990). See

generally, Randy Shilts, *Conduct Unbecoming: Gays and Lesbians in the U.S. Military* (New York: St. Martin's, 1993). See "The Investigations" section later in this chapter for a detailed discussion of the USS Grapple incident and the investigatory process.

35. Jim Lynch, "Witch Hunt at Parris Island," *The Progressive* (March 1989): 26.

36. *ACLU NEWS*, ACLU Press Release, December 29, 1989 (on file at the *Harvard Women's Law Journal*). At least twenty-seven of these women were administratively discharged. Lisa M. Keen, "Board Advises Discharge for Woman With Lesbian Friend," *Washington Blade* (March 3, 1989): 9. Many women chose to resign or accept voluntary discharges rather than face extensive investigations and the possibility of criminal charges. See, e.g., Lynch, 25. See also Harrison Testimony, 8; Testimony of Judith Meade, Defense Advisory Committee on Women in the Services (DACOWITS) 1988 Spring Conference (April 16-29, 1988), 1-2, on file at the *Harvard Women's Law Journal* (hereinafter Meade Testimony).

37. Telephone interview with Captain Kozloski, Public Affairs Officer, Marine Corps Recruit Training Depot at Parris Island (February 5, 1990). See the "Criminal Trials: The General Court-Martial" header in the "Criminal and Administrative Sanctions" section (later in this chapter) for a discussion of one of the criminal trials.

38. National Defense Authorization Act of 1991, Pub. L. No. 102-190, sec. 531, 105 Stat. 1365 (1991).

39. In the Navy, the personnel drawdown had the opposite effect for women of what one might expect, due, in part, to the service's ship-to-shore rotation policies. When pressed, the Navy found it could no longer afford not to fully utilize every sailor, thus making women available to fill sea-going billets vacated by men.

40. See, e.g., "Woman Drops Sex Harassment Suit Against Air Force," *Dallas Morning News* (20 July 1994), describing the case of Sgt. Zenaida Martinez, whose long battle against the Air Force ended when the Secretary of the Air Force personally intervened to set her career back on track.

41. Interviews with military personnel. Throughout the remainder of this piece, we cite to interviews with military personnel who, for their own safety and the sake of their careers, felt the need to remain anonymous and requested omission of the details of their locations, branches, and specialties (hereinafter, Interview or Interviews).

42. Ibid.

43. Ibid.

44. While women have been granted access to most positions by official policies and regulations, in practice, many specialties and assignments remain the exclusive domain of male servicemembers, demonstrating an element of institutional sexism indicative of the hostile environment still faced by women.

45. Jim Spencer, "The Navy's Long History of Harassment," *The San Diego Union-Tribune* (November 28, 1995): B7.

46. Ibid.

47. See note 10.

48. See, e.g., Bob Baker, "Marine Told to Prove He's Gay to Get Discharge," *Los Angeles Times* (October 9, 1985): 3.

49. It appears, however, that the military services may now be "equalizing" the treatment of men and women by increasing witchhunts against men. One example is a witchhunt conducted in the spring and summer of 1994 in Okinawa, Japan in which NCIS agents questioned 21 Marines and one airman about their own sexual orientation and activities and those of their coworkers. Even so, there have traditionally been fewer mass investigations of servicemen than women. Telephone interview with Sue Hyde, National Gay and Lesbian Task Force (October 16, 1989). Those that have occurred include a 1985 investigation of the Army's elite "Old Guard" unit at Fort Myer in Arlington, Va., which resulted in the discharge of four male soldiers; a 1982 investigation of both men and women at Scott Air Force Base in Illinois, resulting in the discharge of forty Air Force personnel, mostly women; and, a 1990 purge of gay men at Carswell Air Force Base in Fort Worth, Texas. Keen, 7; James Waller, "New Trial for Lesbian Marine," *Our Week* (January 21, 1990): 26. See also Jacob Weisberg, "Gays in Arms," *New Republic* (February 19, 1990): 20.

50. This term is used by military women, advocates, and the media to describe mass investigations against women. The term "witch-hunt" has historical significance as a description of the mass trials and extermination of women as witches in Europe and in New England during the 16th and 17th centuries. Modern commentators on this phenomenon have described it as a means by which men in those communities consolidated their power by eradicating women who were perceived to threaten the predominant patriarchal economic, religious, and social structures. See generally Elizabeth Clark and Herbert Richardson, "The Mulleus Maleficarum: The Woman as Witch," in *Women and Religion* (1977): 116-30; Carol F. Karlsen, *The Devil in the Shape of a Woman: Witchcraft in Colonial New England* (1987).

51. Keen, 3.

52. Almquist, note 34. For the competent, athletic drill instructors on Parris Island, "being the ideal Marine made them suspect." *Id.* In effect, patterns of harassment discussed in this article suggest that women in nontraditional fields are punished for performing up to and better than standard.

53. Keen, 11.

54. Harrison Testimony, 2.

55. Ibid., 2-3.

56. Keen, 7.

57. Harrison Testimony, 2.

58. The four-month-long investigation resulted in administrative discharge board proceedings against Harrison and two other sailors. Shortly after Harrison testified at the DACOWITS Spring 1988 Conference about harassment on the USS Grapple (see Ibid) a Navy appeals board cleared her of all charges.

Within three months, Navy officials again pressed charges of homosexuality against Harrison. She was subsequently dismissed from the Navy. Lisa M. Keen, "Navy Discharges Female Soldier Who Denies that She Is a Lesbian," *Washington Blade* (November 10, 1989): 13.

59. Almquist, note 34.

60. Harrison Testimony, 5. One sailor was a chief electronics technician. Another was the first woman to be selected as the Sailor of the Year on the vessel the USS Yosemite. *Id.*

61. Keen, 3.

62. Keen, 3; Lynch, 26.

63. Harrison Testimony, 5.

64. Keen, 11.

65. Harrison Testimony, 5. Investigators have also threatened women with prison sentences. Keen, 3; see also Lynch, 24. Mothers have been threatened with the loss of custody of their children if they did not name others rumored to be lesbians or admit to participating in homosexual activities themselves. Writing about Parris Island in *The Progressive*, Jim Lynch told of Petty Officer Terry Knox, who was threatened with loss of custody of her six-month-old child if she did not sign a statement prepared by NIS agents that she kissed and masturbated with another Marine, Sergeant Mary Kyle. Agents also left her alone in the room with her estranged husband and then observed the heated argument that ensued from behind two-way mirrors. After seven hours of harassment, Knox signed the statement. She later retracted the statement and testified that she signed it only to end the questioning. The statement was ruled inadmissible at Kyle's hearing because Knox was never read her rights. Marine Corps authorities subsequently charged Knox with perjury but later dropped the charges. Lynch, 11.

66. "Jane Wain" is a pseudonym used to protect this soldier from further retaliation. Information on PFC Wain's case is derived from extensive interviews with her, sworn statements of members of her unit, and other official documents, including the report of the investigating officer and that of a subsequent Inspector General investigation. The authors have chosen not to give precise citations in order to protect Wain's identity.

67. This soldier's career and dignity were ultimately salvaged through a six-month effort by Servicemembers Legal Defense Network, its cooperating private counsel from the law firm of Skadden, Arps, Slate, Meagher & Flom, Wain's Congressional offices, and her family, whose perseverance and credible threat of negative publicity made all the difference.

68. UCMJ, Art. 125, 133, 134, (10 U.S.C. 925, 933, 934) (1994). See note 81 (elements of sodomy offence) and note 84 (elements of indecent acts with another offence). Servicemembers accused of being homosexual may also be charged with related offenses such as conspiracy to obstruct justice, fraud, and making false official statements. See, e.g., Transcript of Corporal Barbara Baum Trial, March 28, 1989, 1-4 (hereinafter Baum Trial Transcript), *United*

States v. Barbara Baum (U.S. Navy-Marine Corps Court of Military Review 1990) (NMCMR 89-0-107).
69. 32 C.F.R. pt. 41, app. A Pt. 1.11.1.c (adopted on January 29, 1994); DoDD 1332.30, encl. 8-1; DoDD 1332.14, encl. 4-1.
70. 32 C.F.R. pt. 41, app. A. pt. 1.11.1.b(3) (adopted on January 29, 1994); DoDD 1332.30, encl. 1-1; this definition also applies to enlisted members. See DoDD 1332.14, encl. 4-1. The previous policy contained only the first prong of this definition, requiring that acts be performed for the purpose of satisfying sexual desires.
71. Department of Defense Directive 1332.30 at enclosure 8-1 (Definitions); DoDD 1332.14 at enclosure 4-1 (Definitions).
72. Women encountered this problem under the old policy as well, despite its more narrow definition of homosexual acts. Katherine Bourdanny, Kathleen Gilberd, R. Charles Johnson, Joseph Schumann and Bridget Wilson, *Fighting Back* (1985), 19. See, e.g., Lynch, 25 (marine on Parris Island charged with "indecent assault" for putting her arm around the shoulders of a weeping colleague). With its expanded scope and increased subjectivity, however, the current definition puts women at even higher risk by legitimating such contentions.
73. Richard F. Smith, "Female Marine Under Scrutiny: Affectionate Kiss Touched Off Probe," *The Daily News* (October 1, 1994): 1A.
74. See Meade Testimony, 1-2; Lynch, 25.
75. See Baum Trial Transcript, 205-06.
76. Ibid., 233. The maximum sentence under these charges is 35 years imprisonment, dishonorable discharge, forfeiture of pay and allowances, and reduction to the lowest enlisted grade. *Id.*, 207.
77. Ibid., 61-64.
78. Ibid., 106.
79. Telephone interview with Susan Masling, Attorney for Barbara Baum (February 21, 1990).
80. Ibid. See also comments of attorney Vaughn Taylor, note 88.
81. Consensual sodomy is defined in the *United States Manual for Courts-Martial* as follows:

(1) That the accused engaged in unnatural carnal copulation with a certain other person or with an animal.
Explanation: It is unnatural carnal copulation for a person to take into that person's mouth or anus the sexual organ of another person or of an animal; or to place that person's sexual organ in the mouth or anus of another person or of an animal; or to have carnal copulation in any opening of the body, except the sexual parts, with another person; or to have carnal copulation with an animal.

United States Manual for Courts-Martial, IV-90 (1986).

82. Since the Court's decision in *Richard Solorio v. United States*, 483 U.S. 435 (1987), military prosecutors are no longer required to prove a "service connection" to charge servicemembers for off-post conduct. The *Solorio* Court overruled *James O'Callahan v. J. J. Parker*, 395 U.S. 258 (1969).
83. Baum Trial Transcript, 65-66.
84. UCMJ, Art. 134, note 68. The elements of Indecent Acts With Another are specified in the *United States Manual for Courts-Martial* as follows:

(1) That the accused committed a certain wrongful act with a certain person;
(2) That the act was indecent; and
(3) That, under the circumstances, the conduct of the accused was to the prejudice of good order and discipline in the armed forces or was of a nature to bring discredit upon the armed forces. . . .
Explanation: "Indecent" signifies that form of immorality relating to sexual impurity which is not only grossly vulgar, obscene, and repugnant to common propriety, but tends to excite lust and deprave the morals with respect to sexual relations.

United States Manual for Courts-Martial, IV-131 (1986).
85. Lynch, 27.
86. Keen, 1.
87. "Court Overturns Conviction of Female Marine in Sex Case," 10.
88. *United States v. Barbara Baum*, NMCMR 89-0407 (U.S. Navy-Marine Corps Court of Military Review 1990). In a related case, Staff Sergeants Christine Hilinski and Gloria Gurule were removed from their positions as drill instructors and had their permanent records annotated with negative evaluations that questioned their judgment (virtually nullifying their chances for promotion) because they gave favorable testimony as character witnesses at the general court-martial of Sergeant Cheryl Jameson. Tamar Lewin, "Marine Sues Navy Over Demotion," *New York Times* (January 2, 1990): 16. The Public Affairs Officer at Parris Island, Captain A. J. Kozloski, confirmed at the time that the women were disciplined because their superiors had lost confidence in them as a result of their testimony in the Jameson case. *Id.*, 16. The officer who disciplined Hilinski, Colonel Nunnally, was one of the jurors who was deemed to have extrajudicial knowledge in the Baum trial. "Court Overturns Conviction of Female Marine in Sex Case," *New York Times* (February 19, 1990): 10. See also *ACLU NEWS*, note 36. According to Vaughn Taylor, a Jacksonville, N.C. attorney for several women accused in the Parris Island investigation, the actions against Hilinski and Gurule discouraged others from testifying for their colleagues: "The word is out: You don't testify for women accused of being a homosexual." Cindi Ross, "Corps Deters Witnesses, Attorneys Say," *The State* (August 1, 1988): 1B.
89. Baum, note 88.
90. Keen, 1.

91. Lynch, 27; see also Jennie McKnight, "Marine Escapes Lesbian Witchhunt," *Gay Community News* (July 16-22, 1989): 1.

92. Lynch, 27; Keen, 1.

93. See *Marine Corps Separation and Retirement Manual*, Marine Corps Order P1900.16 dated 27 June 1989 w/chg. 1, Chapter 4, Administrative Separation of Officers for Cause. Administrative discharge procedures are similar for all services. See generally *id.*, Ch. 6 (governing separation procedures for enlisted Marines). See also Air Force Regulations (AFR) 39-10; AFR 36-2; AFR 36-12; Army Regulations (AR) 635-200; AR 635-120; AR 15-6; Navy Regulations SECNAVINST 1920.6A; MILPERSMAN 3610100 through 3640497. In general, officers have more procedural protections than enlisted servicemembers but face harsher sanctions. For example, Marine Corps officers have the option of resigning or challenging charges against them through a tri-level board procedure. Enlisted Marines receive board hearings only if they have six years or more in service or are recommended by their commander for an other than honorable discharge, which is the more serious of the three types of administrative discharge: Honorable, General, and Other than Honorable. See also Bourdanny, note 72, for a detailed discussion of administrative discharge procedures and for advice to attorneys representing servicemembers at such hearings.

94. Meade Testimony, note 36. See also Keen, 1; McKnight, 1.

95. McKnight, 1.

96. Ibid., 1.

97. See note 93 for rules governing administrative discharge boards.

98. Meade Testimony, 1.

99. Keen, 1. See also Meade Testimony, 1.

100. Meade Testimony, 1.

101. Ibid. While provisions in the current policy might prevent board members from making such overtly biased comments on the record, such stereotypes persist today among many military men, who comprise the overwhelming majority of discharge board members. One woman's commander called her "dyke," stating that his suspicion was based on the fact that she wore pumps with short heels instead of tall ones. Another woman's commander was caught starting rumors that she was having an affair with another woman in her unit, on the basis that he considered them both to be "aggressive" and "abrupt" in manner. These are just two of many examples that have occurred since the current policy was implemented. Interviews, note 41.

102. Meade Testimony, 1.

103. Interview with the mother of Jane Wain, October 22, 1995.

104. See discussion under the header "Sexual Harassment" in the "Analysis" section, later in this chapter.

105. Keen, 11. These records are reviewed during investigations for the granting and upgrading of security clearances.

106. Meade Testimony, 1-2.

107. Harrison Testimony, 1.

108. Testimony of Captain Guy Richardson, U.S. Marines. Article 39(a) Hearing of Sergeant Mary Kyle (1980), quoted in Lynch, 26.

109. Williams, 9.

110. Ibid.

111. Schroeder, note 3.

112. Kathy Gilberd, "Both Lesbians and Straight Women Face 'Witchhunts,'" *The Objector* (October 1987): 10. Current examples of women in nontraditional job fields include mechanics, systems maintenance specialists, heavy-equipment operators, pilots, and drill instructors. Nontraditional job sites include Navy ships, Army field units, Air Force flight lines, and the Marines. By contrast, traditional positions include clerk-typist, supply, personnel, and medical specialties.

113. Williams, 43 (quoting 77 Cong. Rec. 2569, 2606 (1942) (statement of Rep. Somers).

114. General Barrows, former Marine Corps Commandant (1982), quoted in Michael Wright, "The Marine Corps Faces the Future," *New York Times Magazine* (June 20, 1982): 74.

115. See Williams, 12-15. In her sociological study of male nurses and female Marines, Williams found that "the [traditional] psychic dispositions psychoanalysts describe are practically caricatured in these two groups." *Id.*, 14.

116. Ibid., 66-67.

117. Tetreault, 55-56.

118. Ibid.

119. Williams, 143, quoting Richard A. Gabriel, "Women in Combat?" *Army* (March 1980): 500.

120. Ibid., 13, citing Nancy Chodorow, *The Reproduction of Mothering* (Berkeley: University of California Press, 1978).

121. Ibid.

122. Ibid., 14, quoting Robert Stoller, *Presentations of Gender* (New Haven: Yale University Press, 1985), 18.

123. Ibid., 64.

124. Ibid., 67.

125. Ibid., 66.

126. Ibid., 66. See also Tetreault, 49.

127. Williams, 66.

128. Ibid.

129. Ibid., 61, quoting Richard A. Gabriel, "Women in Combat?" *Army* (March 1980): 50.

130. See discussion in notes 123, 124, and accompanying text.

131. Williams, 69.

132. Interview, note 41.

133. Williams, 69.

134. Linda Grant De Pauw, "Gender as Stigma: Probing Some Sensitive Issues." *Minerva* (Spring 1988): 31.

135. Williams, 3.

136. Tetreault, 61-62.

137. Williams, 69.

138. Ibid., 64.

139. Interview, note 41.

140. "Military bearing" is the term used to describe subjective impressions of a servicemember's professionalism. Factors which combine to create military bearing include personal appearance and grooming, posture, uniform fit and maintenance, and the way in which a servicemember comports herself. The women's uniforms detract from the military bearing of both short and tall women because the cut fits them poorly. They also tend to make women with large breasts and hips look overweight, which constitutes a serious setback to their promotion potential. Interviews, note 41.

141. Interviews, note 41. The services provide only for basic alterations of off-the-rack uniforms. *Id.*

142. Williams, 63.

143. Ibid.

144. See Tetreault, 49.

145. Interviews, note 41.

146. See "The Investigations" section (discussion of women likely to be targeted in investigations) earlier in this chapter.

147. Women who were targeted in the Parris Island investigation clearly recognize and describe this phenomenon. See, e.g., "Marines Are Said to Suspend Alleged Lesbians," *New York Times* (February 23, 1988): 23 ("The qualities and traits that we demand and are supposed to be training [into] our recruits are the same traits that they're saying make us look homosexual"; "I think the big picture is that our femininity is in question here because we're doing the job we were brought down here to do. . . . They don't like the way some of us look.")

148. Keen, 7 (quoting Vicki Almquist, Women's Equity Action League).

149. Interview, note 41.

150. See generally Catherine A. MacKinnon, *Sexual Harassment of Working Women* (New Haven: Yale University Press, 1979); Barbara A. Gulick, *Sex and the Workplace* (1985).

151. Women in the military are in a particularly vulnerable position with regard to sexual harassment by those within their chain of command. A woman's superiors have control over virtually every aspect of her life. They can give her extra duties, charge her with disciplinary infractions, and write poor evaluations into her file. Servicewomen cannot simply leave their jobs—only a woman's command has the power to release or reassign her.

152. See discussion of investigations, trials, and discharge proceedings in the "History of Abuse" and "The Investigations" sections earlier in this chapter.

153. This is especially true when the woman serves under a sexist chain of command, a situation which is likely to occur in nontraditional job fields. Interview, note 41.

154. De Pauw, 34 (quoting from a letter written to her by an Air Force Equal Employment Opportunity officer with 20 years experience).

155. Interview, note 41.

156. Harrison Testimony, 4.

157. See note 56 and accompanying text.

158. Almquist, note 34; Interviews, note 41.

159. See generally Andrea Dworkin, *Women Hating* (New York: Penguin, 1974); *Pornography* (New York: Plume, 1989); and *Intercourse* (New York: Free Press, 1987).

160. See Dworkin, *Women Hating*, 185.

161. Dworkin, *Pornography*, 24.

162. Ibid., 23.

163. Because strict antifraternization policies prohibit social and sexual intercourse between servicemembers of different ranks, military men are not in a position to have sexual access to their superiors, or to know if another man does. This may partially explain rumors started by subordinates about their superiors; calling a female supervisor a lesbian and thereby diminishing her is one of the few alternatives available to servicemen who feel their masculinity threatened by serving under a woman. Interviews, note 41.

164. De Pauw, 42.

165. See Cindy Koss, "Sex Cases Often Fell Women in Marines," *The State,* Columbia, S.C. (April 8, 1988): 1A.

166. Kozolski, note 37.

167. Williams, 61-62.

168. While the military strictly forbids sexual contact between drill instructors and their recruits, it is widely perceived that male drill instructors have at least some sexual access to women recruits. Interviews, note 41.

169. De Pauw, 33.

170. For discussion of sexual compliance in order to avoid lesbian baiting harassment, see the "Sexual Harassment" header in the "Analysis" section, earlier in this chapter.

171. Williams, 6.

172. See notes 123, 124, and accompanying text.

173. Tetreault, 57, citing Jeanne Holm, *Women in the Military: An Unfinished Revolution* (1982), 104; Stiehm, "Women and the Combat Exception," *Parameters* (1980): 156-57.

174. Williams, 68.

175. Ibid., 79.

176. Interview, note 41.

177. Ibid.

178. We rely on personal experience, interviews, and anecdotes to piece together our assertions in this paragraph. It is extremely difficult to find statistical evidence for the disparate impact of military policies on women of color.

179. It is a risky proposition to seek to describe with any certainty the selection for and timing of promotions. It is a plausible assumption that factors such as appearance and military bearing which are based on a white male standard are even more difficult for many women of color to meet than for white women. One former African American male officer who has prepared and observed many promotion boards went as far as to state, "If you're a black gal, you can hang it up" with regard to promotion decisions. Interviews, note 41.

180. As of September 1989, women of color (African American, Latina, and "other/unknown" groups of women) constituted 37.9% of all women in the services but only 19.1% of women officers. Representation of African American women as the percentage of women in various branches of the military ranged from a high of 43.3% representation in the Army to a low of 23.5% of women in the Air Force. In comparison, the percentage of women officers who were women of color ranged from 19.19% of female Army officers to 11.3% of female Air Force officers. Overall, people of color constitute 28.7% of all military personnel while representing 11% of all officers. Telephone interview with Lt. Col. John Dyeski, Office of Assistant Secretary of Defense for Force Management and Personnel, Military Manpower and Personnel Policy, Officer and Enlisted Personnel Management (February 23, 1990).

181. Almquist, note 34.

182. We believe that this may have been the context which led to the USS Yellowstone incident, in which every African American woman on board was investigated for alleged lesbian activities. See note 34 and accompanying text.

183. See text accompanying note 164.

184. Gilberd, 10.

185. De Pauw, 43.

186. See note 127 and accompanying text.

187. "The Marines are looking for a few good men" and "Kiss your momma goodbye" (Army National Guard) are a few examples of such recruiting slogans.

188. The percentage of women in the armed forces has increased only slightly, to approximately 13%, since these formal barriers were dropped. Many experts on military women are concerned that recruiters may unofficially be turning women away or discouraging them from entering certain job categories.

189. See, e.g., Stephanie Riger and Pat Galligan, "Women in Management: An Exploration of Competing Paradigms," *American Psychologist 35* (1980): 902, 905. (Tokens are likely to be scrutinized more closely, perceived as disproportionately prominent, evaluated more extremely, "pressured to side with the majority against their kind," and expected to conform to stereotypes.)

190. See Kenneth Karst, "The Pursuit of Manhood and the Desegregation of the Armed Forces," 38 *U.C.L.A. L. Rev.* (1991): 499, 541; Riger and Galligan, note 189.

191. Indeed, the unfortunate tendency of senior leaders in the Navy to treat women as sex objects, even after Tailhook, may be directly related to the continued incidents of sexual harassment in this service, despite what many

consider to be the most concerted official effort of any service to stop it. A recent example is Admiral Richard Macke's highly publicized statement, in a case involving the rape of an Okinawa school girl by U.S. servicemen, that for the price of a car the men rented to carry out the attack, the sailor and marines could have hired a prostitute to satisfy themselves.

192. This recommendation was originally made in 1989 by DACOWITS. However, to our knowledge, this recommendation has not been renewed or followed after the change in policy on service by gay men, lesbians, and bisexuals. Nor has it been included in training programs on this policy. The authors are not able to critique existing training programs designed to stem sexual harassment in this article. However, these programs are steps in the right direction and we encourage continued efforts to improve them.

193. Osburn and Benecke, 21-23.

194. "A commander may initiate a fact-finding inquiry only when he or she has received credible information that there is a basis for discharge." DoDD 1332.30, enclosure 8-1. "Credible information exists when the information, considering its source and surrounding circumstances, supports a reasonable belief that a Service member has engaged in homosexual conduct. It requires a determination based on articulable facts, not just a belief or suspicion." Id. (The same standards govern enlisted members. DoDD 1332.14, enclosure 4-1.)

195. "Inquiries shall be limited to the factual circumstances directly relevant to the specific allegations." DoDD 1332.30, enclosure 8-1; DoDD 1332.14 at Enclosure 4-1. "At any given point of the inquiry, the commander or appointed inquiry official must be able clearly and specifically to explain which grounds for separation he or she is attempting to verify and how the information being collected relates to these specific separation grounds." DoDD 1332.30, enclosure 8-3; DoDD 1332.14, enclosure 4-3.

196. Department of Defense Directive 1304.26, "Qualification Standards for Enlistment, Appointment, and Induction," Applicant Briefing Item on Separation Policy, December 21, 1993.

197. See Osburn and Benecke, 23. Servicemembers report a sharp increase in antigay harassment under Don't Ask, Don't Tell, Don't Pursue with epithets about gays becoming a daily, and even hourly, occurrence in many units. In case after case, supervisors have witnessed harassment and have taken no steps to correct it. In an alarming number of cases, leaders in the chain-of-command have actually participated in harassment against suspected gays. Id.

198. Ibid., 24.

199. Ibid. Servicemembers report that, if they do not participate in such activities, they are quickly labeled as gay and harassed. Id.

200. Challenges have been based on equal protection and First Amendment arguments. First Amendment cases contest the discharge of those who merely state that they are gay or lesbian, absent an admission or proof of commission of homosexual acts. Equal protection arguments have focused on the constitutionality of discriminating against homosexuals as a class and on the unequal application of sodomy articles to single out and penalize homosexuals

engaging in consensual sodomy while virtually ignoring consensual heterosexual sodomy. See, e.g., Brief Amicus Curiae of the ACLU for Barbara Baum, *United States v. Barbara Baum* (U.S. Navy-Marine Corps Court of Military Review 1990) (NMCMR 89-0-107). Other relevant decisions include *Ben-Shalom v. Marsh*, 881 F.2d 454 (7th Cir. 1989), cert. denied, 58 U.S.L.W. 3545 (U.S., February 26, 1990) (No. 89-876) (neither First Amendment nor equal protection rights of Army Reserve soldier were violated by Army regulation making status of homosexuality a disqualification for service regardless of conduct); *Watkins v. United States Army*, 875 F.2d 699 (9th Cir. 1989) (no need to reach constitutional issues since Army estopped from barring reenlistment of admitted homosexual solely on the basis of his homosexuality); *Woodward v. United States*, 871 F.2d 1968 (Fed. Cir. 1989), cert. denied, 58 U.S.L.W. 3545 (U.S. February 26, 1990) (No. 89-344) (upheld discharge of Navy Reserve officer for admitted homosexual tendencies on grounds that homosexuality is not protected by the constitutional right to privacy and Navy's antihomosexual policy is rationally related to a permissible end). Subsequently, attorneys for Joseph Steffan included a due process challenge to the policies. See *Steffan v. Perry*, 41 F.3d 677 (D.C. Cir. 1994), (D.D.C. November 15, 1989). For a review of challenges to the policy through 1986 see Rivera, note 28. See generally Jose Gomez, "The Public Expression of Lesbian/Gay Personhood as Protected Speech," *Journal of Law and Inequality* 121 (1983); Notes, "The Constitutional Status of Sexual Orientation: Homosexuality as a Suspect Classification," *Harvard Law Review 98* (1985): 1285; Developments, "Sexual Orientation and the Law," *Harvard Law Review 102* (1989): 1508, 1554-75. Thus far, no one has brought challenges based on gender discrimination in the application and effect of the policy, although the issue has been addressed in an amicus brief filed with the DC Circuit Court of Appeals by the NOW Legal Defense and Education Fund in the *Steffan* case.

201. *Meinhold v. Department of Defense*, 34 F.3d 1469 (9th Cir. 1994); *Cammermeyer v. Aspin*, 850 F.Supp. 910 (W.D. Wash 1994)(currently on appeal before the 9th Circuit); *Able v. United States*, 880 F.Supp. 968 (E.D.N.Y. 1995)(first case filed challenging the current policy; the six plaintiffs prevailed at the district court and the government is appealing to the Second Circuit).

202. See, e.g., *Elzie v. Aspin*, 897 F.Supp. 1 (D.D.C. 1995); *Able v. United States*, note 15. Other servicemembers who have successfully sought injunctions include Naval officers Lieutenant (j.g.) Richard Dirk Selland, Lieutenant Tracy Thorne, Lieutenant Richard Watson, and Air Force Captain Richard Richenberg.

203. *Able v. United States*, note 201; *Thomasson v. Perry*, 895 F.Supp. 820 (E.D.Va. 1995)(now on appeal to the 4th Circuit).

204. See Kirstin S. Dodge, "Countenancing Corruption: A Civic Republican Case Against Judicial Deference to the Military," *Yale Journal of Law and Feminism* 5 (1992): 1, 3-13.

205. See, e.g., *Ben-Shalom*, 881 F.2d at 461, 465; *Woodward*, 871 F.2d at 1077. The finding of constitutionality is therefore, in the opinion of the authors, the result of a double error on the part of the courts. First, we do not believe that rational basis is the level of scrutiny which should be applied to government discrimination against lesbians and gay men. Second, however, even if rational basis scrutiny is applied, the policy should fail, given the lack of a rational relationship between the government's stated rationale and the policy. See note 208.

206. *Ben-Shalom*, 881 F.2d at 463, citing *McGinnis v. Royster*, 410 U.S. 263 (1973).

207. 10 U.S.C. 654 (1994), policy concerning homosexuality in the armed forces.

208. See, e.g., C. Dixon Osburn, "A Policy in Desperate Search of a Rationale: The Military's Policy on Lesbians, Gays, and Bisexuals," *UMKC Law Review* 64 (1995): 1. These arguments are not unknown to the military; in fact, they are bolstered by the military's own research. See, e.g., Theodore R. Sarbin & Kenneth E. Karols, "Nonconforming Sexual Orientations and Military Suitability," Defense Personnel Security Research and Education Center (PERSEREC), PERS TR-89-002, December 1988 (hereinafter First PERSEREC Report); "Report of the Board Appointed to Prepare and Submit Recommendations to the Navy for the Revision of Policies, Procedures, and Directives Dealing With Homosexuals" (hereinafter "The Crittenden Report") (1957); McDaniel, "Preservice Adjustment of Homosexual and Heterosexual Military Accessions: Implications for Security Clearance Suitability" (1989) (hereinafter "Second PERSEREC Report"); First GAO Report, note 10; RAND National Defense Research Institute, *Sexual Orientation and U.S. Military Personnel Policy: Options and Assessment* (1993) (hereinafter "RAND Report"). See also *Watkins*, 875 F.2d at 702-04. Watkins was "the best company clerk" his commander had ever known, and his various units knew he was gay throughout his career, but it "caused no problems and generated no complaints." *Id.*, 702. One of his commanders called Watkins "one of our most respected and trusted soldiers, both by his superiors and his subordinates." *Id.* See note 214 and accompanying text.

209. *Ben-Shalom*, 881 F.2d at 461.

210. Eric Schmitt, "'Be All You Can Be': Fightin' Words?" *New York Times* (November 12, 1995): 6.

211. See Rivera, 323. As of 1983, the General Accounting Office estimated that $23 million was required each year during the period of 1974 to 1983 to recruit, train, and then discharge servicemembers for homosexuality. This figure does not include the cost of investigations, attorneys' fees, or discharge boards, costs which the Department of Defense did not make available to the Government Accounting Office. First GAO Report, 25.

212. See note 207 and accompanying text.

213. See S. Rep. No. 112, 103d Cong., 1st Sess., at 307, 308 (1993)(testimony of Col. Darryl Henderson, retired Research Fellow at the

National War College, and Dr. David H. Marlowe of the Walter Reed Army Institute of Research).

214. "[S]tigmatized individuals understand [that] [i]n order to normalize their relations with nonstigmatized others, they [must] go to great lengths to establish competence and loyalty 'above and beyond'" (arguing that open gay and lesbian servicemembers do not undermine unit cohesion). RAND Report, 321; see also Trial Testimony of Dr. Pepper Schwartz, March 14, 1995, Transcript, p. 146, *Able v. United States* (E.D.N.Y. Docket No. 94 CV 147).

215. See, e.g., Eric Schmitt, "The New Rules on Gay Soldiers: A Year Later, No Clear Result," *New York Times* (March 13, 1995): A1 (superiors and subordinates praise Navy Lieutenant Paul Thomasson after he disclosed his sexual orientation); Jason Gertzen, "Colonel Suggests Honorable Discharge for Gay Captain," *Omaha World-Herald* (June 22, 1994): 14 (Air Force Captain Richard Richenberg's fellow officers, who know he is gay, describe him as a "model officer"); "Gay Marine Sergeant Gets Welcome on Return to Duty," *The Orlando Sentinel* (October 22, 1993): A10 (on Sergeant Justin Elzie's first day back on duty, colleagues welcomed him with remarks such as "Great to have you back and let's get the job done").

216. See First PERSEREC Report, 25.

217. "Military Witch Hunts," *Off Our Backs* (October 1989): 14.

218. See discussion of the Wain case in the "Criminal and Administrative Sanctions" section earlier in this chapter.

219. See, e.g., McKnight, note 91; *ACLU NEWS*, note 36. The military also sought to suppress the First PERSEREC Report, which found no reason to exclude open gay men, lesbians, and bisexuals. See First PERSEREC Report, note 208. See also Michael K. Frisby, "Military Seeks Third Study of Policy on Gays," *Boston Globe* (November 2, 1989): 1.

PART II

Policy Analysis

CHAPTER 4

Promise Unfulfilled:
Clinton's Failure to Overturn the Military Ban on Lesbians and Gays

Craig A. Rimmerman

The next afternoon as Jerry Rosanbalm lay in bed with Karel Rohan, he heard noises—someone was trying to force his way into the apartment. Naked and armed with a tennis racket, Jerry leapt into the hallway to investigate, when the door burst open and a cadre of military police crashed in. With guns drawn and cameras ready, military police shouted their disappointment at not having caught the two in bed. Karel made a vain attempt to hide under the covers as agents pressed into the bedroom and then tried to force Rosanbalm onto the bed for the photographer. After Rosanbalm fought off the agents with his tennis racket, somebody yelled, "Screw it—just arrest him." The agents dragged both men naked out of the bedroom and pronounced Captain Gerald Lynn Rosanbalm under arrest for espionage against the United States.[1]

The situation above, described by Randy Shilts in his book *Conduct Unbecoming*, exemplifies the way that the military has treated lesbians and gays over the past fifty years in this country. Since 1943, when the military issued final regulations banning lesbians and gays from all of its branches, the regulations have remained by and large unchanged. As Shilts points out, "the history of homosexuality in the United States armed forces has been a struggle between two intransigent facts—the persistent presence of gays within the military and the equally persistent hostility toward them."[2]

This chapter examines the circumstances surrounding candidate Bill Clinton's promise to overturn the ban on lesbians and gays in the military, outlines the barriers that he encountered as he attempted to follow through on this promise, and explains why he has broken his campaign promise as President of the United States. In addressing these issues, I will also explore the following questions: How did the debate over gays in the military get resolved at the federal government level? Why was it resolved in a particular way? What are the implications of this analysis for the future of lesbians and gays in the military? For the lesbian and gay movement? For the Clinton presidency and how Bill Clinton deals with intractable problems that appear to have no easy solutions? Why did Clinton's plan to overturn the ban produce such a firestorm of opposition? Why was there such emotional responses on behalf of those opposed to lifting the ban? In answering these questions, I will address the clash of American political institutions in the policy process by briefly discussing the response of the President, Congress, and the court system. Much of my analysis is rooted in personal interviews that I conducted with members of the lesbian and gay community, congressional staff members, and Clinton administration officials. In addition, my analysis undoubtedly reflects the observations that I gleaned as a 1992-93 American Political Science Association Congressional Fellow working in the Washington, DC offices of Senator Tom Daschle (D-SD) and Representative Barbara Kennelly (D-CT).

The central argument is that President Clinton failed to perform his important leadership role in educating the public regarding why he believed that the military ban should be overturned. I explore several reasons for his failure to do so. Clinton realized that he did not have the required votes in Congress to sustain his promise of issuing an executive order to overturn the ban. In addition, compromise comes naturally and easily to Bill Clinton, as his approach to governance is rooted in building consensus. This is what he attempted to do with his "Don't Ask, Don't Tell, Don't Pursue" compromise proposal. A third explanation is that Clinton fashions himself as a new kind of Democrat, one who believes that it is important for the Democratic party to move in a more moderate direction. It made sense, then, for Clinton and his advisors to distance themselves from so-called liberal special interest groups such as lesbian and gay organizations. Finally, Clinton did not want to squander valuable political capital on overturning the ban early in his first term, capital that he would need in his health care and budget fights with Congress.

The blame for the way that the military issue was resolved cannot reside solely with the Clinton administration, however, as the lesbian and gay movement made a number of mistakes as well. After twelve years of hostile Republican rule, the movement was clearly not used to having a "friend" in the White House. It assumed that access to power was tantamount to having direct influence over public policy. The way that the military ban issue was resolved suggests that this is not the case. In addition, there was widespread disagreement in the lesbian and gay community regarding whether the military ban should even be a central priority, given the need for a more sustained federal response to AIDS and the need for federal gay and lesbian civil rights legislation. Finally, the movement did not organize and mobilize at the grassroots level in ways that were necessary to put pressure on elected officials to support overturning the ban. This chapter concludes by discussing the implications of the preceding analysis for the lesbian and gay movement, and by calling for better grassroots organizational support and the need for broad-based education at all levels of society on lesbian and gay concerns.

CANDIDATE CLINTON'S PROMISE AND THE OBSTACLES HE FACED AS PRESIDENT IN OVERTURNING THE BAN

Bill Clinton entered the gays in the military debate at an October 28, 1991 presidential forum at Harvard University. A student asked him whether he would issue an executive order to rescind the ban on lesbians and gays in the military. Clinton responded "Yes," and explained further: "I think people who are gay should be expected to work, and should be given the opportunity to serve the country."[3] He continued with that pledge throughout the 1992 presidential campaign.

As president, Clinton learned quickly that the opposition to overturning the ban was rooted in a number of deep seated concerns, concerns that reflect the longstanding hostility towards lesbians and gays in the larger society. Bruce Bawer points out that an individual might be threatened by homosexuality due to several factors. First is the factor of utter incomprehension: he/she cannot understand how other human beings could have such feelings and could experience sexual attraction to a member of the same sex. The idea is so foreign as to be threatening, frightening, and repulsive. A second explanation is the issue of identification. The individual has experienced homosexual attraction him/herself, and fears that he/she may be gay. It is this possibility that is frightening, threatening, and repulsive. Male sexual insecurity also helps to explain some men's hostility toward extending gay rights: those who harbor these concerns fear being the object of desire. Men are used to being in control in their relationships with women and are not used to being the "object of affection" of other men. This fear is reflected in a Michigan airman's fear of what would happen if the ban on lesbians and gays in the military was lifted: "I couldn't sleep at night. I'd be worried that some homosexual is going to sneak over and make a pass at me."[4]

These concerns underlie some of the more specific arguments offered by those opposed to overturning the ban. It is interesting to note that some of these same arguments were posited by those opposed to Harry Truman's decision to integrate the military racially by executive order in 1948. National security factors were often cited as a central reason to oppose lesbians and gays in the military. This grew out of the hysteria of the McCarthy era.

In addition, those opposed to Clinton's campaign promise contend that the presence of lesbians and gays in the armed forces would undermine the "good order, discipline, and morale of the fighting forces."[5] Norman Schwarzkopf reinforced this point of view in a 1982 sworn deposition where he "characterized homosexuality as being 'incompatible with military service' because it impaired good order, discipline, and morale." The general pointed out that his twenty-six year military career led him to conclude that "homosexuals are unsuited for military service."[6]

The Navy defined a rationale for its gay policies by making several arguments. An individual's daily performance of military duties could be hindered by emotional or sexual relationships with other individuals, would interfere with proper hierarchical and command relationships that characterize the military. There was also the concern that homosexual individuals might force their sexual desires on others, resulting in sexual assaults. In the early 1980s the Pentagon pointed out that gays must be banned in order to "facilitate assignment and worldwide deployment of servicemembers who frequently must live and work under close conditions affording minimal privacy."[7] Furthermore, an internal navy memorandum revealed that "an officer or senior enlisted person who exhibits homosexual tendencies will be unable to maintain the necessary respect and trust from the great majority of naval personnel who detest/abhor homosexuality. This lack of respect and trust would most certainly degrade the officer's ability to successfully perform his duties of supervision and command."[8]

The conservative legal scholar Bruce Fein raised the important connection between masculinity and the criteria for being a good soldier as a justification for opposing attempts to integrate lesbians and gays:

> The lifeblood of a soldier is masculinity, bravery, and gallantry. The battlefield soldier is inspired to risk all by fighting with comrades whose attributes conform to his view of manhood . . . And it is inarguable that the majority of a fighting force would be psychologically and emotionally deflated by the close presence of homosexuals who evoke effeminate or repugnant but not manly visions.[9]

Fein's analysis is an important one because it underscores the importance of how visions of masculinity underlie the debate over lesbians and gays in the military.

All of the above arguments rely on bigoted and negative stereotypes of lesbians and gays. As Richard Mohr points out, "none of them is based on the ability of gay soldiers to fulfill the duties of their stations."[10] But it is these arguments that served to define the broader context of the debate, arguments that both Bill Clinton and proponents of overturning the ban had difficulty engaging in ways that would shift the grounds of the discussion. Had opponents of the ban done a better job in making their case through the media, they would have likely persuaded the broader public and people in positions of power to accept the arguments discussed in the next section.

THE CASE FOR LIFTING THE BAN

Those opposed to the ban offered several arguments. Many pointed out that the ban itself is rooted in discrimination and prejudice against lesbians and gays and we should not countenance any discrimination against individuals or groups in our society. In addition, gays, lesbians, and bisexuals have already fought and died on behalf of this country in wars. As a result, they should be afforded the kind of respect and support that their outstanding service to their country deserves. What this means in practice is that they should be treated with dignity and decency in their daily lives. By its very nature, the ban is rooted in the most ugly assumptions about the connections between sexuality and military performance—assumptions that are not confirmed by any evidence. Indeed, one study provides evidence for overturning the ban. In spring 1992, the Pentagon commissioned a RAND Corporation study of the military ban. The RAND study concluded that "the ban could be dropped without damaging the 'order, discipline, and individual behavior necessary to maintain cohesion, and performance.'" The report also stated that "many of the problems that opponents of lifting the ban anticipate are exaggerated through education and discipline."[11] Unfortunately, the Clinton administration opted to delay the timing of the release of the report in a way that diminished its impact. John Gallagher reports that the report was ready for release long before August 1993, when it was finally made public. Indeed, it was released to the press and public "when the President and everyone was on vacation, so that no one was around to notice it."[12] The release was prompted by a joint congressional letter signed by those in the House and Senate committed to overturning the ban, urging the Clinton administration to make the report's findings public.

Opponents of the ban point out also that many other democracies allow lesbians and gays to serve with dignity in their militaries. All of the NATO countries, except Britain, allow lesbians/gays into their armed forces. Canada's 1992 decision to revoke its military ban caused little or no controversy, and their experience could have been an excellent lesson for the United States.[13] Finally, and perhaps most disturbingly, the ban reinforces the horrors of the closet for lesbians and gays in the military. The closet is then sanctioned by the institutional forces of the United States government in ways that prevent human beings to live open and fully developed lives. In his recent book, Richard Mohr offers an analysis of the horrors of the closet:

> The chief problem of the social institution of the closet is not that it promotes hypocrisy, requires lies, sets snares, blames the victim when snared, and causes unhappiness—though it does have all these results. No, the chief problem with the closet is that it treats gays as less than human, less than animal, less even than vegetable—it treats gays as reeking scum, the breath of death.[14]

The negative consequences of the hostility toward lesbians and gays in the military have taken a number of other forms. There have been economic costs associated with the ban. As Randy Shilts points out, "the cost of investigations and the dollars spent replacing gay and lesbian personnel easily amount to hundreds of millions of dollars."[15] A June 1992 congressional study indicated that "the ban on homosexuals in the armed forces costs the Pentagon at least $27 million a year."[16]

The incalculable human costs have taken a number of forms, as lives have been ruined and careers destroyed. Despairing men and women occasionally commit suicide in the face of the pressure associated with a purge, and the accompanying rumors that often precede one. This should come as no surprise because military policies have created an atmosphere where discrimination, harassment, and violence against lesbians and gays is tolerated and often encouraged. Shilts' analysis of the consequences of the ban provides particularly chilling accounts of how lesbians face significant discrimination and harassment in their daily military lives. For lesbians, "the issues are far more complex than simple homophobia, because they also involve significant features of sex-based discrimination."[17]

BILL CLINTON'S PROMISE TO OVERTURN THE BAN

The first major news story in the period between President-elect Clinton's election and inauguration was his announcement that he planned to follow through on his campaign promise and rescind the ban on lesbians and gays in the military through executive order. At that moment, Clinton had no sense that this promise would be an enduring controversy for the first six months of his presidency. After Clinton's inauguration, the controversy reached its zenith as the issue dominated radio call-in programs and newspaper headlines for a week.[18] In addition, congressional offices were flooded with telephone calls, telegrams, and postcards from irate citizens opposed to Clinton's suggestion that the ban be overturned. The mobilization of the citizenry against rescinding the ban appeared to be carefully orchestrated by the religious right. The Right received a boost when the Joint Chiefs of Staff came out strongly against Clinton's promise and Sam Nunn, chairman of the Senate Armed Services Committee, expressed public concern. Nunn held hearings on the issue in spring 1993, hearings that those in favor of overturning the ban later characterized as being biased in favor of the military. The hearings themselves made for several dramatic moments, most notably Colonel Fred Peck's outing of his own son Scott. Peck, the U.S. Army spokesman in Somalia, testified that he supported the ban because of antigay prejudice in the ranks. He concluded that if his son were in the military hierarchy, "I would be very fearful his life would be in jeopardy from his own troops." Scott Peck later responded to his father by stating: "I have a little more faith in members of the military."[19]

The media played a significant role in defining the context and setting the agenda for the debate. For example, it captured Colonel Peck's dramatic congressional testimony live and televised it into millions of homes. In addition, Sam Nunn and several of his pro-ban colleagues were given a tour of two navy ships so that they could get a more fully developed understanding of the close living quarters experienced by military personnel. He pointed out for the accompanying C-SPAN camera "the closeness of the bunks and shower stalls and asked groups of sailors how they felt about the idea of 'open homosexuals' in the armed forces."[20] The press covered this tour extensively and reinforced the most ugly stereotypes regarding lesbians and gays. The role of the press, Sam Nunn's ability to dominate the debate with his hearings, and the mobilization of the radical right at the grassroots level had the consequence of putting the President and opponents of the ban on the defensive. It was a posture from which opponents of the ban never really recovered.

What was Bill Clinton's role in this entire debate? On May 27, 1993 a Virginia minister asked President Clinton about the issue of gays in the military during a live broadcast of "CBS This Morning." Clinton said in response:

Most Americans believe that the gay lifestyle should not be promoted by the military or anybody else in this country . . . We are trying to work this out so that our country does not appear to be endorsing a gay lifestyle . . . I think most Americans will agree when it works out that people are treated properly if they behave properly without the government appearing to endorse a lifestyle.[21]

Clinton used the worst form of language—"lifestyle," "endorse," "approve," "promote"—from the antigay lexicon in his answer. Members of the lesbian and gay community were quick to respond. David Mixner, Clinton's long-time friend and a leading openly gay member of the Democratic party, said that he was physically sickened by Clinton's response. Mixner and others supporting overturning the ban had good reason to be disturbed. Bill Clinton had begun to equivocate in public on his promise to overturn the ban through executive order. It is clear in retrospect that Clinton was trying to distance himself from lesbian and gay groups for political reasons. What better way to do this but to embrace some of the language of the radical right groups who were so feverishly working to uphold the ban?

But Clinton was also signalling to lesbian and gay groups and their supporters that he would likely compromise on his original promise. Sure enough, he did in fact compromise with his July 1993 Don't Ask, Don't Tell, Don't Pursue proposal. This proposal contained the following details:

1) The policy bars military recruiters from asking if prospective enlistees are gay or lesbian.
2) Homosexual conduct is forbidden both on-base and off-base.
3) What constitutes homosexual conduct?
    a) same-sex intercourse
    b) public acknowledgement of homosexuality
    c) attempting a same-sex marriage
    d) same-sex hand-holding or kissing
4) What constitutes permissible activity?
    a) telling a spouse, attorney, or member of the clergy about your homosexuality
    b) associating with openly gay and lesbian people
    c) going to a gay or lesbian bar
    d) marching in a gay pride march in civilian clothes
5) Military personnel found to have engaged in homosexual conduct could be discharged.
6) Military officials could not launch probes merely to discover if an enlistee is gay or lesbian, but if they suspect, based on "articulable facts," that a person has engaged in prohibited activity, they may investigate to find out if their suspicion is correct.
7) Capricious outing of suspected gays and lesbians by fellow personnel without evidence is forbidden, and any attempt to blackmail a suspected

gay or lesbian member of the armed forces would be punishable by a dishonorable discharge, a $2,000 fine, and a one-year jail term.[22]

Sam Nunn modified Clinton's proposal to toughen it in ways that would ultimately be more punitive toward lesbians and gays in the military. Nunn's efforts were ultimately codified into law by Congress, thus making it much more difficult for opponents of the ban to offer serious structural reforms in the future. (Because the previous ban was enforced through an executive order, which could at least be changed through presidential missive, the codification meant that any future changes to Nunn's congressional policy would require congressional consent.) Nunn's congressional language enabled the specifics of the Clinton plan to take effect while codifying into law a broad statement of policy, one that rejects the idea of accepting lesbians and gays into the military. In addition, the congressional version states that lesbians and gays have no constitutional rights for serving in the armed forces. The irony, of course, is that the last element of the Nunn plan is "exactly what President Clinton had hoped to challenge in his original determination to overturn the ban through executive order."[23]

Why did Bill Clinton support a compromise on this issue? How could he do so, given the very clear promise that he articulated both as a presidential candidate and as a newly elected President of the United States? Individuals both inside and outside the administration identified a number of explanations. Clinton's approach to governance is one rooted in building consensus. This was true when he was Governor of Arkansas, and the first term of his presidency suggests that he is someone who is committed to governing by consensus rather than by adherence to ideology or principle.

In addition, there is little doubt that Clinton was motivated by political considerations as well. His chief advisors—David Gergen, Bruce Lindsey, George Stephanopoulos, Rahm Emanuel, and Thomas ("Mack") McLarty—clearly wanted him to put this divisive "no-win" issue behind the new administration. Clinton and his advisors wanted to make sure that he embraced the center of the political spectrum as a "new kind of Democrat." As a result, for purely political reasons, it made sense that he would want to distance himself from an unpopular special interest—lesbians and gays. For Bill Clinton did not want to associate himself with Democrats such as Walter Mondale and Michael Dukakis, both of whom had reputations as individuals who could be pushed around by liberal special interests.

It is clear, as well, that Clinton realized that without a major fight, he did not have the votes in Congress to uphold his original desire to rescind the ban. This view was reinforced by Representative Barney Frank, who publicly proposed a compromise plan, much to the dismay of many lesbian and gay activists. Frank's explanation for his compromise proposal was that it was better to get something passed for lesbians and gays in the military, rather than nothing at all. According to several interviewees, Clinton shared this spirit of compromise and this rationale underlied his approach to resolving the broader issue.

By backing away from his original promise, Clinton could also appease the Joint Chiefs of Staff. The Joint Chiefs were firmly opposed to rescinding the ban. As Commander in Chief of the armed forces, President Clinton has the authority and power to order the Joint Chiefs to obey his directives. But in this case, Clinton chose not to do so, and ultimately was persuaded that the Joint Chiefs' perspective deserved more attention in the final policy resolution of the issue than the concerns of lesbian and gay activists. The 1992 presidential campaign devoted considerable attention to Clinton's activities during the Viet Nam War. George Bush and the Republicans hammered away at Clinton's opposition to the war and his own lack of foreign policy experience. For Clinton, backing off his support for overturning the ban meant that he could win some points with the military, the group that was seemingly most threatened by his original campaign promise.

Finally, Clinton did not wish to squander valuable political capital during his honeymoon period over such an emotionally charged debate. From Clinton's vantage point, his budget plan, the ratification of NAFTA, and health care were far more important policy initiatives than rescinding the ban. As a result, he did not even lobby members of Congress to overturn the ban, because he knew that he would need their support for the policy concerns he deemed to be of higher priority.

How did Clinton defend his own compromise plan? The President called the plan an "honest compromise," and acknowledged that the plan's specifics were not necessarily identical to his own goals. Almost all interviewees informed me that in the face of intense congressional and military opposition to lifting the ban, Clinton believed that the policy was the closest he could come to fulfilling his campaign promise. As one administration official pointed out: "The President believes that it is a solid advance forward in terms of extending rights to gays and lesbians in the military."

But lesbian and gay activists and their supporters were hardly convinced. Tom Stoddard, the Coordinator of the Campaign for Military Service said, "The President could have lifted up the conscience of the country. Instead, he acceded without a fight to the stereotypes of prejudices he himself had disparaged." Torrie Osborn, Executive Director of the National Gay and Lesbian Task Force, argued that the plan is "simply a repackaging of discrimination." And Tim McFeeley, Head of the Human Rights Campaign Fund, called the Clinton proposal a "shattering disappointment."[24] Bruce Bawer criticized the Nunn proposal and Clinton's support for that proposal in the following way: "This compromise . . . would essentially write into law the institution of the closet: while heterosexuals would continue to enjoy their right to lead private lives and to discuss those lives freely, gays would be allowed to remain in the armed forces only so long as they didn't mention their homosexuality to anyone or have relationships on or off base."[25] But perhaps a *New Republic* editorial best captured the fury of those who expected the President to translate his campaign promise into concrete public policy:

And the most demeaning assumption about the new provisions is that they single out the deepest moment of emotional intimacy—the private sexual act—as that which is most repugnant. Its assumption about the dignity and humanity of gay people, in and out of the military, in public and in private, is sickening.[26]

The anger seen in the comments of gay groups reflected a general frustration with the Clinton administration's ineptness in dealing with the politics of the issue.

To supporters of overturning the ban, the Clinton administration made a number of serious strategic mistakes. Some believe that the administration should have introduced the executive order as he had promised, and then allow Congress to do what it wished, even if that meant passing legislation that challenged this executive order. By embracing this strategy, the President would have been seen as having followed through with a policy promise rooted in principle.

In addition, the administration clearly underestimated the opposition of Congress, most notably Sam Nunn, the religious right, the Joint Chiefs of Staff, and the military. The Clinton administration had no idea that Nunn would attempt to embarrass a new president of his own political party, one who generally supported New Democratic principles.

The administration also did a poor job in establishing an honest and open line of communication with lesbian and gay groups. Indeed, several individuals who I interviewed from a variety of lesbian and gay organizations charged that they were misled about Clinton's intentions regarding rescinding the ban from the outset. Apparently during the transition and the first couple weeks of the Clinton presidency,lesbian and gay groups were told by presidential advisors such as Bruce Lindsey not to lift a finger in terms of organizing grassroots support, because the President would do everything necessary to overturn the ban. In an April 1993 White House meeting, just before the March on Washington, President Clinton told lesbian and gay activists in attendance that he would persuade Colin Powell and the Joint Chiefs of Staff to support his plan to overturn the ban.

Yet another problem was that in the first several months of the Clinton presidency, no one at the White House was really in charge of the legislative strategy for overturning the ban. This was the case until David Gergen joined the Clinton White House. At that point, George Stephanopoulos was given the responsibility for coordinating the Clinton strategy, such as it was.

Indeed, the administration did little lobbying on Capitol Hill. Many of the individuals that I interviewed both inside and outside the Clinton White House pointed out that the administration simply regarded other issues with greater importance, and as a result, refused to expend considerable political capital in dealing with Congress over lesbians and gays in the military. Several also pointed out, however, that the ban might well have received considerable congressional support had the President marshalled the powers of his office to enlist that support.

In retrospect, it is obvious now that Clinton's promise was a poor issue with which to begin his presidency. Some argued that Clinton would have been better off in raising the issue after his first year in office, when he had established the credibility of his presidency and had more legislative accomplishments. Presumably, this would have given him more clout in dealing with Congress.

Finally, it is clear that President Clinton did not perform his important leadership role in educating the public about why he believed it was necessary to overturn the ban. Countless presidential scholars have pointed to the importance of the President's potential role as an educator.[27] In the words of Leon Wieseltier, "It is not leadership to tell people what they want to hear. It is leadership to tell people what they do not want to hear, and to give them a reason to listen."[28]

But it was not only the Clinton presidency that made strategic errors in the debate over lesbians and gays in the military. As the next section points out, the gay and lesbian movement made a number of tactical mistakes, mistakes that undermined their attempt to garner greater public support for overturning the ban.

THE RESPONSE OF THE LESBIAN AND GAY MOVEMENT

At the outset, the mainstream lesbian and gay movement trusted Bill Clinton too much. Delirious with excitement because a supposed friend had been elected to the White House, the movement largely ignored Clinton's past mediocre record on lesbian and gay issues in Arkansas. There were some notable exceptions. Michael Petrelis, a member of the Washington, D.C. chapters of ACT-UP and Queer Nation, distributed "Impeach Clinton" buttons just prior to the November 1992 presidential election. Unlike many of his counterparts in the mainstream lesbian and gay movement, Petrelis recognized that supposedly having Clinton on his side was simply not enough. From the outset, Petrelis and other more radical members of the movement distrusted Clinton's motives, his sincerity, and his seriousness of purpose in rescinding the ban and addressing AIDS in a meaningful way.

Some members of the lesbian and gay community pointed to the movement's inability to mobilize at the grassroots level. The Campaign for Military Service was largely a Washington, D.C. organizing effort, and failed to generate the kind of grassroots support needed in states where there were members of Congress who were wavering in their votes on whether to rescind the ban.

In addition, gay rights advocates were never able to marshall the volume of calls and letters from constituents to win over legislators, who were being deluged with calls and mail organized largely by the evangelical right, who supported the ban. Representative Barney Frank received tremendous criticism from the lesbian and gay community for pointing out the problems associated with the gay and lesbian organizing efforts. Frank said:

We did a very bad job of mobilizing—getting people to write to members of the House and Senate. We spent a lot of our time and energy on things that are irrelevant to a short-term fight in Congress. People assumed that the March on Washington or demonstrations were a poor thing. Those have no effect on members of Congress.[29]

As the above quotation reveals, Frank was particularly critical of the March on Washington's organizers to generate a massive congressional lobbying effort on behalf of rescinding the ban.

There were further complications for those pressing Clinton to follow through on his campaign promise. Some lesbians and gays simply could not get excited about the issue. This lack of grassroots excitement was due to several factors. Many people already thought that the fight had been won by having Bill Clinton in the White House, especially since he promised to rescind the ban. The movement had no real experience in dealing with a President who seemingly supported lesbian and gay concerns. In addition, the issue did not seem nearly as important for a community that had been and continues to be ravaged by AIDS. Finally, many lesbians and gays cut their political teeth in the antiwar movement of the 1960s and did not want to legitimate participation in the military.

With the codification into law of the Don't Ask, Don't Tell compromise, lesbian and gay groups and their supporters have turned to the courts. Their legal challenge will likely rest on one or more of several principles. The first is the right to privacy, where an individual has a right to engage in any private consensual sexual conduct, as articulated in the Supreme Court's earlier decisions allowing contraception, miscegenation, and abortion. A second approach emphasizes the notion that the military's policies against lesbians and gays violates the Fourteenth Amendment's equal protection clause. Finally, the charge is made that even if the federal government could establish homosexual conduct, it would then have to prove why such conduct made an officer unsuitable for the armed forces.

What they have found in the short term is that the courts have been somewhat supportive of lesbian and gay efforts despite the Clinton administration's attempts to pursue a more regressive policy. Interestingly, the Clinton administration has been defending the military's old lesbian and gay policy in court to "set precedents that would make challenges to the new policy more difficult."[30] On June 1, 1994 a Seattle federal judge ordered the military to reinstate Colonel Margarethe Cammermeyer, who was "forced out of the Washington State National Guard after acknowledging that she is a lesbian."[31] Judge Thomas Zilly of Federal District Court "ordered Cammermeyer back to the job she held in 1992, ruling that the military's policy on homosexuals at that time was based solely on prejudice and was a clear violation of the Constitution's equal-protection clause."[32] The judge ruled that "there is no rational basis for the Government's underlying contention that homosexual orientation equals 'desire or propensity to engage' in homosexual conduct."[33]

The Clinton and congressional compromise has also been successfully challenged in the courts. On March 30, 1995 Judge Eugene H. Nickerson of Federal District Court in Brooklyn ruled in *Able v. the United States* that the Don't Ask, Don't Tell, Don't Pursue compromise violated the First and Fifth amendments and also catered to the prejudices and fears of heterosexual troops. To Nickerson, the fact that the new policy attempts to distinguish between sexual orientation and the possibility of acting on such an orientation is "nothing less than Orwellian." Nickerson ruled, as well, that the new policy denies lesbians and gays the protection of the Fifth Amendment by unfairly discriminating against them.[34] Both the Zilly and Nickerson decisions are encouraging to lesbians and gays who embrace the legal approach in the absence of a President and Congress who are unwilling to rescind the ban.

EARLY IMPLEMENTATION OF THE NEW POLICY

Early reports indicate that the first two months of the implementation of the Don't Ask, Don't Tell policy "has not made life easier for many gay servicemen and women and in some ways has made it worse."[35] The central concern is that while the policy may have been designed to enable lesbians and gays "to serve without fear of persecution if they kept their sexual orientation private," it has been carried out by commanders who have misused "the broad new authority granted under the policy to ferret out homosexuals."[36] Eric Schmitt's *New York Times* account also revealed the following:

In addition, while a few gay servicemen and women said they felt the new policy had improved conditions, most of those who were interviewed said it had instead polarized attitudes toward homosexuals and had shifted the burden of proof to the servicemember if accused of engaging in homosexual acts.[37]

The Servicemembers Legal Defense Network released a study of first-year policy implementation in late February 1995. Coauthored by C. Dixon Osburn and Michelle M. Benecke, the study concludes that the Clinton/Nunn policy reveals a pattern of violations that often renders the policy little more than "Ask, Pursue, and Harass."[38]

In its early implementation stages, it is clear that the policy has largely been a failure. Hanna Rosin, for one, writes that "it has not created a climate in which heterosexuals and homosexuals are treated equally; to date, no straight servicemembers have been investigated for consensual sodomy or prostitution. And its attempt to end the witch-hunt by shifting the focus from 'status' to 'conduct' has been totally ineffectual."[39] In addition, Rosin suggests that in the past several months the Pentagon has attempted "to recoup scholarships and bonuses from nine servicemembers discharged for homosexuality—a practice it gave up in 1988."[40] It is obviously too early to offer a full evaluation of the Don't Ask, Don't Tell policy, but the above early reports indicate that those who supported the Clinton administration's original efforts to rescind the ban have reason to be concerned, disappointed, and angry.

THE BROADER IMPLICATIONS FOR THE LESBIAN AND GAY MOVEMENT

There is justifiable rage among some lesbians and gays that Bill Clinton betrayed our community after receiving the majority of our votes in the 1992 election and securing many of our financial resources. But the long-term impact of the debate over the ban is of particular interest. The central question is: Has the public debate about this issue over the past year created a more hospitable climate for lesbians, gays, and bisexuals to live open and honest lives, out of the closet, free from discrimination and harassment? This is a crucial question in light of the following facts:

a) Ours is a society where we endure far too many teenage suicides. Bruce Bawer reports that a 1989 study commissioned by the Department of Health and Human Services "concluded that 30% of teenage suicides were related to 'sexual identity problems' and that as many as a third of all gay teenagers attempt suicide."[41]

b) Ours is a society where people who are suspected of being lesbian or gay are harassed, beaten, and murdered.

c) Ours is a society where people who are suspected of being lesbian or gay can be fired from their jobs.

d) Ours is a society that passes state and local amendments that would deny lesbians and gays the ability to pursue legal redress if discriminated against.

e) Ours is a society that denies gays and lesbians health care insurance in the age of AIDS.

f) Ours is a society where lesbians, gays, and bisexuals have to live lies as they engage with their families, their friends, and their associates in the workplace. Coming out to one's family is the ultimate personification of the "personal is political."

In the end, I am not convinced that the debate over the ban has created a more hospitable environment for lesbians and gays. It is clear, however, that lesbian and gay groups now realize that having a so-called friend in the White House is not enough. In addition, my interviews suggest that these same groups also now recognize that grassroots mobilizing and broad based education on lesbian and gay concerns is of the utmost importance. This is an important strategic lesson growing out of the events surrounding Clinton's promise to overturn the ban.

Duncan Osborne correctly concludes that "the military issue spurred a debate so visible and emotional that it not only revealed the gay community's political strengths and weaknesses as never before but also may have permanently changed the face of gay rights activism."[42] This change can only be for the better. But the radical right is clearly organizing as well. Those politicians who supported rescinding the ban will undoubtedly be targeted by the radical right in the 1996 elections. We will likely see a return to the politics of hate and vitriol.

Ultimately, if we are to create a world in which lesbians and gays can live their lives free from brutality and discrimination, then those of us in academia must do what we can as openly lesbian and gay role models and as educators. We can surely present papers on panels organized around lesbian, gay, and bisexual issues at national conferences. But it is in the classroom where we can really make a difference by potentially opening our students' minds to the importance of extending basic civil rights to all Americans, regardless of their sexuality.

NOTES

1. Randy Shilts, *Conduct Unbecoming: Gays and Lesbians in the U.S. Military* (New York: St. Martin's, 1993), 88.
2. Shilts, 3.
3. Queer Nation, "Queer Activism: The Battle to Lift the Ban: A Chronology, 1991-1993." (Queer Nation, 1993).
4. Bruce Bawer, *A Place at the Table: The Gay Individual in American Society* (New York: Poseidon Press, 1993), 117.
5. Shilts, 17.
6. Shilts, 426.
7. Richard Mohr, *A More Perfect Union: Why Straight America Must Stand Up for Gay Rights* (Boston: Beacon Press, 1993).
8. Shilts, 281.
9. Shilts, 730.
10. Mohr, 93.
11. John Gallagher, "Terrible Timing." *The Advocate* (October 5, 1993): 28.
12. Gallagher, 28.
13. Bawer, 50.
14. Mohr, 114.
15. Shilts, 4.
16. Bawer, 58.
17. Shilts, 4.
18. Bawer, 59.
19. Bawer, 60.
20. Bawer, 60.
21. Bawer, 148-49.
22. Chris Bull, "Broken Promise." *The Advocate* (August 27, 1993): 24.
23. "The Legislative Word on Gays." *Congressional Quarterly Weekly Report* (July 31, 1993): 2076.
24. Bull, 24.
25. Bawer, 61.
26. Quoted in Bawer, 62.
27. For example, see Craig Rimmerman, *Presidency by Plebiscite: The Reagan-Bush Era in Institutional Perspective* (Boulder, CO: Westview Press, 1993).
28. Leon Wieseltier, "Covenant and Burling." *The New Republic* (February 1, 1993): 77.
29. Duncan Osborne, "Military." *The Advocate* (January 25, 1994): 53.

30. Eric Schmitt, "Pentagon Must Reinstate Nurse Who Declared She is a Lesbian." *New York Times* (June 2, 1994): A1.

31. Schmitt, "Pentagon Must Reinstate Nurse," A1.

32. Schmitt, "Pentagon Must Reinstate Nurse," A1.

33. Schmitt, "Pentagon Must Reinstate Nurse," A1.

34. Eric Schmitt, "Judge Overturns Pentagon Policy on Homosexuals." *New York Times* (March 31, 1995): A1.

35. Eric Schmitt, "Gay Troops Say the Revised Policy is Often Misused." *New York Times* (May 9, 1994): A1.

36. Schmitt, "Gay Troops," A1.

37. Schmitt, "Gay Troops," A1.

38. C. Dixon Osburn and Michelle Benecke, "Conduct Unbecoming Continues: The First Year Under 'Don't Ask, Don't Tell, Don't Pursue.'" Chapter 9, this volume.

39. Hanna Rosin, "The Ban Plays On." *The New Republic* (May 2, 1994): 12.

40. Rosin, 13.

41. Bawer, 244.

42. Osborne, "Military."

CHAPTER 5

President Clinton, Public Opinion, and Gays in the Military

Clyde Wilcox
Robin M. Wolpert

In the 1950s and 1960s, a powerful social movement for civil rights for African Americans transformed American politics. In the 1970s, the feminist movement made similar demands for women, with much success. Although neither blacks nor women enjoy full equality in American society today, their demands for civil rights have led to substantial progress. In the 1980s and 1990s, lesbians and gays have also mobilized to seek civil rights protections from the national government.

In the United States, questions of basic civil liberties and rights are often first considered by the elected branches of government—the president and the congress. These popularly elected officials are generally thought to respond to the opinions and prejudices of the general public, since they must defend their policies to voters during their reelection campaigns. Research has shown that the general public does not support basic civil liberties for social groups with unpopular views.[1] It is therefore not surprising that elected officials are reluctant to respond to demands by unpopular minorities for civil rights protection.

Although both the president and the congress respond to electoral pressures, they have different constituencies and responsibilities. It is often easier for a president to propose advances in civil liberties than for Congress to enact them, for the President answers to a national electorate that includes substantial numbers of those who favor expanding civil liberties. Congress, in contrast, contains many members whose constituents ardently oppose these policies. Because Congress proceeds by bargaining and compromise, these conservative members can often use the legislative process to stymie social change. In the 1950s, segregationists held many powerful leadership positions in the Congress, giving an additional advantage to those who opposed basic legislation to ensure equal rights for blacks.

To protect minority rights against majority prejudice, the founders insulated the U.S. Supreme Court from direct popular control. The Court quickly gained the authority to rule on the constitutionality of legislation, and has occasionally overturned laws that discriminated against racial, religious, and other minorities. It has often been the Court that has made the first authoritative pronouncements in civil rights areas. Since the Court lacks implementation powers, elite and popular support is usually necessary for the Court's decisions to have an impact. Even without such support, however, the Court can provide moral authority and leadership on the issue of equality.

The political battle over proposals to lift the ban on lesbian women and gay men serving openly in the military fits this traditional model of civil rights policymaking. Lesbians and gays organized to seek legislation to ensure their ability to serve their country. President Clinton pledged to lift the ban, in part because his electoral coalition included lesbians and gays, civil libertarians, and liberals who supported lifting the ban. Key conservatives in Congress, however, were able to prevent Clinton from fully implementing his policy. Since the enactment of the revised policy in 1993, the Federal courts have been bombarded by suits challenging its constitutionality.[2] Many federal courts have overturned the compromise policy, suggesting that once again it may be the courts that lead the way for greater civil liberties. The experience of the civil rights cases, however, suggests that even if the courts do rule to protect the rights of lesbians and gays, broad popular support will be necessary before those rulings lead to substantial social change.[3]

President Clinton's pledge to eliminate the ban on lesbians and gay men serving in the military was one of the most controversial issues of his early presidency. Although Clinton openly promised to end the ban during the presidential campaign, the issue did not attract widespread attention. Once Clinton assumed office, however, the proposed policy change ran into early, intense opposition from the military establishment and from key members of the U.S. Senate. In the first month of Clinton's presidency, Joint Chiefs of Staff Chairman General Colin Powell publicly announced his opposition to lifting the ban and Senator Sam Nunn (D-Ga) announced on national television that he would prevent the president from enacting his pledge. Conservative Democrats and Republicans in Congress also opposed Clinton's policy and threatened to codify a more explicit ban on service by lesbians and gays.

In the end, Clinton was forced to compromise. The new "Don't Ask, Don't Tell, Don't Pursue" policy allowed lesbians and gay men to serve in the military only if they kept their sexual orientation private. Homosexual conduct—defined as a homosexual act, a statement that the member is homosexual or bisexual, or a marriage or attempted marriage to someone of the same sex—remained grounds for discharge. Applicants for military service, however, would no longer be asked or required to reveal whether they are homosexual or bisexual. In addition, the military would no longer conduct investigations solely to determine a service member's sexual orientation.

The Don't Ask, Don't Tell policy was unpopular with both sides of the controversy. Moreover, press coverage of the issue repeatedly criticized Clinton for spending the first months of his presidency on this controversial issue. Analysis by the Center for Media and Politics reported that 73 percent of the stories on the gays in the military issue carried by the three major networks (NBC, CBS, ABC) were negative. Clinton's popularity plunged precipitously during the controversy, and any hope for a lengthy honeymoon and a productive start to the new administration disappeared. The conventional wisdom is that the controversy over gays in the military contributed to the drop in Clinton's popularity.[4] First, it may have led many voters to conclude that Clinton was a cultural liberal and not the "new Democrat" of the campaign. Although Clinton had publicly made the pledge during the presidential campaign, the Bush administration did not focus on the issue and many voters probably were not aware of Clinton's position. When conservative Democrats learned of Clinton's position and noticed that this was the first policy pronouncement of his administration, they may have concluded that Clinton was a liberal Democrat and lowered their evaluation of him. Second, cultural liberals who favored lifting the ban probably felt that Clinton abandoned his pledge too quickly, thereby dooming the policy to defeat. Finally, those who were not especially concerned about the policy may have lowered their evaluation of the competence of the Clinton administration for allowing this issue to dominate the first days of his presidency.

Although it is likely that the controversy over the lifting of the ban hurt Clinton's popularity, it is also possible that Clinton's initial statement of support, coupled with even more eloquent pronouncements by others inside and outside of the administration, shifted public opinion on the issue. In particular, those who were especially favorable toward Clinton may have responded to his leadership on the issue, and those who were otherwise sympathetic to arguments rooted in equality values may have become more supportive of allowing lesbians and gays to serve openly. Because supporters of lifting the ban on lesbians and gays frequently compared the issue to previous bans on service by women and blacks, it may be that members of these groups were especially open to persuasion. In addition, those who were initially negative toward Clinton may have shifted their attitudes toward increasing opposition to the policy.

In this chapter, we focus on the connection between attitudes on lesbians and gays in the military and evaluations of Clinton. We begin by determining the sources of attitudes on allowing lesbians and gays to serve in 1992 and 1993. We next explore whether these attitudes were a source of evaluations of Clinton in 1993—especially whether those who opposed the lifting of the ban lowered their evaluations of Clinton. Finally, we focus on the possible leadership effects of Clinton on public opinion—whether Clinton's stand may have mobilized increased support for lifting the ban among those who liked him.

THE DATA

The data for this study come from the 1992 National Election Study (NES) and the 1993 NES Pilot survey. These two studies form a short-term panel that began shortly before the 1992 election, had a second wave immediately after the election, and a final wave in the fall of 1993, after the controversy over the gays in the military policy. The data therefore provide an excellent opportunity to study the relationship between opinion on the policy and support for Clinton.

The 1992 post-election wave and the 1993 survey included an item that asked respondents whether they strongly supported, weakly supported, weakly opposed, or strongly opposed allowing homosexuals to serve in the armed services.[5] In both waves respondents were also asked to rate Clinton and "gay men and lesbians— that is homosexuals" on a feeling thermometer ranging from 0 to 100. In the 1992 survey, respondents also rated the military on that scale.[6]

The 1993 survey contained additional questions on reactions toward lesbians and gay men. Respondents were asked whether they believed that homosexuals could change their sexual orientation, whether they believed that homosexuals would try to seduce heterosexuals, whether they believed that homosexuality was natural, whether they believed that homosexuality was against God's will, whether they were afraid of catching diseases from homosexuals, and whether they were disgusted by lesbians and gays.[7]

The 1992 survey also included measures of ideological self-placement and partisanship, as well as items from which we have constructed scales to measure moral traditionalism and equality values.[8] The data also include a number of demographic variables that are potential sources of attitudinal differentiation, including age, sex, race, region, urbanicity, and religious affiliation, doctrine, salience, and practice.

PUBLIC SUPPORT FOR LIFTING THE BAN

In the 1992 and 1993 surveys, respondents were asked about their strength of support or opposition to homosexuals serving in the military. Table 1 shows that support for allowing gays and lesbians to serve increased during this period. In 1992, 33.2 percent strongly favored lifting the ban. By 1993, that figure increased to 44.5 percent. These data show a higher level of support than other polls at the time,[9] perhaps because the 1992 survey included a disproportionate number of Clinton voters.[10]

At the bottom of Table 1 we locate this aggregate change more precisely by crosstabulating positions in 1992 and 1993. Those who held strong positions in 1992 were likely to remain stable: Fully 82 percent of those who indicated strong support for lifting the ban in 1992 held the same position in 1993, while only 10 percent indicated that they weakly or strongly disapproved of allowing lesbians and gays to serve. Slightly more than two-thirds of those who strongly opposed allowing lesbians and gays to serve in 1992 took the same position in 1993, while nearly one in four changed to support for lifting the ban.

Not surprisingly, those who weakly supported or opposed lifting the ban in 1992 were more likely to change their position in 1993. Although there was movement in each direction, the net change in each case was toward more support for the Clinton policy. Nearly half of those who weakly opposed lifting the ban in 1992 favored lifting it in 1993, although nearly a third moved to strong opposition.

Table 1

Support for Allowing Gays and Lesbians to Serve in the Military

	1992	1993
strongly support	33.2	44.5
weakly support	27.8	17.3
weakly oppose	7.6	8.0
strongly oppose	31.3	30.2

Note: Percentage taking each position in each year.

Attitude Change: 1992-1993

	1992		1993	
	strongly support	weakly support	weakly oppose	strongly oppose
strongly support	82	8	2	8
weakly support	44	31	10	15
weakly oppose	27	22	20	31
strongly oppose	13	10	9	68

Note: Percentage of those taking each position in 1992 who held each position in 1993. The number of respondents who held opinions in both 1992 and 1993 is less than the number of respondents who held opinions in either year.

THE SOURCES OF ATTITUDES TOWARD LIFTING THE BAN

We expect the immediate sources of support for allowing lesbians and gays to serve openly in the military to be a constellation of values. One key value should be attitudes toward lesbians and gays themselves. Paul Sniderman, Richard Brody, and Philip Tetlock argue that many Americans determine their attitudes on policy issues based on their affect toward the social groups involved—a "likeability heuristic" that is used by political sophisticates even more than by those with little information about politics.[11] Thus, homophobia is likely to be a key source of opposition to allowing lesbians and gays to serve.

Yet we think it likely that other values will influence attitudes on the ban, for the issue lies at the intersection of a number of important values.[12] One of the most important of these values should be support for equality. Most rhetoric in support of lifting the ban evoked equality as a key rationale. Clyde Wilcox reported that support for gender equality was one of the strongest predictors of support for allowing women to serve in military combat,[13] and we suspect support for political and social equality will increase support for allowing lesbians and gays to serve.

Concern for military effectiveness may decrease support for lifting the ban. Although lesbians and gay men have always served in the military, many with distinction and honor,[14] opponents of the ban repeatedly argued that the presence of homosexuals would produce tensions that would undermine discipline, good order and morale, and mutual trust and confidence among servicemembers.[15] Thus, although some Americans may believe that the ban violates the norm of equality, they may consider it more important to maintain military effectiveness. Unfortunately, we have no direct measure of this attitude in the data, so we use affect toward the military as an admittedly unsatisfactory substitute.

Moral traditionalism should also be a major source of opposition to lifting the ban. Those who hold conservative views on sexual and moral issues should be in favor of banning lesbians and gays from military service, regardless of their level of homophobia. Finally, general ideology and partisanship may influence support for allowing gays to serve.

Although we expect these values to be the major sources of support for allowing lesbians and gays to serve, a variety of demographic variables should have an indirect impact on attitudes through their influence on values, and some may exert a direct impact as well. We expect those with higher levels of education to be more supportive of lifting the ban, along with younger Americans, and those who were raised in urban areas. A variety of studies have shown that men are more homophobic than women, and we expect men to be less supportive of allowing lesbians and gays to serve. Finally, religion should be an important indirect and possibly direct source of opposition to lifting the ban. Evangelicals and conservative Catholics should be more likely to oppose the Clinton policy than mainline Protestants, and Jews and those with no religious involvement should be more likely than mainline Protestants to favor it. Evangelical religious doctrine is likely to be a major source of opposition, and those who attend church regularly or who have high levels of religious salience may also be more likely to oppose the Clinton policy.[16]

In Table 2, we show the results of two regression analyses, the first predicting support for allowing lesbians and gays to serve in the military in 1992, and the second predicting support in 1993. We experimented with a number of specifications and include in the final models only those variables that were either significant predictors or for which we had strong theoretical expectations.

Unsurprisingly, the best predictor of variability in attitudes in both years is affect toward lesbians and gays. Affect toward the military is not a source of attitudes toward allowing lesbians and gays to serve.[17] Those with more traditional moral values were more likely to oppose lifting the ban in both years, and those with strong equality values were more likely to support Clinton's policy in 1992 but not 1993. Democrats were more likely to favor lifting the ban in both years, and opinion was somewhat more split along partisan lines in 1993 than in 1992. After holding partisanship constant, however, general ideology was not a significant predictor.

Contrary to expectations, education was not a direct source of attitudes toward allowing lesbians and gays to serve, nor were blacks more likely than whites to support lifting the ban. Women, however, were *far* more likely than men to support the Clinton policy; and compared to everyone else, those who held evangelical doctrine were far less likely to support the policy. We experimented with a variety of other religious variables, including measures of religiosity, religious salience, and denominational membership, but none was a direct predictor of support once we held moral traditionalism constant.[18]

It is worth noting, however, that education and religion are important *indirect* sources of attitudes. Education was a strong source of equality values, of warmer affect toward lesbians and gays, and of support for less traditional moral values—all strong direct predictors of support for allowing lesbians and gays to serve. This suggests that education influences attitudes on gays in the military primarily by shaping underlying values. In addition, religious denomination was a source of some of these values as well. Jews were distinctively likely to be more liberal, to be more supportive of equality and nontraditional moral values, and to have warmer affect toward lesbians and gays. Those who attended evangelical churches were more likely to hold cool attitudes toward lesbians and gays, and those who held evangelical doctrinal beliefs were less supportive of equality, more supportive of traditional moral values, more conservative, and markedly cooler toward lesbians and gays.

Although these results suggest that attitudes toward gays in the military lie at the intersection of several important values, they also show that homophobia is by far the most important source of attitudes. This result emerges even more clearly in Table 3, which shows the impact of several attitudes toward lesbians and gays on support for allowing them to serve in the military.[19] We include as explanatory variables a variety of specific items on lesbians and gays from the 1993 survey—whether the respondent was disgusted by lesbians and gays, whether the respondent believed that homosexuality was against the will of

Table 2

Sources of Support for Allowing Gays and Lesbians to Serve in the Military

	1992	1993
	b	b
Education	.01	.06
Black	.17	.12
Woman	.66**	.53**
Raised in rural area	-.06*	-.02
Evangelical doctrine	-.34*	-.45*
Equality values	.30**	.10
Moral traditionalism	-.30**	-.27**
Affect toward gays/lesbians	.03**	.03**
Affect toward military	-.00	-.00
Liberal ideology	.01	.08
Democratic partisanship	.08*	.11**
Constant	2.72	1.30
N	548	537
Adjusted R^2	.48	.37

(**p<.01; *p<.05)

God, whether the respondent believed that lesbians and gays could change their sexual orientation, whether the respondent believed that lesbians and gay men try to seduce heterosexuals, and whether the respondent feared catching diseases from lesbians and gays. The most important predictor is whether the respondent was disgusted by lesbians and gays. Indeed, among those who strongly opposed allowing lesbians and gays to serve in 1992, more than two-thirds were strongly disgusted and nearly 75 percent were disgusted (strongly or weakly) by homosexuality. Those who believed that lesbians and gays could change their sexual orientation were more likely to oppose lifting the ban, as were those who feared that lesbians and gays would try to seduce heterosexuals and those who feared disease. Interestingly, despite the frequent framing of the issue as involving religious values, the only item that is *not* a significant predictor is the belief that homosexuality violated God's will.[20]

We expected an interaction between the belief that lesbians and gays try to seduce heterosexuals and the belief that sexual orientation cannot be changed. Older citizens who picture their children or grandchildren in a small tent with a gay soldier (a frequent image used by opponents of the new policy) should be especially worried if they believe that the gay soldier would try to seduce their child *and* that their child's sexuality was malleable. Further analysis revealed that those who believed that sexual orientation was malleable and who also believed that lesbians and gays try to seduce heterosexuals were especially opposed to lifting the ban.

Although visceral reactions tend to be the strongest predictors of attitudes on allowing lesbians and gays to openly serve in the armed forces, more than a third of those who were strongly disgusted by homosexuality favored lifting the ban in 1993. Members of this group were especially likely to hold strong values of equality and were disproportionately black. This suggests that some Americans whose visceral reactions to lesbians and gays were intensely negative were open to persuasion based on arguments on equality.

LESBIANS AND GAYS IN THE MILITARY AND APPROVAL OF CLINTON

Did the controversy over gays in the military affect Clinton's popularity? The issue is one that is likely to have affected approval of the president for several reasons. First, the issue received substantial media attention, making it salient to many Americans.[21] George Edwards, William Mitchell, and Reed Welch have shown that the impact of issues on presidential evaluations varies over time, as does the salience of various values relevant to policy debates.[22] Moreover, Jon Krosnick and Laura Brannon found that events that receive a good deal of media attention affect presidential popularity primarily among those who are knowledgeable but inattentive to politics.[23] For these individuals, stories that receive a good deal of attention become key in their evaluations of the president, at least in the short run.

In addition, the issue invoked visceral reactions,[24] was bathed in symbolism,[25] and involved an "easy" issue[26] on which information was readily

Table 3

Attitudinal Sources of Support for Allowing Gays and Lesbians to Serve (1993)

	b
Homosexuality disgusting	-.30**
Homosexuals can change orientation	-.25**
Homosexuals seduce heterosexuals	-.10*
Fear disease	-.14*
Homosexuality against God's will	-.03

Constant	5.45
N	562
Adjusted R^2	.35

(**p < .01; *p < .05)

available.[27] Each of these factors predicts that the issue would have a strong impact on presidential approval.

More importantly, Clinton had no record on other policy matters to cushion the impact of this controversy. Richard Neustadt has noted that citizens evaluate the president based on current events and policies as well as past performance.[28] In the absence of any evaluations of past performance, the inertial aspect of public evaluations is weak. And the overwhelmingly negative tone of media coverage would likely make otherwise inattentive citizens more negative toward Clinton's handling of the issue.

Although Clinton's handling of the policy was not popular with either group, it aroused far greater opposition among those who opposed lifting the ban. Among those who strongly supported lifting the ban in 1992, a quarter strongly approved of Clinton's handling of the issue in 1993 and an equal number strongly disapproved. But among those who strongly opposed lifting the ban, only 10 percent strongly supported Clinton's handling of the issue (most of whom had changed their position on the policy) while 72 percent strongly disapproved. Thus, although many of those who supported Clinton's policy were disappointed in his early abandonment of his pledge, those who opposed the policy were far more negative.

Despite the fragmentary media and candidate attention to the issue during the 1992 presidential campaign, support for the policy was correlated with evaluations of Clinton in 1992. Clinton voters supported ending the ban in 1992 by a substantial margin, while those who voted for other candidates strongly opposed the policy. Social liberals voted for Clinton, regardless of whether they knew his position on the military issue, in part because they *did* know his view on abortion and other social issues; social conservatives voted for Bush for the same reason. This means that the policy inspired opposition primarily among those who opposed Clinton in the election. Indeed, more than 75 percent of those who opposed lifting the ban in 1992 voted against Clinton.

Yet attitudes toward the ban are associated with changes in Clinton's evaluations. Those who strongly opposed lifting the ban in 1992 rated Clinton seven degrees cooler in 1993 than they had after the presidential election, while those who strongly supported lifting the ban in 1992 lowered their evaluations of Clinton by only a single degree during this period.[29] (Of course, there were other issues at play during 1993, most notably the budget deal that increased income taxes on the wealthy and gasoline taxes on consumers.)

In Table 4, we present two regression models designed to test the impact of lesbians and gays in the military issue on Clinton's job approval and popularity. We first estimate a regression equation predicting job approval for Clinton in 1993, using as explanatory variables approval of Clinton's handling of the economy, foreign affairs, and the gays in the military issue. The results show that although Clinton's handling of the economy was the strongest predictor of job approval for Clinton, his handling of the gays in the military issue was also a significant predictor of job approval.

To see whether Clinton's popularity suffered because of the gays in the military issue, we estimate a regression equation predicting support for Clinton

Table 4

Attitudes on Lifting the Ban and Clinton Job Approval 1993

	Clinton Job Approval
	b
Approve Clinton/economy	.59**
Approve Clinton/foreign affairs	.20**
Approve Clinton/gays in military	.13**
Constant	.24
N	643
R^2	.59
(**p < .01; *p < .05)	

	Affect toward Clinton, 1993
	b
Affect toward Clinton Sept/Oct '92	.48**
Gays in Military '92	2.24**
Clinton raised taxes too much '93	-6.32**
Constant	-0.60
N	657
Adjusted R^2	.43
(**p < .01; *p < .05)	

in 1993. The explanatory variables are support for Clinton in the 1992 pre-election period, support for allowing lesbians and gays to serve, and attitudes toward the tax increases in Clinton's budget.[30] The results, presented at the bottom of Table 4, show that those who opposed allowing lesbians and gays to serve lowered their evaluation of Clinton more than those who favored lifting the ban, although the tax increase had a far greater impact on evaluations. Further analysis reveals that the drop in approval for Clinton was greatest among those who were most strongly opposed to the policy, especially among those who professed to be disgusted by lesbians and gays.

Charles Ostrom and Dennis Simon have reported that the president has several different publics, each of which responds to different issues.[31] In this case, part of Clinton's coalition may have responded positively to his position on lesbians and gays in the military, while other elements may have been more hostile. Further analysis suggests that evaluations of Clinton increased from 1992 to 1993 among those who strongly favored lifting the ban and who approved of Clinton's handling of the issue. Although many of the relatively small number of respondents who had perceived Clinton as a conservative or moderate did lower their evaluations of Clinton based on the issue, overall the issue had no effect on evaluations among those who had voted for Clinton in 1992. Among many who voted for Perot or especially Bush, however, the issue turned their moderate dislike for Clinton into intense hostility.

The electoral implications of this result are important, for Clinton won in 1992 with only 43 percent of the popular vote. Among those who supported him in that three-candidate race, his handling of the gays in the military issue did little damage. But those who voted for Bush or Perot did lower their evaluations of Clinton based on this issue and began to perceive him as more liberal as well. Our analysis (not shown) suggests that among those who did not vote for Clinton but who perceived him as conservative, moderate, or only slightly liberal, his position on gays in the military created the impression that he was very liberal. In a two-candidate election in 1996, this perception could pose a serious problem.

Finally, additional analysis shows that the drop in Clinton's popularity that can be traced to lesbians and gays in the military issue is entirely confined to that portion of the public who are strongly homophobic—i.e., those who expressed disgust at homosexuality. Among those with less extreme or positive evaluations of lesbians and gays, Clinton's popularity did not suffer because of his stand on the issue.

PRESIDENTIAL PERSUASION

Although we have demonstrated that the controversy over gays in the military hurt Clinton's approval, primarily among those who opposed lifting the ban, we have also shown that support for allowing lesbians and gays to serve has increased over time. Thus as Clinton's popularity was dropping among those most opposed to allowing lesbians and gays to serve, support for his initial policy proposal was increasing. Indeed, among those who were not strongly disgusted by homosexuality and who did not initially strongly support lifting the ban, nearly a third became more supportive of Clinton's policy in 1993.

Why should opinion move so sharply toward increased support for lifting the ban? First, it seems likely that for many Americans, the issue was redefined during the debate. Prior to the public discussion, their response was conditioned primarily by their affective reactions to lesbians and gays, but the discussion itself focused attention to other values underlying the debate, including equality. Moreover, Clinton's support for the policy may have had a persuasive effect.

Although there have been a number of studies of presidential persuasion, such analyses pose difficult methodological issues.[32] To see whether Clinton's support of the policy swayed public opinion, we estimated a model predicting attitudes toward allowing lesbians and gays to serve in 1993, using as explanatory variables the respondent's attitudes in 1992 and evaluations of Clinton in 1992.[33] The results are shown in Table 5. Holding attitudes in 1992 constant, we find that those who rated Clinton warmly in 1992 were more likely than those who rated him coolly to support eliminating the ban in 1993. Changes in attitudes from 1992 to 1993, then, were associated with approval of Clinton.

At the bottom of Table 5, we show a more complete equation (including as explanatory variables the basic values from Table 2), a measure of attitudes toward gays in the military in 1992, and support for Clinton in 1992. This model shows that equality values were not especially important in predicting changed attitudes, but that affect toward lesbians and gays was a key predictor. Those who were especially cool toward lesbians and gays were unlikely to become more supportive of allowing them to serve in the military.

Taken together, these results suggest that Clinton did have a persuasive effect on the attitudes of citizens who were not strongly homophobic. Of course, not all attitude change was due to Clinton's leadership. Others inside and outside of the administration made eloquent pleas for the new policy, and those who opposed lifting the ban also exercised leadership effects. Our additional analysis suggests that women were especially likely to increase their support for lifting the ban, while those who held evangelical religious doctrine were especially likely to increase their opposition to the policy.

CONCLUSIONS

Although the highly visible fight surrounding lesbians and gays in the military was a public relations disaster for the Clinton administration, our analysis indicates that the effects of this controversy were more complex than portrayed by the media. Although many lesbian and gay activists were unhappy with Clinton's eventual compromise, our data show that Clinton's popularity fell more sharply among those who opposed lifting the ban. Indeed, the issue hurt him almost entirely among those with sharply negative visceral reactions to lesbians and gays.

Among those who were not so homophobic, and especially among those with weak positions on the issue, Clinton exercised a leadership effect.

Table 5
Attitudes Toward Allowing Gays and Lesbians to Serve 1993

	Attitudes on Service 1993
	b
Gays in the Military '92	.60**
Evaluation of Clinton '92	.01**
Constant	1.03
N	678
Adjusted R^2	.39
(**p < .01; *p < .05)	

	Attitudes on Service 1993
	b
Gays in the Military '92	.50**
Evaluation of Clinton '92	.01**
Equality values	.01
Moral Traditionalism	-.07
Affect toward Gays/Lesbians	.01**
Affect toward Military	-.00
Liberal ideology	.06
Democratic partisanship	.05
Constant	.42
N	534
Adjusted R^2	.48
(**p < .01; *p < .05)	

Although those who disliked Clinton became slightly more liberal on the issue between 1992 and 1993, those who liked him became *far* more supportive of lifting the ban. Our analysis suggests that Clinton and others who argued for lifting the ban persuaded many Americans to support the policy.

It is frequently argued that presidential popularity is an asset that must be husbanded carefully and spent on only those issues where it can matter. Presidents Reagan and Bush were both criticized by conservatives for appearing unwilling to "spend down" their popularity in order to accomplish their policy objectives. The press criticized Clinton in the first months of his presidency for squandering his rather meager honeymoon on an issue that he eventually lost.

Yet our analysis suggests the possibility of a more positive assessment. Clinton's ultimately unsuccessful attempt to allow lesbians and gay men to serve openly in the military can be conceived as a long-term investment in that policy, for opinion did move as a result of the controversy. Of course, as the issue moves through the courts and with Congress controlled by Republicans (many of whom won with the support of the Christian Right), public opinion may not be an important source of policy in the short run. But our analysis does show that the spirited debate on the issue increased support for lifting the ban.

NOTES

An earlier version of this chapter was presented at the Annual Meeting of the Midwest Political Science Association, April, 1995, Chicago. We would like to thank John Bruce and Lee Sigelman for helpful suggestions. The data were made available by the Inter-University Consortium for Political and Social Research. We remain responsible for any errors.

1. See, for example, Herbert McCloskey, "Consensus and Ideology in American Politics." *American Political Science Review* 58 (1964): 350-70; Clyde Z. Nunn, Harry J. Crockett Jr., and J. Allen Williams Jr., *Tolerance for Nonconformity* (San Francisco: Jossey-Bass, 1976); and John L. Sullivan, James Pierson, and George E. Marcus, *Political Tolerance and American Democracy* (Chicago: University of Chicago Press, 1982).

2. For example, *Able v. United States*, 847 F.Supp. 1038 (1994) and *Thomasson v. Perry*, 895 F.Supp. 820 (1995).

3. Gerald N. Rosenberg, *The Hollow Hope: Can Courts Bring About Social Change?* (Chicago: University of Chicago Press, 1991).

4. See, for example, Thomas B. Edsall, "Survey Finds Consensus on Some Major Issues," *Washington Post* (February 10, 1993): A6, and Ann Devroy, "TV Public Puts Clinton on Defensive," *Washington Post* (February 11, 1993): A1.

5. We adjusted these feeling thermometers to take into account individual differences in responses to these kinds of items. We calculated the average thermometer score assigned to social and political groups and then subtracted that score from each feeling thermometer. The resulting score reflects the relative affect of respondents toward Clinton and these groups. For a discussion

of the rationale for this adjustment, see Wilcox (1987) and Wilcox, Sigelman and Cook (1989).

6. The equality scale was composed of items asking whether society should ensure equal opportunity, whether we have gone too far in pushing equal rights in the United States, whether the United States would be better off if we stopped worrying so much about equality, whether it is a problem if some people have more of a chance in life, and whether there would be fewer problems if people were treated equally. Alpha = .71. The moral traditionalism scale was constructed from items asking whether morals should be adjusted to a changing world, whether people should tolerate different moral standards, whether the United States should emphasize traditional family ties, whether new lifestyles contribute to the breakdown of society, and whether sex with someone other than your spouse is always wrong. Alpha = .65.

7. Several polls taken during the controversy show significantly less support for lifting the ban than the NES data used here. For example, an April 22-23, 1993 Newsweek poll indicated that 42 percent approved of lifting the ban while 51 percent disapproved; and a July 29-30, 1993 Newsweek poll showed that 37 percent approved of lifting the ban and 56 percent disapproved.

8. Frequency of church attendance is associated with increased opposition to legal abortion among all religious traditions (Cook, Jelen, and Wilcox, 1992).

9. See note 7.

10. Elizabeth A. Cook, and Clyde Wilcox, "Gender in the 1992 Elections." In Herbert Weisberg (ed.) Democracy's Feast: The 1992 Elections (Chatham, NJ: Chatham House, 1995).

11. Paul M. Sniderman, Richard A. Brody, and Philip E. Tetlock, Reasoning and Choice: Explorations in Political Psychology (New York: Cambridge University Press, 1991).

12. For a similar result on attitudes toward AIDS, see Ted. G. Jelen and Clyde Wilcox, "Symbolic and Instrumental Values as Predictors of AIDS Policy Attitudes." Social Science Quarterly 73 (1992): 737-49.

13. Clyde Wilcox, "Race, Gender, and Support for Women in the Military." Social Science Quarterly 73 (1992): 316-23.

14. Randy Shilts, Conduct Unbecoming: Gays and Lesbians in the U.S. Military (New York: St. Martin's Press, 1993).

15. Pat Towell, "Nunn Offers a Compromise: 'Don't Ask/Don't Tell.'" Congressional Quarterly Weekly Report 51 (1993): 1240-42.

16. See note 8.

17. Although the data do not permit us to test this notion, we suspect that a more focused measure of attitudes toward the impact of lesbians and gays on military morale might have been a significant predictor.

18. For a similar result, see Douglas Alan Strand, "Gay Rights and the Clinton Coalition: Initial Gleanings from the 1993 NES Pilot Study," presented at the 1994 annual meeting of the Midwest Political Science Association, Chicago; and Faith or Fear? Religion, Social Alienation, and the Mass Politics of Family Values, doctoral dissertation, University of California, Berkeley, 1996.

19. The regression equation estimated in Table 3 only includes the specific variables on lesbians and gay men from the 1993 survey. We also ran a more fully specified model which included the variables listed in Table 2. In the more fully specified model, as in the reduced model, all of the specific variables from the 1993 survey were significant except the respondent's belief that homosexuality was against God's will.

20. This is not because of multicollinearity. The various items are not especially highly correlated and alternate specifications that eliminate other items do not elevate the religious item to statistical significance. However, the item of whether homosexuality violates God's will was sharply skewed, with an overwhelming majority supporting the proposition.

21. The gays in the military issue received substantial media coverage. The three major networks (CBS, NBC, ABC) carried 103 stories on the issue in 1993, compared to 329 on the budget.

22. George C. Edwards III, William Mitchell, and Reed Welch, "Explaining Presidential Approval: The Significance of Issue Salience." *American Journal of Political Science* 39 (1995): 108-34.

23. Jon A. Krosnick and Laura A. Brannon, "The Impact of the Gulf War on Ingredients of Presidential Evaluations: Multidimensional Effects of Political Involvement." *American Political Science Review* 87 (1993): 963-75.

24. James Stimson, "Public Support for American Presidents." *Public Opinion Quarterly* 50 (1976): 555-62.

25. Michael MacKuen, "Political Drama, Economic Conditions, and the Dynamics of Presidential Opinion." *American Journal of Political Science* 27 (1983): 165-92.

26. Edward G. Carmines and James A. Stimson, "The Two Faces of Issue Voting." *American Political Science Review* 74 (1980): 78-91.

27. Richard Brody and Benjamin Page, "The Impact of Events on Presidential Popularity." In Aaron Wildavsky (ed.) *Perspectives on the Presidency* (Boston: Little, Brown, 1975).

28. Richard Neustadt, *Presidential Power* (New York: Wiley, 1980).

29. In each case, those who disapproved of Clinton's handling of the issue were cooler toward Clinton. For example, among those who strongly favored lifting the ban in 1992, those who approved of Clinton's handling of this issue were actually 1 degree warmer toward Clinton in 1993, while those who disapproved of his handling of the issue were 4 degrees cooler.

30. Inspection of the residuals indicates that there is no problem with autocorrelation.

31. Charles W. Ostrom Jr. and Dennis M. Simon, "The President's Public." *American Journal of Political Science* 32 (1989): 1096-1119.

32. Lee Sigelman and Alan Rosenblatt, "Methodological Considerations in the Analysis of Presidential Persuasion." In Diane Mutz, Paul M. Sniderman, and Richard A. Brody (eds.) *Political Persuasion and Attitude Change* (Ann Arbor: University of Michigan Press, forthcoming).

33. Once again an examination of the residuals indicated no significant autocorrelation.

CHAPTER 6

The Perils of
Congressional Politics

David M. Rayside

There's no moral leadership in Washington on this—there's arithmetic.
There is only arithmetic!
Administrative official (interviewed 2 September 1993)

As Bill Clinton's inauguration approached, only a few of the exuberant
lesbian and gay activists in Washington took seriously the early sniper fire
from the Pentagon, Capitol Hill, and the religious right. The new President had
made the removal of the ban on gays in the military a signal of his commitment
to lesbian and gay rights, and the transition frenzy after the November election
lent even more credence to the view that the issue would be dealt with
immediately. In an area like military policy, that seemed to lie so clearly
within the prerogative of the executive, doubters about the President's capacity
to lift the ban seemed insufficiently plugged into the kinds of energetic policy
networks that were forging the new optimism.

By midsummer 1993, the memories of glittering inaugural balls and talk of
lesbians and gays being fully a part of the new governing coalition were gone.
The proposal to lift the ban was mortally wounded by March and dead by July,
with further indignities inflicted on its corpse by Congressional and military
opponents in the weeks to follow. In what turned out to be the President's first
major political battle, the initiative was seized by opponents in the Senate,
supported by virtual insurrection in the military's highest command, and
emboldened by a Christian right focusing on gay rights more than ever before.

The failure to repeal the ban, though admittedly a more difficult issue than
many, revealed the daunting challenges facing lesbian and gay organizations
doing battle in Washington. The major groups based in the capital are the
largest and in some ways the most sophisticated gay lobbying organizations in
the world, and yet their resources and strategies were insufficient to the task
at hand. That was partly a product of inexperience in dealing with an ostensibly
supportive administration, but it was also a result of changes in the patterns of
influence on Capitol Hill. Comparison with a number of northern European
countries and Canada reveals that U.S. lesbian and gay activist networks have
many opportunities for entering mainstream political processes. But once

involved in the process, they face hurdles that are no less challenging than in other systems, and in some respects more difficult to overcome. The military factor introduced a barrier with few equivalents in other systems.

Legislative clout has always been greater in the United States than in any of the other liberal democracies of Western Europe and North America, and the decline of presidential authority since the 1970s has further sharpened the contrast. In addition, although the independent influence of the military may well have diminished with the decline of Cold War tensions, the events of 1993 demonstrated a willingness to act in defiance of executive wishes that would find few parallels in other democratic countries. The strength and political influence of extreme antigay forces is also greater than in other countries of the industrialized world. Right wing and religiously based networks play important roles inside and outside the party systems in a number of those countries, but the strength of the religious right in the United States, the growth of its political sophistication, and its fixation on gay rights issues has no equivalent in any.

The difficulty that pro-gay forces faced on this issue was also a product of the extent to which heterosexuality is insinuated into existing law. It is not only that the legal framework governing "family" relationships assumes heterosexuality, as it does in almost all other countries. It is also that the United States contains among the few jurisdictions left in the industrialized world that criminalize consenting sexual activity between two adults of the same sex. All this forms an entwined web of legal marginalization in which weaker strands are supported by others. Despite a political profile given to rights matters that is greater in the United States than in just about any other Western country, progress on sexual minority rights is not concomitantly easier.

THE CONGRESSIONAL CONTEXT

Those seeking to influence political outcomes in American politics have always been challenged by the fragmentation of political authority, even if the dispersion of power has also created opportunities for entry into mainstream politics that are difficult to locate in most other political systems.

Most of the founders of the American Republic were nervous about majorities, and hedged in the democracy they designed with complexity. They conceived of a division of powers not only to prevent executive tyranny, but to slow the pace of change and prevent popular "excess." In the process they created a legislature that was to acquire enormous independence and power, and with comparatively unusual equality between its two chambers. Even in spheres that logically require and constitutionally allow the greatest latitude in executive authority, such as foreign and military affairs, explicit constitutional room is created for legislative policymaking—room that is increasingly used by legislative entrepreneurs.

Even during the middle four decades of this century, when presidential ascendancy was clearest, the role of Congress was more independently powerful than that of any other liberal democratic legislature. The most "imperial" of presidencies could wield nothing like the legislative power of a parliamentary cabinet (providing it was itself united), and the reassertion of Congressional power during the 1970s further sharpened the contrast with other liberal democracies. The first Reagan term stopped and may even have partially reversed the shift, but the growth in Democratic assertiveness in the 1980s restored it.

The separation of powers and the relatively weak party discipline in the United States plants seeds for the fragmentation of influence and authority within the legislature itself. Party voting and partisan cohesion increased in the mid-1980s, and remain higher in the 1990s than they had been in the decades before. (In the 1991 House of Representatives, for example, fully 88 percent of the Republicans and only 21 percent of the Democrats voted as "conservative."[1]) The Democrats are less sharply divided than they have been in more than a century, and both parties learned the benefits of greater unity during the relatively polarizing years of the Reagan and Bush presidencies. What collegiality across parties there was in each congressional chamber has now declined, even in the smaller and more tradition-bound Senate.[2]

But even within more polarized congressional environments, centrifugal forces are very powerful and of a categorically different order than could be found in other systems. In parliamentary systems, a government's survival depends on maintaining a party discipline that it almost always obtains. In northern Europe, even cabinets made up of a coalition of parties can usually bank on the cohesion and loyalty of its distinct parties. The recent rebelliousness of British Conservatives over European issues, and of a few Canadian Liberals over gay rights and gun control, are remarkable for their exceptionalism. Roll call statistics on the U.S. Congress still show significant divisions, for example, between Democrats from the south and their colleagues from other regions—with none of the former and 55 percent of the latter counting as "liberal."[3] Perhaps similar diversity could be found in surveys of the personal beliefs of politicians in the more disciplined parties of other systems: the difference is that in the United States such heterogeneity is fully evident in legislative voting.

The policy initiative that U.S. legislators retain might have contributed to their interest in acting in partisan concert, but more often than not is used to increase visibility among local voters.[4] All this reduces the incentives to tow party lines on either major or minor issues. The increased anti-incumbency mood in the U.S. electorate, the intensification of negative campaigning, and the dramatically augmented capacities of lobby groups to mobilize grassroots efforts either across the country or within particularly targeted districts, intensifies the individual legislator's search for an independent profile and caution over choosing issues that provoke well-organized opponents.[5]

Legislators are also increasingly on their own in their bids for election, and less beholden than ever to the party apparatus for money and people to help in their races. Extra parliamentary party organization has always been uneven across American localities and states, and virtually nonexistent at the national level. At the same time that party ties have increased somewhat within

Congress, party organizations and loyalties have declined in the electorate. Partisan de-alignment is not unique to the United States, but the decline in the role of permanent party organizations in running elections is greater than elsewhere.

The proliferation of subcommittees in both the House and the Senate, and the partial devolution of power to them, creates opportunities for policy entrepreneurship to match the eagerness for profile of politicians with eyes fixed firmly on the next election. Independence is tempered to some extent in the House, where the large size and the volume of business requires more rules and therefore concentrates more leverage in the hands of party leaders. In fact, the disorder created by the dispersion of power to subcommittees has been reversed to some extent, with the majority leadership regaining some influence. But it is also in the House where the Democratic caucus has been most assertive, and readier than ever to challenge such traditional sources of power as seniority. The House was also witness to a dramatic influx of new members in 1992, reducing the weight of traditional constraints on member behavior (reflected to some extent by the lighter hand of then-Democratic Speaker Thomas Foley, in comparison to some of his predecessors). The Senate was once regulated by strong norms about collegiality and deference, but these standards have lessened. Once the unwritten constraints were loosened, the relative absence of rules accorded its members considerable leeway for establishing independent policy profiles. To some extent, this has allowed some liberal senators to champion progressive causes, drawing greater attention to the upper house as a source of potential innovation. And yet the composition of the Senate, and the power retained over committees by its most senior members, gives it a more conservative cast than the House.

The unity that exists within parties, and particularly within the Democrats, is highly contingent on circumstances and on the particular issues at stake. When the majority party faces huge budget deficits constraining its room for maneuver, greater leadership control can be exercised over members in all policy areas dealing with budgeting and appropriations, and that factor is one of the contributors to greater party unity throughout the late 1980s and into the 1990s.[6] Even so, party leaders simply do not have the disciplinary powers they might once have had, and cannot easily oblige recalcitrant members to vote in ways that conflict with personal beliefs or home district pressure, especially in the Senate.[7]

There can be particular difficulty in whipping votes in favor of controversial positions, with legislators more concerned than ever about what issues might be used successfully against them the next time around.[8] On certain high profile issues, they become extremely sensitive to indications of district opinion, no matter how orchestrated the signals. Some policy positions, such as the pro-choice view on abortion, have shed enough of the "controversial" tag that declaring clear positions is more possible, but pro-gay positions in particular seem now firmly in the kind of category that legislators wish to avoid.

Elected politicians in parliamentary systems, to be sure, are seldom noteworthy for their courage on gay-related issues. In Canada and Britain, too, such matters are often among the rare questions that are left to "free" votes (without the imposition of formal party discipline), leaving legislators more exposed. Nevertheless, individual politicians in such systems are less on their own than their congressional counterparts in defending themselves against attack, and negative campaigning directed at individuals is less pervasive. In such systems, too, the electoral fate and career ascendance of a member of the legislature can be shaped substantially by the favor curried with party leaders (even highly unpopular ones), in a way that has virtually no parallel in the contemporary American system. Party leaders therefore have more unspoken leverage over legislative compatriots, even in the rare cases of free votes.

The U.S. system proliferates the sites from which both progressive and regressive initiatives can emerge. If favorable openings are thereby provided, the work required to ensure success is monumental and the outcomes almost invariably unpredictable. Initiatives that frontally attack or indirectly undermine progress already made are given just as many opportunities to come forward, often without warning. This confronts proponents of progressive change with a task more daunting than that faced by activists in virtually any other political system, while also creating more openings for political intervention.

SENATORIAL LEVERAGE

During the primary season and the general campaign leading up to the 1992 election, Bill Clinton had committed himself unequivocally to lifting the ban on gays in the military, with little in the way of opposition publicly voiced or mobilized against the pledge. Because the promise seemed to lie within the realm of presidential prerogative, expectations were high that it could be fulfilled quickly, even in the face of objections.

In fact, the initiative stayed only momentarily in the hands of the victorious Clinton. Even before the January inauguration, congressional opponents moved into a position to check presidential movement on the issue, and they soon appeared able to engineer a checkmate. The Democratic chair of the Senate Armed Forces Committee was the central player opposing a lifting of the ban; this position was emboldened and strengthened by the Republicans' willingness to play aggressive antigay politics, by the readiness of the religious right and veterans groups to mobilize grassroots opposition, and by the active collusion of antigay elements in the military hierarchy.

Congress had formal authority in the establishment of rules for the military and the authorization of expenditures. Although rulemaking had more often than not been delegated to the President, it did provide a formal means by which presidential action could be counteracted. The Uniform Code of Military Justice (UCMJ) is an embodiment of Congressional prerogative, and the fact that it retains a sodomy provision prohibiting anal and oral sex ensured that Congressional opponents of lifting the ban on gays would have a critical legislative lever. The need for congressional approval to change the UCMJ meant that even a forthright executive order lifting the ban would leave intact a comprehensive prohibition on lesbian and gay sexual contact.

Although the House has always had the power to exercise leverage over military issues because of its powerful role in appropriations politics, the Senate has also established influence over the broader range of issues related to foreign and defense matters. In that chamber, opponents could benefit from the greater ease of deviating from party lines, and the wider openings for amendment provided by laxer procedural rules.[9] They could also benefit from the considerable media exposure available to Senators, which is not nearly as available to the more numerous members of the House.

Sam Nunn's Aces

The chair of the Armed Service Committee was in a particularly strategic position, in part because of the power still held by committee chairs in the Senate. (Such power has been considerable in the House, but more circumscribed by caucus, by party leadership, and by subcommittee prerogative.) The Senate's sheer burden of legislative work makes challenges particularly difficult to mount from outside the membership of a particular committee.

In the Senate as a whole, and within his committee, Sam Nunn could count on majority support for his views. He could rely, first, on all but a few southern Democrats. Even if the North-South split had been tempered in recent years, it was still pronounced and as likely to surface on either gay related or defense related issues as any (see Table 1).[10] Nunn's lead on a number of issues was strengthened beyond southerners by perceptions of him as moderate—not fanatically right wing or strongly tied to conservative Christian forces. Although this hardly counts as progressive, Nunn had the most liberal voting record on gay-related issues of any of the southern Democratic Senators prior to the ban issue.[11] Some even suggested that his opposition made it easier for others to oppose the lifting of the ban without fear of being branded extreme.

There were, of course, reliable supporters of pro-gay positions in the Senate, including the four women Democrats. But few were vocal enough or strategically positioned at the outset to challenge Nunn's leading position. Even if Democrats on the Armed Services Committee were in the end about evenly divided on the ban, only Senator Ted Kennedy acquired significant profile in registering opposition to Nunn's drive. Without a substantial chance of winning the day in votes, few Senators were willing to carve out a high profile on a controversial issue such as this.

Nunn's influence in the Armed Services Committee was especially secure, since those who served on it were likely to be disproportionately supportive of the military, thus making lopsided majorities in favor of relatively conservative positions easier to obtain than they would be within most other committees. Leverage was also increased by cozy links to the military hierarchy unrivalled in Congress. Before the election, as chair of the House Armed Services Committee, Les Aspin was the closest competitor, but the military hierarchy itself had been wary of Aspin, in part presumably because he was not a sufficiently uncritical cheerleader.

Even as Secretary of Defence, Aspin could be outmaneuvered by Nunn. The military was concerned about Aspin's interventionist style of policymaking and an agenda that could well result in significant budget cuts.[12] The fact that, whatever his personal views, Aspin might be the instrument of President Clinton's intention to end the ban on lesbians and gays in the military intensified the readiness of military officers to work closely with Nunn in challenging executive authority.

Executive Vulnerability

The new President's vulnerability on military issues further strengthened Nunn's hand. During the election, Clinton's opponents, and much of the press corps, had emphasized his mild-mannered and otherwise unremarkable opposition to the American conduct of the Vietnam War, and his avoidance of the draft. The very fact that he had not served in the military was oddly translated into a challenge to his capacity to make reasoned decisions about military issues.

Clinton's authority was always more challengeable than that of most presidents because of the particular circumstances of his election. It was easy enough for other politicians and observers to conclude that Clinton's election had been a negative vote—a rejection of George Bush. The entry of a substantial third party candidacy also robbed the victor of the symbolic power of support by more than half of the electorate—a source of legitimacy more important in a system with a separate executive election than in parliamentary systems in which minority voter support is more common. As one insider has suggested, "Remember this guy's a 43% President—always has been."[13]

The early days after the 1992 election seemed to reinforce the room for maneuver among Congressional Democrats wishing to dissent. Clinton's reputation in Arkansas had been as a politician eager to please, and initial meetings with members of Congress reflected a relatively passive style reflective of that temperament.[14] Subsequent voting patterns revealed what some insiders sensed from the beginning—that Democratic Senators and House members would have no particular difficulty voting against the President.

Senator Nunn and other opponents of lifting the ban had an added advantage in the new President's campaign message of focusing attention on economic issues. Once it became clear that there were more difficulties in giving effect to Clinton's promise on the ban than had been anticipated, the White House was strongly motivated to distance itself from the issue.[15] To have engaged in the kind of presidential arm-twisting that might have made a difference would, in their view, have made them even more vulnerable than they already were to charges of being sidetracked.

Republicans Playing the Antigay Card

The hands of Democratic opponents of Clinton's plans on the ban were greatly strengthened by Republican antipathy to virtually all gay-related causes. The near unanimity of that party's opposition, and their commitment to maintaining the existing ban intact, helped Nunn to appear a moderate on the issue, thereby building his strength among Democratic colleagues.[16]

It was no surprise that Nunn could count on Republican alliances in opposing the President. What was something of a surprise to the White House and to others working to sustain Clinton's promise was the ferocity of the Republican onslaught.[17] The gay bashing of the party's August convention, after all, had seemed to do more harm than good, and the Bush campaign avoided the military ban issue altogether.[18]

Republicans like Robert Dole and Newt Gingrich, in the leadership of both the Senate and the House, were probably not personally uncomfortable around lesbians and gays. But what one activist said about Gingrich could easily be said of the two of them:

I've never found Gingrich to be an ideological homophobe. I think Gingrich is a political homophobe, and I think if he sees it to be in his political benefit to gay bash he will, and if he sees it not to be in his political benefit to gay bash he won't.[19] As Marvin Liebman says about them, "Gays and lesbians really don't matter: we're out of the rhetoric; if we begin to matter, they'll not be with us but against us—they will turn against us in a second."[20]

There were warning signs as early as November 15th, 1992. On that day Sam Nunn voiced his opposition to lifting the ban on national television, and Senate Republican leader Robert Dole expressed similar views on another of the Sunday television news shows, flagging his party's readiness to "pounce on the issue."[21] Another sign came on December 9th, when the Republican Research Committee (the research arm of the House Republican Conference) sponsored a meeting on gays in the military, providing a forum for strategic thinking about responding to the issue from Congress.[22] By this time it was becoming clear that there would be only a few Republicans who could resist the temptation of playing on what they perceived to be Clinton weakness on military issues, and using an issue with which they could tag the new President as "liberal."

Late in January, once the Clinton strategy on the military issue was clear, Senate Republican leaders and Armed Services Committee members met to plan their own tactics.[23] There was already talk of them encoding the ban by tacking it onto the much-sought-after Family Leave Bill or an appropriations bill needed to pay for the military's Somali operations. They were focusing their strategy on the Senate, where amendments were procedurally easier to introduce, and where the support of Sam Nunn could be counted on. Some were hesitant about focusing on social issues after an election dominated by concerns over the economy, and some were concerned about appearing to be gay bashing.[24] But no one was publicly dissenting on the side of supporting the Clinton proposal. The appearance of Republican unity was reinforced by the absence of dissenters on the House side. There may have been as many as twenty-five or thirty moderate Republicans who did not want the opposition to lifting the ban to go too far; there were perhaps ten or so with strong views. But in the words of one aide, "They certainly didn't want their names in the paper."[25]

Nunn, not thought by congressional observers to be a man of particular political courage, was therefore able to challenge his own party's President as forthrightly as he did because he held three crucial aces: the deference on military issues coming from his own Democratic colleagues, the alliance of all but a handful of Republicans, and the active collusion of the Joint Chiefs of Staff. By the end of January, he would be able to add a fourth ace: the capacity of right wing forces to mobilize grassroots opposition to Clinton's plan.

SAM NUNN AND THE SENATE SHOW TRIALS

Democratic Congressman Barney Frank, normally disinclined to attack members of his own party, was moved to comment after Nunn's first defiant Senate speech on the ban, "I don't think [Clinton] could have predicted that Sam Nunn would show more passion on behalf of discrimination than he's shown on any issue since he came to Congress."[26]

Nunn had more than enough motivation to take advantage of the room for maneuver provided by law and political circumstances. The relationship with the military was symbiotic, providing Nunn with valuable political leverage in Washington, ensuring him his share of spending benefits specific to his district, and creating for him a valuable national constituency of enlisted service members and veterans. Appearing strong on defense issues and conservative on social issues also provided a degree of protection against electoral challenge from right wing forces in his home state of Georgia.

But antigay personal beliefs were also important. His voting record and his response to activist pressure signalled his opposition to pro-gay positions on a number of fronts, and on two occasions, he had been unwilling to support gay Washington staffers when they faced difficulties with gaining the security clearances or the military cooperation they needed in order to serve the Senator.[27]

Nunn's preparedness to confront the President on the issue of the gay ban was thought by some observers to be partially motivated by his pique at not having been appointed to the cabinet, or resentment at having his own longer term presidential ambitions undercut by the success of a fellow southern Democrat.[28] A sense of thwarted ambition could well have played a role in provoking the Senator, although there can be no serious doubt that his strong views on gays in the military were rooted in other factors, and that other inducements to confront the President were sufficient to provoke him.

Seizing the Initiative

Sam Nunn had always seemed ready to confront Clinton directly and publicly about the ban. Six months before the election, he had bluntly warned Clinton in person that "the military isn't ready for it."[29] Appearing November 15th on "Face the Nation" (only days after the election), Nunn expressed his support for the existing ban and called on the President-elect to refer the issue to Congress so that he could hold committee hearings before a policy was formulated.[30]

By early January 1993, the White House and the office of the Defense Secretary began considering a "cooling off" period—an idea that was crystallized in a January 18th memo from Les Aspin to Clinton, leaked to the press soon after its delivery. During the six-month period, discharges or reassignments based on sexual orientation would cease, and in the meantime a draft executive order would be prepared by Aspen. That same memo indicated the weak position that Clinton was in on Capitol Hill, citing Senate majority leader George Mitchell as estimating no more than thirty secure votes. It also flagged the difficulties in circumventing the strategies likely to be used by opponents—for example, tagging a codified ban to a bill that the Administration badly wanted (like the Family Leave Bill).

During the week of January 25th, a firestorm of protest letters and phone calls swept Congress and the White House, mobilized by the religious right and veterans organizations. Only late in that week did calls in favor of lifting the ban begin to register in Washington offices, though never even close to the volume against. This was Nunn's fourth ace, emboldening Clinton opponents and intimidating a number of his supporters. Midway through this firestorm, on the 27th, Nunn voiced strong opposition to the Clinton commitment on the Senate floor, sending a volley across the bow of the administrative ship that, even at this stage, surprised many Democrats. If there had been any doubt up to this point that he would seize the initiative on the issue, there could no longer be a shred of it left.

By this time, Nunn had become a central player in negotiations between the White House and the Pentagon over how to proceed. There seemed no longer to be any disagreement about the value of a six-month delay, but considerable debate over the regime that would apply in the interim—the White House wanted a major shift, while Nunn joined Pentagon officers in pressing for as modest a shift as possible from the existing ban.[31] The Clinton announcement on January 29th signalled an important victory for Nunn and the Joint Chiefs, for it allowed commanders to continue processing new and existing discharge cases, though relegating those destined for "separation" to the limbo of "standby reserve" pending final determination of the policy issue. The only concession made to the White House was that recruits would no longer be routinely asked about their sexual orientation.[32]

Senate Hearings

With the Administration more shell-shocked than ever by the opposition to lifting the ban, the field was clear for Senator Nunn to work his mischief. He quickly set out to schedule hearings and manage them in such a way as to maximize their advantage, not only in the kinds of witnesses and the visuals that would be offered up to the media, but also in the manner in which they were organized. Proponents of lifting the ban were being constantly surprised by last-minute word on new or different witnesses, and their resources were therefore drawn in even more disproportionately to the Senate hearing process.[33] Nunn was also successfully framing the public debate in narrow military terms, with "unit cohesion" as the central issue.[34]

By the end of the first day of Committee hearings, on March 29th, it was clear that most members had formed their opinions, with enough Democrats opposed to lifting the ban to secure Nunn an overwhelming majority. Even at this early stage, Nunn was talking of the possibility of adopting permanently the six-month interim policy he had played so prominent a role in crafting, allowing lesbians and gays to serve as long as they didn't identify themselves as such. On the second day of hearings, on March 31st, military witnesses who began their testimony opposing the lifting of the ban seemed to fall into line behind the Nunn proposal.[35] In some quarters, "don't ask, don't tell" was being talked of as a compromise, though in fact it differed only fractionally from the status quo.

In President Clinton's own pronouncements, there was subtle preparation (perhaps unconsciously) for compromise in the distinctions being emphasized between "status" and "conduct."[36] The distinction was to some extent meant to respond to opposition arguments that stereotyped lesbian and gay existence as focused only on sexual activity, which was in turn characterized as predatory and unconstrainable. The President's assurances that he was talking only of an end to discrimination based on "status," that he favored the maintenance of a strict code of conduct, and that he had no intention of proposing any changes in the military's existing codes, seemed to be moving away from his original pledge. Before long, Nunn was able to then cite such statements as suggesting agreement between the two views.[37]

The Senate Armed Service Committee held its second round of hearings at the end of April, retaining its initiative on the issue and monopolizing the public spotlight. Once again, witnesses were chosen to undercut attempts to lift the ban entirely, among them the Desert Storm deputy commander Lt. General Calvin Waller, an African American called to refute the analogy between antigay and antiblack discrimination. Senator Ted Kennedy tried to challenge the way in which the hearings had been stacked, but in a recorded vote only Kennedy opposed the chair. And once again, the signs of an emergent compromise were clear—a compromise that would remove routine questioning about homosexuality at the point of recruitment, but characterize even the declaration of being gay as inappropriate conduct leading to dismissal.[38]

Then, on May 10th, the Committee embarked on the first of its field hearings, staging a photo opportunity tour of a submarine to provide a closeup view of the most tightly packed environment in the military, complete with bunked sailors asked to react on camera to the prospect of openly gay colleagues.[39] The media lapped it up, and the story received precisely the coverage that was intended by its stage managers. The ground was now slipping even more rapidly than it had been since late January.

In a May 11th hearing back in Washington, the Armed Services Committee heard testimony from General Norman Schwartzkopf. The "hero of the Persian Gulf War" talked of the threat to military discipline and morale posed by a lifting of the ban, though he endorsed the Nunn proposal under questioning and asserted that "declared" homosexuals were the problem.[40] Dramatic testimony was heard the same day from a Marine colonel who acknowledged that he had a gay son but justified the ban out of fear for the safety of gays in the military, and who in the process helped secure the fiction that opposition to the presidential initiative was unhomophobic.

Even Senators on record as favoring a lifting of the ban were now talking only about allowing lesbian and gay servicemembers to "discreetly acknowledge their sexual orientation," while prohibiting overt or disruptive activity.[41] Nunn made clear throughout the month of May that he was immovable on the subject, citing the military's sodomy law as prohibiting homosexual activity on or off base.

HOUSE ALLIES AND THE COMPROMISE IMPERATIVE

The original Clinton proposal was always expected to find more support in the House than in the Senate, in part because the chamber's rules allow the majority leadership more control over debate and amendments, and in part because there were more outspoken supporters. Openly gay Representative Gerry Studds had begun taking on the issue years before, in 1989 publicizing a Pentagon report that undermined the rationale of excluding lesbians and gays as security risks. In 1991, then-House Representative Barbara Boxer (later elected to the Senate) responded to the increased visibility of lesbian and gay military personnel prepared to challenge the existing policy by proposing a nonbinding resolution urging the President to lift the ban.[42]

In May 1992, Armed Forces Committee member Patricia Schroeder moved more aggressively towards legislatively forcing the executive's hand, introducing the Military Freedom Bill. Within a few weeks sixty House members had signed on as cosponsors, with Schroeder herself sensing, perhaps naively, a "reservoir of good feelings on this issue" among her colleagues.[43] There was even talk of enough congressional support to attach an amendment to the Defense Authorization Bill, awkward even for a Republican President to veto. Hearings were being talked about in positive terms as a means by which the issue could be aired.

The large wave of newly elected House members following the 1992 election promised even more support for pro-gay initiatives, not least because of a sharp increase in women (from 29 to 48) and blacks (from 26 to 39).[44] Committee reassignments in the new Congress also placed into the chair of the Armed Services Committee a strong supporter of Clinton's promise to lift the gay ban. Ron Dellums was an African American highly respected by his Democratic colleagues, and himself a former Marine. This gave him some important advantages in countering Senator Nunn's headlong drive to undercut any attempt to lift or substantially modify the ban, even though he lacked most of the aces that Nunn was able to play.

Dellums had wanted to launch his own committee hearings in March, in part to counteract the bias he knew would shape the Senate hearings. He was persuaded to delay by activists who were themselves not advanced enough in their own campaign to be prepared for a second set of hearings, and by supporters in the White House and Congress who feared that earlier hearings would provide House Republicans an opportunity to force an early vote on the ban issue.[45] Even if Dellums' view had prevailed, he would have had difficulty attracting as much limelight as Nunn on the Senate side (the much higher public profiles of Senators invariably gave them an advantage over House members in attracting media attention). In addition, Dellums, long a critic of the military, would never have been able to benefit from the kind of assistance that Nunn received from the military hierarchy itself—assistance that was crucial in developing and maintaining a high media profile.

Dellums was also hampered from the beginning by clear indications that he did not have support for his position among anything close to a majority of his committee. One of his many Democratic opponents on the issue was Ike Skelton, strategically located in the chair of the Subcommittee on Personnel. Dellums was disinclined to the sort of manipulativeness that characterized his Senate counterpart's moves on this issue, but even if he had been so inclined, he simply did not have the leverage or support that Sam Nunn did in the Senate.

Two days of full committee hearings finally began on May 4th, with Personnel Subcommittee hearings to be held on questions of implementation at a later date. By early May, there seemed no way to deflect attention from the Nunn hearings, so artfully constructed to grab headlines. The media paid only scant attention to the House Armed Services Committee, and whatever positive effect they might have had was swamped a few days later by the media shots of concerned Senators and sailors in a cramped submarine.

By this time, too, Dellums, Schroeder, Studds, and their allies faced a groundswell of resentment from their House colleagues about having to deal with the issue at all. Even before the inauguration of Senator Nunn's hearings, most members of the House (and probably the Senate) were driven mostly by a desire to be rid of the issue—to have it go away in whatever form would allow it to go away. Democratic members of Congress, besieged since the end of January and constantly asked to comment on the issue by constituents and their local press, were entreating Dellums to end the debate. This was a view for which there was sympathy in the Democratic leadership, which saw the gays in the military issue as throwing off the whole legislative agenda. By then, many Republicans shared this view, so there was probably a majority of the whole House and certainly a majority of the Armed Services Committee indicating frustration with the continued focus on the issue.

The Barney Frank Compromise

At the time that the military issue was being debated, Barney Frank was the only openly gay member of Congress apart from Gerry Studds. Frank had not devoted the attention to the ban that Studds and his aides had, but had developed a higher profile on other gay-related issues both in Congress and the gay media, and was widely thought to be the brightest member of the House and one of its most effective legislators.

On May 13th, in a general and speculative way (and more pointedly on the 18th), Barney Frank began talking of compromise on lifting the military ban.[46] He developed a "don't ask, don't tell, don't listen, don't investigate" proposal that imagined lesbians and gays being open about their sexual orientation while off duty and off base, but not while on duty. The compromise proposal was motivated primarily by Frank's conclusion that there were simply not enough votes in Congress to sustain the President's commitment for lifting the ban, and that support for a highly unfavorable Nunn policy of "don't ask, don't tell" was congealing fast both in Congress and elsewhere. That, Frank claimed, was "inviting a situation in which the ban in its most repressive and restrictive and unfair form is not only continued but written into law, so we'd be worse off than we were before."[47]

In making the move that he did, Frank was reflecting the ethos of the institution he worked in and with:

> Being able to effect a compromise—that's a basic rule with this place. I can say, "By the way, my position is [that] only a total lifting of the ban is acceptable; now let me negotiate a compromise." Nobody around here is stupid enough to let you do that. It's like poker—if you haven't got the stakes, stay out of the game. I saw a compromise coming, and I saw that compromise being negotiated without any of us. You can't be part of the compromise if you are not willing to compromise.[48]

Soon afterwards, with some sadness in his voice, one Capitol Hill staffer described the ethos of Congress in terms that sustain Frank's view of the indispensability and the ubiquity of compromise:

> [Frank's] perspective would be [that] it is more fair to us than the way it is now. It may not be what we are entitled to; it may not be what should happen; but he believes that it is as good as we'll get. So that is the way we look at things around here. We try to get two million dollars for this project and someone says, "we can't give you two million, but we will give you a million if you do this." The way he thinks about it is, "my goal is to get rid of this blatantly discriminatory practice, period. If that isn't possible, then I want to improve the quality of life for lesbians and gays as much as I possibly can, even if it is on the surface hypocritical and unfair and contradictory."[49]

Frank pushed the logic behind presenting a compromise further, claiming that a preparedness to participate in a process of compromise on this issue provides political strength down the road.

> Because of this, I am in a position to help get more. It is one thing to have a compromise done to you over your screaming objections; it is another if you help participate. That is why I think we are going to get out of this not just some gains for gays in the military but very

significant victories with regard to security permits and discrimination against gay people.[50]

To his critics, Frank was providing cover for a President too willing to abandon principles. To someone like Frank, having to constantly negotiate gains on an array of issues, and in need of allies in the White House as well as on Capitol Hill, helping the President was a normal part of the job. To fail in that, or even more obviously to criticize the President too strongly, would risk burning bridges vital to the longer road ahead. In that sense, Frank was acting in a partisan fashion, but in a way that he would freely acknowledge. It was his view that whatever the opposition to gay rights in the Democratic Party, the support for them was almost non-existent in the Republican Party. In the long run, and the short run, his loyalty was strategically important.

Frank also believed that the particular bargain he was proposing was an inherently unstable one because of its potential limits on free speech, and could well prepare the ground for future advances in the courts or in administrative regulations. (The litigation record on gay rights issues had been mixed, but most likely to elicit favorable decisions when based on the First Amendment right to free speech.)

Frank's talk of compromise immediately created a gulf with the activist groups with which he had so often worked closely, as well as with some of the Capitol Hill allies who had worked on the issue. Frank himself had grown impatient with activist groups:

> I begged them to get a letter-writing campaign going. . . . The groups were making a fundamental error. They thought that having a president on your side means you've won. Having the president on your side is a necessary condition, but it's not a sufficient condition. I told the groups, "You're deciding what to have for desert when we haven't even killed the chickens for dinner yet."
>
> CMS [Campaign for Military Service] kept saying, "We have until July 15," and I said, "No we don't." Members of Congress don't wait until the week before a vote to lock in their positions. They had to figure out their positions right away to answer the hundreds of letters they were getting. A majority had locked in against us in January. You can't turn that around later.[51]

Frank's impatience peaked during the gay rights March on Washington in late April, an event that had absorbed so much activist energy in the weeks before but that had produced little in the way of letters to and visits with members of Congress.

> The March was an important cultural event; it was an important self-actualizing event; but it had no short term political impact for us. So by May I was very discouraged about our inability to make the transition from a marginal to a mainstream political group. And that is the

problem when people have the preference for the tactics of the margins—sit-ins, demonstrations. When is the last time the NRA had a sit-in, or a demonstration, or a shoot-in? They don't do that. Who is more influential?[52]

The talk of compromise provoked all but universal criticism from activist groups.[53] Many called the proposal a sellout for encoding the closet and offering solace to cowardly Democrats. Some activists and Capitol Hill insiders, including Gerry Studds, focused more on what they argued was precipitous timing and lack of consultation.[54]

Not surprisingly, the White House reacted with delight at the help they had been given, and Clinton himself phoned Frank to express his gratitude. The Administration had long abandoned the hope of lifting the ban entirely, but had hesitated in clearly stating a compromise:

> The White House was concerned with the political fallout of a unified, national gay and lesbian community in all of its manifestations —electoral, political, grassroots—denouncing, hating, condemning the White House. Barney Frank pulled the middle out of that unified front and made it seem like the reasonable, sensible, politically astute gays (i.e., himself and all others who thought like him) could understand the compromise based on political reality.[55]

For the administration, the organized community became irrelevant, with the only significant spectrum of opinion remaining being that between Barney Frank on the left and Sam Nunn on the right. Within ten days administration officials were signalling the President's willingness to compromise on the issue, in ways that seemed to reflect the Frank version of "don't ask, don't tell."[56]

But at the same time there were indications of further slippage. On May 27th, President Clinton talked of being very close to a compromise that would address the "legitimate concern" that "our country does not appear to be endorsing a gay lifestyle."[57] Sam Nunn seized on that, and on the President's regular references to imposing strict rules on conduct, to assert that Clinton was now closer to his own views than to Frank's, at the same time flatly rejecting the possibility of service personnel publicly acknowledging their homosexuality.[58]

In a rearguard action given very little publicity, key lesbian/gay activist groups had narrowed their core demands to three in June: no discharges based on status, the protection of private speech, and the equitable application of sodomy provisions to allow private off-base consensual sexual conduct. The activists still believed in the possibility of attaining those objectives, and in some respects they were reinforced in that belief by White House representatives persistently talking of the issue being in flux, and repeating the president's objective that "status alone should not disqualify people from serving."[59] Hope for movement seemed to be kept alive in mid-June, when even the conservative *Washington Times* reported a survey showing that 143

House members favored lifting the ban, with 81 more still undecided.[60] The same survey showed an unfavorable shift in the Senate from a poll earlier in the year, but still with 32 opposing the ban and 28 undecided. Gay activist polling suggested the possibility of a progressive shift if accompanied by clear Presidential leadership.[61]

But the number count on the side of lifting the ban was soft, and the polling misleading. By late June, a letter circulated by pro-gay members of the House calling on the President to lift the ban garnered only 69 signatures, some of them reluctant.[62] More than ever, Democrats in Congress were resentful at being forced to solve what they perceived to be the President's problem, and "appalled" at the story returning once again to the front pages.[63] It seemed increasingly that the particular form of the compromise mattered less than that the contentious and difficult issue was moved off the agenda.

ENCODING THE NUNN BAN

By June 22nd, there was no longer any serious question about Nunn's victory. Les Aspin was reported as supporting an alternative closely resembling the Senator's version of "don't ask, don't tell"—one asserting that sexual orientation (meaning, of course, only homosexual orientation) was a personal and private matter, and that homosexual conduct was inconsistent with high standards of combat effectiveness. At the same time, incredibly, White House officials were indicating that the option favored by the Defense Secretary was "not necessarily incompatible" with Clinton's pledge to lift the ban on gays in the military.[64]

In July (in particular in a Senate speech on the 16th) Nunn made clear his intention to proceed with codification whatever the President announced at the expiration of his six-month deadline, using as a vehicle the almost-unvetoable Defense Authorization Bill. Ike Skelton, chair of the House subcommittee on military personnel, had even tried to schedule a vote on the matter at the end of June, and made clear his intention to try again should a Presidential announcement deviate even in small detail from his (and the military's) wishes.

On July 19th, Clinton announced a policy that largely matched the Nunn view, eliciting open expressions of disappointment from allies on Capitol Hill, including Barney Frank. They had been lobbying hard against the most restrictive proposals coming out of the Pentagon, in part on the basis of defending the President's commitments. They were now faced with a policy declaration that bought in almost entirely to the military's preferences, but adopted by Clinton as an "honorable compromise" and characterized as a "substantial advance" over the previous policy. Proponents of lifting the ban were now on the other side of the fence from Clinton.

On July 23rd, the Senate Armed Services Committee voted 17 to 5 in favor of the Nunn amendment (only Democrats voting against, including Senators Kennedy and Robb but not Glenn). The amendment included a statement on the incompatibility of homosexual conduct with military service; it expressly permitted the reinstatement of questioning of recruits about sexual orientation; it provided no illustrations of off-base conduct that might be permitted; and it omitted the Clinton policy's stated objective of enforcing sodomy laws equally for heterosexuals and homosexuals—all of this using language carefully crafted to immunize the new policy as much as possible from judicial challenge.[65] The Nunn amendment was far more restrictive than Clinton's already restrictive version announced only days before, and was enough to please even some of Congress's most conservative members.[66] The utterly fatigued White House immediately signalled its approval, having already acquiesced to the principle of encoding.[67]

At about this time, Rep. Ike Skelton and his House Armed Services Committee allies were persuaded to follow the Nunn lead that had been so unassailably established from January, by incorporating the Senate Armed Services Committee wording into the House version of the Defense bill. So strongly had the pendulum swung against Clinton that some of the committee members that had worked alongside Skelton in opposing any lifting of the ban were wary of Nunn having talked too much to the President and having gone "soft" on the issue as a result. They were convinced to adopt the language that Nunn had developed on the grounds that it was basically a reversion to the old policy, in some respects even tougher and more defendable in court. In any event, using the language in the House version would avoid forcing the issue to a Senate-House Conference Committee. On July 27th, Ron Dellums proposed an amendment lifting the ban altogether but lost 12 to 43. (Only one Republican supported Dellums; twenty-two Democrats— mostly from southern and border states—opposed him.)

On September 9th, the Senate as a whole voted 63-33 to codify the Nunn policy on gays in the military, after rejecting a pro-gay amendment proposed by Senator Barbara Boxer. Thirty of the thirty-three votes for the Boxer amendment came from Democrats, but twenty-five Democrats (including Majority Leader Mitchell) sided with Nunn.[68] The division between southern Democrats (7 percent voting with Boxer) and the rest of the caucus (69 percent voting "yes") was stark, even more than among other gay-related votes that year (see Table 1).

On September 28th, the House adopted the Nunn language by a vote of 301 to 134 (Democrats voting 140 to 121, Republicans 12 to 161). There had been votes on two amendments, one to reinstate the pre-Clinton ban, and another to delete references to the ban in the bill in order to allow presidential discretion (formally proposed by Rep. Martin Meehan).[69] By this time, Democrats were sufficiently fed up with the issue that even a recorded vote was a troublesome imposition.[70] Even some of the clear-cut supporters of lifting the ban were discontent. As one aide put it:

> It makes little sense, legislatively, to force members to walk the plank when the vote itself will have no real life consequences—when you know it's a losing vote. The general wisdom is "don't put your friends through that; don't put them in a situation where they have to prove their loyalty to you in a manner which will put them in jeopardy back home."[71]

Table 1
Congressional Voting on Military Ban and All Lesbian/Gay Related Issues, 1993

	#S		%Vote on Ban*		%+Votes on >50% of Qs		%+Votes on 100% of Qs		Average Scorecard Vote	
	Dem	Rep	Dem	Rep	Dem	Rep	Dem	Rep	Dem	Rep
SENATE										
South	14	12	7%	0%	86%	0%	7%	0%	62%	22%
MdWst	15	9	60	0	93	22	33	0	89	37
West	11	15	73	0	100	20	45	0	88	37
NE	16	8	75	38	94	50	63	0	90	60
Total non-So.	42	32	69	9	95	31	43	0	87	43
Total	56	44	54	7	95	23	34	0	81	37
HOUSE										
South **	85	53	31%	0%	40%	0%	15%	0%	45	2%
MdWst	61	43	61	7	57	5	16	0	60	11
West	55	38	91	5	96	3	42	0	86	9
NE	59	42	73	14	78	12	34	0	75	27
Total non-So.***	179	123	74	9	77	7	31	0	73	16
Total ***	264	176	60	6	65	5	26	0	64	12

Source: Human Rights Campaign Fund, "Votes of the 103rd Congress, 1st Session."

Notes: Senate votes comprise: Feb. 4 procedural vote to block entrenching existing military ban; Feb. 18 vote to codify prohibition on immigration of HIV+ individuals; Feb. 18 vote on National Institutes of Health Re-authorization that included AIDS initiatives; May 24 confirmation of nomination of Roberta Achtenberg as Ass't Sec'y for Fair Housing; July 27 vote to allow D.C. to implement domestic partnership registration; Sept. 7 confirmation of nomination of Joycelyn Elders as Surgeon General; Sept. 9 vote on Barbara Boxer amendment to prevent codification of "don't ask, don't tell"; Nov. 4 vote on Dianne Feinstein amendment to increase penalties for hate crimes; Nov. 16 vote on bill penalizing physical obstruction to abortion clinics.

House votes comprise: Feb. 4 procedural vote to block entrenching existing military ban; Mar. 11 vote on Sam Johnson amendment to defund a phone HIV counselling program; Mar. 11 procedural motion agreeing with Senate amendment on immigration of HIV+ individuals; June 30 vote on Henry Hyde amendment to prohibit federal funds being spent on abortion; June 30 vote on Ernest Istook amendment prohibiting D.C. spending money on domestic partnership registration; Sept. 28 vote on Martin Meehan amendment to prevent codification of "don't ask, don't tell"; Sept. 28 vote on Duncan Hunter amendment requiring military to ask recruits about homosexuality.

*Refers to votes on Boxer amendment in Senate and Meehan amendment in House.

**16% of the 67 white southern Democrats, and 88% of the blacks from the region, voted "yes" on the Meehan amendment. In the Congressional Black Caucus overall, 87% voted "yes." (David A. Bositis, *The Congressional Black Caucus in the 103rd Congress* [Washington, D.C.: Joint Center for Political and Economic Studies, 1994]).

***Totals include four House members not included in regions, from American Samoa, Guam, Puerto Rico, and Virgin Islands.

In the House, the regional differences so evident in the upper house were also present, though tempered by the recent growth of black representation from the south. Only 16 percent of white southern Democrats supported the Meehan amendment, while 74 percent of the non-southern Democrats did (see Table 1). Southern black Democrats voted 88 percent with Meehan, and 87 percent of the Congressional Black Caucus as a whole voted "yes."[72]

On November 17th, the budget bill to which the amendment was attached was finally sent to the President for signature, without ceremony. By then regulations had been issued, with some modest signs of pulling back from the worst that could have emerged from the Nunn language. Some on Capitol Hill even ventured to say that gays in the military are "much, much better off" in comparison to the worst case potential, even as the first reports coming in about the new policy being misused by homophobic commanders cast doubt on such optimism.[73]

BUTTRESSES TO CONGRESSIONAL OPPOSITION
Sam Nunn and his allies had substantial advantages over the new President even when the policy preferences and prejudices of members of Congress are considered in isolation from other factors. Their advantage was buttressed, as has already been made evident, by forces beyond Capitol Hill—some of them of a peculiarly American cast.

Legal Framework
There were aspects of the existing state of law that strengthened the hand of those who opposed lifting the ban. The formal criminalization of consensual same-sex activity in more than twenty states has long been a brake on progress at other fronts. In addition, the sodomy provisions of the congressionally dependent military justice code were always a barrier to full legal equality in the armed forces, and delimited even Clinton's early proposals for lifting the ban. From the beginning of the debate, in fact, the President's inability to change those provisions justified a particularly discriminatory differentiation between status and conduct—one that reinforced widespread double standards about closeting sexuality. Apart from the legal barriers it provided to enacting protections against discrimination, this statutory web contributed to the perception of lesbian and gay sexuality as sordid and quasi-criminal.

Constitutional guarantees of equality were not strong counterweights. There had been successful litigation on behalf of lesbians and gays seeking equal rights protections under the 14th Amendment, but appellate courts had rarely moved to scrutinize antigay discrimination with the same care as discrimination on racial or gender grounds. Gay-related litigation in cases strengthened by free speech arguments was more likely to be successful, but litigation based on privacy grounds had provided mixed results. Higher courts were particularly reluctant to challenge military discretion or executive prerogative in such areas even if a number of the legal challenges to the pre-Clinton ban had been successful in their early rounds.[74]

The Canadian case is a clear contrast. Consensual same-sex activity among adults was decriminalized by the federal government (with exclusive jurisdiction over criminal law) in 1969. And unlike Britain, no exception was made to retain sodomy provisions for the military. In addition, the Charter of Rights and Freedoms enacted in 1982 contained equality provisions that were more flexible and comprehensive than those in the American Bill of Rights. Although sexual orientation was not explicitly included in a list of grounds for which discrimination was prohibited, the general language of the equal rights guarantee was soon widely believed to encompass grounds such as that. Court decisions, including one rendered by the Supreme Court in May 1995, have since confirmed a growing judicial consensus that antigay discrimination is implicitly covered by the Charter[75] (even if some disturbing room has been created for exceptions to that coverage). Sexual orientation is also explicitly included in the human rights codes of most of the Canadian provinces.

The Canadian military had long resisted openly admitting lesbians and gays to the forces, using arguments strikingly similar to those used in the U.S. military. Their resistance had appeared to be weakening in the early 1990s as even Conservative governments promised to end discrimination against gays and lesbians (without following through). What resistance remained finally collapsed in October 1992 on the brink of a court case that they realized they were going to lose on constitutional grounds.

The ban on gays in the British armed forces is less challengeable than the Canadian ban was on legal or constitutional grounds, and as in other countries there is a strong web of laws that presume—and therefore enforce —heterosexuality. The legal challenges now being mounted to the military ban also confront a deep seated judicial reluctance to challenge the British tradition of parliamentary supremacy. But the fact that most European countries have no such ban strengthens challenges to it, and increases the possibility of successfully appealing to the European Court of Human Rights.[76] Though bitterly opposed to change, some military leaders agree with one of the two judges in a 1995 decision upholding the ban that the policy might not survive an appeal at the European level. In the written decision for that case, Lord Justice Brown was moved to comment further that

. . . the tide of history is against the Defence Ministry. Prejudices are breaking down; old barriers are being removed. It seems to me improbable, whatever this court may say, that the existing policy can survive much longer.[77]

Military Opposition

The opposition of the U.S. military to lifting the gay ban was an enormously powerful impediment to change. Here too there are striking contrasts with the Canadian case, and with most other countries in the industrialized world. Its power to resist rested on its relative size, its prominence in American economic and political life, and the kind of popular support that usually accompanies status as an imperial power— amplified by the war successfully waged against

Iraq. The public support for the military is in contrast to popular distrust of political authority—a distrust that has longer standing and currently a more cynical edge than in most other liberal democratic systems.[78] Many Americans (oddly, it seems) perceive the military as the only part of government that works.[79]

Opponents were able to build upon that support, and to define the issue as an exclusively military one of cohesion in the ranks. This they were able to do even though the objections of the military command routinely constituted an admission of its own prejudice of its readiness to acquiesce in the bigotry of enlisted personnel beneath it, and of the inability of military officers to effect compliance with unwelcome orders. With only modest exceptions, the strength and popularity of the military immunized it from criticism for the baser motives that provided the foundation for resistance to Clinton's commitment.

There had been precedents for military protests of civilian policy in the past, but none in the last half century against a president whose own legitimacy on military matters was as vulnerable to challenge as Clinton's. As a result, the opposition was more overt and more organized than any within memory, enough that even unnamed Pentagon sources wondered if it constituted insubordination. Military opposition to Clinton had been evident long before the November 1992 election. The chair of the Joint Chiefs of Staff had signalled his opposition to lifting the ban in the spring of that year, and in mid-June of that year a variety of military and veterans organizations affirmed their support for the existing policy.[80] Right after the election anonymous sources inside the Pentagon began talking to the press of "nearly wholesale resistance among military brass."[81] The opposition of General Colin Powell was particularly important, given his immense popularity in Washington and the rest of the country. His own African American background gave him particular influence in deflecting claims about discrimination, and in countering arguments about parallels to racial exclusion. It also immunized him to some extent from justifiable criticisms of personal prejudice.[82]

By January there were reports of senior officers copying and circulating "The Gay Agenda," a fanatically homophobic video prepared by Christian Right.[83] According to one Pentagon official, "The Marines are passing it out like popcorn," with the Marine Commandant one of those said to be most actively distributing it, even to some members of Congress.[84] Organized phone-ins were reported from some military bases, and dissenters from the gathering storm of orthodoxy were discouraged from giving voice to their views.[85] It was clear that military leaders were orchestrating a virtual campaign against the president, using command structures ideally suited to political mobilization.

The new Secretary of Defense, Les Aspin, was no match for the unified service chiefs. In any event, Aspin was not personally convinced of the wisdom of fully lifting the ban, and disinclined to expend political capital in the Pentagon by overly pressing the chiefs on the issue.[86] Aspin had acquired a relatively pro-gay reputation as a member of Congress, and his failure to provide more support and leadership as Defense Secretary caught some activists off guard.[87] Even if he had been more supportive, the military hierarchy was distrustful of him as well, and fully prepared to work with Congressional allies like Sam Nunn in order to undermine his authority.

By June the Joint Chiefs were virtually dictating terms to the Secretary of Defense, by the end of the month pointing with approval to his willingness to defer to military leaders on "social issues" such as this.[88] And according to some observers, Pentagon officials were leaking proposals emerging from negotiations over details in order to help secure their position against possible White House erosion. On June 25th, Aspin formally presented to the Joint Chiefs a proposal that differed only microscopically from the position they favored, and once again leaks signalled their unwillingness to be moved.[89]

There are few other liberal democratic political systems where the military has the sort of independent legitimacy accorded the U.S. armed forces. Superpower status and the size of the military establishment contribute to that standing, as does recurrent U.S. engagement in armed engagements abroad. Military figures like Colin Powell and Norman Schwartzkopf benefit from a kind of celebrity status that is rarely if ever accorded their counterparts in other countries.

In almost all other countries, military hierarchies also have few opportunities to effect end runs around executive authority. The extent of cabinet dominance over legislatures in Canada, Britain, and most of continental Europe precludes the kind of alliances used with congressional supporters in the United States. Military establishments in other countries are also smaller than the American, even on a per capita basis, with a lower political profile to match.

Mobilized "Public Opinion" and the Religious Right

Public opinion is more obsessively cited in Washington than in any other national capital, and indicators of public sentiment more closely scrutinized in explaining policy choices than anywhere else. Yet there are clear variations across issue areas in attentiveness to that opinion. On major economic issues that affect the climate of investment, for example, gauges of public sentiment are sporadically sought and modestly weighted. In the conduct of foreign relations and military policy in general, public opinion is either only casually considered or thought to accord wide latitude to policy makers. Gay-related issues are firmly lodged within that category of issues which provoke close attention to public opinion or mobilized opinion. In respect to attitudes both in the general public and among those people moved to communicate to Congress, opponents of Clinton's plan to lift the ban had considerable advantages.

Although survey evidence has indicated a large and slowly growing majority of Americans favoring equal rights for lesbians and gays, a clear majority also "disapprove" of homosexuality.[90] A 1988 electoral survey found that Americans felt more negatively toward lesbians and gays than toward any other social group asked about, including illegal aliens.[91] The moral disapproval is to some extent rooted in perceptions of religious doctrine, and also in persistent stereotypes about sexual predation and child molestation. The persistence of prejudice, combined with a widespread reluctance to talk about sexuality in general and sexual difference in particular, creates the potential for considerable volatility in public sentiment about specific issues. The relatively recent arrival of gay rights issues onto public agendas exaggerates that volatility, and creates room for protagonists in debate to shape public perceptions.

Public opinion surveys on the issue of gays in the military provide striking evidence of volatility. Polls taken between 1977 and 1991 showed an increase in public support for allowing gays to serve, from 51 percent to 69 percent, this at a time when the ban on their serving was total.[92] But by the time of the late January firestorm, one similarly worded poll found that support for gays being allowed to serve had fallen to 47 percent, and three others showed a slide down to the low 40s.[93]

A number of Capitol Hill insiders have talked of public opinion as a major problem for politicians sorting out the issue of the gay ban. Some emphasized that removing the gay ban was simply not a high priority for people in their districts.[94] What lay behind this sentiment is the belief that ardent support for gay rights was largely restricted to a small minority that was all but invisible in most parts of the country. This view was routinely accompanied by the belief that there was also deep seated popular antipathy to homosexuality. In other words, there were more opponents who cared about the issue than proponents.

The same judgment would once have been made about abortion, but politicians tend to see opinion as both more negative and more volatile on the subject of homosexuality. On abortion people had well-worked out positions, and politicians have in most cases been forced to publicly declare their positions. As an aide to a southern democrat argued:

This issue is more volatile, and stirs up more passions. . . . As recently as seven or eight years ago, no candidate wanted to talk about abortion, particularly on the more liberal side of the issue—well, on both sides really. . . . People want to know what side you're on. And so, you figure you're going to alienate some people, but you're going to have to take a stand or else you're going to please no one. And there has also been some shift in public opinion that makes it more profitable to say I'm for gun control or I'm for choice. But we haven't reached that point yet with gay rights. I think we may; I think public opinion is moving there.[95]

Many legislators, of course, use public opinion as a shield for their own prejudice or ignorance. In confronting sexual orientation issues, a number of gay positive politicians in Canada, Britain, and the United States itself have taken pains to explore the range of opinions in their constituencies, often uncovering strands of decency not evident in polling or in letters. What is different about the American case is the high likelihood that powerful antigay forces will actually use the issue electorally. The preparedness of the religious right to throw their extraordinary resources against pro-gay initiatives, and the readiness of Republican opponents to exploit antigay rhetoric, engenders great fear among most politicians in the middle ground, and many on the liberal side. These factors weigh much more heavily in the United States than in other political systems. Voter turnouts are lower than in any other liberal democracy in the industrialized world, for reasons that include the sheer number and complexity of decisions appearing on the ballot, the initiative required to appear on the voter registration lists, and the extent of cynicism about the political process. In that kind of institutional and attitudinal climate, the capacity of social movements and political organizations to mobilize letters and phone calls on particular issues comes to stand for the potential to mobilize voters at election time. In other words, even if mobilized opinion is widely recognized as distinct from public opinion, the former comes to stand as an electorally important representation of the latter, at least in some circumstances. Barney Frank talks about this:

> People's ability to organize mail is a pretty good marker for their ability to organize votes. The fact that one group is able to get thousands of people in your district to write you letters and make phone calls, and another group is not, is not irrelevant when it comes to who's going to mobilize people to vote in the primaries and the general election. . . . If you know these are people who are totally out of sympathy with the overwhelming majority of the public, that lessens their impact. But if you know that the public is divided—[what legislators attend to] is the public opinion that registers itself. I guess it's not public opinion, it's voter opinion, and it's what motivates most people.[96]

Of particular significance in strengthening the hands of conservative legislators in Washington was the active participation of the religious right—this too a distinctive feature of the American political landscape. Only in Catholic Europe have religious groups had a capacity for political mobilization that comes even close to that within the grasp of the U.S. Christian right. But even in countries like Italy, Austria, France, and Belgium, Roman Catholic political groups have long had to confront well-organized, explicitly anticlerical forces. In any event they have been weakened by declining religiosity (to levels below that in the United States), and by growing preparedness even on the part of believers to ignore the political and religious directives of the Catholic hierarchy.

The U.S. religious right is rooted in local churches and local preachers with considerable influence over their following, buttressed on some issues by the conservative leaders of the Roman Catholic hierarchy and by right-wing leaders of other religious faiths. The messages of the Protestant right are powerfully reinforced by religious media resources, fundraising capacities, and central political organizations without parallel in other countries. In other countries of the industrialized world, political mobilization by right-wing Protestant forces is not close to the scale of their American counterparts. Even in Canada, so much influenced by U.S. patterns and so widely tuned in to American media outlets, less than 10 percent of the population belong to the denominations that form the basis of the religious right, in contrast to between 25 percent and 40 percent in the United States.[97] Fundamentalist mobilizing can make a difference in Canada, but the language used to effect it is more likely than in the United States to be thought unacceptably extreme.[98]

The U.S. Christian right had been strengthened by its success in bridging religious and political differences during the Reagan and Bush years, spurred in part by the opportunities opened up within the Republican Party for the exercise of conservative political influence. Focusing on homosexuality assists in such bridging by creating a common enemy about which few would dissent. For an expanding conservative coalition, the prominence given the gay ban in the weeks after the election was "a bonanza for building organizations and raising money."[99]

The church-centered facilities and national media resources available to the religious right enabled it to generate the firestorm of protest against lifting the ban in the last week of January. For most of that week, the Congressional switchboard was handling more than five times its typical daily total of 80,000 calls, in some offices producing tallies that ran 100 to 1 against Clinton's plan. Those who had been around Capitol Hill for a number of years claimed that only a few other issues elicited reactions even close to the scale of this one. Even if most people on Capitol Hill recognized that there was considerable orchestration behind the waves of telephone calls and letters, the scale was a reminder of the potential electoral influence of the groups behind the campaign.

The leading organizations tended to be those firmly lodged in the extreme right, though they were strengthened and in some ways legitimized by the additional voices of otherwise moderate evangelical groups, some of which had harbored large numbers of Clinton supporters.[100] The campaigning by religious conservatives and moderates, in addition to that so feverishly engaged in by veterans groups, also stirred fears in the wider public enough to elicit a great deal of letter writing and telephoning by people perceived in Capitol Hill offices as average Americans.

Lawmakers are accustomed to organized efforts to derail controversial nominations and legislation, and interest groups certainly have weighed in on both the Baird nomination and lifting the gay ban. But many members have expressed surprise at the level of what one Senate aide termed "genuine, authentic, public outrage" from usually silent quarters.[101]

One congressional aide talked of the campaign's effectiveness in similar terms, highlighting the fact that it did not appear to be coordinated:

I think it was one of the most effective grassroots campaigns that have ever been run. I would say that what made it so effective was that it appeared not to be organized by an interest group or by a lobbying organization, because letters came and they were handwritten by people in their words—they weren't scripted, computer-driven letters or postcards.[102]

Because of the religious right's capacity to mobilize grassroots support with strong views on issues such as this, the pressure stands out in a city overflowing with lobbyists and with organizations claiming widespread and deep grassroots. Fundamentalist groups in particular have devoted constituencies with strong and heartfelt views on subjects such as these, and when they communicate those views to politicians they stand out from the sorts of messages usually mobilized by political action groups. As one journalistic observer commented in the midst of the gay ban controversy,

> Unlike other powerful interest, [the gospel lobby] does not lavish campaign funds on candidates for Congress nor does it entertain them. The strength of fundamentalist leaders lies in their flocks. Corporations pay public relations firms millions of dollars to contrive the kind of grassroots response that Falwell or Pat Robertson can galvanize in a televised sermon.[103]

The decline of party organization and party loyalty in the electorate increases politicians' exposure to the mobilizing of groups like those in the religious right. The cynicism about politicians that has always been part of the American political culture—and that has increased so markedly in the last generation—further increases the vulnerability to negative campaigning, and intensifies nervousness about taking on causes thought unpopular.[104]

LESBIAN/GAY ACTIVIST WEAKNESSES AND DISADVANTAGES

It was during the 1980s that lesbian and gay activists most dramatically increased their entry into mainstream political processes at the national level. Prior to that, the prospects for activist entry into or influence over any branch of the federal government seemed slim enough to weaken the logic and reduce the support for devoting substantial resources to the enterprise. Sexual minority politics had always been intensely local, and the widespread American distrust of political authority and progressive/left pessimism about state policy seemed more intensely felt with more senior levels of government.

Not coincidentally, the growth in attention to Washington politics occurred during a twelve-year period of Republican ascendancy in the executive branch, which threatened what few gains had been made to that point. It was also during the development and spread of the AIDS epidemic, drawing more and more lesbians and gays to the view that positive state intervention on gay related issues was essential.

The emergence of national organizations during that period and the development of activist groups within the national parties had virtually no parallel in other countries. Even accounting for population differences, Washington-based groups were larger, more sophisticated, and more experienced in the politics of the mainstream than activist organizations anywhere else. (However, they were never as powerful as a number of mainstream media accounts suggested, particularly in the lead-up to the 1992 election and the period immediately following it.[105])

In mobilizing support for lifting the military ban, Washington activists built on their experience by maintaining contact with a large number of Capitol Hill supporters in both parties. They were also effective in the use of some of their media contacts. As Mary Fainsod Katzenstein points out, they were able to make highly theatrical use of clean-cut, intelligent lesbian and gay service personnel declaring their determination to keep serving their country, providing images that important media outlets found "irresistible."[106]

But they were no match for the other side. There was nothing of the resources that their opponents were able to muster, and strategic miscalculations delayed mobilizing the resources they had. The national groups had never focused on building a mass base—their combined memberships totalling no more than 100,000 lesbians and gays—and little attention had been paid to building the kinds of mailing lists that constitute a critical resource for other lobby groups. The movement as a whole, in fact, had a bifurcated approach, using on the one hand the crisis oriented oppositionist tactics of the National Gay and Lesbian Task Force, on the other hand the lobbying techniques associated with the Human Rights Campaign Fund.[107] Some critics argue that national organizations oriented to traditional lobbying have to develop institutionally in order to do that job better—specifically to secure long-term staffing, and to expand information systems. A number of informed observers (though not all) believe that the insider resources built up by these national organizations have in fact been deployed well, but that activist groups are missing the crucial grassroots connections. According to Barney Frank,

The only problem they have is that the troops don't do their job. Lobbying on high priority issues, high visibility issues, is a matter of getting people to write and call. The basic problem with the gay and lesbian constituency is that it doesn't have the write-and-call outlook. . . . We suffer on the political left from a lot of self-fulfilling prophecies—"politicians don't care, they don't listen, it's all big money." Money counts on low priority, low visibility issues where there is no public opinion. But if there's any significant public opinion on an issue, it will swamp money any day.[108]

The failure to mobilize sufficient grassroots lobbying was only in part a function of the priorities of national organizations of course. It was also a function of a political quiescence and cynicism that is characteristic of the broader American population.[109] Lesbians and gays have even more reason than the average American for doubting that communicating to a member of Congress will make a difference. Writing to an elected politician is an expression of faith in the system that few of them had reason to muster.[110] Other groups of course face the same barriers, but manage to overcome them.

The religious right has mechanisms that are ideal for energizing and channelling political beliefs—well suited to both persuading people to write or phone, and helping them in formulating their arguments.

If lesbian and gay organizations were limited in the kinds of resources they could marshall for grassroots mobilization, they were also thought by some critics to have misjudged some of their strategy.[111] For example, the preoccupation with media-compelling stories of lesbian and gay military personnel led to an underuse of images and perspectives representing the experience of racial minorities, thus reinforcing the (largely accurate) perception of gay activist leadership in Washington as overwhelmingly Caucasian. This reduced the power of the parallels being pointed to between homophobic and racist discrimination, and probably diminished the breadth of alliances supporting the campaign.

The most widely heard criticism dealt with the slow start and buildup of the campaign to lift the ban. The Campaign for Military Service (CMS) was formed only after the firestorm of late January, and it seemed slow to organize, despite the political and financial support of heavy hitters like David Mixner and David Geffen. It concentrated its early labors on relatively low-key lobbying and on the development of media-focusing strategies such as the "Tour of Duty" (a cross-country bus tour); some of that work was useful, but some was unproductive. As late as March 22nd, the head of the Campaign for Military Service was still talking only of a grassroots campaign "revving up."[112] Delays were partly a product of distrust between the new group and the established Washington-based lesbian and gay organizations, and the relative inexperience in national politics of some of the CMS leaders. Delay was also a result of a belief that an effective campaign needed to peak only toward the end of the six-month period that Clinton had set aside for a decision, a belief that seemed to persist even when there were signs of dramatic slippage in Congress.

The difficulty of organizing a response, including a grassroots response, was exacerbated by the fact that the military ban had never been a high priority issue on gay activist agendas. Those who were on the forefront of lesbian/gay politics shared to varying degrees an antipathy towards an institution thought to represent all the hierarchical and male heterosexual values that their movement abhorred. More than any other part of the state, the military was widely thought irretrievable and irredeemable. The National Gay and Lesbian Task Force had developed a Military Freedom Project in 1988, in the wake of antilesbian witch hunts at Parris Island.[113] Lesbians were in fact at the fore in such work, persistently pushing their male colleagues to take the issue seriously. But it was still thought a marginal issue by most activists, until Bill Clinton made it a front-burner issue.

The slowness of the existing national organizations to mobilize in 1992 and early 1993 also had a lot to do with the excessive optimism that accompanied Clinton's election to the Presidency. Even ex-Task Force head Urvashi Vaid, more prepared than most to be skeptical of party leaders, was quoted as anticipating that lesbians and gays "have broken through every barrier that existed in mainstream politics," and would now be "part of the governing of this country."[114]

The hopes and expectations built up by the Clinton promises and implicit in the electoral support accorded him were reinforced in the weeks following the election, with the military ban becoming even more the focus of attention. Immediately after the election, David Mixner, one of the three people seen to be most insinuated into the President-elect's networks, was interviewed by the *Washington Blade*:

> Mixner said he hopes and expects that an executive order banning discrimination in all federal agencies—and ending the military ban on gays—will be signed within the first 100 days of the new administration. "I can tell you this," Mixner said. "There is not one second of doubt in my mind that Bill Clinton will sign such an executive order."[115] Mixner repeated his expectations a week later, even speculating that the ban would be lifted in the first week of the new administration.[116] When the issue was raised at an emergency meeting called by the Human Rights Campaign Fund to discuss the election, Mixner said, "don't worry, it's a done deal."

Some critics argue, appropriately, that Washington-based activists ought to have known enough about the climate for gay issues in the capital, and what it takes to get things done in Congress, to have recognized the impediments to removing the ban. But even among some of the insiders on Capitol Hill, there was considerable optimism. As one gay congressional aide reports,

> I remember the original discussions quite vividly, right around the time of the election. . . . A lot of it now, with hindsight, seems to have been remarkably naive in its premises. The working assumption was that this would not necessarily be an easy thing to do, that it would involve a great deal of delicacy, but ultimately it would happen and the only question was how quickly and what form it would take.[117]

Clinton and his advisors continued to foster such optimism, long after they were hit by the wave of protest at the end of January. After Clinton appalled lesbian and gay activists with a trial balloon about restrictions on the deployment of gay service personnel, White House aides hastily arranged a meeting with activists on March 26th. At that meeting, officials affirmed continuing commitment to the President's original position.[118] Even though the issue had been largely lost by then, no one was publicly acknowledging it. Among themselves, White House advisers were already talking of some version of "don't ask, don't tell," knowing that it would be regarded by lesbians and gays as a betrayal, but would offer up only bland assurances that no final decision would be made until July 15th.[119]

The difficulty facing activists lay partly in their inexperience in dealing with a sympathetic administration, and in operating within a political climate that was other than overwhelmingly negative. Unprecedented openings had been created, and were still being created for a kind of insider politics that all too easily created the illusion of power. But as openings for change inside the administration increased, so did disagreements about how to proceed. Part of that was rooted in the ego-driven one-upmanship that is so integral to Washington culture, but part of that is seated in age-old differences over the role of compromise and caution in effecting change, the role of professionalism in working inside political systems, and the importance of legal change itself.

The point remains, however, that even if the sensors of lesbian and gay activists had been more accurate, and their connections to a mass of supporters more developed, they could not have matched the volume of mail and phone calls that the extraordinary media and church networks provide for the religious right. And even if they had been able to match the volume of public response mobilized by that right, they would not have prevailed against a Congressional majority buttressed by the U.S. military. Tanya Domi of the Task Force, and Bob Hattoy, openly gay Clinton administration appointee, make the same point:

> Even if we had done things differently, we would not have won, because the White House walked, the Pentagon did nothing to help us, and we were left really holding the bag, at the same time dealing with a very vigorous right wing that is—in every single appeal that they do, in every single piece of direct mail, in every piece on radio and television, every think tank that's working on right wing issues—focusing on the ban and on the gay and lesbian people of America.
>
> All of a sudden the White House, in one corner here, and the gay and lesbian community . . . all had to go into high gear to do probably the most difficult task that the community has faced—to lift the ban in the military. . . . It was the most difficult because we were up against the military might of the United States of America—we're up against the Pentagon—we're up against the most institutionalized homophobia that you could find in America today.[120]

CONCLUSION

Eliminating discrimination against lesbians and gays in the military proved more difficult by far than most proponents of change had believed. Postmortems among activists almost immediately pitted those who had always believed in accommodating to prevailing American norms of political representation against those who sought a revival of direct action tactics, and between those who attributed failure to the cowardice of politicians and those who blamed the failure of gay organizations to mobilize grassroots support. All but a few shared the peculiarly American optimism that victory was attainable but for the failing of individual participants in the process.

Despite the temptation among protagonists to assign blame for failure to lift the ban on one or another single factor, the impediments to success were various, and for the moment, probably insurmountable. And while there was to be sure individual prejudice, weakness, and misjudgment, there were also institutional hurdles that stand in the way of progressive change on a variety of fronts. But it does reveal the barriers to progress on a number of fronts explicitly identified with sexual orientation. That does not preclude advances on behalf of lesbians and gays (or other marginalized groups) even in the aftermath of defeat on the military, but it makes change extraordinarily difficult to attain, especially at the federal level. That was true before the 1994 election that produced a Republican majority in Congress; it is even more true today.

The campaign to lift the ban, though benefiting from raising an issue of explicit discrimination that could easily be characterized as an "old chestnut," brought lesbians, gays, and their allies face to face with a military establishment of unusual size and political power, and in some ways this issue may not be typical of the broad range of lesbian and gay issues. It is not that the heterosexist cultures of the military in most other countries is so different. In general, the intimacy of contact and the importance of bonding in largely male environments depends on a masculinized culture that denies homosexuality. Even if particular units and commanders tolerate specific deviation, the institution as a whole must deny it in order to maintain a culture upon which it feeds. A few of the northern European countries that are less sexually conservative than Anglo-American societies might provide useful examples of variations in military culture, but even in those countries that have no ban or have recently removed it, the impediments to culture shift are formidable and the acceptance of sexual difference easily exaggerated.

There were a number of other impediments to progress that spoke to the chances of progress on lesbian and gay issues beyond the military. Though there was real interest in lifting the ban within the new administration, most notably on the part of the President, there were recurrent indications from Clinton himself of a relatively shallow understanding of what real equality in the armed services required. A number of participants in the process of trying to lift the ban have also suggested that the White House abandoned its indispensable role in managing the firefight that broke out at the end of January, until a point (in June) when the fight was lost. Some such criticism overstates the room for maneuver in relation to a Congressional majority determined not to be moved on this subject, but the criticism accurately points to the governmental inexperience of many in the new administration, and the lack of commitment to lesbian and gay rights of some.

Proponents of lifting the ban also faced a powerful religious right that builds on the comparatively high religiosity of Americans, their relative sexual conservativeness, and their anxieties about the rapidity of social change. It is not so much that antigay popular sentiment is greater in the United States than elsewhere, but that it can be more readily tapped by political and religious networks that treat lesbian and gay visibility as a symbol for all that is threatening about the modern world.

The mainstream media do little to correct the imbalance created by the religious right, armed as it is with huge media outlets. Even in the more established networks and newspapers, religious and secular extremists are routinely pitted against lesbian/gay rights advocates in the name of balance. In the case of most talk show radio, there is not even a pretense of balance. Even if there are important changes in the way in which gay content is insinuated into dramatic programming, the hand-wringing among television producers about lesbian and gay content, and in particular about open displays of affection, reinforces public perceptions of sexual variation as deviation and pathology. Even some of the more progressive media voices in the United States display a caution about gay-related stories that is more pronounced than in their media counterparts in other countries— including those in an otherwise very homophobic country like Britain.[121] Often, too, they feed increasingly widespread myths about lesbians and gays constituting a privileged minority with considerable political clout.

These factors impinge on proponents of reform in ways that are reinforced by aspects of the American legal and political systems. Gay rights advocates confront a statutory web that discriminates against sexual difference in ways that feed popular stereotypes and reinforce double standards about the closet. They also face a governmental system deliberately constructed to slow the pace of change. Activist groups face the extraordinary challenge of, first, maintaining lobbying contact with hundreds of legislators and officials in a very complex political system, and, second, generating enough grassroots pressure to be noticed above the din created by thousands of lobbyists. Not all groups seeking influence and power in Washington need that kind of grassroots capacity: corporate entities are the most obvious example of a "special interest" able to wield power without much attention to popular pressure. But those on the margins have little else that counts as political currency.

The Congressional arena alone is a complex and fragmented one, burdensome to lobby and heavily circumscribed by a culture of electoral nervousness that is unfriendly to radical change. The fact that both congressional chambers remain so heavily male—substantially more than most of the legislatures of the industrialized world—reinforces the resistance of change on issues of gender and sexuality. It is easy to exaggerate the political impact of an increase in women's entry into electoral politics, but congressional voting records on gay-related issues do display a gender gap (also evident in the population at large) that is a sobering reminder of the extent of impediment posed by a male-dominated legislative order.

But even in such a legislative arena, gains are possible. Part of the distinctively American lure into the political mainstream is the possibility of effecting change even against the odds. The very proliferation of political levers in Washington creates openings and hopes for the exercise of political influence, enticing progressive movements into the legislative and electoral process more regularly than in more tightly controlled parliamentary systems. For lesbian and gay activists, the potential for progressive shifts in policy has never entirely disappeared at any point since the early 1990s, and neither has the possibility of successfully mobilizing against attacks from legislative opponents.

Despite the despondency over the failure to lift the military ban, a number of those most involved in the campaign were able to speak of progress. In the words of one activist:

During the Bush administration, we had people who wouldn't talk to us at all; we had people who would talk to us but had no idea what we were talking about—hadn't formulated an opinion and weren't really interested in formulating one. We had a handful of friends, but not a very solid handful of friends—a handful of friends that were so decidedly liberal than they weren't very useful. The most radical 20% of Congress in your camp and you haven't gone very far in terms of making the issue penetrate into other political spheres. We're in a vastly different place—the 169 votes on the House side in the military issue, I think, demonstrates how far we came in the course of that nine months. And there are a lot of people beyond the 169 that got a lot closer to understanding this issue but wouldn't take a political plunge on that vote.[122]

Barney Frank adds that a substantial number of his legislative colleagues opposed lifting the ban on grounds that were more circumspect than they would have been even a few years ago. They were more inclined than ever to say that the military was a special case, and partly so because of prevailing prejudice among heterosexuals, and that they had no objection to equality rights in general.[123] He acknowledges that most of his congressional colleagues did not want to even talk about the ban, but here too he saw a shift from an earlier time—a shift from a "no way!" response to gay rights to an "oh shit!" reaction.

That's good for us, because the role of Congress has always been to be negative, not positive. That is, we have never realistically thought in the fifteen years I've been here that the House was going to do, or the Senate was going to do, something positive for us. Our agenda has uniformly been to prevent the House and Senate from inflicting bad things on us—either overturning good things the Clinton administration has done, or just adding negatives. So to the extent that people want to avoid that, that works in our favor. . . . When I first got here, there was no sense that they wanted to be rid of this issue: many of them looked forward to it; it was an easy way to go. The fact that they feel conflicted by it now is a sign of progress— obviously it's not nearly enough, but it also works to our favor. And our threat to make everything a roll call is part of that issue.[124]

A number of Washington insiders point to a number of pro-gay administrative moves by the Clinton administration as an indicator that sexual minority issues were not swept off the political age ᵈᵃ entirely by the defeat over the military ban. Most notable among these were ᵊignificant increases in

AIDS funding obtained by the administration, and a directive from the Office of Personnel Management citing existing law as prohibiting discrimination against federal employees on the basis of sexual orientation, accompanied by a flurry of agency-specific directives to the same effect. Such voices recognize the threat to gains posed by the strengthening of socially conservative forces after the 1994 election, but offer an important corrective to the view that the 1993-94 period was marked only by setback.

The contradictory messages that can be pulled out of the first two years of the Clinton Presidency illustrate a continuing dilemma for lesbian/gay and other progressive movements. The U.S. system creates inescapable inducements to organize within the political mainstream, but in the process it sows the seeds for separation between, on the one hand, those wrapped up in mainstream political mechanisms, and on the other, the average citizen, community member, and even local activists. The potential for this sort of tension or isolation exists in other political systems, in part because of stronger ideological divisions about the merits of working with existing state institutions. But it is a very strong feature of gay politics in the United States, despite the weakness of voices representing a radical rejection of the existing political and economic order.

The sheer complexity of the system hand wraps up those closest to it in its intricacies and alienates those more distant from it by its incomprehensibility. The preoccupation with legislative action of those inside the center of political systems often leads to an absorption in legal remedies that seem marginal to many ordinary citizens and front-line activists. Any campaign for legal change, in any country, will be pressured to adapt to existing legal frameworks in ways that may compromise longer term transformative goals. The pressures to appear moderate, and to compromise, are even greater in the United States than in other systems, in part a product of the complex processes by which political decisions are made, and in part because of the relative weakness of radically critical political alternatives. Activists oriented exclusively to insider politics risk absorption in a political culture that exaggerates the impact of legal change and imposes severely judgmental limits on what are thought to be realistic goals and acceptable tactics. Perhaps as much as in any system (though in very different ways the British system may have a similar impact), those who are preoccupied by insider politics believe that their strategic needs must take precedence in the communities they seek to represent, and that other forms of community activism should be hewn to these needs. This inevitably creates a gulf between those whose political value lies in being able to play the legislative game and those who seek to mobilize activist pressure for fundamental change from outside that system.

Some Washington-based activists are sufficiently allegiant to the political order within which they work that they understate the tilt of the playing field against gay rights, and overstate the potential for success. This leads them to an exaggerated belief that, for example, the military ban could have been lifted with more effective lesbian and gay mobilizing. They are not necessarily wrong in the criticisms they level at lobbying groups that do not mobilize in ways that seem to make a difference, but they may overstate the extent to which the legislative system responds to the kind of pressure they wish had been applied. In the end, arguably, the national lesbian and gay groups could never have reversed the slide away from the position they favored even if they had done all that their critics (on and off Capitol Hill) had urged.

None of this is meant to suggest that lesbian/gay organizations have erred in focusing as much energy as they have on engagement with mainstream political institutions. To engage in that way was and is necessary and inevitable, more so in the American political system than in any other because of the constant need for vigilance. And in order to work effectively in the legislative and administrative arenas that Washington-based activists need to work, they must understand the structures and norms that give shape to decisionmaking processes. The failure to lift the ban, however, served as a reminder that political activism focusing only on political maneuvering inside the Washington beltway and on providing election support for openly lesbian/gay politicians and heterosexual allies is insufficient for effecting change. Even if they might differ on the kinds of political action most likely to have political impact, lesbians and gays as diverse as Urvashi Vaid, Michelangelo Signorile, and Barney Frank have all drawn from the defeat on the military ban the lesson that national groups have to build more substantial grassroots foundations. Apart from other reasons, such foundations are required for tactical reasons in a political system that has set the stakes as high as it has for being noticed in Washington. U.S. national politics requires more of those whose rights claims are defined as "special interests" than any other political system, challenging the organizational skills even of the most sophisticated activist networks.

The failure to lift the ban also constitutes a timely reminder that our location on the political agenda is a fragile place frighteningly close to the edge. If we are in the mainstream, we are at best on the fringe, and too often not even there. The claims to equal rights may well be frameable in traditional liberal language, but they do represent, and are perceived by many to represent, a challenge to entrenched constructs of gender, sexuality, and family. In a political culture so often riven by anxiety about social change, and in which questions of sexuality have so regularly stood for a broader discomfort with changing social relations, politicians remain loath to speak of homosexuality at all.

Located in the fragile position they are on the national political agenda, American lesbians and gays have to recognize that there is no single tactical approach to political change. To argue that progress will come only if activists and their followers blend in with mainstream conceptions of normalcy is just as misguided as to claim that mass mobilization and direct action are all that will extract change from an otherwise irretrievable political order. Even if U.S. social movement activists have often treated mainstream/oppositionist and insider/ grassroots as mutually opposed tactics, the progress that has been effected to this point in their country and others has often come from the coordinated or uncoordinated activities of individuals and groups representing the full range of strategies so evident in the last quarter century.

NOTES

The research for this chapter is part of a larger project on gay/lesbian experience in "mainstream" political processes in Canada, Britain, and the United States, funded in part by the Social Sciences and Humanities Research Council of Canada. My American work has benefited from the extraordinary cooperation of Rep. Barney Frank, from members of his staff in Washington and Massachusetts, and from a large number of activists and "insiders" who agreed to confidential interviews between 1992 and 1995. Advice, assistance, and support have come from Ben Davidson, Mark Blasius, Tim Cook, Audrey Dennie, Leonard Hirsch, Gerry Hunt, Elizabeth Lorenzin, James Murray, Shane Phelan, Jean Smith, Judi Stevenson, Neil Thomlinson, and the National Resource Center at People for the American Way.

1. See Norman J. Ornstein, Robert L. Peabody, and David W. Rohde, "The U.S. Senate in an Era of Change," in *Congress Reconsidered*, 5th ed., ed. by Lawrence C. Dodd and Bruce I. Oppenheimer (Washington: Congressional Quarterly Press, 1993), 16.

2. These points are made by a number of authors, including the contributors to Dodd and Oppenheimer, eds., *Congress Reconsidered*; and Morris P. Fiorina and David W. Rohde, eds., *Home Style and Washington Work* (Ann Arbor, MI: The University of Michigan Press, 1989). They are given the emphasis of personal experience by David Price, *The Congressional Experience: A View from the Hill* (Boulder, CO: Westview Press, 1992), chaps. 5, 6, and 10. The Republican leadership in both the House and the Senate had shifted to less conciliatory approaches, evident in the styles of Senator Robert Dole and especially Rep. Newt Gingrich (Republican House Whip during the 103d Congress).

3. See Ornstein, Peabody, and Rohde, "The U.S. Senate in an Era of Change," 16.

4. The preoccupation with service to the home district in order to secure re-election is most associated with Richard Fenno, *Homestyle: House Members in Their Districts* (Boston: Little, Brown, 1978); and Morris Fiorina, *Congress: Keystone of the Washington Establishment*, 2d ed. (New Haven, CT: Yale University Press, 1989).

5. This is a point made in Roger H. Davidson and Walter J. Olesjek, *Congress and its Members*, 4th ed. (Washington: Congressional Quarterly Press, 1994). One member of Congress is quoted as saying, "Through their computers these groups get to more of my voters, more often, and with more information than any elected official can do" (p. 302).

6. On this point, see Lawrence C. Dodd and Bruce I. Oppenheimer, "Maintaining Order in the House," pp. 41-66 in *Congress Reconsidered*, ed. Dodd and Oppenheimer.

7. See Price, *The Congressional Experience*, 88-89.

8. On the increase of negative campaigning, see, for example, Fiorina, *Congress*, part 2; and Price, *The Congressional Experience*, 155-56. The separation of powers increases the ease of shifting blame or evading responsibility for taking a stand.

9. The Senate, for example, does not require that amendments by substantively related to the bill under deliberation.

10. In the 102d Congress, for example, Ornstein, Peabody, and Rohde categorized 55 percent of northern Democrats and none of the southerners as "liberal," with 8 percent of the northerners and 53 percent of the southerners classified as "conservative" ("The U.S. Senate," 16).

11. The Human Rights Campaign Fund counted him as voting favorably on two thirds of the nine issues they used to evaluate members of the 103d Congress during its first session, but only two out of five votes in their overview of the entire 103d Congress ("Votes of the 103d Congress, 1st Session," and "Highlights of the 103d Congress").

12. See Elizabeth Drew, *On the Edge: The Clinton Presidency* (New York: Simon & Schuster, 1994), 45.

13. Interview, 2 September 1993.

14. Drew, *On the Edge*, chap. 7.

15. White House officials were straightforward in talking of there being no intent to lobby Congress during the six-month cooling off period announced at the end of January, and gay activists have confirmed that there was no one in the Administration "managing" the issue until June (Clifford Krauss, "Agreement is Setback for Republican Amendment," *New York Times* 31 January 1993; and interviews with activists, 30 June and 2 September 1993).

16. Of the 31 Senators who had signed on as cosponsors of the Employment Non-Discrimination Act by the end of the 103d Congress, only three were Republicans, and of the 136 House members cosponsoring it, only six were Republicans (Human Rights Campaign Fund, "Highlights of the 103d Congress"). In the final votes on the ban, one of the Republican cosponsors in the Senate and two in the House failed to support pro-gay positions.

17. On the surprise, see Richard Berke, "Timing Awry, Clinton Trips Into a Brawl," *New York Times* (29 January 1993).

18. William Schneider, of the American Enterprise Institute, was quoted as being "astonished" that the Republicans did not pick up on Clinton's promise on the ban as an opening to the "family values" issue. In Chris Bull, "D-Day," *The Advocate* (10 August 1993): 32.

19. Interview, 7 February 1995.

20. Interview, 7 February 1995.

21. See Pat Towell, "Roles for Women, Homosexuals Among Clinton's First Tests," *Congressional Quarterly Weekly* (21 November 1992): 3679-80.

22. Kristina Campbell, "Republicans Examine Issue of Gays in Military," *Washington Blade* (11 December 1992): 13.

23. Bill Gertz and Rowan Scarborough, "GOP Senators Plan Offensive," *Washington Times* (26 January 1993).

24. These hesitations were shared by Alan Simpson, the Party's whip, who, though a conservative on many issues including homosexuality, was quoted as denying that there was Republican unity on the strategy of seeking codification of the ban. See Krauss, "Agreement is Setback for Republican Amendment," and Carrol J. Doherty and Pat Towell, "Fireworks Over Ban on Gays Temporarily Snuffed Out," *Congressional Quarterly Weekly* (6 February 1993): 273. By the time of the hearings into the ban in late March, some of the Republicans on the Senate Armed Services Committee like Strom Thurmond, the ranking minority member, seemed to be avoiding the kind of extreme antigay rhetoric that had so often come from some of the colleagues' mouths.

This is not an issue of being for or against homosexuals as a group or homosexuality as a lifestyle. . . . The record is replete with instances of dedicated and heroic service by many gays in the ranks of our armed services. (Quoted in Bill McAllister, "Senate Opens Hearings on Gay Ban," *Washington Post* 30 March 1993.)

25. Interview, 13 February 1995.

26. Quoted in Peter Freiberg, "Nunn Vows Hearings on Gay Ban Will be Unbiased," *Washington Blade* (5 February 1993): 15.

27. On pro-gay votes listed by the National Gay and Lesbian Task Force, Nunn's support was 46 percent in the 1987-88 Congress, 70 percent in 1989-90, and 36 percent in 1991-92 (Freiberg, "Nunn Vows Hearings on Gay Ban Will be Unbiased," 17).

28. Although Nunn himself claimed to have had no interest in the Defense portfolio, he did indicate a preparedness to consider Secretary of State.

29. Interview with activist, 7 February 1995; and Drew, *On the Edge*, 43.

30. Lou Chibbaro Jr., "Clinton Stands Firm as Many Advise Him to Back Off Promise," *Washington Blade* (20 November 1992): 15.

31. Gwen Ifill, "Aides Say Clinton Will Lift Gay Ban Despite Opposition," *New York Times* (29 January 1993).

32. Eric Schmitt, "Compromise to Revise Rules on Homosexuals in Military," and Gwen Ifill, "Clinton Accepts Delay in Lifting Military Gay Ban," *New York Times* (30 January 1993).

33. Campaign for Military Service activist, 30 June 1993.

34. Melissa Healy, "Nunn Likely to Narrow Debate on Military Gays," *Los Angeles Times* (29 March 1993).

35. Melissa Healy, "Military Experts Back Proposal to Let Gays Keep Their Privacy," *Los Angeles Times* (4 April 1993). Note the language of the headline, suggestive of a nod in the direction of gays.

36. Lisa Keen, "Clinton Stands Firm on Vow to Repeal Military's Gay Ban," *Washington Blade* (13 November 1992): 15. As the President was finalizing the plan for a six-month delay, he said to a reporter, "I agree that any sort of improper conduct should result in severance. . . . The narrow issue on which there is disagreement is whether people should be able to say that they are homosexual . . . and, do nothing else, without being severed." In Lisa Keen,

"Clinton 'Pretty Close' to Plan on Ban," *Washington Blade* (29 January 1993): 1.

37. Senator Nunn and Committee Republicans at first seemed dubious about distinguishing status and conduct, clearly concerned that removing bars against status would allow open declaration of homosexuality. Their nervousness may have been allayed somewhat by one "expert" social anthropologist who testified at the hearings that speaking was a form of behavior. Carrol J. Doherty, "Heated Issue is Off to a Cool Start as Hearings on Gay Ban Begin," *Congressional Quarterly Weekly* (3 April 1993): 852.

38. This is not the only instance in which forms of speech (for example, the wearing of T-shirts) have been treated as "conduct."

39. Some accounts tried to balance the event's staging, for example Eric Schmitt, "Gay Shipmates? Senators Listen as Sailors Talk," *New York Times* (11 May 1993).

40. Eric Schmitt, "Compromise on Military Ban Gaining Support Among Senators," *New York Times* (12 May 1993). Schwartzkopf speculated that a lifting of the ban risked demoralizing U.S. troops "just like many of the Iraqi troops who sat in the deserts of Kuwait, forced to execute orders they didn't believe in." The Nunn approach had by this time gained support from the ranking Republican and a number of other members from both parties, though opposed by Senators Kennedy and Levin, both Democrats.

41. Armed Services Committee member Charles Robb was quoted as saying, "That's where the dividing line is now." Pat Towell, "Nunn Offers a Compromise: 'Don't Ask/Don't Tell,'" *Congressional Quarterly Weekly* (15 May 1993): 1240.

42. John Gallagher, "A Congresswoman Confronts the Pentagon," *The Advocate* (31 December 1991): 51.

43. Interview with congressional aide, 10 June 1993.

44. In the general public as well as among national politicians, women are less homophobic than men; among national politicians (though not in the general public), African Americans are less opposed than whites to pro-gay measures. Voting patterns derived from Human Rights Campaign Fund, "Votes of the 103rd Congress, 1st Session." On African Americans in Congress, see Bositis, *Congressional Black Caucus*, pp. 134, 150. On public opinion analyzed by gender and race, see John Gallagher, "What America Thinks of You," *The Advocate* (6 October 1991): 92.

45. See Towell, "Nunn Offers a Compromise," p. 1240; and John Gallagher, "Feds Appeal Meinhold Ruling," *The Advocate* (6 April 1993): 19. Frank himself believed that early House hearings would have been useful. (Interview with Barney Frank, 9 February 1995).

46. For a useful account of the reasoning behind and reactions to the Frank compromise, see Chris Bull, "No Frankness," *The Advocate* (29 June 1993): 24-26.

47. Interview with Bob Edwards on "Morning Edition," National Public Radio, 19 May 1993, printed as Barney Frank, "We Are Very Late in the Game," *Washington Post* (21 May 1993).

48. Interview, 30 June 1993.

49. Interview, 29 June 1993.

50. Interview, 30 June 1993.

51. Bull, "D-Day," pp. 34, 35.

52. Interview, 30 June 1993.

53. See, for example, Corrie Wofford, "Frank's 'Compromise' Denounced," *Washington Blade* (21 May 1993): 14; and Urvashi Vaid, "Compromising Positions," *The Advocate* (29 June 1993): 96.

54. Studds was quoted in the press as criticizing Frank for "prematurely raising the white flag." Eric Schmitt, "Gay Congressman Offers a Plan on Homosexuals in the Military," *New York Times* (19 May 1993). Frank himself acknowledges that Studds was annoyed at him, though only temporarily (interview, 30 June 1993).

55. Interview, 2 September 1993.

56. See Thomas W. Lippman and Ruth Marcus, "President Seeks Gay Ban Compromise; Nunn Rules Out a 'Haven' in Military," *Washington Post* (28 May 1993).

57. See Peter Freiberg, "Many Wonder What Military Compromise Will Emerge," *Washington Blade* (11 June 1993): 21.

58. Bill Gertz, "Nunn: No OK for Gays," *Washington Times* (31 May 1993); and Pat Towell, "Clinton Calls Compromise Close, But Nunn Won't Deal on Gays," *Congressional Quarterly Weekly* (29 May 1993): 1380.

59. This being claimed even as late as July 14, Lisa Keen, "Gays 'Bracing for the Crash,'" *Washington Blade* (16 July 1993): 1, 13.

60. Lisa Keen, "Was Memo a Smokescreen by Pentagon?" *Washington Blade* (25 June 1993): 27.

61. Tom Sheridan of the Campaign for Military Service asserted that if Clinton took a principled stand on lifting the ban, 45 Senators and 172 House members would support it, with 15 Senators and 101 House members undecided. Pat Towell, "Aspin Seeks a Deal on Gays That the Brass Will Bless," *Congressional Quarterly Weekly* (26 June 1993): 1670-71.

62. Interview with congressional aide, 1 July 1993.

63. Drew, *On the Edge*, 169.

64. John Lancaster and Ann Devroy, "Aspin Backs a 'Don't Ask, Don't Tell' Policy on Gays," *Washington Post* (23 June 1993).

65. The amendment included the following: "the presence . . . of persons who demonstrate a propensity or intent to engage in homosexual acts would create an unacceptable risk to the high standards of morale, good order and discipline and unit cohesion that are the essence of military capability." A July 19th memo to Clinton from Attorney General Janet Reno confirmed that some of the adjustments made even in Clinton's own policy improved its immunity to constitutional challenge over the old policy.

66. Even conservative extremists like Jesse Helms seemed satisfied with the Nunn amendment when it eventually reached the Senate floor. Kitty Cunningham, "The Senate's Last Word on Gays," *Congressional Quarterly Weekly* (11 September 1993): 2401.

67. Among the Republicans who declared themselves satisfied with the final version of the Nunn amendment was fanatically right-wing Rep. Robert Dornan. See "Victory Over Homosexual Lobby," *Free Americans* (July-August 1993): 9; "Two Cheers for Nunn's Legislative Maneuver," *Human Events* (7 August 1993): 5; and William P. Hoar, "Mr. Clinton Loses Again," *The New American* (6 September 1993): 13-14.

68. Lou Chibbaro Jr., "Senate OKs Policy on Gays in Military," *Washington Blade* (10 September 1993): 11.

69. Some activists, and Rep. Dellums, had wanted a stronger amendment, lifting the ban entirely, but most were persuaded that the vote would have been humiliatingly low (interview with congressional aide, 8 February 1995).

70. Interview, 18 October 1993.

71. Interview with congressional aide, 8 February 1995.

72. David A. Bositis, *The Congressional Black Caucus in the 103d Congress* (Washington, D.C.: Joint Center for Political and Economic Studies, 1994), 134, 150.

73. John Gallagher, "Some Things Never Change," *The Advocate* (17 May 1994): 46-47; Sara Miles, "Don't Ask, It's Hell," *Out* (February 1995): 61-65, 108-110; and Sheila Walsh, "Report: Military Sidesteps 'Don't Ask, Don't Tell,'" *Washington Blade* (3 March 1995): 1, 29.

74. A lower court judgment rendered in March 1995 ruled the new ban unconstitutional, but there is no indication that this, and other court decisions on the pre-Clinton ban, will survive appeals up the judicial ladder.

75. See Bruce Ryder, "Equality Rights and Sexual Orientation: Confronting Heterosexual Family Privilege," *Canadian Journal of Family Law* 9 (1990): 39-97; and Douglas Saunders, "Constructing Lesbian and Gay Rights," *Canadian Journal of Law and Society* 9/2 (1994): 99-143. On the most recent Supreme Court decision, see Sean Fine and Margaret Philp, "Divorced Mothers, Gay Couples Lose in Court," and Margot Gibb-Clark, "Lawyers Split on Ruling's Effect," *Globe and Mail* (26 May 1995).

76. Increasing use is being made of European laws in challenging antigay discrimination, and although the record until now is mixed, there may be stronger grounds in some such cases of explicit statutory discrimination. See K. Waalkijk and A. Clapham, eds., *Homosexuality: A European Community Issue/ Essays on Lesbian and Gay Rights in European Law and Policy*, International Studies in Human Rights, vol. 26 (Dordrecht, The Netherlands: Martinus Nijhoff, 1993), and my own review of the book in *Journal of European Integration* 17/2-3 (1994): 391-93. For a somewhat contrasting view, see Peter Tatchell, *Europe in the Pink: Lesbian and Gay Equality in the New Europe* (London: GMP, 1992).

77. See Kathy Marks and George Jones, "Fight to Keep Homosexual Forces Ban," and Peter Almond, "Homosexuals Will Hurt Forces Morale," *Daily Telegraph* (8 June 1995).

78. The contrast with Canada, with a longer tradition of positive regard for political authority, is analyzed by Seymour Martin Lipset, *Continental Divide: The Values and Institutions of the United States and Canada* (New York: Routledge, 1990).

79. See Jeffrey Schmalz, "Homosexuals Wake to See a Referendum: It's on Them," *New York Times* (31 January 1993).

80. See, for example, Joyce Price, "Gay Ban Backed in Ranks," *Washington Times* (18 November 1992).

81. See, for example, *USA Today* (12 November 1992). For the next six months, the marines appeared to have been the most rabid (see "The Battle of the Gay Ban," *Newsweek* 5 April 1993, 42). According to a House Republican Research Committee survey in June 1993, 97 percent of active duty admirals and generals supported the ban on homosexuals serving in the U.S. military, and 99 percent agreed that openly lesbian/gay personnel would "significantly disrupt unit cohesion and readiness" (Rowan Scarborough, "Military Brass Want Ban to Stay," *Washington Times*, 1 July 1993).

82. A. M. Rosenthal talks of Powell's stature and popularity in, "General Powell and the Gays," *New York Times* (26 January 1993). See also Bull, "D-Day," 36. His own prejudice is indicated by his juxtaposition of sexual orientation to "benign" characteristics such as race, adopting the religious right distinction used to justify continuing discrimination against gays and lesbians. On his vehemence, see Drew, *On the Edge*, 45-46.

83. Carleton R. Bryant, "Pro-Ban Forces Circulate Graphic Video on Gays," *Washington Times* (26 January 1993); and Art Pine, "Issue Explodes Into an All-Out Lobbying War," *Los Angeles Times* (28 January 1993).

84. The quote is from Pine, "Issue Explodes Into an All-Out Lobbying War."

85. The phone-ins were reported in Pine, "Issue Explodes Into an All-Out Lobbying War."

86. Bob Hattoy, remarks delivered at a panel on gays in the military, Annual Meeting of the American Political Science Association, Washington, 2 September 1993.

87. Jeffrey Schmalz, "Gay Groups Regrouping for War on Military Ban," *New York Times* (7 February 1993).

88. John Lancaster and Ann Devroy, "Clinton's Gay Ban Policy Crystallizes," *Washington Post* (24 June 1993).

89. Rowan Scarborough, "Aspin Fails to Sway Generals With Gay-Ban Presentation," *Washington Times* (26 June 1993).

90. This argument is laid out in more detail in David Rayside and Scott Bowler, "Public Opinion and Gay Rights," *Canadian Review of Sociology and Anthropology* 25 (November 1988): 649-60. American polling data since that publication indicate a persistently high level of support for general equality rights, with perhaps a slight lowering of the rate of moral disapproval of

homosexuality. A late summer 1992 *New York Times*/CBS News poll showed 80 percent in favor of equal rights to job opportunities, but only 38 percent believing that homosexuality was an acceptable alternative life style (cited in Jeffrey Schmalz, "Gay Politics Goes Mainstream," *New York Times Magazine* (11 October 1992): 41.

91. Based on "feeling thermometers" that give respondents a scale from "0" to "100" degrees in order to register their feelings. Average response to gays and lesbians was 29, to environmental activists 77, illegal aliens 39, blacks 62. Cited in Kenneth Sherrill, "On Gay People as a Politically Powerless Group," in *Gays and the Military: Joseph Steffan versus the United States*, ed. Marc Wolinsky and Kenneth Sherrill (Princeton, NJ: Princeton University Press, 1993), 98.

92. See Mary Fainsod Katzenstein, "The Spectacle as Political Resistance: Feminist and Gay/Lesbian Politics in the Military," *Minerva: Quarterly Report on Women and the Military* 11 (Spring 1993): 5; and *USA Today*, 22 September 1992 and 12 November 1992.

93. The first was a *Washington Post*-ABC News Poll (*Washington Post*, 27 January 1993); the second, showing 41 percent approval, was a *Wall Street Journal*-ABC News Poll, the question phrased in terms of "Bill Clinton's goal of allowing gays and lesbians to serve in the U.S. military" (*Wall Street Journal*, 28 January 1993); the third was a more generally phrased question in a *New York Times*-CBS Poll conducted just a few days later, and showing 42 percent support (*New York Times*, 1 February 1993); and the fourth a *Los Angeles Times* poll two weeks later, showing 40 percent in favor (28 February 1993). The *New York Times* poll showed a considerable gender gap, with 52 percent of women favoring removal of the ban, and only 31 percent of men. Some decline had been registered by the time of the 1992 election, a *Newsweek* poll showing 59 percent support, and a Gallop Poll showing 57 percent, both cited in *USA Today*, 12 November 1992.

94. Interview with congressional aide, 9 February 1995.

95. Interview, 18 October 1993.

96. Interview, 9 February 1995.

97. According to W. Craig Bledsoe about 25 percent of U.S. voters identify with the Christian right. ("Postmoral Majority Politics: The Fundamentalist Impulse in 1988," paper presented to the annual meeting of the American Political Science Association, San Francisco, 1990, 13.) According to surveys cited by Seymour Martin Lipset, 38 percent of Americans hold a literal, fundamentalist view of *The Bible* (*Continental Divide*, 89).

98. See, for example, David M. Rayside, "Gay Rights and Family Values," *Studies in Political Economy*, 26 (Summer 1988): 649-60.

99. Peter Applebome, "Gay Issues Mobilizes Conservatives Against Clinton," *New York Times* (1 February 1993).

100. Gustav Niebuhr, "Push on Gay Ban Roils Religious Community," *Washington Post* (29 January 1993).

101. Kevin Merida and Helen Dewar, "In Boom of Phone and Fax Activism, Citizens Give Government an Earful," *Washington Post* (1 February 1993). A similar sentiment was voiced by a Republican congressman quoted in Schmalz, "Homosexuals Wake to See a Referendum."

102. Interview, 13 February 1995.

103. Weisskopf, "'Gospel Grapevine.'"

104. See Fiorina, *Congress*, part 2; and Price, *The Congressional Experience*, 138, 166.

105. For example, Jeffrey Schmalz's *New York Times Magazine* article "Gay Politics Goes Mainstream" begins with the claim that gay men and lesbians were becoming "major players" in the presidential election (p. 18). Writing in *Newsweek* in the aftermath of the springtime March on Washington, just as the ground was slipping under the ground of Clinton's gay ban pledge, Howard Fineman talked in terms of homosexuals becoming a "powerful and increasingly savvy bloc" ("Marching to the Mainstream," 3 May 1993, 42).

106. Katzenstein, "The Spectacle as Political Resistance," 8-9. The description of such images as irresistible is Jeffrey Schmalz's, quoted in Chris Bull, "And the Ban Played On," *The Advocate* (9 March 1993): 36-42.

107. One NGLTF insider agreed that it had been operating too much with "crisis mentality" born of oppositional organizing, arguing that "Going into a Democratic administration, the value of a mobile SWAT team, that went around and denounced things, is much more limited" (interview, 8 February 1995). Another agreed that "We don't have any legs in the movement" (interview, 29 June 1993).

108. Interview, 9 February 1995.

109. There is a great deal of political science literature on the persistence of apathy and disengagement. For a sometimes-perceptively critical view, see John C. Berg, *Unequal Struggle: Class, Gender, Race, and Power in the U.S. Congress* (Boulder, CO: Westview Press, 1994).

110. A point that Barney Frank makes (interviews, 30 June 1993 and 9 February 1995).

111. See, for example, Lou Chibbaro Jr., "Gay Groups Scramble to Respond," *Washington Blade* (29 January 1993): 1, 16; and Schmalz, "Gay Groups Regrouping for War on Military Ban."

112. Eric Schmitt, "Months After Order on Gay Ban, Military is Still Resisting Clinton," *New York Times* (23 March 1993).

113. Lesbian activists were at first more prepared to treat the military issue as a priority, not least because the rate of removal from active duty because of homosexuality was higher for women (8.1/10,000) than men (3.4/10,000). See Schmalz, "Homosexuals Wake to See a Referendum."

114. Peter Freiberg, "Gays Now 'Part of the Governing Coalition,'" *Washington Blade* (6 November 1992): 21, 14. The same sentiment was expressed by Vaid in a high-profile *New York Times* story on gay issues in the election (Jeffrey Schmalz, "Gay Areas are Jubilant," 5 November 1992).

115. Freiberg, "Gays Now 'Part of the Governing Coalition,'" 14.

116. "We're in a place we've never been," *Washington Blade* (13 November 1992): 1, 21.

117. Interview, 8 February 1995.

118. Richard L. Berke, "White House Gets a Warning Against Retreat on Gay Issue," *New York Times* (27 March 1993).

119. Interview, 2 September 1993.

120. Both comments from remarks at a panel on gays in the military, Annual Meeting of the American Political Science Association, Washington, 2 September 1993. Similar points were made by political scientists Larry Sabato and Craig Rimmerman, quoted in Bull, "D-Day," 32.

121. I have written about the English case in "Homophobia, Class and Party in England," *Canadian Journal of Political Science* 25 (March 1992): 121-49.

122. Interview, 7 February 1995.

123. Interview, 2 September 1993.

124. Interview, 9 February 1995.

CHAPTER 7

Seeking Another Forum:
The Courts and Lesbian and Gay Rights

Richard Pacelle

For a two decade period bounded by *Brown v. Board of Education* (347 US 483, 1954) and *Roe v. Wade* (410 US 113, 1973), the U.S. Supreme Court created a virtual constitutional revolution. The Court extended equal protection, incorporated significant portions of the Bill of Rights to the states, and created new rights. The *Brown* decision gave voice to groups that were shut out of the political process. The decisions had enormous symbolic significance, although there is evidence to suggest that the impact of *Brown* and *Roe* was limited.[1]

The cases that mark the Court's most liberal activist period, *Brown* and *Roe*, are especially relevant for lesbian and gay rights. *Brown* breathed life into the Equal Protection Clause of the Fourteenth Amendment. *Roe* expanded the Court created right of privacy, a right based on a number of constitutional provisions. Lesbian and gay activists using the courts have often relied on the doctrinal progeny of these two cases, framing their arguments in equal protection and privacy terms. Favorable, albeit indirect, precedents were available for those seeking to expand lesbian and gay rights.

A judiciary that is active in policymaking gives additional credence to pluralistic notions of American government. Groups that have been disadvantaged in the political process or denied access to the other branches have attempted to use the courts to achieve their policy goals.[2] Lesbians and gays are examples of such a politically powerless group.[3]

The use of the courts is often instrumental. Groups seek favorable decisions to create precedents for future litigation efforts. Positive decisions also create the conditions for spillovers to the elected branches. Success in the judiciary adds legitimacy to group demands and can reduce the barriers to the elected branches, thereby creating the necessary access. Often success in Congress and the executive branch is imperative if judicial decisions are to be enforced. Certainly, it took the Civil Rights Act of 1964 and executive intervention to realize any of the promises of the *Brown* decision.[4]

There are pitfalls in using the courts, however. Some argue that the judiciary lacks the ability to construct coherent public policy.[5] Groups pour their resources into a slow moving judiciary, which lacks capacity. Thus, courts may be a trap for groups. Their victories energize opponents, who move to block those gains in the other branches. Victories in court may breed false confidence and sap the movement of vitality. Symbolic victories are mistaken for substantive gains. Thus, "courts act as 'fly paper' for social reformers who succumb to the 'lure of litigation.'"[6] In fact, some argue that courts serve an ideological function of luring social movements to an institution that is structurally constrained from addressing their needs.

These constraints are real and serve to limit the prospects for social change. Courts are better suited to operating at the margins, rather than as the core of a social movement. Such constraints were not as critical for the lesbian and gay rights movements at the outset. First, gay rights advocates did not have a full range of alternative options; second, even symbolic victories would serve an important purpose. Courts may be useful as triggering mechanisms to provide momentum for a nascent social movement or to remove lingering obstacles.[7] A few significant legal victories could create an environment for legislative or executive victories.[8]

The military ban on lesbian and gay personnel represented an imposing challenge for lesbian and gay rights advocates. Few institutions so openly discriminate against lesbians and gays as the military establishment. Yet, the military has long been recognized by the Supreme Court as "legitimately different." The Court has tended to defer to the military when its policies or regulations are challenged.[9] Because the elected branches of government and the military establishment were unlikely to remove the ban voluntarily, lesbian and gay activists would need to use the judiciary. To overcome the entrenched doctrinal support for military policies, advocates for lesbian and gay rights would need to create a countervailing set of favorable precedents in other areas of law and try to transplant them into challenges to the military ban.

In his quest for the presidency, Bill Clinton assiduously courted the lesbian and gay vote. During the campaign, Clinton announced that if elected he would repeal the military ban on lesbians and gay men.[10] President Clinton's plan to remove the military ban represented a recognition of the rights of lesbians and gays and access to one of the elected branches. There were important symbolic and practical overtones to this policy. President Truman's integration of the military was considered a first step toward the *Brown v. Board of Education* decision.[11]

Having presidential or Congressional imprimatur on policy provides the legitimacy a favorable Court ruling would. But unlike a judicial decision, recognition of a right or allocation of values by the political branches carries additional practical weight. The president and Congress are more likely to provide the tangible resources that give policies a greater chance to succeed.[12] Because the courts had been unsympathetic, Clinton's lifting of the ban might have reversed the strategies that worked for race litigation. The Legal Defense Fund of the National Association for the Advancement of Colored People (NAACP) used the courts to earn victories, recognition, legitimacy, and public acceptance that could be translated into gains in the political branches. Lesbian and gay rights activists attempted to use the elected branches in hopes that the courts would follow later.

This chapter examines the litigation efforts of groups interested in gaining and protecting lesbian and gay rights. These groups have not had a great deal of success in the judiciary, the traditional forum for the disenfranchised and the protector of individual rights. It is important to place the current battles over the military ban in the context of the litigation strategies and battles that have preceded it. In some ways, this is a symbolic issue, but it is a practical issue of political power.

It is difficult to understand the practical and symbolic nature of the military ban without reference to past efforts to claim lesbian and gay rights. Indeed, the litigation that challenged the military ban on lesbians and gays and the decisions in those cases did not arise in a vacuum. Past litigation efforts in cases concerning lesbian and gay rights structured the strategies and arguments made in favor of removing the military ban. The failure to attain their goals in the judiciary made the opportunity to gain access to the elected branches more important. The lack of litigation success that penetrated the legal system made Clinton's entreaties so important and his failure to deliver on the promise so devastating to lesbian and gay rights activists. The issue is important in and of itself, but a decision to rescind the ban whether it emerged from the executive or judicial branch would have potential spillover effects for a variety of other issues that concern lesbians and gay men.

Analysts have demonstrated that to understand policy in any institutional context, one must study the development and roots of that policy.[13] Arguably understanding the evolution of policy is most important in the judiciary, where past decisions form a supporting structure if the precedents are favorable or a formidable set of barriers if they are not. Thus, it is important to begin not with the first cases that directly involved the military ban, but to examine the cases that led activists for lesbian and gay rights into the courts, the development of litigation strategies, and the decisions that emerged from these cases.

To understand the use of the courts by advocates for lesbian and gay rights, I trace the rise and transformation of groups involved with lesbian and gay rights,[14] focusing on their efforts to use the courts. The analysis examines the transition from defensively using the courts to the aggressive pursuit of legal strategies. Litigation strategies are a function of the underlying political environment, the nature of judicial doctrine, the ideological balance of the courts, and the policies emerging from state legislatures, Congress, and the executive.[15] I examine the emergence of litigation strategies, the cases that led to *Bowers v. Hardwick* (478 US 186, 1986), and the nature of strategies in the wake of that decision. The chapter demonstrates the constraints that litigants faced when they directly challenged the military ban on lesbian and gay personnel. Those constraints and barriers were constructed over a period that began a generation before the military ban cases first reached the courts.

POLITICAL LITIGATION: USING THE COURTS

The judicial process is not amenable to the coherent construction of policy without the assistance of groups that monitor policy, read the entrails of decisions, and sponsor or join subsequent litigation. Successful groups can sequence cases to structure the evolution of policy and the nature of judicial debate.[16] The Legal Defense Fund of the NAACP implemented a careful strategy that culminated in razing *de jure* segregation in the South. The work building up to the *Brown v. Board of Education* precedent provides the classic example of systematic, incremental litigation designed to pursue long-term goals.[17] For decades, groups have used the courts as a vehicle of social change.[18] The fact that the Court is not a self-starter maximizes the utility of groups.

"Repeat players" pursue policy goals in the courts by litigating strong cases to achieve favorable precedents that will penetrate the judicial system, and by settling weak cases to avoid harmful precedents. Such groups tend to have impressive legal and financial resources and the ability to predict which cases have the best chance of creating the precedents they desire. Such groups are able to litigate strategically and rationally, although more recently, this task is getting more difficult.[19] These systemic advantages mean that precedents and the law will often favor the repeat players.[20]

Even groups with the most resources cannot hope to litigate every issue that concerns them. Such groups will be affected by many decisions and need to keep a viable presence in a number of areas. Groups lacking sufficient resources can enter pending cases through an *amicus curiae* ("friend of the court") brief, which serves to inform the Court about the impact of a decision on a group that is not directly involved in the case. *Amici* briefs can frame the issues in a case in a different context and help specify alternatives to consider. In effect, such briefs serve the same functions as group testimony before congressional committees: they marshall specialized opinion, provide general and technical information, and provide an informal tally of public opinion.[21]

Lesbian and gay individuals, until recently, represented examples of what Marc Galanter called "one-shotters."[22] As the name implies, one-shotters use the courts infrequently and are not interested in long-term gains. Rather, their litigation efforts are directed toward settling the instant case. Because of manifest and latent societal prejudice and hostility, many lesbians and gay men would not reveal their sexual orientation and remained "in the closet."[23] They were politically powerless and without a coherent judicial strategy. Groups purported to speak on their behalf, but there were only vague estimates of the numbers they represented. The activist organizations did not have the experience to act effectively on their own in the courts. In recognition of their lack of experience, these groups initially concentrated their efforts in other directions and sought outside assistance.

THE RISE OF INTEREST GROUPS CONCERNED WITH LESBIAN AND GAY RIGHTS

Prior to the Stonewall riot in 1969 that served as a galvanizing moment for lesbian and gay rights, groups like the Mattachine Society (formed in the 1950s), the East Coast Homophile Organization (ECHO), and the Society for Individual Rights (SIR) formed grassroots organizations.[24] Although some groups were more concerned with civil rights, none were legal organizations. Like early groups in other social movements, they tended to adopt assimilationist arguments and accommodationist tactics. These groups initially took a relatively low public profile.[25] They were active in the lesbian and gay communities. The goal was to achieve legitimacy in those communities before seeking broader acceptance. Discrimination against lesbians and gay men was widespread and induced advocate groups to use courts defensively to stop individual acts of harassment. The long-term goal would involve getting rid of offending laws and using the various branches of government in a more proactive fashion.

Despite widespread repression and police harassment, lesbians and gays began to win protections in some courts. Two early sets of cases involved gay bars and the loss of federal employment. These were strictly reactive, one-shotter cases. The litigation efforts, which were hardly scripted or coordinated, involved cases brought after arrests at a gay bar or in the wake of a dismissal from a government position. The goal was not to create a precedent, but to reverse a conviction or win back a job. Because the cases were not strategically sequenced, attorneys for lesbian and gay rights had to take whatever cases were available. Not surprisingly, many of these cases arose in areas where the Mattachine Society, SIR, and ECHO were active. In other areas, harassment went undetected or without redress.

In California, New York, and New Jersey, lesbian and gay rights advocates won some victories. Most notable was a 1959 victory in the California courts. The state legislature passed a law permitting the revocation of liquor licenses if the bars became "a resort for drug users, pimps, prostitutes, and sexual perverts." The law, which was used almost exclusively against lesbians and gays, was declared unconstitutional in *Vallegra v. Department of Alcoholic Beverage Control* (347 P.2d 909, Cal. 1959).[26] In some senses, however, the victory was more symbolic than real. The court's decision recognized a distinction between status and conduct. Thus lesbians and gays could not be punished for their status. They could be punished, however, for illegal conduct. In many circumstances, illegal conduct that was "an offense to public morals" could be alleged to justify arrests and uphold convictions.

The second set of early cases involved government employees. In actions that foreshadowed the military ban on lesbians and gays, government employees in the armed forces who were charged with being lesbian or gay and then fired had no procedural safeguards.[27] In *Harmon v. Brucker* (355 US 579, 1958), the Supreme Court sanctioned judicial review of administrative discharges, but did so in a way that had the least possible impact. The Court used a *per curiam* decision, which carries less weight than a signed opinion. Second, the Court refused to consider the broader constitutional issues based on the Fifth and Sixth Amendments. Interestingly, in recounting the facts of the case in the decision, the Court did not mention the reasons for Harmon's discharge from the Army. Rather, the opinion said that the dismissal was predicated on the preinduction activities of the petitioner. The reluctance to address homosexuality directly would be a long-standing trait for the Supreme Court.

Harmon and a companion case were argued by attorneys for the American Civil Liberties Union (ACLU). The Worker's Defense League and the Servicemen's Defense Committee filed *amici* briefs on behalf of Harmon. This broadened the issues in the case beyond a question of lesbian and gay rights and shifted the focus to appropriate procedures. This would make the case more palatable to a Court that was not ready to consider lesbian and gay rights directly, but would limit the impact of a favorable precedent on the gay rights movement.

For a long period of time, civil service employees could be dismissed for engaging in any form of lesbian and gay conduct, because such activity was prima facie evidence of immoral activity. Federal courts usually upheld the dismissals, though there were a handful of victories for lesbian and gay rights. Occasionally, a federal court demanded some proof of a causal connection between the conduct at issue and unfitness for service. In *Norton v. Macy* (417 F.2d 1161, D.C. Circ. 1969), the District of Columbia Court of Appeals established a "rational nexus test" for all dismissals of government employees terminated for off-duty immoral conduct. As a result, lesbian and gay conduct per se was no longer adequate grounds for dismissal.[28] This became an important bellwether case. Its impact was limited because it was a lower court case, but other lower courts faced with similar issues consulted and cited the decision.

It is not unusual for a Court of Appeals decision to have spillover effects in three directions. First, a decision that is favorable (or unfavorable) to a particular group typically leads to the expansion (or contraction) of other rights. Second, when one federal court—typically a respected one like the Court of Appeals for the District of Columbia—issues an important decision, it diffuses to other circuits. Courts in other parts of the nation are not required to follow another circuit, but often look to the doctrinal developments from respected judges and circuits. Finally, repeat players will take legal arguments that are successful in one jurisdiction and use them in courts in other parts of the country.

In post-*Norton* cases, other federal courts were willing to adopt the "nexus test," thus shifting the focus to what sorts of conduct were sufficient to justify job termination. In the wake of the *Norton* case, private lesbian or gay conduct might not be sufficient grounds for job termination. The decisions, however, seemed to hold that the more public the lesbian or gay conduct, the more likely an employer would be found justified in firing an employee.[29]

Without the capacity, resources, or experience to create a reputation or simulate the advantages of a repeat player, activists for lesbian and gay rights attempted to enlist the assistance of established groups, particularly those with good reputations and experience in litigation. The group that best fit these requirements was the ACLU. Unfortunately, early efforts to incorporate the organization were not fruitful. Initially, the ACLU balked and refused to support lesbian and gay rights groups, speak on their behalf, or assist in the construction of their cases.[30]

During the 1950s, the ACLU was periodically approached to provide legal assistance for lesbians and gay men who had suffered discrimination. The cases were to be challenged at the local level, but the attempt to involve the ACLU was based on the desire to increase the stakes and move litigation to the national level. The requests came at a time when the ACLU was struggling for an institutional identity, and its successes were still rather limited. The organization had achieved some progress in expanding free speech, but World War II and the ideological Cold War that flourished in its wake forced the ACLU to concentrate its resources and pick its battles carefully.

The national organization was primarily interested in expanding freedom of expression. In the minds of the leadership, prudence dictated moving slowly and concentrating its resources on direct First Amendment cases. The ACLU was willing to concede that the Court's distinction between pure speech (which would get the ultimate protection) and conduct (which could be regulated by the government) was reasonable. This construction had consequences for lesbian and gay rights. By drawing a line between speech and belief (which was protected) and sexual conduct (which was not constitutionally protected), the ACLU generally refused to handle lesbian and gay rights cases.[31] This abdication had dramatic symbolic and practical consequences. Lesbians and gays were an easy target for McCarthyism. In the absence of support from the ACLU, there was no defense for lesbian and gay rights. Thus it was easy to codify laws that declared that lesbian and gay individuals were security risks.[32] Once sanctions had been placed into regulations, removing legal stigmas would be a laborious and costly task.

Less than a generation earlier, the ACLU had refused to support the rights of those branded as Communists. The leadership wanted to avoid being tied too closely to the Communist Party. The rejection of the entreaties of lesbian and gay rights activists reflected a similar desire to distance the organization from an unpopular group. The refusal to support lesbian and gay rights split the membership, as had the decision to ignore the pleas of alleged Communists. Some local affiliates of the ACLU intervened to assist lesbians and gay men who were the victims of discrimination in their jurisdictions. Several affiliates, most notably those in Southern California and Washington, D.C., fought to reverse the national office's policy.

In 1957, the ACLU issued its first national policy statement on issues concerning lesbians and gays, conceding the constitutionality of sodomy statutes and admitting homosexuality was a valid rationale for security clearances. The organization did step in to protect the due process rights of lesbians and gay men as in the *Harmon* case. The ACLU opposed the police entrapment that often went on at the state and local levels and proposals for the compulsory registration of lesbians and gays.[33]

The ACLU was criticized for its reluctance to endorse lesbian and gay rights. Because there was not a powerful gay rights movement in the 1950s and 1960s, some speculate that members of the ACLU, particularly the older leadership, shared the types of stereotypical views of lesbians and gays that were often used as a rationale for harassment.[34] By the early 1960s, however, the political environment had changed dramatically. Changes in the composition of the Warren Court created the most liberal court in American history.[35] First Amendment issues were increasingly resolved in the ACLU's favor, allowing the organization to turn its attention to other issues. In addition, the ACLU attempted to transplant favorable First Amendment precedents to other areas of law.

Shortly after the *Griswold v. Connecticut* (381 US 479, 1965) decision that created the constitutional right to privacy and was a symbol of the revolution wrought by the Warren Court, several board members pushed for the inclusion of lesbian and gay rights as part of the ACLU agenda. Finally, in 1967, after additional precedents buttressed the *Griswold* decision, the ACLU took the position that all private consensual conduct, heterosexual as well as lesbian or gay, should be protected by the privacy rights recognized in *Griswold*. In 1973, the ACLU created the Sexual Privacy Project to work on the privacy challenges to governmental regulation of sexuality.[36]

On the eve of the Stonewall riots, the shape of the legal topography for lesbian and gay rights was decidedly uneven. The Supreme Court's obscenity decisions, beginning with *Roth v. United States* (354 US 476, 1957), provided greater protection for freedom of expression. This had the spillover effect of providing more latitude for lesbian and gay publications, which were frequently the target of censorship. A subsequent decision directly considered gay magazines. *Manual Enterprise v. Day* (370 US 478, 1962) involved a postmaster who withheld delivery of 405 copies of magazines after a hearing found that the magazines had no literary, scientific, or other merit. The decision appeared to liberalize the "prurient interest" standard of the *Roth* test. The Court held that the materials must be "so offensive as to affront current community standards of decency," but that decency had to be "self-demonstrating."[37]

Federal employees who were fired for being lesbian or gay had some success in challenging dismissals, but such protections were not uniform across the nation. Lower courts had provided an inconsistent patchwork of laws and precedents. Lesbian and gay rights were partially a function of which state an individual called home. This was an issue that the Supreme Court was sensitive to regarding African Americans. After *Brown*, the Court nationalized the law to protect racial minorities. The justices showed no inclination to offer similar protection to lesbians and gays. That was partially a function of the ACLU's refusal to get involved. Thus, lesbian and gay rights were not systematically brought to the courts to provide favorable decisions for future litigants. Lesbian and gay rights needed precedents that would penetrate through the judicial system and provide the foundation for those later cases that would invariably raise more difficult questions.

The early legal victories established the conduct/status distinction that continues to dominate lesbian and gay litigation. Discrimination solely on the basis of status and conduct that was totally private found some protection in the courts. Once behavior crossed from purely private into the public sphere, however, the protection would normally be removed.[38]

The influence of policy entrepreneurs is conditional. Advocates must await the occurrence of a "policy window," a propitious opportunity for action. A policy window opens as a result of a change in a political stream or because a problem reaches prominence. New issues achieve agenda status by moving through open policy windows. To reach the decision agenda, the convergence of solutions and policy alternatives needs to be attached to a problem. If that occurs, the problem is likely to find support in the political stream.[39] The Warren Court appeared to open a potential policy window, but the ACLU was reluctant to add its authority and reputation until that window (if it ever existed) was closed.

Policy windows can close quickly. The Supreme Court's refusal to grant lesbian and gay rights any agenda space was an example of a policy window that was left unopened. Petitioners sought entry through a variety of existing windows including criminal law, education, and public employment. The claims invoked First Amendment, equal protection, privacy, and due process arguments. The failure seemed to be in the political stream. It appears that a majority of justices felt the nation was not ready for definitive rulings concerning lesbian and gay rights.[40]

There was little systematic litigation strategy prior to Stonewall. Gay rights litigation was reactive. There was little outside assistance from reputable repeat players. In addition, the lesbian and gay rights movement was constrained by unfavorable direct precedents, favorable indirect precedents that were not exploited, and a legal system that was unwilling or unable to address the concerns of the lesbian and gay community. In this context, lesbian and gay activists began to create their own litigation strategies.

TO THE STREET AND TO THE COURTS: THE EMERGENCE OF A LEGAL STRATEGY

The Stonewall riot is widely considered the beginning of the modern gay liberation movement. Stonewall was a shock to the social system that spilled over to the political and legal realms. Of course, the lesbian and gay liberation movements cannot be viewed in isolation from other radical movements of the 1960s. The Stonewall riots provided a shift in lesbian and gay arguments for civil rights in a decidedly more radical direction. The movement would no longer be assimilationist and accommodationist. Rather than have others define the context of their rights, these groups set out to define their own ideas of what was appropriate behavior.

Stonewall was followed by the formation of new groups, many of whom broke rank with existing homophile organizations.[41] Among the most prominent of the new forces were the Gay Liberation Front (GLF) and the Gay Activists Alliance (GAA).[42] These new groups did not turn immediately to the courts. Like many groups of the day, these organizations assumed that conventional politics and policies were deaf to their goals. As a result, they took to the streets. The silence of the proverbial closet was broken by a newfound visibility as the ranks of persons willing to be counted as lesbian or gay grew.[43]

Advocate groups also pursued an elite strategy to work at the fringes of conventional politics through important expert communities. Representatives of these groups began to assemble at political forums to question candidates about their position on lesbian and gay issues. The most successful challenge was a campaign to get the American Psychiatric Association (APA) to reverse its position and remove homosexuality from its registry of mental disorders.[44] The medical profession's definition of mental illness had important legal consequences. The victory within the APA was equivalent to winning an important victory in the courts by creating a precedent.[45] Another significant development in lesbian and gay rights law occurred when the American Law Institute, in publishing its Model Penal Code, dropped any prohibition of sodomy. Beginning with Illinois in 1961, 21 states decriminalized sodomy by adopting the Model Penal Code.[46] Lesbian and gay rights activists also successfully lobbied the Civil Service Commission to remove hostile policies.[47]

By the early 1970s, the gay rights movement began to split into radical and conservative camps, a common occurrence in most social and political movements.[48] The GAA had become more structured, and separated itself from the more radical GLF. The Alliance itself dissolved and began anew in 1973 as what would become the National Gay and Lesbian Task Force. Part of the impetus for the split from the more radical elements of the movement was the desire to pursue a litigation strategy based on that of the NAACP.[49] Groups purporting to speak for gay men and those representing lesbians went through similar rifts.[50]

The defining characteristics of the lesbian and gay rights movement in the immediate post-Stonewall years were the increased visibility of its more radical demands for the freedom to be different. If the more diverse elements of the lesbian and gay rights movement were more visible, they were absent from the litigation efforts. In the search for the perfect plaintiffs to bring test cases, strategists for gay litigation wanted mainstream, otherwise conservative-looking lesbians and gay men to carry the banner into court. In this respect, the military cases provided the ideal plaintiff profile: loyal, patriotic, relatively conservative individuals, who just happened to have a different sexual orientation.

The ACLU ultimately played a significant role in shaping litigation efforts and strategies. The ACLU leadership propagated an "enclave theory." Society was comprised of many groups whose members were systematically denied the full protections of the Bill of Rights. The ACLU wanted to identify those groups and work to expand their rights.[51] The rights consciousness of the period and the spillover effects from other social movements provided further impetus.

The role of the ACLU in lesbian and gay rights litigation was both direct and indirect. First, recognition by the ACLU provided the legitimacy lesbian and gay rights activists had sought for two decades. Second, the ACLU brought cases that did not involve lesbians or gay men directly, but would have implications for their rights. Third, the establishment of the Sexual Privacy Project helped spawn a variety of groups directly concerned with lesbian and gay rights and dedicated to litigation efforts. The role of the ACLU was magnified by the fact that these new litigation groups were frequently headed by former members of the ACLU.[52]

In 1973, the Lambda Legal Defense and Education Fund (LLDEF) was formed as a litigation arm. The LLDEF was a public interest law firm to be run by lesbians and gay men.[53] Unfortunately, as late arrivals to the practice of litigation, advocates for lesbians and gays faced a more complicated and hostile environment. It was complicated by the proliferation of groups using the courts, which were increasingly hostile due to the packing of the federal judiciary with judges with a conservative social vision, who espoused a limited view of judicial power and constitutional rights.

Compare the courts facing civil rights activists in 1954 (*Brown*) and 1973 (*Roe*) to those that lesbian and gay groups faced in the 1980s. Nixon, Reagan, and Bush packed the Supreme Court with conservative justices, who passed litmus tests on judicial restraint, law and order, and "traditional family values." In many ways, lower courts are more important than the Supreme Court. Over 95 percent of the cases that begin in the federal courts have a final determination in the district courts. The significance of the lower courts is magnified in lesbian and gay rights litigation because the Supreme Court is often unwilling to review cases in these areas, making the lower court decisions the final word. Reagan and Bush were responsible for packing the lower courts, filling over half the seats with younger, more conservative jurists who were hostile to the expansion of rights.[54]

By the time of the *Roe* decision, litigation had become a complex process. Groups representing the marginalized in society had achieved success and continued to proliferate and crowd the courts. Conservative groups, often representing the "haves" of society, also began to utilize the courts. They had recognized that the gains they had accrued in the other branches were being undermined by liberal groups using the judiciary. As the number of Republican appointees grew, conservative activist groups felt the courts would be more sympathetic to their social and economic agenda.[55]

The confluence of these factors did not bode well for lesbian and gay rights activists. A brief overview of some of the significant cases shows that a variety of factors limited the movement toward equal rights for lesbians and gays. First, negative decisions structured the government's arguments in subsequent cases and often became the essence of later decisions. Second, the Supreme

Court often refused to get involved in the cases. This limited the effect of a negative decision, but also blunted the opportunities for positive precedents that could percolate throughout the judicial system. The reluctance of the Court to consider these issues also limited the influence of litigation groups. With limited resources, the groups could only get involved in a handful of cases. They preferred to conserve resources for the Supreme Court and the best test cases. Unfortunately, the Court was unwilling to accept these cases, preferring to let the issue remain in the lower courts. This had important symbolic and practical consequences. It created a patchwork of laws and precedents that provided some protection and broader recognition in some jurisdictions, and severe limits on rights in other parts of the country.

Further complicating the process for advocates of lesbian and gay rights was the fact that when the Supreme Court did get involved in these cases, its decisions tended to hurt the movement. Cases of first impression have traditionally caused a great deal of trouble for the Court. The judicial process is based on the construction of policy analogy, and the Court views new cases in the context of existing issue areas.[56] This is not surprising that the justices need to justify their decisions in reference to related precedents and litigants, for both sides will raise favorable precedents from neighboring areas of law. The Supreme Court often makes a tentative initial decision and then returns to the issue over the next few years to modify and perhaps overturn the earlier decision.

One of the earliest Supreme Court cases, *Boutilier v. Immigration and Naturalization Service* (387 US 118, 1967), is a prime example of some of the difficulties that lesbian and gay rights faced in the Court. The case was decided in the context of the policies of the Immigration and Naturalization Service (INS), rather than in a framework emphasizing civil rights. The Court had often been deferential to INS policies in past decisions. The ACLU had filed an *amicus curiae* brief on behalf of Clive Michael Boutilier, advancing a number of arguments that had been successfully employed in other cases.

The INS was notorious for shrouding distinctions between status and conduct in decisions on aliens. Because the Court accepted the case, a decision concerning status and conduct would have broad applicability. Prior to the APA removal of homosexuality as a mental disorder, the INS routinely deported lesbian and gay aliens on the grounds that they were afflicted with "a psychopathic personality." The Court upheld this policy in *Boutilier*, ruling that aliens could be deported for moral turpitude, which would include crimes of a sexual nature. The Court held that Boutilier was gay when he entered the country and could be excluded under the Immigration and Nationality Act of 1952, as one "afflicted with [a] psychopathic personality." The Court ruled that Congress clearly intended to include lesbians and gays within that description. The Court further ruled that the term "psychopathic personality" was not void for vagueness nor repugnant to the Fifth Amendment's due process clause.[57]

The dissenters, in an opinion authored by Justice William Douglas, argued that the term "psychopathic personality," like "communist," was so broad and vague as to be nothing more than an epithet. Years before the APA ruling that removed homosexuality from its lists of mental disorders, Douglas dismissed the contention that homosexuality equated to a psychopathic personality or some form of mental illness. He further took the majority to task for blurring the distinction between conduct and status (a debate that was occurring in other areas of law, most notably in the free speech cases).

Just below the surface in many of the early cases was the specter of the antisodomy laws. The issue was certainly at the forefront of the gay rights movement and its litigation efforts. The decision to attack sodomy laws marks the transition from reactive to more proactive litigation. Rather than merely challenge a dismissal, the Lambda Legal Defense and Education Fund and the National Gay and Lesbian Task Force, often with the assistance of the ACLU, would attack the sodomy law on its face. These cases also provided gay rights groups with the opportunity to raise the conduct/status distinction more directly.

The presence of sodomy laws represented an assault to the dignity of all gay men and women. The fact that such laws were rarely enforced was of little solace. In some symbolic ways it made the situation even worse. The mere existence of such laws seemed to mean that insulting a class of citizens was their main purpose.[58] Many claim that "sodomy laws are the bedrock of discrimination against gays."[59] The arguments for attacking the validity of sodomy laws could be cast in terms of their practical consequences. Legal reform was necessary not because the laws were inherently objectionable, but because of the real and apparent spillover effects into areas of public policy that did matter (such as housing, employment, immigration, and the military). They provided opponents of lesbian and gay rights with a quasi-legal basis for opposition.[60] On a practical level, these laws seemed vulnerable to constitutional challenge in light of the privacy decisions.

The goal was to overturn sodomy laws on the grounds that they restricted a fundamental right to privacy. This would create a precedent that might be useful in reversing discrimination in employment, immigration, and military laws.[61] A decision on the issue could serve to clear up the obfuscation of the conduct/status distinction. Further, because a number of states had repealed their sodomy laws in light of the American Legal Institute's model penal code, lesbians and gays in one part of the country had more rights than those living in other regions merely by virtue of their residence.

The Supreme Court had carefully dodged the issue of the constitutionality of sodomy laws, despite the increasing numbers of such cases in the wake of the *Griswold* decision. Finally, in a *per curiam* decision (*Wainwright v. Stone*, 414 US 21, 1973), the Supreme Court ruled that state sodomy laws prohibiting the "abominable and detestable crime against nature" (the common law description of sodomy) were not unconstitutionally vague because the Florida courts had specified the content of the crime by construing the statute to prohibit oral and anal sex. Two years later, a federal district court in Virginia was asked to rule on the constitutionality of a sodomy statute in *Doe v.*

Commonwealth's Attorney of Richmond (403 F. Supp. 1199, E.D. Va. 1975; affirmed, 425 US 901, 1976).

Relying primarily on *Griswold*, attorneys for Doe argued that the statute violated the right to privacy under the First and Ninth Amendments, due process under the Fifth and Fourteenth Amendments, free expression under the First Amendment, and the prohibition against cruel and unusual punishment under the Eighth Amendment. The lower court rejected the arguments, citing the critical language in Justice Arthur Goldberg's concurring opinion in *Griswold*, which differentiated homosexuality and adultery from marital intimacy, which would be constitutionally protected under the right to privacy. The district court adopted the traditional judicial restraint position, claiming that it could not substitute its judgment for that of the legislature that passed the law. The court used a rational basis test, the standard that is most restrictive of individual liberties and most deferential to state power.

Doe was summarily affirmed by the Supreme Court without opinion. The effect of the decision was toxic for lesbian and gay rights. New York and Pennsylvania courts distinguished related cases from *Doe*, but many state courts relied upon it. In addition to denying lesbians and gay men constitutional protection for their most private, intimate relationships, *Doe* was used to support other antigay discrimination, thus having the negative spillover effects that were part of the rationale for attacking the sodomy laws.

The distinction between conduct and status, which had arisen in early litigation involving gay bars and the immigration cases, became even more evident and problematic in these post-*Doe* cases. Courts increasingly clouded the distinction by upholding rules banning homosexuality with no explanation as to whether the ban was based on conduct or status. The failure to enunciate a clear distinction between conduct and activity represented a negative judgment against lesbians and gay men as a class.[62]

The impact of the *Doe* precedent produced negative spillover effects in immigration cases as well. The INS denied applications to individuals who had admitted to any lesbian or gay relations. Courts citing *Doe* argued that this was a crime of moral turpitude, and the mere admission of intimate relations was sufficient evidence.[63] In the early 1980s, the INS adopted an earlier variation of the "Don't Ask, Don't Tell" policy. After court decisions forced the INS to modify its policies excluding lesbian and gay aliens, the INS adopted a policy excluding lesbian and gay foreigners only when they identified themselves or were so identified by others.[64]

Not every issue area was marked by negative decisions, however. The *Norton v. Macy* precedent provided some protection for public employees under the due process clause if they could demonstrate a liberty or property interest in their jobs. Employers would have to show that lesbian or gay conduct affected the employee's job performance before the employee could be fired. In federal employee cases, the government could not generally cite sexual orientation as sufficient grounds for dismissal without showing some connection between that orientation and job performance.

However, individuals who were denied job opportunities due to their sexual orientation could not utilize the property or liberty interest arguments. A prospective employee would have only a potential expectation of the job, which was not considered a liberty or property interest. The job applicant would have to make the more difficult claim that the denial of employment punished constitutionally protected lesbian and gay conduct.[65]

The court's failure to protect lesbian and gay conduct from criminal prosecution in *Doe* made it easier in subsequent cases to deny protection to lesbians and gay men who lost job opportunities as a consequence of engaging in "criminal" sexual conduct. In general, the practical result was that those who were not open about their sexual orientation and stayed in the closet had a chance to win the case, while those who were open about their private affairs often lost. In a case involving the refusal to hire a gay activist as a police officer, *Childers v. Dallas Police Department* (513 F. Supp. 134, N.D. Tex. 1981; affirmed 669 F.2d 732, 5th Cir. 1982), the federal court was explicit about this, emphasizing the differences between cases in which governmental employees were too open about their sexual orientation and those cases in which they were not. The court argued that its reading of those cases showed that only plaintiffs who remained closeted won their cases.[66]

In this largely unfavorable context, the numbers of challenges to the military ban on lesbians and gays proliferated. In 1982 President Reagan ordered the Department of Defense to revise the policy so that it was a total ban that was uniform throughout various military branches. In response to the regulations, most lesbian and gay service members remained closeted.[67] When lesbian and gay military personnel revealed their sexual preferences, they were discharged from military service. The resulting cases were designed to reverse the discharges, but with the presence of groups like the Lambda Legal Defense and Education Fund and the National Gay Rights Task Force, the cases had the broader aim of creating a favorable precedent that would penetrate the system, be useful in challenging other dismissals, and ultimately be used to reverse the directive itself.

THE MILITARY BANS ON LESBIANS AND GAYS: BUCKING PRECEDENT, TRADITION, AND DEFERENCE

The public employees cases provided some protections, even if they were not extensive. In cases involving lesbians and gays in the military, however, the results were much less favorable. While *Norton v. Macy* had established the principle that the government could not use sexual orientation as a grounds for dismissing employees unless there was a rational connection between that orientation and job performance, that principle had never been extended to military employees.

The *Matlovich v. Secretary of the Air Force* (591 F.2d 852, D.C. Circ. 1978) case provided the court with the opportunity to close the gap between the military and employment cases. Citing *Doe*, which the Supreme Court had recently upheld, Judge Gerhard Gesell ruled that Leonard Matlovich had no constitutional right to engage in sodomy. Gesell held that the regulation was not so irrational that it might be branded arbitrary. This case was significant because it was the first to hold that because criminal laws against sodomy were constitutional, governmental discrimination against lesbians and gays would not violate equal protection unless a plaintiff could show that the discrimination was not rational. Most subsequent cases in other courts followed the analysis of *Matlovich*. The combination of low level rational basis review and judicial deference to the military led to a number of litigation losses.[68]

The case demonstrated the strategic principles that go into mapping litigation plans. David Addlestone, who represented the ACLU on the Matlovich litigation team, advised against taking the case to the Supreme Court regardless of the outcome in the lower court, because he felt that the justices would not be sympathetic to the case. Matlovich wanted to ignore the advice and take the case to the Supreme Court. The ACLU withdrew its resources from the effort, but the Lambda Legal Defense and Education Fund was willing to step into the vacuum.[69]

The strategic choices of the two groups reveal the differences between the LLDEF and the ACLU. The experience and expertise of the ACLU led it to exit from the case. As generalists in the process litigating across a variety of issue areas, the ACLU was concerned that the adverse decision it predicted would have negative consequences that might spill over to other areas of law. The LLDEF did not face the same constraints, and had less reason to be concerned with spillovers to other doctrinal areas and little to lose by going to the next level.

Some lower courts recognized a right to privacy in consensual lesbian and gay conduct. Invariably, however, the courts still ruled that the government's interest in military regulation outweighed those privacy interests. In only one pre-*Bowers* decision, *BenShalom v. Secretary of the Army* (489 F. Supp. 964, E.D. Wis. 1980), did the court distinguish sexual preferences from conduct and find that mere preferences were constitutionally protected. Miriam BenShalom refused to admit lesbian conduct and won her case.[70] The decision acknowledged that there was no proof that she had engaged in lesbian activity.[71] Thus, the case provided a good set of facts for establishing a favorable precedent.

The Federal District Court in Wisconsin held that the military regulation directly infringed on a soldier's right to meet with other lesbians and gay men and discuss current problems or advocate changes, even when no unlawful conduct was involved. These activities could subject the soldier to dismissal from the service, even though they represented traditional modes of expression that were protected under the First Amendment. The Army's interests in protecting national defense and maintaining discipline under the "peculiar" conditions of military life have traditionally been given great respect by courts. In this case, though, the court ruled that those regulations were substantially outweighed by the chilling effects imposed on the First Amendment rights of soldiers.[72] The Court ruled further that the Army's policy of discharging people simply for being gay offended privacy interests rooted in the First Amendment. One legal expert claimed, "At that particular moment in history, gay rights in the military seemed within reach."[73]

The *BenShalom* case was an aberration, however. The military dismissals and cases they spawned were rarely specific as to the nature of the sexual conduct alleged. Prior to *Bowers v. Hardwick*, there was a belief that private consensual sexual conduct enjoyed some constitutional protection, therefore the conduct could be admitted. The litigation strategies in military cases emphasized the private, consensual nature of the conduct and maintained that it was irrelevant to job performance.[74]

As the *BenShalom* case demonstrated, there were a few victories, though they were typically limited. The key was to find the case that could unlock the door to the Supreme Court and create a favorable precedent that could create spillover effects. A few cases suggested a change in the prevailing climate and appeared destined to get to the Court. In *Nemetz v. INS* (647 F.2d 432, 4th Circ. 1981), the Fourth Circuit Court of Appeals recognized the patchwork of conflicting lower court decisions. Part of the recognized role of courts is to establish consistency in the law, so that individuals would know the extent of their rights. In this case, the INS was willing to defer to state laws concerning moral turpitude (Virginia sodomy statute), a traditional state police power to protect the health, safety, and morals of its citizens. Attorneys for Nemetz argued that the Constitution required a "uniform rule of naturalization."

The Court of Appeals for the Fourth Circuit agreed with Nemetz's attorney. The court opined that the development of a federal standard for making that determination would provide the only certain means of creating a constitutionally required uniform rule. A number of states had decriminalized private, consensual sex between adults. At oral argument it was conceded that if Nemetz lived in one of those states, the INS would be unable to oppose his petition on the ground of bad moral character. In any state in which sodomy was not a crime, Nemetz could have freely admitted to committing acts of sodomy without placing his petition in jeopardy. In other words, according to the court, but for an "accident of geography," Nemetz would be a naturalized citizen.

This was the type of case that the Supreme Court normally enters. First, it involved individual rights, the most prevalent cases on the Court's docket. Second, the case involved a lower court conflict. The Court frequently grants certiorari when there is a clear conflict between two lower courts.[75] The lower court did all it could to call attention to that fact. Despite these factors, the Supreme Court denied certiorari in the case. This had the positive effect of upholding the favorable lower court decision, but a denial of certiorari carries no precedential value so the effects were limited.

There were other candidates for Supreme Court review progressing through the legal system. The Court summarily affirmed a Tenth Circuit opinion dealing with the regulation of public speech about homosexuality. *National Gay Task Force v. Board of Education Oklahoma City* (729 F.2d 1270, 10th Circ.

1984) was a constitutional challenge to a statute authorizing the dismissal of a teacher for engaging in public conduct related to sexual orientation.[76] The case did not involve sexual conduct, but rather activities that might be directed at repealing the law, thus implicating free speech concerns.

The trial court upheld the statute. The Court of Appeals reversed, claiming that the statute limited protected speech and was thus overbroad. The Court of Appeals ruled that the law which punished teachers for "public homosexual conduct," defined as "advocating, soliciting, imposing, encouraging or promoting public or private homosexual activity in a manner that created a substantial risk that such conduct would come to the attention of school children or school employees."[77] The court held that a teacher who lobbied the legislature to urge repeal of the Oklahoma antisodomy statute would be "advocating" and "encouraging" sodomy, but such statements, which were aimed at legal and social change, were at the core of First Amendment protections. Despite the favorable decision, the case presented no issues regarding private sexual conduct. Because this involved public activity, the right to privacy was not implicated or addressed in the opinion.[78]

The Supreme Court voted to accept the case, creating the potential for a long awaited decision on lesbian and gay rights. That was unlikely, because the First Amendment question would probably overwhelm the more direct lesbian and gay rights issues. Justice Lewis Powell did not participate in the case and the final vote was equally divided. This had the effect of affirming the lower court decision but limiting any long-range impact, because it did not create a precedent. This was not a positive harbinger for future success. The Court took a relatively easy case, involving free speech, and was unable to reach a positive decision.

This paved the way for the *Bowers v. Hardwick* case, which represented an opportunity for the Supreme Court to weigh in on a question related to lesbian and gay rights. The facts of the case are significant and demonstrate the dynamics of organized litigation. First, the state of Georgia initially declined to prosecute the case; rather, Michael Hardwick was instrumental in actively pursuing the case.[79] Second, this seemed to be an ideal test case. In retrospect, critics have argued the folly of using this case as a vehicle for a favorable precedent to begin to dismantle decades of discrimination. That criticism is misplaced.[80] There have been few test cases that seemed to present strategic litigants with a better opportunity to get a favorable decision. Despite that, some justices were apparently loathe to bring the issue to the docket for fear of an unfavorable decision that would create a negative precedent.[81] In truth, groups (and justices) often misjudge cases of first impression, because it is unclear which frame of reference the Court will utilize or what context will be used to view the new case. Third, new areas of law are often based on extreme fact situations in the early cases. Because of these facts, litigants are anxious to get the case to the appellate courts. These elements were present in the *Bowers v. Hardwick* case.

In oral argument, Georgia claimed the purpose of the act was largely "symbolic." To Richard Mohr this meant that the laws allowed states "to express hatred of gays officially and systematically without directly addressing the issue."[82] Assistant Attorney General Michael Hobbs urged the Court to adopt a rational, minimum level of scrutiny. He catalogued "a parade of horribles" that would occur if the justices struck down the law. Hobbs suggested there was a link between the sodomy law and the growing AIDS epidemic.[83] The state's argument appeared to influence Justice White, who was assigned the majority opinion.

Litigation strategy and the development of arguments were important agenda items for the Ad Hoc Task Force to Challenge Sodomy Laws. By 1985, the Task Force had become an official project of the LLDEF. National meetings of lesbian and gay rights litigators included attorneys from ACLU affiliates in states with sodomy statutes. These advocates created a think tank and forum for discussions of constitutional theory and litigation strategies.

Laurence Tribe, who argued *Bowers* before the Supreme Court, was an active participant in the Task Force.[84] Tribe based his arguments on the privacy decisions. Like recent abortion arguments, which are generally directed at a single justice (Sandra Day O'Connor), Tribe's argument was largely aimed at Lewis Powell, the unknown factor in the case and certain to be the tie breaking vote. Tribe argued for a heightened level of scrutiny and the fundamental rights that would inhere in privacy.[85] He argued that the case represented a mere extension of previous privacy decisions. Attorneys for lesbian and gay rights felt the arguments were strong and well received by the justices. They believed that the end of sodomy statutes as the legal basis for codified discrimination against lesbians and gays was at hand.[86]

The lesbian and gay community has since been critical of Tribe's approach. In particular, Tribe was criticized for not stressing the impact of this case on the question of the legitimacy of lesbians and gays and their private relationships, as well as his decision to de-emphasize personhood arguments in favor of locational privacy arguments.[87] The proof was visible in the majority's lack of understanding of the stakes and of the broad stigma the decision had on lesbians and gays.[88]

In *Bowers v. Hardwick* the Court considered the substantive due process question: does *Griswold* extend to private consensual same-sex sexual conduct? By a 5-4 vote, the Court held that the constitutional right to privacy did not extend to private consensual gay sodomy. In the *Hardwick* decision, the Court upheld the statute criminalizing sodomy against the due process challenge. The Court held that the statute was rationally related to the state's interest in upholding morality. Tribe raised no First Amendment argument, and the Court subjected the statute to only relaxed rational basis scrutiny.[89] The decision left lower courts confused about First Amendment and equal protection questions,[90] even though those issues were not raised or considered.

Hardwick altered the course of lesbian and gay rights litigation, because the decision represented a major setback in the fight to end discrimination.[91] In the post-*Hardwick* era, lesbian and gay rights litigators have been forced to develop constitutional arguments that circumvent the adverse holding.[92] Most directly, it foreclosed the use of privacy arguments, which were central to the early cases. Litigators typically avoid privacy arguments and claims that sexual conduct is constitutionally protected. The conduct/status distinction, used sporadically by advocates of lesbian and gay rights in the post-*Doe* years of litigation, has now become the central focus in shaping new challenges to discrimination against gays and lesbians. Relying on the conduct/status distinction, lesbians and gay men are careful to separate questions about what they do in private from who they are in public.[93]

If there was anything positive about the decision, it was an element of new visibility. A decade earlier, the Supreme Court dodged full review and summarily affirmed a lower court's decision upholding a similar sodomy statute in *Doe v. Commonwealth's Attorney of Richmond*. *Doe* had already done what *Hardwick* did, but the latter was more notorious and galvanized outrage more effectively.

Whatever *Bowers v. Hardwick* meant constitutionally, the case has had profound effects on the lives of lesbians and gay men. In the wake of the decision, there was a renewed round of gay bashing by legislatures and courts, what Dunlap referred to as "the second epidemic."[94] The decision was especially devastating in one other sense: this appeared to be a good test case. The negative decision under these "ideal" conditions did not portend well when the inevitable issues concerning the military arose. Even before the *Bowers* decision, courts had shown deference to the military's policies; had the Supreme Court declared the Georgia sodomy law unconstitutional, there was a possibility that positive spillover effects may not have reached the armed forces. It was certain that negative effects would reach the military cases and that the precedent in *Bowers* would be used to justify the military restrictions. Because *Bowers* focused on sexual conduct rather than identity, it invited rationales like those the military now advances, which separate sexual identity from sexual conduct.[95]

As the primary symbol of legal suppression, *Bowers* has been to the lesbian and gay rights movement what *Plessy v. Ferguson* (163 US 537, 1896) was to the civil rights movement, and what *Dred Scott v. Sandford* (19 How. 393, 1857) was to abolitionists. Each of these decisions reflected the Court's failure to recognize the equality of a minority.[96] It has been necessary at some times to use the courts in a reactive manner, when there was an arrest, an offensive law, or a destructive voter initiative.[97] Ultimately, lesbian and gay rights advocates had to question whether the courts were a legitimate forum.

SEEKING ANOTHER FORUM

In light of *Bowers* and negative decisions in *BenShalom* (on rehearing) and *Woodward v. Moore* (451 F. Supp. 346, D.D.C. 1978; affirmed 871 F.2d 1068, Fed. Cir. 1989), both of which were refused by the Supreme Court, advocates argued that the courts were not sympathetic. The military decisions led leaders of the movement to recognize that civil rights for lesbians and gays were not destined to come from the federal judiciary for years, if not decades.[98] Nan Hunter, director of the ACLU Lesbian and Gay Rights Project, sounded a new direction for the movement: "We can win this issue in any one of three arenas: the courts, the Congress, or the Defense Department itself. In the past, efforts have been concentrated only in the courts, but we believe that the future resolution of this issue may lie in Washington."[99] In particular, the courts were probably a blind alley for those challenging the military ban on its face.

The military has fought hard to keep its ban on lesbian and gay service personnel in place. The arguments in favor of banning lesbian and gay personnel from the military have included the need for discipline, morale and unit cohesion, and the privacy of heterosexuals in the armed forces. The military sounded similar themes when it attempted to continue its policy of racial segregation in the 1940s.[100]

Service in the military has not traditionally been considered the equivalent of civilian employment. The protections of the Bill of Rights are available to military personnel, but those guarantees do not apply to the same extent as in the civilian setting.[101] Unlike civilian employment, which could be controlled by civil rights legislation, regulations governing entry into the armed services routinely differentiate on the grounds of height, weight, age, physical condition, education, and mental capacity. There has never been a recognized right to serve in the armed forces. Further, once an individual enters the military, all duties, privacy, assignments, apparel, length of hair, living conditions, and freedom of movement are dictated by superiors. Failure to conform to regulations can result in dismissal, discharge, or court-martial. In addition, a member of the military has no liberty or property interest in continued service.[102]

Lesbian and gay rights advocates previously tried to work through the executive branch in challenging military regulations. Although the issue of admission and retention of lesbians and gays in the military had not been a primary part of the lesbian and gay rights agenda, it became important when Jimmy Carter was elected president. With the stroke of a pen, Carter could have issued an executive order ending the military ban on lesbians and gays. Carter's advisors were convinced, however, that an executive order would be overturned by Congress, thus retaining the ban and giving it more weight. Randy Shilts argues that the Administration gave gay rights leaders assurances they would revisit the issue if Carter was re-elected in 1980.[103]

The issue reached the public agenda during the 1992 campaign. If lesbians and gay men needed further incentive to support Bill Clinton, the atavistic attacks of Pat Buchanan, Pat Robertson, and others at the Republican National Convention raised the stakes even higher. Lesbians and gay men responded with large campaign contributions, heavy voter turnout, and a large majority for Clinton.[104] Given his relatively small "mandate," a strong case could be made that Clinton owed his election to these groups. The new president seemed poised to make good on his promise. One could argue that the honeymoon period would be the most propitious time to enunciate a radical change in policy. The countervailing argument is that a president should not expend his precious, finite resources on controversial issues at the outset, but take advantage of the window of opportunity to build up political capital that could be spent on the controversial issue later.

Whatever the optimal strategy, Clinton mishandled the situation. By announcing the policy and then rescinding it in the face of pressure, Clinton appeared weak and vacillating. The initial policy alienated a military that was already wary of a commander in chief it considered a draft-dodger. The reversal cost him the support of a group that worked hard on his election. In fact, the resolution was tenuous, given that the courts were reintroduced into the issue area.

The Clinton administration's "honorable compromise" of "Don't Ask, Don't Tell, Don't Pursue" represents a variation on the conduct/status distinction. The earlier broadly based condemnations of lesbians and gays by the military had been translated into a revised version, which condemned lesbian and gay sexual activity. The Don't Ask, Don't Tell policy appeared to offer nothing more than a newly phrased warning for lesbians and gay men to return to the closet.[105]

The military ban illustrates how the boundaries of legal doctrine shape political debates and decisions. In the aftermath of *Bowers v. Hardwick*, the federal judiciary divided over the conduct/status debate, with most courts ruling that discrimination based on sexual orientation was not accorded heightened scrutiny under the equal protection clause because it was constitutionally permissible under *Hardwick* for a state to criminalize sodomy. Without a privacy based defense against criminalization of that conduct, advocates had to argue that sexual orientation represented status and was not contingent on conduct. The line between status or conduct was an artifact of legal doctrine and the outcome of the sodomy cases. The distinction was amplified in arguments over the military ban. President Clinton claimed that his opposition to existing military discrimination was based on the fact that it involved mere status. In response, congressional opponents such as Senator Sam Nunn, who took the lead on the issue, argued that there was no status without conduct.[106]

FORCED BACK INTO THE COURTS

Clinton's decision to abandon his promise for political expedience had the effect of forcing rights activists back into the courts. The prospects are not encouraging. The courts are still overwhelmingly conservative, and the military has traditionally been given broad latitude by the courts. In areas outside the military, in supposedly ideal test cases, lesbian and gay rights advocates have not been successful.

The adverse precedent in the *Bowers* case forced groups arguing for lesbian and gay rights to reassess their legal strategies. New rights and issues do not arise whole; rather, they are tied to existing issues. As such, new issues carry baggage that constrains and channels their development. The litigation strategies of groups interested in gay rights had normally included the privacy doctrine, which was on shaky constitutional grounds, and equal protection, which the Supreme Court has been systematically limiting for years. The trends of judicial federalism and the Supreme Court further suggest that lesbian and gay rights will continue to be an issue dominated by the lower federal courts, meaning that the scope of those rights will vary from jurisdiction to jurisdiction.[107]

Lesbian and gay groups have been caught in a doctrinal bind. To use equal protection under the Fifth and Fourteenth Amendments as a justification, litigants had to argue that distinctions on the basis of sexual preference require a higher level of scrutiny. Distinctions on the basis of race are considered a suspect classification and merit strict scrutiny. Gender discrimination has been defined as a semi-suspect classification requiring moderate scrutiny standards. Most other groups have been denied even the moderate level of scrutiny. Rather for other classifications, the state need only show a rational policy. Alternatively, groups could rely on the right of privacy. The Court has declared that privacy is a fundamental right, thus triggering strict scrutiny. The constitutional right to privacy has been under judicial siege. From the start, *Griswold v. Connecticut* was seen as a naked form of judicial activism and the subject of criticism. More damaging for lesbian and gay rights, the concurring opinion by Goldberg in *Griswold* explicitly distinguished between the protected private relations of a married couple and the less protected privacy rights of unmarried heterosexuals and lesbian and gay couples. More directly, the Supreme Court rejected the application of the privacy argument to homosexuality in *Bowers v. Hardwick*. The problems inherent in using the privacy doctrine do not fall on lesbian and gay rights alone. Women's groups have had similar problems and the ebbing abortion doctrine is the proof.

A related theory of law, substantive due process, has been advocated as an alternative.[108] Lesbian and gay rights groups could argue that sodomy laws and military regulations were patently unfair and that the courts would be justified in declaring them unconstitutional. Under substantive due process, legislation would be subjected to judicial review when questions of "essential justice" are raised.[109] Many argued that the privacy and abortion decisions represented a new substantive due process. Yet substantive due process has been an exhausted, controversial doctrine that asks the judiciary to do too much in a normative sense. Further, the very description "substantive due process" represents a negative buzz phrase which creates immediate opposition with no debate. Some claim that *Bowers* did irreparable harm to substantive due process as a legal doctrine.[110]

Perhaps the lone remaining outlet is the First Amendment. The Don't Ask, Don't Tell policy implicates notions of free speech. If the courts decided to rely on the First Amendment, then government laws that restrict free speech would be held to strict scrutiny. Unlike privacy and equal protection, there is a well-established body of favorable speech and expression precedents. But the First Amendment route is less direct. It threatens to take the focus of the case away from the rights of lesbians and gays. The strategy of using the First

Amendment has been recommended by Nan Hunter: "My experience as a litigator tells me that the First Amendment has provided the most reliable path to success of any of the doctrinal claims utilized by lesbian and gay rights lawyers."[111] (Hunter was originally an attorney from the ACLU, which stressed the First Amendment in its litigation.)

One area in which *Doe* failed to have any negative impact was litigation over university recognition of lesbian and gay organizations. *Wood v. Davison* (351 F. Supp. 543, N.D. Ga. 1972) was the first reported case in which First Amendment associational rights of a lesbian and gay group were recognized. A series of other decisions in favor of lesbian and gay groups followed. Courts have generally held that noncriminal conduct by lesbians and gays (such as discussing lifestyles and socializing with others) were fully protected constitutional rights. Despite the widespread success in these cases in the lower courts, no lesbian or gay group has been endorsed by the Supreme Court. The Court has steadfastly refused to accept such cases, thus declining an opportunity to issue a clear statement and create a precedent.[112]

The First Amendment was used to block one expression of lesbian and gay rights, when the Supreme Court unanimously ruled that private organizers of the St. Patrick's Day parade could exclude lesbian and gay groups from participating in *Hurley v. Irish-American Gay Group* (115 S.Ct. 2338, 1995). The decision, which was narrow, could actually prove a boon to lesbian and gay rights groups in the military cases in the future. The implications of the decision suggest that identifying themselves as lesbians or gays may be seen as a form of expression worthy of protection. But symbolically, the parade decision was perceived as yet another rebuff to lesbian and gay rights activists. The negative spillovers attendant to those perceptions could be more important and damaging.

An important theme that could emerge from the lesbian and gay rights litigation is the relationship between expression and equality. The growth in the lesbian and gay rights movement has generated speech about sexuality. Lesbian and gay rights advocates are fighting a battle in all governmental arenas over the scope of public discourse. Cole and Eskridge urge lesbian and gay rights activists to advance claims that speech about sexuality should be treated as protected speech, like political speech.[113] This might create a category to treat sexual speech as part of a shared social dialogue. Such expression signals the conceptualization of sexuality—specifically homosexuality—as a political idea. By their sexual conduct, lesbians, gay men, and bisexuals are seeking their own identities and voices, and the First Amendment could be used to afford them the same rights as other groups.

Because virtually all conduct is potentially expressive, the critical First Amendment question is the reason why the government is regulating the particular conduct. If those reasons are unrelated to the expressive elements of the conduct, the regulation is subject to relaxed scrutiny and generally upheld. If, however, the regulation is tied to what the conduct communicates, the law must be treated as if it was regulating speech itself, and subjected to strict scrutiny. The name given to the Don't Ask, Don't Tell policy suggests that it is designed to regulate expression. Some argue that the rationale for regulating sodomy—upholding community morals—is inextricably related to what sodomy expresses to the community. If that is a viable argument, then sodomy statutes are regulating expression and thus would need to satisfy strict scrutiny, not rational basis review. Lesbian and gay rights advocates are confident that the government cannot meet the more stringent standard.[114]

In defending exclusions of lesbians and gays from the service, the government argues that courts should defer to military judgment. The purpose of this argument is to lower the level of judicial scrutiny back to rational basis, or to transform a weak set of governmental interests into a compelling interest.

The government has successfully evaded First Amendment review in the past by arguing that it was not punishing servicemembers for saying they were gay, but that it simply used those words as evidence of gay identity. Under the regulation, the government claimed that it is not concerned with identity, but argued that its concern was with lesbian and gay conduct. The military expressly disclaimed concern with whether an individual was in fact gay. Rather, the government argued that its concern was specifically with individuals who tell others, by proclaiming that they are lesbian or gay in word or deed.

At least one judge has rejected the government's contention and agreed with the justifications offered by the First Amendment. Judge Eugene Nickerson of the New York District Court found the Don't Ask, Don't Tell policy was a violation of the free speech rights of the members of the service. In *Able v. United States* (44 F.3d 128, 2nd Cir. 1995), Nickerson held that the speech at issue involved the value of promoting individual dignity and integrity and as a result, it was protected by the First Amendment from efforts to prohibit it because of its content. The government's position essentially amounted to a "heckler's veto."

Judge Nickerson wrote that: "To presume from a person's status that he or she will commit undesirable acts is an extreme measure. Hitler taught the world what could happen when the government began to target people not for what they had done but because of their status." He further held that:

Defendants therefore designed a policy that purportedly directs discharge based on "conduct," and craftily sought to avoid the First Amendment by defining "conduct" to include statements revealing one's homosexual status. To say "I have a homosexual orientation," a mere acknowledgment of status, is thus transmogrified into an admission of misconduct, and misconduct that the speaker has the practically insurmountable burden of disproving . . . The court regards the definition and treatment of these terms to be nothing less than Orwellian.

Nickerson recognized that the policy essentially forced lesbian and gay members of the armed forces to stay in the closet.

Not content to rest the opinion on First Amendment grounds, Nickerson held that military policy violated the equal protection clause of the Fifth Amendment "because the Act gives to persons of one status, heterosexual, the chance to exercise the fundamental right of free speech and prohibits it to those of another status, homosexual, defendants must at least show that the policy is 'tailored to serve a substantial governmental interest.'" The judge held that the government did not meet that standard. Activists for lesbian and gay rights had sought a favorable precedent based on equal protection grounds.

The decision represented the culmination of litigation strategies, but as repeat players know, the game is never finished in the courts. Indeed, the government announced immediately that it would appeal the decision. Given the conservative nature of the judiciary (Nickerson was a Carter appointee), the prospects for ultimate success in the Courts of Appeals and the Supreme Court (which are more important in the creation of a viable precedent) are not encouraging.

In his book *The Hollow Hope*, Gerald Rosenberg argues persuasively that courts cannot induce positive social change. Lesbian and gay rights advocates would certainly second that assessment. Rosenberg notes that victories sap the energy of the social movement and invigorate opponents.[115] If that is true, then there is hope. As states pass measures that directly or indirectly restrict lesbian and gay rights or seek to limit the ability of lesbian and gay individuals to use civil rights laws as other victims of discrimination,[116] the prospects for legal change actually may get brighter. Overly restrictive laws open a policy window. First, unfair laws can create a more favorable climate for public opinion. Clinton's leadership on the gays in the military issue, before the about-face, moved public opinion in a positive direction.[117] Second, and maybe more importantly, bad laws provide the opportunity to get to court with very strong arguments that could lead to the web of precedents that are necessary to change the law. Some could have positive spillover effects for related issues of lesbian and gay rights. Substantive due process arguments that focus on the unfairness of laws may have some applicability. The problem, however, is that such a strategy is costly, uncertain, and takes a great deal of time. At the current time, in the current environment, that may be the best that advocates for lesbian and gay rights can hope for.

NOTES

The author would like to thank Paul Clark and Michael Jordan for their assistance and research efforts.

1. Gerald Rosenberg, *The Hollow Hope: Can Courts Bring About Social Change?* (Chicago: University of Chicago Press, 1991).
2. Lee Epstein, *Conservatives in Court* (Knoxville: University of Tennessee Press, 1985).
3. Kenneth Sherrill, "On Gay People as a Politically Powerless Group." In *Gays and the Military*, ed. Marc Wolinsky and Kenneth Sherrill (Princeton: Princeton University Press, 1993). Sherrill filed an affidavit in the *Steffan v.*

Cheney (920 F.2d 74, D.C. Circ. 1990) case. Joseph Steffan was discharged from the military because he was gay. Sherrill argued that lesbians and gay men lack political power to obtain redress for grievances through the majoritarian branches of government. He claimed that gay people were despised, stigmatized, outnumbered, and lack adequate political resources. As a result, Sherrill (1993, 116) argued that the judiciary must intervene to protect the rights of lesbians and gay men.

4. Rosenberg, 1991.

5. Donald Horowitz, *The Courts and Social Policy* (Washington, D.C.: Brookings Institute, 1977). Horowitz argues that judges are generalists and unable to make policy in complicated areas. He contends that the process is not amenable to coherent policy making because cases are not sequenced. Horowitz also argues that the courts cannot enforce their decisions. He further argues that issues are polycentric, thus a decision in one area has consequences for other areas of law that may not be related to the issue in question. These concerns are certainly relevant to advocates of lesbian and gay rights.

6. Rosenberg 1991, 341.

7. Rosenberg 1991, 339-42.

8. Lee Epstein and Joseph Kobylka, *The Supreme Court & Legal Change: Abortion and the Death Penalty* (Chapel Hill: University of North Carolina Press, 1992).

9. Walter Krygowski, "Comment: Homosexuality and the Military Mission: The Failure of the Don't Ask, Don't Tell Policy." 20 *Dayton Law Review* (1995): 875-933. In two notable cases, the Court refused to allow women to be subject to the selective service (*Roskter v. Goldberg*, 453 US 57, 1981) and upheld military dress codes over a free exercise of religion challenge by an Orthodox Jew who wanted to wear a yarmulke (*Goldman v. Weinberger*, 475 US 503, 1986). Subsequent decisions by Congress and the executive branch have overturned these decisions.

10. Krygowski, 1995.

11. Rosenberg, 1991. Clinton claimed he "would do for gays what Harry Truman did for blacks in 1948—eliminate the military's discriminatory policies by executive order" (Krygowski 1995, 875).

12. Gerald Rosenberg, "The Real World of Constitutional Rights: The Supreme Court and the Implementation of the Abortion Decisions." In *Contemplating Courts*, ed. Lee Epstein (Washington, D.C.: Congressional Quarterly, 1995).

13. John Kingdon, *Agendas, Alternatives and Public Policies*, 2nd edition (New York: Harper Collins, 1995); Frank Baumgartner and Bryan Jones, *Agendas and Instability in American Politics* (Chicago: University of Chicago Press, 1993).

14. There are a number of studies that discuss the rise and transformation of groups interested in gay rights. See John D'Emilio, *Sexual Politics, Sexual Communities* (Chicago: University of Chicago Press, 1983) and *Making*

Trouble (New York: Routledge, 1992); Barry Adam, *The Rise of a Gay and Lesbian Movement* (Boston: Twayne Publishing, 1987).

15. Epstein and Kobylka, 1992.

16. Frank Sorauf, *The Wall of Separation* (Princeton: Princeton University Press, 1976).

17. Jack Greenberg, *Crusaders in the Court* (New York: Basic Books, 1994).

18. Epstein and Kobylka, 1992.

19. Stephen Wasby, "How Planned is 'Planned Litigation'?" 32 *American Bar Foundation Research Journal* (1984): 83-138.

20. Marc Galanter, "Why the 'Haves' Come Out Ahead: Speculations on the Limits of Legal Change." 9 *Law & Society Review* (1974): 95-160.

21. Kay Lehman Schlozman and John Tierney, *Organized Interests and American Democracy* (New York: Harper & Row, 1986).

22. Galanter, 1974.

23. Sherrill, 1993.

24. D'Emilio, 1983.

25. Nan Hunter, "Identity, Speech, and Equality." 79 *Virginia Law Review* (1993): 1695-1719.

26. Patricia Cain, "Litigating for Lesbian and Gay Rights: A Legal History." 79 *Virginia Law Review* (1993): 1570-71.

27. Cain, 1572.

28. Cain, 1576-77.

29. Cain, 1577-79.

30. William Donohue, *Twilight of Liberties: The Legacy of the ACLU* (New Brunswick, NJ: Transaction Press, 1994), 46.

31. Samuel Walker, *In Defense of American Liberties* (New York: Oxford University Press, 1990), 312.

32. Randy Shilts, *Conduct Unbecoming: Lesbians and Gays in the U.S. Military Vietnam to the Persian Gulf* (New York: St. Martin's, 1993), 108.

33. Walker, 312.

34. Cain, 1583.

35. Lawrence Baum, "Measuring Policy Change in the U.S. Supreme Court." 82 *American Political Science Review* (1988): 905-12.

36. Walker, 312.

37. Henry Abraham and Barbara Perry, *Freedom and the Court: Civil Rights and Liberties in the United States*, 6th ed. (New York: Oxford University Press, 1994).

38. Cain, 1579.

39. Kingdon, 172-76; Baumgartner and Jones, 5-7.

40. Arthur Hellman, "Case Selection in the Burger Court: A Preliminary Inquiry." 60 *Notre Dame Law Review* (1985): 10006-7.

41. Adam, 1987.

42. D'Emilio, 1983.

43. D'Emilio, 1992.

44. Richard Mohr, *Gays/Justice: A Study of Ethics, Society, and Law* (New York: Columbia University Press, 1988), 23.

45. Cain, 1582.

46. Hunter, 1993.

47. Shilts, 249.

48. Adam, 1987.

49. Shilts, 249.

50. D'Emilio, 1983, 168-75. Lesbians and gay men had common interests, but they had separate agendas. Thus the movement was hampered by a lack of concentrated effort and a single mission. Lesbian groups like the Daughters of Bilitis had different priorities than gay rights groups such as child custody (Mohr 1988, 199-203).

51. Walker, 299.

52. Tom Stoddard, an ACLU official from the New York Civil Liberties Union, left the Union to become executive director of the Lambda Legal Defense and Education Fund (Donahue 1994, 46). As the AIDS crisis grew and brought new types of discrimination, Nan Hunter left the ACLU's Reproductive Freedom Project to head the Gay and Lesbian Rights Project (Walker 1990, 313).

53. Cain, 1584-86.

54. Sheldon Goldman, "Reagan's Judicial Legacy: Completing the Puzzle and Summing Up." 72 *Judicature* (1989): 318-30; "Bush's Judicial Legacy: The Final Imprint." 78 *Judicature* (1993): 282-93.

55. Epstein, 1985.

56. Richard Pacelle, *The Transformation of the Supreme Court's Agenda: From the New Deal to the Reagan Administration* (Boulder, CO: Westview Press, 1991).

57. Cain, 1593-94.

58. Mohr 1988, 59.

59. Cain, 1587.

60. Mohr 1988, 53.

61. Mohr 1988, 56-57.

62. Cain, 1589-92.

63. Cain, 1594.

64. Mary Dunlap, "Gay Men and Lesbians Down by Law in the 1990's USA: The Continuing Toll of *Bowers v. Hardwick*." 24 *Golden Gate University Law Review* (1994): 1-39. By 1983, the new INS policy had been held invalid as inconsistent with federal law and unconstitutional according to a federal district court. By 1990, the Immigration and Nationality Act was amended to eliminate the statutory predicate to lesbian/gay exclusions. If the analogy to the current military policy is true, Don't Ask, Don't Tell would meet a similar fate.

65. Cain, 1599-1600.

66. Cain, 1601-03. Childers openly labeled his relationship with a male companion a marriage. Childers was a gay rights activist and represented by the ACLU. One of the claims was that the Texas sodomy statute was

unconstitutional as a violation of the right to privacy. To make this claim, Childers needed to admit the conduct covered by the statute (Cain 1993, 1601-03). As a test case, this involved some of the worst facts. First, he was denied employment, not fired, so liberty and property arguments were not available. Second, he was an avowed activist and the court noted they tend to fare less well than those who admitted nothing. Conversely, by removing property arguments and openly admitting behavior sanctioned by the statute, the ACLU could get an unvarnished case that focused directly on privacy.

67. Krygoski, 876-77.

68. Shilts, 234-40; Cain, 1596-98. Among the most notable were *Steffan v. Cheney, Woodward v. Moore, Berg v. Claytor*, 436 F. Supp. 76 (Dist. Ct. D.C. 1977), *Dronenberg v. Zech*, 746 F.2d 1579 (D.C. Circ. 1984), known for the concurring opinion of Judge Robert Bork, and *Beller v. Middendorf*, 632 F.2d 788 (9th Circ. 1980).

69. Shilts, 286.

70. Cain, 1597.

71. It is the nature of the judicial process that petitioners may not even reap the benefits of a favorable decision. The government refused to reinstate BenShalom, who found herself faced with a second round of litigation when her enlistment expired. She won at the district court level, which ordered reenlistment, but the holding was reversed by the court of appeals (*BenShalom v. Marsh*, 881 F.2d 454, 7th Cir. 1989), and the Supreme Court denied certiorari.

72. 489 F.Supp. 964, at 973-74.

73. Shilts, 347.

74. Shilts, 1993; Cain, 1993.

75. Pacelle, 1991.

76. Cain, 1607.

77. 729 F.2d 1270, at 1275.

78. Cain, 1607-08.

79. Peter Irons, *The Courage of Their Convictions* (New York: Penguin Books, 1988).

80. Dunlap, 1994.

81. Justice Marshall's papers discuss the deliberations in *Bowers v. Hardwick*. Justices Brennan and Marshall had voted to grant certiorari in a previous case, but could attract no other votes on the merits. Only Justice Byron White, who would author the decision, and Chief Justice Burger initially favored granting *Hardwick* (a pro-gay rights decision in the lower court). If Brennan and Marshall signed on, the vote in favor would be four, the number needed to accept the case. The only indication of the individual positions of the justices came from the *National Gay Task Force* case, in which the vote was 4-4 with Justice Powell not participating. Powell had apparently indicated that he might side with the justices who had supported lesbian and gay rights. The possibility for a favorable ruling tempted Brennan and Marshall to vote to grant certiorari. Brennan was risk averse, afraid that the ultimate decision by the Court was

likely to reverse the favorable decision of the lower court. Thus he cast a defensive denial. Justice Rehnquist agreed to grant certiorari and a fourth vote was needed. Marshall decided to take the risk and signed on as the necessary fourth vote. Marshall miscalculated because Justice Powell voted to uphold the Georgia sodomy law (Cain 1993, 1607). According to one account, Powell originally voted to strike the law. Ultimately, he could not accept Blackmun's rationale extending the right to privacy to lesbians and gays (Shilts 1993, 523). Since retiring, Powell has publicly stated that he should have voted against the sodomy law, as noted in John Jeffries, *Justice Lewis Powell: A Biography* (New York: Scribners, 1994), 530. John Jeffries (1994, 514) has a different version, claiming Rehnquist and White initially voted to grant certiorari and it was Brennan and Marshall who both voted to grant believing they could pick up the five votes to win on the merits and instead "set the stage for their own defeat."

82. Mohr 1988, 60.

83. Irons 1988, 387. One of the many *amici* briefs in the case brought by a variety of health care organizations argued that the state's logic was flawed concerning AIDS. The brief argued that sodomy laws harmed the public health effort by driving the disease underground (Irons 1988, 387-388).

84. Cain, 1993.

85. Irons, 389.

86. Shilts, 522-23.

87. In an article on gay rights litigation, Patricia Cain (1993, 1616-17) wonders if the case would have been decided differently if it had been argued by an openly gay lawyer who could have personalized the threat to dignity and self-respect posed by the statute. Was it a mistake to focus narrowly on the privacy argument? Would the decision be different if *Baker v. Wade* (774 F.2d 1285, 5th Circ., 1985), a concurrent case with a fuller record, had reached the Court first?

88. Dunlap 1994, 23. The view that Tribe made a tactical error was not shared by all. One of Thurgood Marshall's clerks, Daniel Richman, praised Tribe for the oral argument. Richman did not believe the focus on privacy was misplaced: "You can't fault Tribe for taking what seemed to be the most likely line of attack and not trying to cater to the idiosyncratic view of a single justice" (Cain 1993, 1617). Had Tribe adopted a more extreme tack, he might have lost Powell from the start. The different perspectives stem from the views of an insider used to the process by which new issues evolve from existing ones, and outsiders, who might expect novel arguments and not recognize normal constraints.

89. David Cole and William Eskridge, "From Hand-Holding to Sodomy: First Amendment Protection of Homosexual (Expressive) Conduct." 29 *Harvard Civil Rights-Civil Liberties Law Review* (1993): 319-51.

90. Cain 1993, 1606.

91. Former Solicitor General Charles Fried, law reviews, some lower court judges, and retired Justice Powell, who voted with the majority, have argued

that *Bowers v. Hardwick* was wrongly decided and believe it will eventually be overruled. Charles Fried, *Order and Law: Arguing the Reagan Revolution* (New York: Simon & Schuster, 1991), 83; Jeffries 1994, 530.

92. Dunlap, 1994.

93. Cain, 1993.

94. Dunlap, 1994.

95. Cole and Eskridge, 1993.

96. Cole and Eskridge, 1993.

97. Jane Schacter, "The Gay Civil Rights Debate in the States: Decoding the Discourse of Equivalents." 29 *Harvard Civil Rights and Civil Liberties Law Review* (1994): 283-317.

98. Shilts, 687-98.

99. Shilts, 698.

100. Cole and Eskridge, 1993. The history of the military's resistance to desegregation suggests the military's rationale regarding unit cohesion was suspect. Although most white soldiers did not want to serve with black soldiers when President Truman ordered desegregation in 1948, integration was relatively smooth, in part because integration led white soldiers to rid themselves of prejudices. That same phenomenon has been observed in nations that allow openly lesbian and gay personnel to serve (Cole and Eskridge, 1993).

101. Krygowski, 888.

102. David Schlueter, "Gays and Lesbians in the Military: A Rationally Based Solution to a Legal Rubik's Cube." 29 *Wake Forest Law Review* (1994): 393-434.

103. Shilts, 348.

104. Clyde Wilcox and Robin Wolpert, "President Clinton, Public Opinion, and Gays in the Military," chapter five in this volume.

105. Dunlap, 22-23.

106. Hunter, 717.

107. Richard Pacelle, "The Dynamics and Determinants of Agenda Change in the Rehnquist Court." In *Contemplating Courts*, ed. Lee Epstein (Washington, D.C.: Congressional Quarterly, 1995).

108. Cain, 1993.

109. C. Herman Pritchett, *Constitutional Civil Liberties* (Englewood Cliffs, NJ: Prentice Hall, 1984), 292.

110. Ronald Kahn, *The Supreme Court & Constitutional Theory, 1953-1993* (Lawrence: University of Kansas Press, 1994), 292.

111. Hunter, 1695.

112. Cain, 1610-11.

113. Cole and Eskridge, 1695-96.

114. Cole and Eskridge, 1993.

115. Rosenberg, 1991.

116. Schacter, 1994.

117. Wilcox and Wolpert, chapter 5 in this volume.

PART III

Policy Implications

CHAPTER 8

The Spectacle of Life and Death:

Feminist and Lesbian/Gay Politics in the Military

Mary Fainsod Katzenstein

This article has three agendas. First, I offer an explanation for a set of rather specific political events. Why did President Clinton campaign on the military and homosexuality issue? Why did he make it one of his first Presidential deeds? Second, I describe how the lesbian/gay movement used the media to create what could be best termed a political "spectacle"[1] as a means to achieve the specific policy objective of ending the military ban. Third, by contrasting the media spectacle that prefaced the controversy over the homosexual ban with the media spectacle that preceded the reversal of the legislation barring women from combat pilot positions, I wish to offer some observations about the efficacy of political theater in achieving particular policy ends.

The lesbian/gay movement sought to promote and the feminist movement to capitalize on the media's capacity to dramatize both the ordinary and the unusual. The tale this account suggests is that, if the aim of protest is immediate policy change rather than longer term attitudinal shifts, then not simply any media dramatized act of political protest will do. It may take nothing less than the drama of death for the political theater to galvanize policy change.

It is hard to imagine social movements in the last decade of the twentieth century having an impact without reliance on the media as one tool in their strategic repertoire.[2] Social movement organizers are certainly not newly cognizant of the media's power to dramatize. The innovation of movement activists who organized around the lesbian/gay ban, however, was to realize that individual narratives make good television copy. Television, in particular, affords the power to make a movement's claims "real." Television can bring the voice, the face, and thus often the pathos of individual lives to the screen. By individualizing a movement's story—portraying individuals who somehow exemplify the movement's message—lesbian and gay activists hoped that television could bring a movement's message home to a public trained in the medium of talk show intimacy.

The importance of television was evident in earlier histories of social movements. Sidney Tarrow observes that television newscasting was important to the civil rights movement of the 1950s, bringing "long-ignored grievances to the attention of the nation, particularly to viewers in the North," and helping to convince viewers of the moral righteousness of the activists' politics by contrasting "the peaceful goals of the movement with the viciousness of the [Bull Connor] police."[3]

And yet, reaching out to the public in the hope of reconstructing popular understandings has to be, by and large, a long-term movement strategy. The cultural shift a media promoted spectacle may aim to achieve is likely to be, at best, slow and incremental. Rare is any instant policy effect of such a strategy. Its impact on policy is likely to be most immediate, I argue in this chapter, when that which the media brings alive is a narration not only of lives lived righteously—but also of righteous death.

THE CLINTON DECISION

Thinking about why President Clinton initially committed himself to ending the homosexual exclusion points to the importance of cultural politics in general. Over a period of time, the creation of political spectacles transmitted by the media may help to shift the popular perceptions from which politicians take their cues. Yet, political theater is rarely apt to have short-term policy effects.

A caveat: when we attempt to analyze particular policy outcomes, historical events have generally crystallized. The historical moment is done and over. There is archival material that helps to document intentionality. There are extensive records of who said what, who did what, who thought what. Lacking these materials, I am necessarily entering into the world of speculation. I offer these thoughts, then, not in the form of social science hypothesizing but, instead, as program notes, hoping that as the performance on stage unfolds, themes will be revealed to which the ear might not otherwise attend.

A second caveat, this one political. I am describing the spectacle largely as it was being composed rather than as it was being received. The tale I recount is scripted by lesbian and gay and by feminist activists in and around the nation's capital. But even as many activists sought to open up the military to lesbians/gays and to heterosexual women as a basic right of citizenship, many others were skeptical about the desirability of defining citizenship in terms of a right to join the armed forces.[4] If the latter group stood to be persuaded at all, it was only perhaps by evidence that the political campaign to secure military citizenship might establish a broader societal acceptance of lesbians and gays and a blurring of gender lines, of men and women, whether in uniform or not. This essay cannot resolve this debate since little is known about how movement crafted media images were in fact being read by the general public.[5] The more modest claim of this chapter is that even a professional and creative media campaign was not able, in and of itself, to secure the "right to serve," whatever the merits of such a goal. Such a campaign, I speculate, would have required an even more dramatic media message—evidence that those who claimed entitlement were not just loyal citizens, not just willing to sacrifice their lives for their country; what an effective media campaign would have required, is the evidence that such sacrifice had already occurred.

What motivated Bill Clinton, initially, to promise to end the ban on homosexuals in the military was most probably a commitment to a view of justice that reflected ongoing changes in social values rather than a primarily interest-based calculation that he would gain more (votes, money) than he would lose. The lesbian/gay movement's focus on using political theater to change social values was vindicated, in a sense, by the very example of President Clinton. Social mores *were* changing, faster it seemed than judicial actions or congressional legislation. It is understandable, therefore, that lesbian and gay activists might have wanted to concentrate their energies on trying to get a message across through the media to the public at large—seeking to effect a further long-term shift in social values and seeking, thereby, to create an opportunity for politicians to act as Clinton was initially inclined to do. In this context, the many public/media appearances of Keith Meinhold, Tracy Thorne, Joseph Steffan, and Magarethe Cammermeyer may indeed have long-term importance. But in the short term, this political theater had little impact in the policy realm: it did not prevent Congress from scuttling the Clinton initiative and Clinton, himself, from listing off his initial course.

Clinton's initial promise to end the homosexual exclusion did appear to be grounded in an underlying shift in social values. Here a three-fold distinction should be made. There is a difference among motivations based on morality, intent based on social values, and reasons based on political exigency. Imagine, as Margaret Levi suggests, a decision continuum. At one end, some people base decisions on singularly opportunistic interest calculations. At the other end, some act on purely moral principle.[6] In the middle of the continuum, decisionmaking is informed by social values that are based on moral principle, but that are at the same time cost sensitive.

If President Clinton's decision was merely opportunistic, we would need to imagine his calculating a surge in electoral support from the lesbian and gay electorate, at least in the key states of California and New York. Senator Al D'Amato's endorsement of lifting the ban (taken prior to the Senate race against the liberal District Attorney Robert Abrams) might have been seen in such terms. Perhaps the pre-campaign, pre-election timing of Clinton's promise invites similar speculation, although, unlike D'Amato who faced a liberal opponent in what had been a largely liberal state, Clinton's electoral calculations would have had to be quite different. Perhaps the clearest interest argument was that President Clinton stood to expect that, in return for the promise of an executive order, he could raise significant campaign contributions from the white, male, gay, and well-to-do activist community. He did, in fact, raise such funds: the lesbian/gay PACs, by most accounts, contributed at least five percent of the campaign's costs—as large as the Jewish lobby.[7] An executive order, moreover, would raise no fiscal opposition from the ever attentive taxpaying public. Available to the Clinton campaign in June 1992 was a Government Accounting Office report that said the discharge of approximately 1500 gay and lesbian service members a year was costing the taxpayer $28,000 to replace each enlisted military person and $121,000 to train each officer replacement, a figure which omits the costs of legal fees paid to military lawyers to prosecute such cases in military and civilian courts.[8]

There are problems, however, with imputing merely opportunistic motives to Clinton's decisions. For one thing, it is vehemently repudiated by people who know President Clinton well. Individuals close to the Presidential campaign say that he committed himself to lifting the ban because he thought it ought to be done.[9] The oft-noted phrase Clinton used in a campaign fundraiser in Los Angeles where he said to those gathered, "I have a vision, and you are part of it," appeared to claim an identity connecting himself to lesbian and gay politics different from the distanced rights language, for instance, of Senator D'Amato.[10]

But even assuming such testimonials to Clinton's principled motivations would need to be discounted as coming from those who might seek to cast a favorable gloss on the presidential image, there are other reasons to be skeptical of the opportunism interpretation. The President had to have known that such a position carried risks. Focus groups run by public opinion analysts indicated that public support was soft: when focus group participants were asked to discuss the issues of homosexuality at any length, support dropped off significantly. For "Weak Willie, the draft-dodger," as he was referred to by angry military veterans, this could not have seemed to him without electoral hazards.

On the other hand, the Clinton "Don't Ask, Don't Tell" compromise marked a retreat from a strongly principled position. As Margaret Levi writes, "Those making choices based on moral principles do what they believe is right no matter how others are acting and no matter the penalties they may have to pay for their behavior."[11] The costs of ordering military compliance and risking a showdown with Congress over an unchanged executive order were clearly, in Clinton's view, too high politically.[12] Instead of pursuing a compromise, Congressman Barney Frank observes, Clinton might have decided to lose the issue, making it clear that he would rather fail to win than compromise his principles.[13] However, cost-benefit calculations were clearly the reigning force when Clinton opted for Don't Ask, Don't Tell and conceded in his Presidential Address of July 19, 1993 that "It is not a perfect solution. It is not identical with some of my own goals. And it certainly will not please everyone. . . ."[14]

What I am suggesting is that first proposing and then lifting the ban, for Clinton, were decisions of the sort located somewhere between the extremes of purely principled and opportunistic. Margaret Levi describes that middle place along the continuum as one governed by "social values." Social values are ethically constrained in contrast to mere opportunism. "In contrast (however) to moral principles," she writes, "social values are cost sensitive." Individuals are more likely to act on social values when the costs of doing so are low or there are positive incentives reinforcing their normative inclinations.[15]

What is important to see here, is that as social values change, so do interests. Presidential ethics are likely to be "cost sensitive," and those cost calculations are in turn assessed against the changing norms of popular cultures. President Clinton can act in a principled way on the issue of homosexuality because changing social values enhance the probability that principle and interest are likely to converge.

Social values, themselves, embrace two different forces: shifts in public culture, and changes in public opinion. Transformations in public culture found expression in President Clinton's own personal experience. The gradually increasing cultural acceptance of "coming out" must have been part of what encouraged David Mixner's decision to make his homosexuality known to the Clintons some years ago. A prominent civil rights and peace activist from Los Angeles who has been a Clinton friend since their Oxford days in the late 1960s, Mixner shared with the Clintons his commitment to the civil rights of lesbians and gays, a commitment made passionate by seeing hundreds of his friends die of AIDS. Bob Hattoy, diagnosed with AIDS during the campaign, was Clinton's personal choice for speaker at the New York Democratic Convention.

If these friendships helped form Clinton's personal convictions, increasingly pro-civil rights popular opinion (of which Clinton would certainly have been aware) made his personal convictions likely to be acceptable publicly. Gallup polls had been showing support for gay rights climbing dramatically. The June 1992 GAO report cited national Gallup polls that showed the percentage of the public who believed that homosexuals should be employed in the military increasing slowly between 1977 and 1987 from 51 percent to 55 percent, rising to 60 percent by 1989 and to 69 percent by 1991.[16] Although this support was considered "soft," there was no doubt that popular culture was shifting.

The Clinton decisions were not simply a matter of a presidential candidate asserting a moral truth of which he may have long been convinced, nor were they mere opportunism. They were a matter of Clinton's following a cultural shift, taking his cues from a society in which social norms were in flux. The crucial question, itself, then shifts. The question, then, should be less "why did the President decide as he did?" but more "what forces cause this cultural evolution?" This question takes us back to the subject of this chapter—the spectacle as a method of movement politics.

SECRETS AND SPECTACLES

The movement strategies pursued by lesbian and gay activists who sought to challenge the military ban combined the public and private in unusual ways. Theirs was not the very public spectacles of protest, marches, demonstrations, and riots made familiar by the 1950s and 1960s civil rights struggles. Nor was theirs the stories (like the ones James Scott tells so eloquently) of how everyday resistance is practiced by individuals in the realm of the semi-private: gossip, absenteeism, pilfering, the arsenal of daily resistance, were not the methods deployed here.[17] This is an account, rather, of how the private became publicized, how secrecy turned into spectacle. Here we see how the once-silent participated in, even choreographed, elaborate public performances.

A preview of the spectacle: CBS *Nightwatch*, or it could be *20/20*, *Nightline*, *Donahue*, or the *Today Show*. The host is interviewing Joseph

Steffan, a former midshipman at the Naval Academy expelled from Annapolis weeks before graduation. Raised in the Midwest, Catholic, a choir boy in his local church, Steffan was the kid next door. Clean-cut, an excellent student, exceptional in track, he took as his date for the senior prom the high school's homecoming queen. From his small town in Minnesota, Joe Steffan entered Annapolis. At the Academy, he ranked in the top ten in his class, became battalion commander his senior year, and received the unique honor of twice singing, solo, the national anthem at the Army-Navy game.[18]

The TV monitor shifts to a film clip of Joe Steffan, standing on a platform as the Army-Navy game is about to begin, bearing erect, singing the anthem against the red, white, and blue backdrop of the American flag waving in the stadium breeze. The television studio camera again trains its lens on Joe Steffan's face, his sincere gaze, his serious eyes. Joseph Steffan, who at the academy confided his homosexuality to only a handful of friends, and who on that account was expelled only weeks before graduation, is now "out" to the USA.

In January 1993, at the Clinton inauguration's lesbian and gay Triangle Ball, Joseph Steffan again sings the national anthem while, according to the *Village Voice*, "an honor guard of homosexuals purged from the military carried in the flag."[19]

As spectacular as these media transmitted images were, I argue that their effect on policy was limited. What they lacked (as the contrast with the issue of combat exclusion demonstrates) was not the specter of lives lived loyally; what was absent, rather, was the imagery of lives given over to dutiful death.

The public spectacle—a term I take from Foucault—is usually depicted as a political act meant to secure popular acquiescence to state power. In *Discipline and Punish*, Foucault describes public hangings in eighteenth-century France as an affirmation of state authority.[20] In his grimly memorable opening chapter, Foucault relates the story of Damiens, the regicide, confessing to his guilt in the public square before the populace that was to see in the public spectacle of the hanging the confirmation of the king's truth and the king's power.

As Foucault recounts, the entire criminal procedure right up to the sentence remained secret, taking place without the public or the accused having knowledge either of the charges or of the evidence.[21] The "truth" was arrived at in secret. What gave truth its power was the public confession.

The theatrical and extraordinary nature of public tortures ensured a popular audience. The requisite public confession (the placard borne around the victim's neck, and the avowal of guilt) was supposed to reveal to the assembled crowd the fairness of the sovereign's punishment.

Can the public spectacle be a tool of political opposition, just as it can be a site of state and elite domination? Is there an analog to the spectacle as exemplary punishment in the spectacle as exemplary protest?

Four likenesses:

(1) The spectacle as a challenge to political domination is visually impressive and theatrical, but instead of a display of terror, it is the display of courage.

(2) It works in the same way: it reveals a secret. As with the public hanging, it is the revelation of a "truth" or "secret" that has, heretofore, been hidden. In the public hanging, the suffering and the confession of the accused is evidence of the sovereign's claim. In the case of exemplary protest, the victimization and injury is evidence of the truth claims of the accused.

(3) The purpose of the public hanging is to bring the message of the sovereign to the people. The purpose of the spectacle as opposition is, similarly, to bring the truth of the people to the public.

(4) And, finally, it doesn't always work. Just as public hangings sometimes caused the crowd to riot, the public spectacle as protest may fail to persuade.

There are two kinds of spectacles. One kind of spectacle may become available as a strategy of political protest through historical accident—as it did in the case of military women and the combat exclusion. Or it may be specifically created, and carefully strategized, as was the case with the homosexual ban.

STRAIGHT WOMEN, COMBAT EXCLUSION, AND THE SPECTACLE

Over the spring and summer of 1991, Congress passed an amendment to the Defense Authorization Act which finally cracked open the exclusionary policies that had prohibited women from fighting in combat roles. Still to be fully implemented in practice, the law at least now reads that women aviators can serve as fighter pilots on airforce and navy planes, and that (as of 1993) women can serve on surface warfare ships.[22]

What did it finally take to open this jealously guarded male preserve to women? Very simply, the dramatic spectacle of women at war—41,000 women sent to the Gulf.[23] Although the distinction between combat and noncombat jobs is a largely specious one in modern warfare (where the front line is not necessarily the place most vulnerable to attack), it took the dramatic, televised reporting of the war to demonstrate that military women were hardly out of harm's way, no matter what formal distinctions about a male-only combat force were being made.

The media spectacle began with Panama and the reports of Captain Linda Bray, who commanded a military police unit assigned to capture a kennel holding guard dogs that turned out to be defended by Panamanian forces.[24] During the Gulf War, reports flooded the newspaper about women leaving behind loved ones, and military women in Saudi Arabia accustoming themselves to their new responsibilities. Ironically, these stories got more play than they might have otherwise, because of the severe restrictions on journalists' mobility and their capacity to report on the military action itself. Much of the media reporting focused on uniformed women as mothers, leaving behind young children.[25]

But what made the 1991 spectacle decisive was that the media made visible military women "dying in combat." The phrase, of course, is a political construction. Throughout American history, women have been part of American wars and have died serving as uniformed members during wartime —as nurses, and as transport, communications, or intelligence operators.[26] The deaths of women in the Gulf War were decisive, however, because for the first time, uniformed women had come to be recognized by the American public as integral to the military itself. Although in some ways no different from the circumstances of American uniformed women killed in previous wars, the deaths of American women in the Gulf War were transmitted by the media and understood by the public as the deaths of women in combat.

What the American television public saw, for the first time, was the "spectacle" of women's deaths in combat when on the 25th of February, the Al Khobar barracks were bombed by Scud missiles, taking 28 lives, including those of three women soldiers. The capture of Specialist 4 Melissa Rathbun-Nealy at the end of January and later, of Major Rhonda Cornum received extensive press coverage with the predictable questions raised in the press about whether either had been subject to sexual assault as prisoners of war. On February 24, as Jeanne Holm relates it, Major Marie T. Rossi was interviewed on the eve of the ground assault into Iraq. "Rossi had stolen the hearts of TV viewers during an interview on CNN. 'Sometimes you have to disassociate how you feel personally about the prospect of going into war and . . . possibly see the death that is going to be out there,' she had said. 'But . . . this is the moment that everybody trains for—that I've trained for—so I feel ready to meet the challenge.'"[27] One week later, Major Rossi, a pilot with the 159th aviation battalion of the 24th infantry brigade, was killed along with three others when her plane struck a tower on her return from a supply mission.

The dramatic months of large numbers of women being sent to the Gulf and of women being captured and killed opened the way for political organizing on Capitol Hill. Over late spring and summer, an intensive and sophisticated lobbying effort was led by women determined to end the combat exclusion laws. When the legislation to open combat aviation positions to women was introduced in the Senate, women pilots flew into Washington and, some in full military attire, joined with women lobbyists, visiting congressional offices and briefing those who sought to know whether women could "do the job."[28]

The dramatic spectacle of military women in the Gulf—fighting, captured, dying—was, I would argue, absolutely critical to the congressional action that dropped the legislative proscription against women aviators. Efforts had been made earlier to drop the combat restrictions. In fact, in May 1979, the Department of Defense urged Congress to repeal the combat exclusion.[29] But 1991 was the first time Congress seriously confronted the 1948 ban. The importance of the Gulf War and of women's lives lost to war was captured in a remark that proved to be prescient. In March 1991, one feminist activist in Washington who had led efforts over the last years to secure equality for women in the military commented: "Can you see the fathers of these women testifying before a Congressional committee and being told, 'What women in combat? No, your daughter didn't fight and die for her country.' This war will be what brings down the combat exclusion."[30]

THE EXECUTIVE ORDER AND THE HOMOSEXUAL EXCLUSION

For lesbian and gay activists, the spectacle as political protest in 1992-93 was specifically choreographed rather than capitalized upon, as had been the case with the Gulf War and women. Given the persistent repudiation that lesbian/gay claims had met in the courts and the untouchability of gay issues at the congressional legislative level, it is understandable that much of gay activism has focused on cultural politics. For the lesbian/gay movement, the development of political theater and of the spectacle as a mode of political action has a long history. Purposefully created theater has included a broad, imaginative range of actions: the AIDS quilts, the marches on Washington, ACT-UP protests, and the flamboyant gay pride parades with drag queens in wedding dresses and glorious wigs (recalling the Holly Woodlawn comment, "Man or woman? what difference does it make as long as you look fabulous"[31]).

For the last years, the airwaves have treated the issue of homosexuality in part as the spectacle of AIDS: Magic Johnson, the late Arthur Ashe, and Ryan White brought home to the viewing public the reality that straight, gay, or lesbian, there is a shared human tragedy. Talk shows with lesbian and gay guests, films and Broadway performances (*Torch Song Trilogy, Personal Best, Early Frost, Normal Heart, As Is*) have conventionalized through public performance lifestyles previously viewed as aberrant. Talk shows on radio and television began to normalize homosexuality as a matter of open public discussion.

The deployment of the spectacle as resistance reached a fine art with the issue of the homosexual ban in the military. The media (public talks, newspaper interviews, television appearances) were the predominant mode by which the campaign to end discrimination in the military has been fought. It is not that other avenues of political action had not been utilized. Lesbians and gays had been challenging the military's ejection of homosexuals for decades in the courts, and legislation to overrule the ban was submitted to Congress. But there had been only an occasional court victory, mostly on minor technicalities, and no success on the congressional front. In some ways, this was the history of the lesbian/gay movement writ large: the limited judicial and legislative progress at the national level directed the movement towards a cultural politics which targeted the general public and a symbolic politics which was self directed (exploring issues of identity and diversity). Gay marches and parades were a different kind of theater and were aimed not so much at moving popular culture as they were affirming for the movement itself a new found freedom and self-recognition. The media spectacle which featured uniformed members of the military blended past strategies: it sought changes in policy much as had the conventional legislative and judicial politics of the past, but it did so while utilizing the strategies of cultural politics. Lesbian and gay members of the armed forces, in a made-for-the media spectacle constructed on the confessional, sought to influence policymakers by bringing their stories to the country.

Unprecedented, to my knowledge, in the history of civil rights litigation, lesbian and gay organizations and individuals in case after case took their stories on the road even as their cases were being litigated in court. Margarethe Cammermeyer (like Tracy Thorne, Keith Meinhold, and Joseph Steffan) set out on the media and lecture circuit soon after her case went to court. These appearances were inevitably major public events. Here is an excerpt from the notes I took while hearing Cammermeyer at the Kennedy School at Harvard during the spring of 1992:

> The auditorium, known as the Forum, is crowded and abuzz. Kennedy school students with backpacks and casually attired have arranged themselves towards the back on the elevated bleachers and the balcony seats. The first ten or twelve rows near the stage look like a who's who of the gay community in Boston. Everyone is dressed to the nines. Congressman Barney Frank is expected but hasn't yet arrived. On the dais are Margarethe Cammermeyer, in full military regalia; Sandra Lowe, her lawyer; Lawrence Korb, former Assistant Secretary of Defense and one of the few ex-Pentagon officials who supports changing the regulations. The room is abuzz. Sandra Lowe, a vibrant, African American woman with dreadlocks, appears much shorter than her client, Colonel Cammermeyer. Sandra Lowe comes to the podium. Hardly a typical lawyer by appearance or self description, she begins autobiographically. A lesbian, she says, she is a lawyer with Lambda Legal Defense Fund. She recounts stories of her own life—the child of once-communist parents, she has had little love for the military. She explains why she took on the Cammermeyer case, why it is important. . . . Cammermeyer rises from her seat, walks to the podium. Tall, ramrod posture, straight out of central casting, she tells her story in eloquent prose without notes. The mother of four sons, a Mormon, she has been a nurse with the Washington National Guard for over twenty years. Up for a promotion to the top job as Director of the Nurse Corps, in a security clearance, she is asked whether she was homosexual. She refused to lie. . . . It is a stellar performance and the audience rises to its feet and applauds long and loudly.

For months prior to and following the Clinton election, the major networks and the regional press were filled with stories, much the same. Hardworking, patriotic women and men who happen to be gay or lesbian serve their country with indisputable proficiency and are expelled from the military for wanting nothing more than to continue to serve their country.

These media events do not happen without orchestration. On May 19, 1992 legislation was introduced in Congress to overturn the ban. That same day Tracy Thorne comes out on *Nightline*; Keith Meinhold on ABC. Tanya Domi of the National Gay and Lesbian Task Force speaks of these appearances as "incredibly courageous acts of civil disobedience, using the method of the media."[32] Not only does it take courage to come out so publicly, but the act of publicly challenging the military is not without reprisal. (Tracy Thorne, awaiting the outcome of his court suit, was assigned to a toxic waste cleanup project.) Two lesbians from Minnesota (one in the army guard, the other a naval reservist) also come out in the public media. Their stories are all over the regional press.

I ask Alexander Robinson, a Washington ACLU lobbyist, whether the purpose is to present uniformed lesbians and gays to the public as "your average American kid." "The point is," he corrects me, "that they are your well-above-average patriotic citizens, all of them, red, white, and blue, extraordinary military records, willing to die for their country."[33] "Are there particular ideas—points to be covered in these appearances?" I ask Tanya Domi. "Yes, there are messages to be gotten across," she says. She ticks them off without a moment's hesitation:

-We're proud, patriotic Americans and only want to serve our country.
-This is a responsibility of citizenship. How would you feel if in wartime gays and lesbians declined to serve.
-We do serve, we're there.
-Gays and lesbians have distinguished themselves in war and in peacetime.
-The cost of discharging gays and lesbians is excessive. We need to spend our dollars differently.
-These are middletown Americans. Gays and lesbians should have opportunities to get education and to get skills just like anyone else. We should share the responsibilities and share the benefits.
-This is discrimination against a group of people simply because of who we are.[34]

It is an extraordinary public spectacle. Part of what makes the drama compelling is the sight of individuals being prosecuted not for deception or corruption (standard media fare in a cynical age) but being persecuted, rather, for their honesty. This is, also, a far cry from images of students setting draft cards on fire. "Look," one civilian activist says to me, "I may be ambivalent about the military. These folks aren't." The theatrical moment is intensified also by a sense of titillation—the serviceman or woman confessing to what has long been a closely guarded secret. These images of upright, presentable gay or lesbian servicemen and women likely works in part because it is set against other portraits of homosexuals harbored by the public: the more "outrageous" spectacle of the gay pride marches where dramatic cross dressing and flamboyant, demonstrative, "in your face" political theater. These uniformed men and women, after all, look and sound like—indeed *are*— the kids next door.

POLITICS BY THE BOOK

Why the choice of public spectacle? In both the case of the combat exclusion and the ban on homosexuality, the public spectacle is in some sense the method of last resort. Where claims for political equality have been frustrated in other political arenas and where it is possible to circumvent more routinized institutions of representation, the public spectacle becomes an attractive mode of political resistance.

Particularly in the case of lesbians and gays in the military, other avenues of political redress have secured almost no significant policy changes. Neither Congress nor the courts have provided effective routes for lesbians and gays seeking to change the ban on homosexuality. Neither legislation nor any Court decision by 1992 had caused the military to dismantle the proscription against homosexuals. Legislative initiatives to overturn the homosexual exclusion have been repeatedly introduced (by Senators Tsongas, Adams, and Metzenbaum, and Congresswomen Boxer and Schroeder, among others). But such legislation has never come close to winning sufficient support for passage. More astonishing, lesbian and gay members of the military had fought discrimination in the courts for decades—with consistently scant results. Some early court successes led the military to revise their policies to provide a stronger defense against challenges to the ban in 1982. But until the recent Meinhold case, in which a federal court declared the homosexual ban to be unconstitutional, the successes have been almost entirely on technicalities.[35]

The feminist story as it concerns equal opportunity for women is a little different. Politics by the book, in the case of feminists (who may be unwanted but are not at least illicit in the military) has been up to a point more successful. Feminists have been able to organize in the military through professional officers associations and, most prominently, as associates of the Defense Advisory Committee on Women in the Services (DACOWITS) with offices in the Pentagon. Many members of these groups are wary of addressing issues about homosexuality lest any association with lesbianism discredit their efforts at securing respectability. Only a few years ago, for the first time, did DACOWITS gingerly address the question of witch-hunting under the umbrella concept of sexual harassment. But on other issues—lifting the earlier two percent limit on women's numbers in the military, pushing the doors open to the service academies, forcing the services to address problems of harassment, opening up an ever wider range of occupational specialties, convincing the military to reissue more appropriate footwear and uniforms—DACOWITS has been at least one of a number of organizational voices pushing for change.[36]

Referred to by Phyllis Schlafly as the "feminist thought-control brigade of the U.S. military,"[37] DACOWITS has without doubt caused the military to accede to women's claims on numerous occasions. But the point beyond which the Committee had been unable to push the military is over the issue of combat exclusion. Despite the Committee's recommendation that the bar on utilizing women in combat roles be overturned (a proposal that had been translated into a legislative motion by Congresswoman Schroeder), the military and Congress were (until 1991) intransigent.

During the 1970s and 1980s, case after case challenging gender discrimination was brought before the courts. This litigation proved remarkably successful until the issue of combat arose and the brakes on equal opportunity were applied. In successive instances, the courts directed the military to provide dependency allowances to husbands of servicewomen on the same basis as wives, to permit women to serve on ships, to drop the ban on pregnant servicewomen, and to open particular military jobs to women.[38]

Unlike the history of lesbian and gay judicial challenges, litigation around sex discrimination repeatedly elicited favorable responses from the bench. This was all the more surprising given the deferential approach that the courts had taken toward the military in the years preceding. In what has been called the *Stanley* line of cases, the courts time after time rejected claims against the armed services.[39] Throughout the 1970s, the Courts turned down first amendment cases brought against the military. In 1986 the Court ruled that a plaintiff had no first amendment right to wear a yarmulke, and in 1987, in *Stanley*, the Court decided that the plaintiff who was earlier the unconsenting subject of a military experiment with LSD had no claim against the institution. In each of these cases, the Court repeatedly asserted that "military life calls for a different (that is, lower) standard of review than civilian life."[40] Yet in sex discrimination cases, the courts were perfectly prepared to hold the military to the same expectations as the courts held civilian institutions.

With the 1981 *Rostker v. Goldberg* case, however, the Supreme Court drew its line in the law.[41] In *Rostker*, the Court was finally drawn close to the defining mission of the institution, the issue of combat. Confronting a claim that the male-only draft registration was discriminatory, Justice Rehnquist, writing for the Court, held that registration was directly related to conscription, hence to combat, and that the Court needed to pay a "healthy deference to legislative and executive judgments in the area of military affairs." The nucleus of a masculinist military was now at issue and the Court drew back.

Politics by the book (organizing to influence Congress, bringing cases to the courts) worked fine for feminists up to the point where what William Brundage calls the demarcating "essence" of the military—who serves in combat—was called into question.[42] Without the dire spectacle of women dying in combat, it is unlikely that combat exclusion against women could have been successfully challenged.

A similar argument can be made about other population groups. One of the catalysts of the Truman Executive Order of 1948 desegregating the military was a violent incident that received wide publicity the year before, the blinding of Isaac Woodard. An African American army sergeant, Woodard was returning home by bus from Fort Gordon, Georgia when he was beaten by a local sheriff or policeman and blinded for life. Largely because Woodard was a returning veteran, the incident received an "outpouring of sympathy, shock, and assistance."[43]

The spectacle of patriotic, uniformed gays and lesbians, out to the American public, was dramatic theater. But what was lacking was the imagery (although likely not the reality) of lesbians and gays dying in battle. The brutal murder of Allen Schindler received extensive publicity.[44] But its occurrence, not on the battlefield but in a park bathroom in Japan, was framed by the press as a crime of homophobic violence rather than as a heroic soldier's death. As the authors of an important military history have written, "Indeed, the absorption of immigrants into the American melting pot has been achieved historically through the 'blood test'—you proved you loved America through allegiance and sacrifice and dying for the country in its wars (that is, paying the 'price in blood')."[45] Lacking images of lesbians and gays dying in battle, the spectacle of patriotic gay and lesbian soldiers telling the truth about who they were seems not to have been enough.

CONCLUSION

In 1991 Congressional action ended the combat exclusion that barred women from combat aviation, thus legally dismantling the exclusive male-only combat preserve. Two years later, a similar dismantling of discriminatory policies toward lesbians and gays failed when the Congress opposed the Executive Order and President Clinton backtracked on his opening term declaration to end the ban. At some level, the contrast is less stark than it might seem. The end of the combat exclusion permits—but does not require—the integration of women into combat ranks, leaving much up to the military command itself. But just as the Truman 1948 Executive Order at least opened the way for the racial desegregation of the military, the ending of any legally sanctioned discrimination is a crucial first step. That this step was taken in the case of gender and the combat exclusion and was not taken in the case of the lesbian/gay exclusion invites explanation.

It is not enough to say, real as it may be, that there is greater popular acceptance or less overt fear of women's rights than of lesbian/gay rights. This does not help to explain why the combat exclusion barring women aviators would finally be dropped in 1991 and not five years earlier or ten years later. It is also not enough to say that the women who lobbied against the combat exclusion were more effectively organized than were lesbian and gay activists (although the lesbian/gay lobbying efforts gathered momentum only somewhat belatedly as it became clear that the Clinton executive order was going to face Congressional trouble). Not even a flawless lobbying campaign beginning months earlier would have been a match for the political right on the lesbian/gay issue (any more than a flawless lobbying campaign could at this point in time establish the right to Medicaid abortions). There are some issues that simply cannot be won at a given point in time, short of some dramatic happening.

What social movements can do in these historical moments is to draw attention to such dramatic happenings. In the social movement literature, such attention making and interpretative work is described as "framing"—doing the meaning-making work that portrays a given situation as unjust.[46] Some collective action frames are directed at mobilizing a movement following; others at influencing decisions and policies made by state elites. This chapter describes the limitation of framing as a device to influence policy. Movements are limited by the kinds of events whose meaning they may hope to interpret. Dramatic happenings are more easily interpreted than created.

This dramatic happening was what the lesbian/gay movement intentionally attempted to produce, ultimately unsuccessfully, in 1992-93. Such theater, by contrast, was unintentionally (and successfully) available to be interpreted in 1991, bringing an end to the congressional combat exclusion of women. The spectacle of patriotic, uniformed lesbians and gays, exhibiting great personal courage by coming out to the American television public, was high drama. It put a face on the grievous injustice done to lesbians and gays whose proven excellence in their jobs was indisputable and whose military careers were ended based on their sexual identities alone. And yet the drama was probably not theater enough. This was not Damiens, the regicide, whose gruesome hanging "proved" the authority of the sovereign. Nor was it the story of women in the Gulf, Lieutenant Marie Rossi and twelve others, whose tragic, media broadcast deaths laid bare the hypocrisy of the argument that women were not already serving in combat. Had the movement and the media been able to convey (as was done in 1948 and in 1991) that lesbians and gays had served *and died* in combat, 1993 might have turned out differently. What the story of American social movements may suggest is that if a movement is to assert a group's claims to citizenship by demanding equal access to a nation's military, the spectacle of patriotic death is a minimal condition.

NOTES

This is a revised and updated version of "The Spectacle as Political Resistance: Feminist and Gay/Lesbian Politics in the Military" that appeared in *Minerva: Quarterly Report on Women and the Military* Vol. XI, No. 1 (Spring 1993): 1-16. I am grateful to Sandra Bem, who invited me to address this topic at the Friday Women's Studies seminars at Cornell; to Michael Busch for providing me with a constant stream of current materials; to Kathryn Abrams, Benedict Anderson, Zillah Eisenstein, Peter Katzenstein, and Sidney Tarrow for their comments; and particularly to Uday Mehta, for his imaginative insights. I was assisted by the Jonathan Meigs Fund and the Peace Studies Program (project support from the John D. and Catherine T. MacArthur Foundation). For this article, I spoke with a number of lesbian, gay, and feminist activists in Washington and New York, with several producers of television programs that featured lesbian and gay members of the military, with Clinton pollster Stanley Greenberg, and with Congressman Barney Frank. I am deeply appreciative of their willingness to spend time discussing the many questions I posed.

1. I use the term "spectacle" to capture the way events and ideas are either purposefully or inadvertently dramatized, such that the media deems them newsworthy.

2. On collective action repertoires, see Charles Tilly, *From Mobilization to Revolution* (Reading, MA: Addison Wesley, 1978). See also Timothy Cook and David Colby, "The Mass Mediated Epidemic: The Politics of AIDS in the

Nightly News," in Elizabeth Fee and Daniel M. Fox, eds. *AIDS: The Making of a Chronic Disease* (Berkeley: University of California Press, 1992).

3. Sidney Tarrow, *Power in Movement: Social Movements, Collective Action and Politics* (Cambridge: Cambridge University Press, 1994), 126. Tarrow notes that media also played a third role in providing a medium of communication within the movement itself (1994, 126).

4. Writing about the "heady" experience of watching Joe Steffan sing the national anthem at the inaugural ball, *Village Voice* columnist Donna Minkowitz interjects (albeit metaphorically rather than descriptively) the critical words: "I had to keep reminding myself that the military was at that moment bombing hotels in Iraq." In "High Anxiety: I Was a Stepford Queer at the Inaugural Ball." *Village Voice* (2 February 1993): 30.

5. Part of the concern of those who were critical of the efforts expended to establish the rights of lesbians and gays to be a recognized part of the military was the desexualized portrayal of lesbian/gay uniformed servicemembers. Mary Ann Humphrey's edited collection of autobiographical accounts of lesbians and gays in the military offers a much broader representation of sexual and personal identities than that portrayed in the broadcast media. See, for instance, accounts of Leonard Matlovich and Perry Watkins, in Mary Ann Humphrey, *My Country, My Right to Serve: Experiences of Gay Men and Women in the Military, World War II to the Present* (New York: Harper Collins, 1988).

6. Margaret Levi, "The Contingencies of Consent." Draft manuscript, Department of Political Science, University of Washington (1992).

7. Jim Teschner, interview with the author, December 1992. The *Newsweek* article "Gays and the Military" states that gay supporters contributed $3 million to the campaign (1 February 1993): 53-54.

8. Government Accounting Office, *Defense Force Management: DOD's Policy on Homosexuality* (June 1992). President Clinton used a figure of half a billion dollars "to get rid of 16,300 homosexuals in the military" in a town meeting. In "Clinton in a Town Meeting Calls for Dedication and Sacrifice." *New York Times* (11 February 1993): A27.

9. Interview, Stanley Greenberg, February 1, 1993. A *Newsweek* article notes that Clinton's first public comment on the issue, dating back to his October, 1991 appearance at the Harvard Kennedy School of Government forum, "was only mildly remarkable at the time—the kind of gesture a moderate Democrat would make to impress the avant-garde, and one that seemed to bear no significant political price. It was simple: Clinton, once elected, would do for gays what Harry Truman did for blacks in 1948—eliminate the military's discriminatory policies by executive order, starting a social revolution with the stroke of a pen" ("Gays and the Military," 53). The importance of the shift in social values can be seen in the fact that other moderate Democrats in the White House (Presidents Kennedy, Johnson, and Carter) had not been pressured to issue such an order, nor had they, on their own, raised the issue.

10. In a letter to constituents, Senator D'Amato explains his position supporting the end of the gay ban in "rights" terms: "With this argument, I am defending

the most elementary American principle, that of individual freedom. Gays and heterosexuals have served in the military in the past with honor . . . I can't imagine a more basic conservative position than to believe in individual responsibility and individual freedom . . ." (Dated February 12, 1993).

11. Levi, II, 9.

12. Craig Rimmerman, "Promise Unfulfilled: Clinton's Failure to Overturn the Military Ban on Gays and Lesbians." Paper presented at the annual meeting of the American Political Science Association, September 1-2, 1994.

13. Interview, May 6, 1995, Ithaca, NY.

14. *Congressional Quarterly Weekly Report*, 1993, 1976. Well known columnists were quite scathing in their critique of the Clinton compromise, seeing it as the abandonment of principle. See Bob Herbert, "Clinton Caves In." *New York Times* (18 July 1993): 19 and Ellen Goodman, "Putting Gay Troops in the Closet is No Compromise." *Ithaca Journal* (12 July 1993): 12A.

15. Levi, II, 10.

16. GAO *Defense Force Management* report, 39.

17. James C. Scott, *Weapons of the Weak: Everyday Forms of Peasant Resistance* (New Haven: Yale University Press, 1985).

18. Joseph Steffan, *Honor Bound: A Gay American Fights for the Right to Serve His Country* (New York: Villard Books, 1992).

19. Minkowitz, 30.

20. Michel Foucault, *Discipline and Punish: The Birth of the Prison* (New York: Vintage, 1979).

21. Foucault, 35.

22. In May, 1991, the House of Representatives repealed Section 8549 and modified Section 6015, 10 *U.S. Code* as proposed by Representatives Patricia Schroeder and Beverly Byron. In July, after a much more controversial discussion and vote, the Senate recommended the establishment of a Presidential Commission (most of whose proponents hoped to delay enactment of the repeal), but at the same time went along with the House repeal by a voice vote, led by Senators Roth and Kennedy. Senators Glen and McCain's efforts to block repeal thus failed. See Georgia Sadler, "Women in Combat: The United States Military and the Impact of the Persian Gulf War." Paper presented at the Women's Research and Education Institute Conference, December 1994 and Holm, 1992, Chs. 27 & 28. In the wake of Tailhook, Congress repealed 6015 as part of the National Defense Authorization Act for fiscal 1994 with the support of Navy leadership including Admiral Frank Kelso who in 1991 had opposed opening up combat ships to women.

23. Figures vary on the numbers of women sent to the Gulf. This report suggests that women were seven percent of the half million troops sent to the Gulf. In Mark E. Gebicke, "Women in the Military: Deployment in the Persian Gulf War." United States General Accounting Office, Report to the Secretary of Defense, GAO/NSIAD-93-93 (July 1993).

24. Michael R. Gordon, "Woman Leads G.I.'s in Combat in Panama, in a 'First' for Army," *New York Times* (4 January 1990): 1.

25. See Cynthia Enloe's powerful piece "Womenandchildren," *Village Voice* (25 September 1990).
26. Information on women casualties is scarce—presumably in part because official records are scanty. Through WWII, no death gratuities were offered to the parents of women killed in war. On deaths in World War I, II, and Vietnam, see Peter A. Soderbergh, *Women Marines: The World War II Era* (Westport, CT: Praeger, 1992, 146-7 and Jeanne Holm, *Women in the Military: An Unfinished Revolution* (Novato, CA: Presidio Press, 1992), 10, 11, 92, 206, 242.
27. Holm, 1992, 460. The dedication page of Holm's book displays a large photograph of Major Rossi.
28. Holm, 473-511; Mary Fainsod Katzenstein, *Liberating the Mainstream: Feminist Organizing in the U.S. Military and the American Catholic Church*, forthcoming.
29. Holm, 338.
30. Carolyn Becraft, Interview, March, 1991.
31. Mark Thompson, ed. *Gay Spirit: Myth and Meaning* (New York: St. Martin's Press, 1987), 50.
32. Tanya Domi, interview with author, January 1993.
33. Alexander Robinson, interview with author, 1993.
34. Interview with Domi, 1993.
35. William B. Rubenstein, "Challenging the Military's Antilesbian and Antigay Policy." *Law and Sexuality* 1 (1991): 239-65; Jeffrey S. Davis, "Military Policy Toward Homosexuals: Scientific, Historical, and Legal Perspectives." *Military Law Review* 131 (Winter 1991): 55-109; Kenneth L. Karst, "The Pursuit of Manhood and the Desegregation of the Armed Forces." *UCLA Law Review* 38 (February 1991): 499-581.
36. On DACOWITS, see Mary Fainsod Katzenstein, "Organizing the Terrain of Mainstream Institutions: Feminism in the United States Military." In *Going Public: National Histories of Women's Disenfranchisement and Women's Participation within State Institutions*, Mary Fainsod Katzenstein and Hege Skjeie. Oslo: Institute for Social Research, 1990.
Available from the Western Societies Program, Uris Hall, Cornell University, Ithaca, NY 14853.
37. Phyllis Schlafly, "The Feminization of the U.S. Military." *The Phyllis Schlafly Report* 23 (September 1989): section 1.
38. Judith Hicks Stiehm, *Arms and the Enlisted Woman* (Philadelphia: Temple University Press, 1989).
39. Stephanie Levin, "The Deference That Is Due: Rethinking the Jurisprudence of Judicial Deference to the Military." *Villanova Law Review* 35 (1990): 1010-61.
40. Levin, 1990.
41. *Rostker v. Goldberg*, 101 S. Ct. 2646.
42. Personal communication, Major William Brundage, Department of Political Science, Air Force Academy, Colorado Springs. The idea of changing

institutional core is central to Brundage's doctoral thesis on gender policies and the military to be submitted to the Department of Government, Harvard University.

43. Bernard C. Nalty, *Strength for the Fight: A History of Black Americans in the Military* (New York: Free Press, 1986), 205; Lee Nichols, *Breakthrough on the Color Front* (New York: Random House, 1954).

44. Programs such as *Dateline* did special reports, as did the mainstream press. See Jesse Green, "What the Navy Taught Allen Schindler's Mother." *New York Times Magazine* (12 September 1993): 58-63. The lesbian/gay press in particular covered the incident.

45. Martin Binkin and Mark J. Eitelberg, *Blacks and the Military* (Washington, D.C.: Brookings, 1982). With the collaboration of Alvin J. Schexnider and Marvin M. Smith. These authors mention Michael Novak's observation that ethnic Poles were over twelve percent of American deaths in World War I, although only four percent of the population. See Michael Novak, *The Rise of the Unmeltable Ethnics: Politics and Culture in the Seventies* (New York: Macmillan, 1972), xxi-xxii. They also mention that the term "fighting Irish" derives from the large number of Irish deaths in the Civil War.

46. For a helpful summary of the work on "framing" by David Snow and Robert Benford as well as related literature, see Tarrow, 122.

CHAPTER 9

Conduct Unbecoming Continues:

The First Year Under "Don't Ask, Don't Tell, Don't Pursue"

C. Dixon Osburn
Michelle M. Benecke

INTRODUCTION

February 28, 1995 marked the first anniversary of "Don't Ask, Don't Tell,Don't Pursue," the military's new regulations on homosexuals. There are two striking results during the past year, one good and one bad.

The good news results not from the policy but from federal court and military commands with strong leadership. In cases where courts have allowed lesbian and gay servicemembers to serve openly, there have been no problems. In fact, the opposite has proven to be the case. As reported in *U.S. News and World Report* on February 6, 1995 in regard to Petty Officer Keith Meinhold, who won his case before the Ninth Circuit Court of Appeals last year, "Meinhold . . . has been not only tolerated by the majority of his colleagues—he has been embraced by them." Meinhold's flight crew was recently named the most combat effective in the Pacific fleet.

Colonel Margarethe Cammermeyer has also received strong support. After she won her court case in June 1994, she immediately received calls from her unit welcoming her back to the Washington State National Guard. Petty Officer Mark Phillips was given a chocolate cake by his crewmembers on the one-year anniversary of his coming out to his unit. And Captain Rich Richenberg's coworkers threw a surprise birthday party for him in February 1995 as he continues to fight to stay in the military. These servicemembers are only a handful of those who have been serving openly for the past one to three years, and who, as clear documentation shows, have had a positive impact on their unit's good order, discipline, and morale.

The bad news results from the implementation of Don't Ask, Don't Tell, Don't Pursue in the field. The new policy promised to stop questions about sexual orientation, witch-hunts, and harassment. Through a lack of proper training and willful disregard of the new policy, many commanders continue to ask, witch-hunt, and harass suspected homosexual servicemembers in direct violation of the new policy. The result has been that the discharge rate for homosexuals in fiscal year 1994 has not declined, and the cost of training replacements for those discharged has exceeded $17.5 million. The costs of conducting investigations, holding discharge hearings, administering the new policy, and defending the policy in federal court are far higher. This report details four specific violations of the new policy occurring in the field. The report documents cases where military officials have (1) asked servicemembers about their sexual orientation; (2) punished statements of sexual orientation that are permissible under the new policy or expanded the situations where telling is prohibited; (3) pursued or witch hunted suspected homosexuals; and (4) condoned harassment based on sexual orientation. This report does not include other clear violations, including situations, among others, where suspected homosexuals receive improper or inadequate legal representation within the military; are treated in an unevenhanded manner with respect to potential criminal prosecution; and are "outed" to their units and family by commanders in direct violation of the Privacy Act.

This report is based on violations of Don't Ask, Don't Tell, Don't Pursue documented by the Servicemembers Legal Defense Network (SLDN), located in Washington, D.C. SLDN is the sole national legal aid and watchdog organization for those targeted by the military's new policy on homosexuals, and the only means currently available to document abuses. The Department of Defense has instituted no method of identifying and correcting abuses of the new policy.

SLDN's documented cases reflect only the tip of the iceberg of all servicemembers affected by the Don't Ask, Don't Tell, Don't Pursue policy. Many servicemembers are discharged by the Department of Defense for homosexuality without ever having contacted SLDN, and others are removed from service for homosexuality through ulterior means such as denial of reenlistment. SLDN's outreach is limited by its scarce resources, but even with such constraints, it received over 400 calls for direct assistance in the past year, suggesting that SLDN's figures represent only a fraction of the total violations of the new policy.

SLDN is headed by two attorneys, C. Dixon Osburn and Michelle M. Benecke. Mr. Osburn is a former legal/policy advisor to the Campaign for Military Service, the national coalition that worked to lift the ban legislatively. Mr. Osburn holds a J.D. and M.B.A. from Georgetown University, and an A.B. from Stanford University. Ms. Benecke is a former Captain and Battery Commander in the U.S. Army, and former staff attorney at the Campaign for Military Service. She has written extensively on the military policy's disproportionate impact on women. Ms. Benecke is a graduate of Harvard Law School and holds a B.A. from the University of Virginia.

BACKGROUND/DEFINITION OF TERMS

From March 1, 1994 to the present, over 400 servicemembers contacted SLDN needing assistance. The servicemembers were typically between the ages of 18 and 25 and had limited financial resources. The types of assistance requested ranged from basic information about how to comport one's behavior under the new policy to intensive efforts to stop witch-hunts or prevent death threats from being carried out. Of the 188 calls requiring intervention, SLDN's staff attorneys, in conjunction with aides in Republican and Democratic Congressional offices and with cooperating attorneys from SLDN's network of over 200 attorneys from the finest law firms in the country, carefully monitored and documented violations of the Don't Ask, Don't Tell, Don't Pursue policy.

This report documents common command violations of four regulatory provisions in the Don't Ask, Don't Tell, Don't Pursue policy. Those provisions are called, not surprisingly, "Don't Ask," "Don't Tell," "Don't Pursue," and "Don't Harass." "Don't Harass" was never added to the common title of the new policy, but is nevertheless an explicit component of the policy.

What is "Don't Ask?"

The "Don't Ask" regulations state that "servicemembers will not be asked about or required to reveal their sexual orientation." Violations of Don't Ask monitored by SLDN include (1) direct questions about sexual orientation, such as "Are you gay?"; (2) surrogate questions about sexual orientation where a servicemember is not asked directly about his or her orientation, but is asked through creative phrasing, as in "Do you find men attractive?"; and (3) inadvertent questions where a commander does not realize that the question requires disclosure of sexual orientation, such as when a commander, out of concern for someone in his or her unit, asks what is troubling the servicemember, and the answer is that the servicemember is grappling with issues related to sexual orientation. The question would not pose a problem for a heterosexual servicemember but it does for the homosexual servicemember.

What is "Don't Tell?"

With respect to "Don't Tell," the new regulations do not prohibit all statements about sexual orientation. Indeed, the new regulations do not forbid statements made to lawyers, chaplains, spouses, or security clearance personnel. In violation of the new policy, however, security clearance personnel continue to punish servicemembers who state they are gay by removal of or protracted delays in granting the clearances or, also in direct violation of the new policy, by threatening servicemembers with the denial of their clearance if they do not confess to their sexual orientation and any sexual activity. Additionally, the Pentagon has expanded Don't Tell, in ways that the public is not aware, to include statements to family members, close friends, doctors, and mental health professionals. Thus, violations of Don't Tell include incidents where statements to family members, close friends, doctors and mental health professionals, and security clearance personnel have resulted in discharge or the threat of discharge of homosexual servicemembers.

What is "Don't Pursue?"

The "Don't Pursue" portion of the new regulations states that (1) "sexual orientation is a personal and private matter"; (2) "inquiries shall be limited to the factual circumstances directly relevant to the specific allegations"; and (3) "credible information exists when the information, considering its source and the surrounding circumstances, supports a reasonable belief that a servicemember has engaged in homosexual conduct." Additionally, it is widely understood that the new regulations would "bring an end" to witch-hunts, as President Clinton stated on July 19, 1993, and General Colin Powell reiterated upon the issuance of the new regulations. Some military commands continue to pursue homosexual or suspected homosexual servicemembers in a variety of ways. Violations of Don't Pursue include (1) witch-hunts, (2) improper searches and seizures, (3) expanding investigations beyond the instant allegation, and (4) misapplication of the credible information standard.

While there is some overlap among these four prongs, each prong can be roughly defined as follows. *Witch-hunts* are situations where inquiry officials ask servicemembers or take other affirmative steps to identify suspected homosexuals or those they suspect have engaged in homosexual acts. *Improper searches and seizures* include illegal, warrantless searches, as well as zealous investigations where commanders confiscate personal and private property such as diaries and letters. *Expanding investigations beyond the instant allegation* includes situations, among others, where a servicemember who has been alleged to have engaged in homosexual conduct on a specific occasion is investigated for any additional conduct in which the servicemember may have engaged in order to fish for information that could lead to criminal prosecution or lower discharge characterization. *Misapplication of the credible information standard* contemplates situations where a commander has not seriously evaluated the "source and the surrounding circumstances" of the allegations as required by the new regulations. Examples include situations where the commander has failed to examine or take into account (a) the retaliatory motives of an individual making the allegations, (b) the lack of consistency and coherence in the allegations, (c) recanted testimony, (d) exculpatory evidence, and (e) inadvertent discoveries in which no one knows about a servicemember's sexual orientation except through, for example, the discovery of a private letter by a commander during a surprise inspection.

What is "Don't Harass?"

Lastly, the "Don't Harass" portion of the new regulations makes explicit that "the Armed Forces do not tolerate harassment or violence against any servicemember, for any reason." Violations of Don't Harass include death threats, physical harassment, and verbal harassment made against servicemembers who are or are suspected of being homosexual. "Don't Harass" violations also include downgraded performance evaluations, denial of reenlistment, and failure to promote due to sexual orientation.

The cases received by SLDN spanned every branch of military service[1] and were geographically dispersed. Thirty-six percent of SLDN's cases came from military personnel in the U.S. Navy, 29% came from the U.S. Army, 26% from the U.S. Air Force, 8% from the U.S. Marine Corps, and 1% from the

Table 1

Findings: SLDN Cases By Service

Service	Total # Cases	% Total Cases	Men	Women	Gender n/a
Air Force	49	26%	38	9	2
Army	55	29%	31	24	0
Navy	68	36%	56	11	1
Marine Corps	15	8%	12	3	0
Coast Guard	1	1%	1	0	0
TOTAL	188	100%	138	47	3

U.S. Coast Guard. Of the 188 cases followed, 138 servicemen contacted SLDN for help (73%), and 47 servicewomen contacted SLDN (25%). The percentage of women who contacted SLDN is disproportionate to women's representation in the armed forces, which is thirteen percent.

Of SLDN's 188 cases under the new policy,[2] SLDN documented 37 cases where there were violations of Don't Ask (20% of its cases); 18 cases where there were violations of Don't Tell (18% of its cases); 65 cases where there were violations of Don't Pursue (35% of its cases); and 62 cases where there were violations of Don't Harass (33% of its cases). (See Table 2.)

The Navy and Army accounted for the most cases involving violations of Don't Ask, accounting for 35% and 30% of such cases respectively. The Army accounted for the most cases misapplying or redefining Don't Tell, accounting for 50% of all such cases. The Air Force accounted for the most cases involving violations of Don't Pursue, accounting for 37% of all such cases. The Navy accounted for the most cases involving violations of Don't Harass, accounting for 37% of all such cases.

The total number of cases involving violations does not total the 188 cases received by SLDN, because some cases did not involve any regulatory infractions by military officials. Thus, the total number of cases involving violations reported above is 182.

The total number of cases involving violations also does not take into account multiple violations occurring in the same case. In the past year, SLDN documented 65 violations of Don't Ask, 21 violations of Don't Tell, 114 violations of Don't Pursue, and 140 violations of Don't Harass, for a documented total of 340 overall violations during the past year. The multiple violations indicate that in cases where there is one incident of asking, pursuit, or harassment, others are likely.

Table 2
SLDN Cases Involving Violations Of
"Don't Ask, Don't Tell, Don't Pursue, Don't Harass"
By Service
(Total #, %)

Service	Don't Ask	Don't Tell	Don't Pursue	Don't Harass
Air Force	8 (21%)	5 (28%)	24 (37%)	15 (24%)
Army	11 (30%)	9 (50%)	16 (25%)	17 (27%)
Navy	13 (35%)	2 (11%)	15 (23%)	23 (37%)
Marine Corps	4 (11%)	1 (5.5%)	10 (15%)	6 (10%)
Coast Guard	1 (3%)	1 (5.5%)	0 (0%)	1 (2%)
TOTAL	37 (100%)	18 (100%)	65 (100%)	62 100%

It is clear that some commanders continue to violate Don't Ask, Don't Tell, Don't Pursue, Don't Harass in a myriad of ways. The following are a few examples of how the new policy on homosexuals is being improperly implemented in the field.

Examples of Violations of "Don't Ask"
Violations of Don't Ask include asking direct, surrogate, or inadvertent questions about sexual orientation.

Asking Direct Questions About Sexual Orientation
One Chief of Boat asked a sailor, "You're not going to tell me you're a f___ faggot, are you?" In Japan, CID Special Agent Jose Abrante asked a marine point blank: "Are you gay?" In Florida, recruiters asked one recruit whether

she is homosexual five times, both verbally and through use of outdated written forms. In the Washington, D.C. area, a security clearance investigator asked, "I'm not going to ask you if you're homosexual, but if I did ask, how would you respond?"

Asking Surrogate Questions About Sexual Orientation
An inquiry official asked a male sergeant, "Do you find men attractive?" An executive officer asked a PFC whether she had "homosexual tendencies." A security clearance investigator asked an Army Major about her female roommate, "Do you have a physical relationship with your roommate?" Another security clearance investigator at Ft. William, Alabama, asked during an interview whether the individual knew "any homosexuals."

Asking Inadvertent Questions About Sexual Orientation
Out of concern, a Naval commander asked one of his unit members why he had not reported to work one day. The servicemember honestly told him that he and his male partner had a family emergency, and was subsequently discharged for his statement. Another commander asked why a servicemember's security clearance had been held up. The reason was that the member had followed regulations and was honest with the investigators about his orientation.

Violations of "Don't Tell"
Violations of "Don't Tell" include using statements from family members, doctors and psychologists, and security clearance personnel for purposes of discharge.

Using Statements from Family Members
Air Force Captain Earl Brown's parents were asked in detail about their son's sexual orientation, and statements made by Brown to his mother and father were included among the statements for which he was to be discharged. An Air Force doctor's mother says she was shocked when an inquiry official contacted her to ask about her son's sexual activities. Indeed, the Department of Air Force issued a memorandum on November 3, 1994 specifically directing inquiry officials to "interview . . . parents and siblings" to obtain information to be used as a basis for discharge.

Using Statements from Doctors and Psychologists for Purposes of Discharge
Corporal Kevin Blaesing, with the Marine Security Force in Charleston, South Carolina, was turned in by his Naval psychologist for asking questions about sexuality during private counseling sessions. His commander, Lt. Col. Martinson, ordered that he face discharge proceedings despite advice from his legal advisors not to proceed. Another servicemember in the Air Force was advised by his psychologist that disclosure of his sexual orientation would be conveyed to his commanding officer for purposes of discharge; the servicemember, however, stated that his priority was mental health services and

that he could not obtain full and adequate treatment without some discussion of issues related to his sexuality. He now faces discharge.

Using Statements Made During Security Clearances for Purposes of Discharge
In violation of the new policy, security clearance personnel continue to punish servicemembers who state they are gay by removal of or protracted delays in granting the clearances. In direct violation of the new policy, servicemembers are also threatened with the denial of their clearance if they do not confess to their sexual orientation and sexual activity.

Violations of "Don't Pursue"
Violations of "Don't Pursue" include (1) witch-hunts, (2) improper searches and seizures, (3) expanding inquiries beyond the instant allegations, and (4) misapplying the credible information standard.

Witch-Hunts: Asking About the Orientation and Conduct of Others
SLDN documented 15 actual or attempted witch-hunts under the new regulations where commanders and inquiry officials asked military members to identify other servicemembers who were or were suspected to be homosexual. In Japan, over twenty-one servicemembers were questioned regarding the sexual orientation and private lives of their coworkers. At New River Station, North Carolina, immediately after briefing his unit about the military's new policy on March 1, 1994, a Marine Master Sergeant told his troops that, despite the regulations, they had "a moral duty and an obligation" to turn in suspected homosexuals. At Pope Air Force Base, North Carolina, a commander reportedly asked for a list of all Combined Federal Campaign (CFC) contributors to gay and AIDS organizations; the commander dropped his order once the incident was publicly reported.

Improper Searches and Seizures
Overzealous commands continue to conduct or condone illegal searches and seizures of items belonging to suspected homosexual servicemembers. Additionally, they continue to confiscate personal and private items, as well as circumstantial evidence, that should have no bearing on an inquiry, per regulation. Commanders and inquiry officials routinely seize personal diaries, private letters, address books, personal computers, erased computer files, photos of friends, copies of popular gay-themed books and videos like "Torch Song Trilogy," HIV pamphlets, academic notes from classes on human sexuality, and, in one serviceman's case, even a pair of men's platform shoes.

Expanding Inquiries Beyond the "Instant Allegations"
Commands routinely expand the scope of an investigation beyond the instant allegations. Thus, a person who has admitted to being gay will be asked to additionally confess to homosexual acts in order to gather information that could lead to criminal prosecution or lower discharge characterization.

Servicemembers who are under investigation for allegations of homosexual acts are often questioned about other acts beyond the instant allegation. Inquiry officials in North Carolina, for example, asked more than 25 servicemembers to speculate about the sexual orientation and activities of one marine, beyond the two allegations she faced.

Misapplying Credible Information Standard

A seaman faces discharge after his roommate, while snooping in the seaman's personal desk, discovered and read several letters from which he concluded that the seaman might be gay, and turned the letters over to the command. In another case, a seaman was asked by his superior if he was gay and he answered truthfully; the command has decided to proceed with a discharge board despite the clear Don't Ask violation.

Violations of "Don't Harass"

Violations of "Don't Harass" include (1) death threats based on sexual orientation; (2) targeted physical and verbal harassment based on sexual orientation; and (3) downgraded performance evaluations, denial of reenlistment, and failure to promote due to sexual orientation.

Improper Response to Death Threats

SLDN received 10 cases where servicemembers were threatened with their lives for being or being suspected of being gay. One commander in Misawa, Japan, Captain Miller, reportedly told a heterosexual servicemember, "You're going to die," after the servicemember's recommended separation for alleged homosexual conduct had been overturned. A new recruit at Parris Island was told she was not "going to walk out of here alive" if she reported being physically assaulted for being suspected of being a lesbian. A seaman reports finding a noose next to his berthing onboard ship, having previously found a note scrawled on a magazine photo that read "Die Fag." The Pentagon has established no means whereby servicemembers can report death threats with a guarantee that the report will not be used as a basis to start an investigation against them.

Improper Response to Harassment (Physical/Verbal) and Extortion

As with death threats, the Pentagon has established no means whereby servicemembers can report harassment with a guarantee that the report will not be used as a basis to start an investigation against them. SLDN has received 69 reports of targeted physical and verbal abuse based on their perceived orientation. A majority report describes command climates rife with derogatory comments about gays. One servicemember reports that someone gouged his new car with keys and scrawled into the paint the word "fag."

Downgraded Performance Evaluations, Denial of Reenlistment, and Failure to Promote Due to Sexual Orientation

Lt. Colonel Trask admitted on the record at a discharge board that he downgraded the evaluation of and recommended against promotion for Captain Rich Richenberg, an officer who ranked in the top ten percent of all Air Force officers prior to Lt. Col. Trask's actions, solely because Richenberg is gay. After Corporal Kevin Blaesing, Marine of the Quarter for his unit, succeeded in having his recommended separation overturned, his commander, Lt. Colonel Martinson, downgraded his performance evaluations contrary to the recommendations of Blaesing's supervisors and gave Corporal Blaesing the lowest possible recommendation for reenlistment, thus effectively killing Blaesing's opportunity to reenlist and continue his military career.

Notably, there is little to no harassment of open lesbian and gay service personnel who have remained in service due to court order or discharge board recommendation. In fact, all documentation shows that those individuals enjoy the wide support of their colleagues, coworkers, and commands.

These cases make clear that either through a lack of training or willful disregard of the new policy, some commanders continue to ask, pursue, and harass servicemembers in direct violation of the new policy.

Table 3
DOD Discharges Of Servicemembers For Homosexuality

Fiscal Year	Air Force	Army	Navy	Marine Corps	Total	% Total Armed Forces
1991	151 15.9%	206 21.7%	545 57.4%	47 5.0%	949 100%	.04
1992	111 15.7%	138 19.5%	401 56.6%	58 8.2%	708 100%	.04
1993	152 22.2%	156 22.9%	334 49.0%	40 5.9%	682 100%	.04
1994	180 30.1%	136 22.8%	245 41.0%	36 6.0%	597 100%	.04
Total	594	636	1525	101	2936	.04

The result of the widespread violations is that the rate of discharge for homosexuals has not declined as expected. Despite the belief that the interim and new regulations would be as President Clinton remarked, "a major step forward," the rate of discharge of homosexuals from 1991 to 1994 has remained constant at .04% of the total active force.

The distribution of discharge cases by service as reported by the Pentagon, however, has markedly changed for two services. The Navy's percentage of homosexual discharge cases compared with other services has declined from 57.4% of total discharges in 1991 to 41% of total discharges in 1994. On the other hand, the Air Force has contributed more to total discharges during the same time frame. In 1991, the Air Force accounted for only 15.9% of total homosexual discharges; in 1994, the Air Force accounted for 30.1% of total homosexual discharge cases. The Pentagon's figures suggest that the Air Force has significantly increased efforts to target and discharge homosexual servicemembers over the last four years, and especially during fiscal year 1994.

The dollar costs of the military's policy on homosexuals continue to be high. Based on figures the Pentagon supplied to the General Accounting Office in 1992, the last time the Pentagon provided such information, the cost of training servicemembers to replace those discharged for homosexuality totaled $17.5 million in fiscal year 1994 (see Table 4). The costs from 1991 to 1994 totaled $86.5 million. These figures are not adjusted for inflation and do not include the costs to investigate servicemembers, the costs of holding and preparing for administrative discharge hearings, or the costs of administering the policy. Nor do the figures include the significant cost of defending the policy in federal court. SLDN has no independent estimates of the costs of the Department of Defense (DOD) policy.

Table 4
Costs Of Training Replacements For Servicemembers
Discharged Under Homosexual Conduct Policy

Year(s)	# Discharged	Costs[3]
1980-1990	16,919	$498,555,244
1991	949	$27,964,355
1992	708	$20,862,764
1993	682	$20,096,617
1994	597	$17,591,907
TOTAL	19,855	$585,070,887

In summary, it is clear that many military commanders continue to ask, pursue, and harass servicemembers in direct violation of the new policy. Evidence of the continuing violations comes not only from servicemembers' cases documented by SLDN and its cooperating attorneys, but from memoranda issued by the Department of the Air Force, Department of Navy, and others. The question is why these abuses have occurred.

ANALYSIS
Reasons for Command Violations
There are four common reasons for command violations of Don't Ask, Don't Tell, Don't Pursue, Don't Harass: (1) commanders and others lack information; (2) commanders and others do not understand the policy; (3) insubordination by commanders, investigators, and prosecutors; and (4) commanders and others have no incentive to learn or follow the rules.

Commanders and Other Leaders Lack Information
Some command violations can be attributed to lack of information about the new policy. A major problem has been inadequate distribution of the new regulations. Throughout the past year, numerous commanders, defense attorneys, and servicemembers have contacted SLDN in search of current copies of the DOD and service regulations because they were not available in their commands. As recently as early February 1995, SLDN was required to ship these regulations to an overseas trial defense office.

Commanders and Others Do Not Understand the Policy
Other command violations stem from insufficient training, and therefore understanding, of the policy. Even the Pentagon concedes that training on the new policy has been handled less diligently than other personnel policies, such as those on sexual harassment.[4] The most striking gap in training has been the failure of the Department of Defense to issue sufficient guidance regarding the intent of the new policy to military leaders as well as servicemembers. This is an especially critical oversight in light of the broad discretion afforded commanders under the policy. Without an understanding of the intent of the policy, many commanders and prosecutors have focused their efforts on how to skirt the letter of the regulations.

Insubordination by Commanders, Investigators, and Prosecutors
An alarming number of command violations documented by SLDN result from outright insubordination, not lack of information or inadequate training. These violations are fueled, in part, by a climate of backlash in many units. The controversy over President Clinton's proposal to lift the ban charged the atmosphere in the military and focused unprecedented attention on the private lives of servicemembers. Since that time, everyone from private to general officer has speculated about who in the ranks might be gay. In this climate, many commanders and others have taken the Congressional vote against lifting the ban as a license to go after those whom they suspect are gay. As Lawrence J. Korb, former Assistant Secretary of Defense for Personnel and Readiness under President Reagan, recently stated, "I think the military feels they have

beaten Clinton back on this issue and they're not going to change."[5] As a result, many servicemembers are actually worse off than before.

Commanders Have No Incentive to Learn or Follow the Rules
A major problem is that the Department of Defense has established no means to monitor cases and to correct violations and misapplications of the policy. Although Department of Defense regulations provide that commanders and others who violate the policy be disciplined, this provision has been roundly ignored. SLDN knows of no commander or other military member who has yet been disciplined for abusing the policy, despite numerous complaints.

The military's treatment of servicemembers who are harmed by command violations of the policy exacerbates the problem of accountability. Servicemembers presently have no official means of redress for command violations. As just one example, a young sailor is currently being discharged solely because he responded truthfully to his supervisor's direct question about his sexual orientation, even though the command admitted on the record that the supervisor's action violated the new policy. To date, DOD and the services have been unwilling to provide a common sense resolution to this and similar situations.

The clear message to commanders is that they do not have to take the new policy seriously and that, if so inclined, they may violate it with impunity.

Analysis of "Don't Ask" Violations
"Don't Ask" is a simple, well-publicized mandate. Unlike some other provisions, there is no ambiguity in this part of the regulations. Nevertheless, commanders and other leaders continue to ask servicemembers about their sexual orientation, often repeatedly. While a few commanders have done so inadvertently, the overwhelming majority have violated Don't Ask through direct questions about sexual orientation and surrogate questions designed to circumvent the letter of the regulations. The facts and circumstances surrounding these violations indicate that almost all were deliberate. The degree of thought and ingenuity evident in devising many of the surrogate questions further indicates a climate of insubordination in many commands.

Analysis of "Don't Tell" Violations
Most military leaders fail to understand that the new policy does not preclude all statements regarding sexual orientation and that it recognizes a zone of privacy for all servicemembers.[6] Over the past year, military leaders have established two clear trends that violate "Don't Tell." They have (1) punished statements of sexual orientation that are permissible under the new policy, and (2) expanded the situations where telling is prohibited in order to reach the most private spheres of servicemembers' lives.

The most prominent cases involving the first trend have occurred in the context of security clearance investigations. Security clearance regulations encourage gay servicemembers to be forthcoming about their sexual orientation and to reveal whether their family and close associates are aware of it. The regulations state that "information about homosexual orientation or conduct obtained during a security clearance investigation will not be used . . . in separation proceedings." The regulations further state that a servicemember may decline to answer questions about sexual orientation without adverse consequence. In reality, however, security clearance personnel continue to threaten servicemembers with denial of clearances for either stating or declining to state their sexual orientation. Denial of a security clearance effectively kills the servicemember's career. Additionally, some commands have attempted to use the information obtained during security clearance for purposes of discharge, in direct violation of the new policy.

The chief problem with the security clearance regulations is that they are inconsistent with the other sections of the military's policy on homosexuals. Those charged with implementing the security clearance regulations in light of the other policy provisions do not know whether or not to ask about sexual orientation and how to respond to the answers forthcoming. Servicemembers do not know how or if to respond to questions about sexual orientation, given the regulations' conflicting guidance. Thus, confusion results and homosexual servicemembers typically receive the short end of the stick.

Servicemembers and their families have also been shocked by the Department of Defense's expansion of situations where telling is prohibited. At least some commanders have violated this prong of Don't Tell as a direct result of guidance from the top levels of the Pentagon. A Department of the Air Force memo from Judge Advocate General Headquarters to all Staff Judge Advocates and military judges dated November 3, 1994, actually instructs inquiry officers to question parents about the sexual orientation and activities of their children to obtain information for purposes of discharging their sons and daughters. The memo also instructs officers to interrogate close civilian friends and mentors, such as high school guidance counselors, to determine whether a servicemember has ever discussed their orientation.

Additionally, the Department of Defense instructs psychologists to turn in servicemembers who seek private counseling about their sexual orientation. In response to public outcry in the wake of one case, the Department of Defense General Counsel's office simply announced that the military would not treat statements to psychologists as privileged and confidential. The response entirely brushes aside the issue of whether such private statements are the kind of statements contemplated as a grounds for discharge under the new policy.

This attempt to enforce a gag rule in the context of communications with family and professional health care providers is chilling. Most Americans would be appalled to learn that their tax dollars are being spent on such unprecedented invasions into relationships that are generally considered private and confidential.

A related problem is the outing of gay servicemembers by their commanders. Although a detailed analysis is outside the scope of this report, it should be noted that some commanders have told their units, and even a servicemember's spouse and parents, that the servicemember was under investigation for homosexual conduct, in direct violation of the Privacy Act. Outing is not only a violation of servicemembers' privacy, but it has also jeopardized the safety of servicemembers in commands where harassment is tolerated.

Analysis of "Don't Pursue" Violations

The words "Don't Pursue" do not actually appear in the policy or regulations. Instead, the concept is communicated through two primary standards. First, commanders or investigators may not initiate an inquiry or investigation unless, considering the source and surrounding circumstances, they have credible evidence that a servicemember has engaged in homosexual conduct. Information based on opinion, rumor, and capricious claims does not constitute credible information. Second, inquiries and investigations must be limited to the scope of the instant allegation.

Don't Pursue was intended, in part, to stop the military's infamous witch-hunts of suspected homosexuals. Like Don't Ask, this concept has been well-publicized and communicated through the ranks. General Colin Powell testified before the Senate Armed Services Committee that the new regulations held forth that, "We won't witch hunt. We won't chase. We will not seek to learn orientation."[7] Nevertheless, SLDN documented fifteen attempted and actual witch-hunts over the past year. Most were initiated in deliberate violation of the new policy.

Among those commanders who wish to follow the regulations, most do not comprehend the actual standards of Don't Pursue. Some commanders know that they must be able to articulate a basis to begin an inquiry against a servicemember. Army and Air Force commanders are supposed to write down their justification for beginning an inquiry. A significant problem, however, is that the vast majority of commanders do not know what constitutes credible information. The policy itself provides little guidance on how to interpret this inherently subjective and vague standard.

A major consequence is that commanders apply the policy inconsistently throughout the services and even in the same commands. Additionally, commanders routinely initiate inquiries and investigations against servicemembers based only on hearsay or circumstantial evidence, contrary to the clear intent of the regulations. These trends are evident in the following examples.

In the case of Corporal Blaesing, who asked questions of his psychologist, his first commander did not consider his questions as evidence of homosexual conduct and allowed him to continue service. When this commander later retired, his successor revived the case, notwithstanding the fact that the Navy psychologist testified that she did not know Blaesing's orientation and that he had not stated it to her. As a result, Blaesing was forced to face discharge proceedings and was recommended for separation.

In identical cases from the Air Force, two commanders inadvertently discovered private letters belonging to one of their airmen that contained language that could be interpreted as hints about homosexuality. One commander made no issue of the letters and allowed the airman to stay; the other investigated and discharged the airman based solely on the letters.

SLDN has also found that most commanders are not even aware of the standard to limit inquiries to the scope of the instant allegation. Thus, even where inquiries are properly initiated, they inevitably become fishing expeditions into all aspects of a servicemember's private life. In the case of Lance Corporal Elena Martinez, an inquiry that was not initiated properly, her supervisor directly solicited coworkers to make allegations of homosexual conduct against her. Two male Marines lodged allegations that Martinez had danced with both men and women at a popular local club and that, on another occasion, she had given another woman a goodbye peck on the cheek. Based on this report, the command initiated an inquiry in which they questioned over twenty-five coworkers and civilian acquaintances, including former landlords, inviting them to speculate about every detail of Martinez's private life. Further, her supervisor directly ordered coworkers to monitor and report on Martinez's social activities. Even if the basis of this inquiry had been legitimate, the command's wide-ranging campaign into Martinez's personal life clearly violated the requirement to limit inquiries to the scope of the instant allegation.

Many commanders and investigators use this tactic of expanding investigations beyond the scope of the instant allegation in a deliberate effort to dig up information to support a less than honorable discharge characterization or criminal charges against servicemembers who are or are perceived to be gay.

Analysis of "Don't Harass" Violations
Like "Don't Ask," the mandate against harassment is unambiguous. It forbids harassment of any kind against any servicemember. This mandate is not unfamiliar to commanders. In the wake of the Tailhook scandal, it has become a standard order. Nevertheless, SLDN's cases show that harassment and death threats against suspected gay servicemembers are worse than ever.

Poor leadership is the primary reason for the high incidence of harassment. A majority of servicemembers who have called SLDN report that their supervisors have witnessed incidents of harassment and have taken no steps to correct it. In an alarming number of SLDN's cases, members of the chain-of-command have actually participated in harassment against suspected gays. In addition, some commanders have retaliated against gay servicemembers through downgraded performance evaluations or by denying them reenlistment. These actions send a clear message that harassment is condoned.

SLDN's data also show a high correlation between harassment and "Don't Pursue" violations. In units where commanders pursue gays, servicemembers report that they feel great pressure to prove that they are not gay. One way to do so is to make derogatory comments about gays in the company of coworkers and to directly harass other servicemembers who are perceived as gay. Servicemembers report that if they do not participate in such activities, they are quickly labeled as gay and harassed.

In light of these findings, it is not surprising that the majority of servicemembers who have called SLDN report that derogatory comments and harassment of suspected gays have been a regular occurrence in their units since the national debate.

Servicemembers who wish to complain about harassment or death threats face significant obstacles. There is no guarantee that commands will not use a report of harassment or death threats as a basis for investigation and discharge of the threatened servicemember. At best, servicemembers who have dared to file complaints have simply been ignored by their chain-of-command. As a result of the lack of response and threat of discharge, most incidents of death threats and harassment go unreported.

In stark contrast, there has not been a problem with harassment in those units with openly gay servicemembers, many of whom are serving by court order. Nor has there been a problem in units with commanders who have made it clear to their troops that they will not tolerate harassment. This suggests the truth of the old maxim that "troops follow the flag." In short, harassment occurs because of a unit's leadership, not despite it.

CONCLUSION AND RECOMMENDATIONS

SLDN concludes that many military officials continue to ask questions about sexual orientation, conduct witch-hunts, and condone harassment of lesbian and gay servicemembers in direct violation of Don't Ask, Don't Tell, Don't Pursue. SLDN further concludes that the chief reasons for the continuing violations are lack of information, lack of adequate training and guidance regarding the new policy, and in some cases, willful disregard of military policy by commanders and others.

SLDN recommends that the Department of Defense ensure the proper implementation of Don't Ask, Don't Tell, Don't Pursue by providing (1) adequate information to and training for all servicemembers about the new policy, (2) common sense remedies to servicemembers who are harmed by command violations, and (3) clear accountability for violations of the policy by military officials.

Provide Adequate Information and Training

The Department of Defense should ensure that full DOD Directives, Guidance, and Service Regulations reach the field. Attorneys and commanders often possess only the message text of the service regulations sent to the field on February 28, 1994, with no guidance on how to interpret those regulations. At a minimum, military officials should have the full DOD Directives, Commander's Guidance, DOD Guidelines dated July 20, 1993, and all DOD and service guidance necessary to interpret the regulations.

Additionally, the Department of Defense should clearly and strongly communicate the intent of the new policy to stop antigay harassment and pursuits of suspected homosexual servicemembers. At present, the intent of the new policy has not been adequately disseminated to the field and, thus, is not widely known or understood. In order to apply the legal standards of the new policy, commanders must, as with all regulations, understand the "commander's intent" behind the policy itself. Advisors to the command, particularly military attorneys and Inspectors General, must also understand its intent. Clear intent is vital given the current hostile command climate in many commands, the wide discretion afforded commanders, and the ambiguity of some policy standards. At a minimum, all existing command and advisory channels should be vigorously utilized to communicate and reinforce the intent of the policy. All servicemembers and unit leaders need to be trained on the policy and the expectations for their behavior.

The Department of Defense should also issue further guidance on legal standards. Even armed with all existing materials, there is still a clear need for more information on the meaning of the new standards. The credible information standard needs particular elaboration. Credible information should be defined to exclude reports of harassment or death threats; information obtained by the command through illegal means; use of private statements to parents, siblings, and psychologists; or inadvertent disclosures, such as when a supervisor discovers a letter after snooping through the personal possessions of a unit member.

Provide Common Sense Remedies for Command Violations

"Don't Ask, Don't Tell, Don't Pursue" means nothing if servicemembers must pay the price for improper questions, witch-hunts, and harassment. Enforcement of military regulations and act of law is not discretionary. Thus, homosexual servicemembers who are discovered through improper methods should be afforded a common sense remedy, like other victims of command impropriety. Decisionmakers, for example, are not permitted to disregard claims by women that they have been retaliated against for reporting sexual harassment and rape. Where claims are substantiated, they must take steps to correct the retaliation.

The Department of Defense should establish measures to ensure command compliance with the new regulations. Advisors to the command, including military prosecutors and Inspectors General, must understand their role to ensure that credible information exists at the outset of an inquiry or investigation, not merely to justify poor, let alone illegal, actions by the command. Where an inquiry is appropriate, military lawyers need actively to advise inquiry officers, who typically have no legal training or experience with the regulations, on the parameters of the inquiry.

The Department of Defense should also order Staff Judge Advocates (SJAs) to monitor violations by investigative agents. SJAs should make clear to base Military Criminal Investigative Organizations that investigative violations will not be tolerated and ensure that agents are trained in proper and improper investigative tactics.

The Department of Defense should also issue strong, clear guidance regarding harassment and threats. The one sentence in the Don't Ask, Don't Tell, Don't Pursue regulations forbidding harassment has proven inadequate.

A top-down policy of zero tolerance is required instead. As a minimum, servicemembers must be able to report death threats and harassment and their underlying basis without fear that the report will be turned against them for purposes of investigation and discharge. Based on SLDN's experience, many complaints are likely to require disclosure of a servicemember's sexual orientation or details of their private lives. For this reason, and because even legitimate questions regarding a servicemember's safety can result in "incriminating" answers, complainants should be exempted from discharge and investigation and should be afforded counsel. It is reasonably foreseeable that if the Department of Defense does not take corrective actions now, deaths of actual and perceived homosexual servicemembers, like slain sailor Allen Schindler, will occur.

The Department of Defense should prevent the use of security clearance interviews as a loophole for targeting suspected homosexuals. DOD should take strong steps to ensure compliance by Defense Investigative Service (DIS) agents with DIS regulations and the intent of the DOD directives. The present situation putting servicemembers' careers and liberty in jeopardy for truthful responses regarding their sexual orientation is untenable. Already, without such attention, the security clearance process has become a back channel to obtain information for commands and pursue suspected homosexuals.

Provide Adequate Review and Accountability
Those who are willfully disobeying the letter and intent of the new policy on homosexuals will continue to do so unless they are held accountable for their insubordination. Those violating the new regulations out of ignorance will also continue to do so as long as there is not incentive to learn and abide by the policy.

The Department of Defense needs to amplify disincentives to prevent violations of the policy. Currently, guidance is needed regarding procedures to initiate discipline against commanders and others who violate the policy, as provided for in the DOD directives. To date, no commander has been disciplined for violating provisions in Don't Ask, Don't Tell, Don't Pursue despite many complaints. Further, information obtained as the result of violations should be excluded and inquiries/investigations found to have been initiated without credible information should bar prosecution and discharge. Security clearance regulations should bar transfer of information to the military command. Annotations in servicemembers' files based on information obtained as the result of improper command actions should be prohibited.

These three broad recommendations—information and training, common sense remedies, and accountability—are only a handful of recommendations specifically targeted to the violations detailed in this report. The recommendations are intended to bring commanders and other military officials into compliance with military regulations and law. The recommendations are intended to ensure that "Don't Ask" means don't ask; "Don't Tell" does not mean interrogate family, doctors, and psychologists; "Don't Pursue" means don't pursue; and "Don't Harass" means don't harass.

SLDN will continue to monitor the Department of Defense's implementation of its newest policy on homosexuals and report on its progress in complying with the policy's provisions.

NOTES

1. These figures indicate the Service with the most cases involving particular violations. The figures do not reflect, as a percentage of total active force in each Service, which Service had the highest rate of cases with violations of Don't Ask, Don't Tell, Don't Pursue, Don't Harass.
2. Multiple violations per case make total violations exceed total cases. Thus, findings that state total number of SLDN cases involving violations present the most conservative picture of violations servicewide.
3. Costs are based on figures and percentages reported in a General Accounting Office study, *Defense Force Management: Statistics Related to DOD's Policy on Homosexuality* (June 1992). The GAO reported that the Department of Defense discharged 16,919 servicemembers for homosexuality from 1980-1990 at a cost of $498,555,244. The cost figures for 1991-1994 are based on the ratio of discharges in year X divided by the costs in year X set equal to the ratio of discharges in years 1980-1990 divided by the costs in years 1980-1990. The cost figures have not been adjusted for inflation.
4. Art Pine, "Few Benefit From New Military Policy on Gays," *Los Angeles Times* (February 6, 1995): A1, A8.
5. Ibid.
6. In announcing the new policy, President Clinton charged DOD civilian and military leaders to "carry out this policy with fairness, with balance, and with due regard for the privacy of individuals." See "Text of President Clinton's Announcement of the New Policy," *Washington Post* (July 20, 1993): A12. The new regulations also state that "sexual orientation is a personal and private matter."
7. Federal News Service, Testimony Before Senate Armed Services Committee, July 21, 1993.

CHAPTER 10

Constructing the *'Other'* Soldier:

Gay Identity's Military Threat

Gary L. Lehring

This is not a military dictatorship. It is not the former Soviet Socialist Republic. Here, the rule of law applies to the military.
   Federal District Court Judge Terry Hatter[1]

Military Justice is to Justice, what Military Music is to Music.
   Georges Clemenceau

The federal policy governing participation in the Armed Forces is an important area within which to research the treatment of minority groups in the United States. For what is public policy if not a snapshot of the values, beliefs, and preferences of a culture at a given point in history? Today one would hardly advocate the segregation of African Americans or the forced sterilization of the poor and mentally handicapped, although both have been official government policy at specific times in this country's history, and both were widely accepted and supported among the general population.[2] While not to suggest that all public policy decisions are doomed to be judged as unenlightened mistakes by the generations that follow, it is clear that federal policy texts are interesting "material" for theoretical investigation as the privileges, convictions, predispositions, and prejudices of a culture are all too present in the "rational" outcomes of the policy process. Rather than reprehend these values and beliefs as "soft" as many policy analysts do, I believe these decisions, *because* of their softness, reveal much about the political climate and the culture that produce them. Policy decisions do not function unidirectionally; in other words, they do not flow simply from the institutions of government to the people. Indeed, much of what government representatives do is carefully crafted to meet with the approval of the people, to embody their desires and opinions. In this sense the policymaking process is interactive, permeable, and subject to change; not at all the reasoned and studied decisionmaking process some policy analysts describe. Reflecting as well as initiating beliefs and values, the decisions of public policy help shape the values of a culture and are in turn shaped by them, creating *official* meanings and accepted understanding, while granting legitimacy and recognition.

Never was this more true than with the decisions that govern membership in the United States military. Military policy is historically significant to the gay and lesbian political history because the massive military mobilization of young men in World Wars I and II helped to constitute and expand an urban gay community. More importantly, it is in military policy that homosexuals first appear as concerns to the federal government, which subsequently developed official policies to describe who and what "homosexuals" are. Imported wholesale from the evolving medical experts of the early twentieth century, these definitions and descriptions became the basis for decades of official prejudice and discrimination against lesbians and gay men in all walks of life. This official construction of the homosexual also configured the terms of debate for a nascent lesbian and gay political movement. In the pages of medical guidelines advising draft board physicians how to identify homosexuals, and in the military court proceedings of those soldiers who contested their military discharges, there exists more than a historical record of discrimination against lesbians and gays. These texts contain the birth and delineation of a new political group, a new official state identity, as well as the rationales and legitimating strategies used to justify legally constituted prejudice and state sponsored discrimination.

In modern representations of lesbians and gays, elements of three different epistemological systems of representation can be seen functioning, overtly or covertly, within public policy texts. These three systems are: the Judaeo-Christian prohibitions of sodomy as an act contrary to "nature"; the late nineteenth-century medical "discovery" of "homosexuality" (a term invented by the same medical establishment that would prescribe its treatment and cure); and the psychiatric, psychological, and developmental models of homosexuality that emerged in the twentieth century. These epistemologies—these ways of understanding sex—were produced by the practitioners of institutions that came to have a great amount of authority in the society within which they operated, combining practitioners, institutions, and epistemology in a common effort: the production of "truth." Although the medieval theologian, the nineteenth-century medical doctor, and the twentieth-century psychiatrist each differ from one another, they come together in the position they share in relationship to the state. The role of "expert" or "authority" is a powerful one, often carrying with it a great capacity to influence state policymakers, be they king, legislature, or judge. Historically, each of these epistemological systems had some authoritative claim to the possession of a truth about sexuality and sexual difference that they were more than willing to share with the rest of society. These practitioners, these mouthpieces of various epistemologies, sought (and often were granted) the opportunity to "speak 'Truth' to power," with the consequence that their opinions (their "truths") spilled over into the public policies of the modern state.

It is important to keep in mind that the intersection among epistemology, the institutions of its production, and the state shifts over time. But as each shift occurs, the new discourse of authority, the new epistemology, never succeeds completely in replacing earlier ones. In fact, even as new epistemologies, social institutions, and discourses replace older ones as *the interpreter of "truth"* and *the* language of authority, older explanations are never completely abandoned. Sifted and repackaged within the framework of the controlling paradigm or epistemological system, their influence continues. As Jeffrey Weeks has noted, "[a]ll the major elements of the medieval taboos are present in the modern hostility toward homosexuality, but the contents of the kaleidoscope have been shaken and the pattern is different."[3]

For example, for many centuries it was the Catholic Church that controlled the production and dissemination of knowledge and truth about the purpose and intention of sexual acts. Procreation was the aim and goal of all sexual acts in this epistemological system. In the nineteenth and twentieth centuries medical science supplanted the religion's monopoly on the truth about sexual acts, yet the moral authority of the Church's pronouncements never completely ceased. Although procreation is never explicitly posited as a standard on "normal sexuality" in the nineteenth-century medical epistemology, nonproductivity does infiltrate the Darwinian, evolutionary understanding of homosexuality, shaking the kaleidoscopic pattern of the cultural representation of sexual difference while maintaining all its former elements.

The issue of homosexuality and military service provides a perfect opportunity to examine how widely disseminated these constructions of homosexuality have become. Often expressed by military personnel and elected public servants, these epistemologies of sex have exploded in the official public discourse of the United States. These diverse tenets often overlap and contradict one another, but they come together in their efforts to construct the homosexual as one "unfit for military service." The reasons generated are almost always unrelated to job performance, or any objectively verifiable standards of military readiness or effectiveness. By the military's own evaluative standards, lesbian and gay personnel have excelled. But the fear of homosexuals runs deep, and despite overwhelming evidence that they make excellent service personnel, hostility toward and discrimination against lesbians and gay men continues to be tolerated by many in the United States.

Still, it is not the separation of homosexuals from the armed forces that is the most revealing aspect of these policy decisions, nor is it the perceived or actual consequences of this separation for the individuals involved. Rather, it is the ways in which these decisions—employing the authority and legitimacy of the United States Government—politically construct the homosexual, all homosexuals, in a manner that makes their exclusion appear rational.

In this chapter, I will examine how the three different models of "homosexuality" discussed above found their way into the military policy texts of the United States, where they are employed by the military to make policies appear rational and necessary. I will conclude with observations about how the military's policies excluding lesbians and gay men—as well as the gay community's efforts to overturn the ban—are locked in the same ontological debate about who and what gay people are. I will begin with a brief introduction to the military's ban against lesbians and gay men.

GAY PERFORMANCE IN THE MILITARY

The provision of a common defense is one of the general principles enumerated in the preamble to the United States Constitution that explains the very reason why a government is necessary and desired. Also, defense of country traditionally has been considered a defining characteristic of citizenship. In fact, it has been suggested that the legal disabilities women incurred in classical Greece with regard to property rights, rights within marriage, and rights of inheritance occurred because they were prohibited from bearing arms.[4] The prohibition of certain groups from military service adversely affects those excluded in other areas where rights and privileges of citizenship are involved. For example, undesirable discharges from the military have been used historically to hinder service personnel's future attempts to find employment.[5] As the largest single employer in the United States, the military is both substantively and symbolically important. But federal civil rights laws do not prohibit discrimination based on sexual orientation, and the courts have upheld the military's right to exclude lesbians and gays. Although aversion to homosexuals is present in all facets of society, in no other part is the hostility toward them as absolute or as codified as it is in the armed forces.

When one thinks of the gays in the military issue, most people think of Bill Clinton's failed attempt to allow lesbians and gay men to serve openly in the military that came shortly after he took office in 1993. In reality, the military has excluded homosexuals for over seventy years, and the justifications for this exclusion have evolved over time. Still, one of the most interesting elements of the recent manifestation of this debate has been the unswerving insistence of the military that homosexuality is incompatible with military service, despite overwhelming evidence and arguments to the contrary. Often this evidence comes from within the military establishment itself.

In 1957, the *Report of the Board Appointed to Prepare and Submit Recommendations to the Secretary of the Navy for the Revision of Policies, Procedures and Directives Dealing with Homosexuality* addressed one of the principal justifications for the ban against lesbians and gays: their sexuality makes them more susceptible to blackmail by enemy agents and spies, who might threaten to reveal their sexuality. Called the Crittenden Report (after its chair Captain S. H. Crittenden Jr. U.S.N.), the findings were a surprise to the Navy. The report concluded that:

> The concept that homosexuals pose a security risk is unsupported by any factual data. Homosexuals are no more a security risk, and in many cases are much less of a security risk, than alcoholics and those people with marked feelings of inferiority who must brag of their knowledge of secret information and disclose it to gain stature. Promiscuous heterosexual activity also provides serious security implications. Some intelligence officers consider a senior officer having illicit heterosexual activity with the wife of a junior officer or enlisted man is much more of a security risk than the ordinary homosexual . . . The number of cases of blackmail as a result of past investigations of homosexuals is

negligible. No factual data exist to support the contention that homosexuals are a greater risk than heterosexuals.[6]

Not finding the conclusions of this study to their liking, the Navy subsequently suppressed the study for twenty years until a court order forced its release.[7] Twenty-four years after this report was first submitted, and with no new evidence to contradict its findings, the 1982 Defense Department Directive concerning homosexuals still included the phrase "to prevent breaches of security" among its summary of reasons why "homosexuality is incompatible with military service."[8] By the end of his tenure as the Secretary of Defense, even Dick Cheney would admit that this particular justification for the ban was "a bit of an old chestnut."[9] In fact, in November 1992, Cheney told then President-elect Clinton that the Department of Defense's policy excluding homosexuals was "just a quaint little rule, but we're not going to change it."[10]

In 1988, a second study conceived, financed, and overseen by the Department of Defense reached a similar finding. This study, conducted by the Defense Personnel Security Research and Education Center (PERSEREC), found that homosexuality "was unrelated to job performance in the same way as is being left- or right-handed."[11] Like the Crittenden Report before it, the PERSEREC report was suppressed by the Pentagon. This report was not made public until Congressional Representatives Gerry Studds of Massachusetts and Patricia Schroeder of Colorado received copies of the report anonymously, and then released it to the press in October 1989. Included with this report were the memos from the Pentagon chastising the researchers at PERSEREC for their findings. The memos directed PERSEREC to fundamentally rewrite the report to remove all claims that homosexuals are suitable for military service.[12] A second PERSEREC report, released by Studds and Schroeder at the same time, went even further than the first, suggesting that "homosexuals also showed better preservice adjustment than heterosexuals" as well as "greater levels of cognitive ability than heterosexuals."[13]

A fourth report, a $1.3 million study conducted by the RAND Corporation, also concluded that the ban could be lifted without adversely affecting the "order, discipline and individual behavior necessary to maintain cohesion and performance."[14] Commissioned by the Pentagon, the RAND Corporation study was completed in the Spring of 1993 but again was withheld by the Pentagon until Democratic Senators threatened to hold up the following year's defense appropriations bill if the study was not made public. The report was released in August, but the timing of the release seemed carefully calculated to ensure the least amount of publicity. As one National Gay and Lesbian Task Force spokesperson claimed, August is the month when "no one in government is around."[15] Also, by August, the highly sensationalistic Senate Armed Forces Committee hearings on the issue of allowing lesbians and gay men to serve openly in the military had wound down, having culminated in a Committee tour through the cramped quarters of a U.S. Navy warship.

Each of these four reports cast doubt on the Pentagon's assertion that homosexuality is incompatible with military service. In fact, one report claimed that homosexuals made *better* soldiers than heterosexuals.[16] This opinion was echoed, albeit ironically, by Vice Admiral Joseph S. Donnel, Commander of the Navy's surface Atlantic fleet. In a 1990 memorandum to the officers in charge of nearly 200 ships and 40 shore installations in the eastern half of the United States, Donnel characterized lesbians as generally "hardworking, career-oriented, willing to put in long hours on the job, and among the command's top performers."[17] Contrary to the way it sounds, Donnel's description was not intended to be an endorsement of lesbians serving in the Navy. Rather, it was a description formulated to help senior officers identify the lesbians among their crew so they could be investigated and discharged from the service.

In 1992, a General Accounting Office report could find no rational basis for the military's ban. This report concluded that "no reasons to support this policy exist, including public opinion and scientific evaluations of homosexuality. If a more tolerant attitude were enforced it would lead to better functioning of all."[18] The ban was also attacked as a costly and inefficient policy by the GAO report. Relying upon information provided by the Department of Defense, the report said that 16,919 service men and women had been discharged for homosexuality between the years 1980 and 1990. Adjusting for inflation, the cost of recruiting and training replacements for those discharged was placed at $498 million.

Documenting an amazing waste of highly trained personnel and money, the GAO report tells only half the story. The Defense Department acknowledged to GAO researchers that the figures used for numbers of discharges for homosexuality did not include lesbians and gays separated under other categories of misconduct. Department of Defense officials also admitted that coterminous with the adoption of the 1982 gay ban, local military commanders were given greater flexibility in discharging personnel under other categories. The likely practical effect of this is that many more lesbian and gay service people were discharged because of their sexual orientation, but were persuaded by commanders to accept discharges under regulations unrelated to sexual orientation as a way to avoid being "outed" by the military.

The GAO's financial estimates are incomplete as well. The report notes that the GAO was "not able to calculate the original investment cost of training and compensation, the cost of investigating alleged or actual homosexual cases, or the cost of out-processing servicemen and women who have been identified as homosexual."[19] When these expenses are added in, the cost increases perceptibly. One estimate puts the cost of the Pentagon policy at three to four times the number suggested by the GAO report.[20] Expenses in military readiness and financial costs aside, if the objective of the Department of Defense policy was to make sure that there are no homosexuals in the military, it is an objective that has failed.

In the face of such overwhelming evidence that no legitimate interest or rational explanation exists for its exclusionary policy, the military has relied on stereotypic judgments of homosexuals and homosexuality that are rooted deeply in American culture. In the section that follows, I will detail these contrary constructions of lesbians and gay men that appear in the military court records and public policy texts governing the treatment of homosexuals. The acceptance and promotion of age-old stereotypes and homophobia by the official instruments of the state have a legitimizing effect, codifying prejudice and thereby making legal reform for lesbians and gays more difficult than ever.

CONSTRUCTING THE "OTHER" SOLDIERS' SEXUALITY

The public record of lesbians and gays in the military suggests that homosexuality comes to define an accused individual absolutely; it is the "damned spot" of Lady Macbeth that no amount of rubbing will remove, and all previous assessments of an individual are jettisoned and new ones formed that comport fully with this new-found flaw. All parts of a person's life are affected, and the term "homosexual" becomes synonymous with "lecherous deviant," "emotional immaturity," "liar," and "criminal," as the military and military's courts race to find reasons why even lesbians and gays with exemplary service records should be discharged from the service. In one such case, a military court upheld the discharge of a soldier who was "morally unreproachable except for his sexual perversion."[21] The understatedness of this remark is almost humorous, as homosexual "perversion" has never been a small exception in the eyes of the military, nor in the eyes of society.

As early as 1919, homosexuals were becoming defined as a greater problem by the military. As Acting Secretary of the U.S. Navy, Franklin D. Roosevelt approved the establishment of a military vice squad that was to investigate homosexual activities. In 1921 it was revealed that many of the investigators (none of which had any professional investigative training), as a matter of standard operating procedure, had engaged in sodomy in order to entrap suspected homosexuals. Roosevelt's Republican opponents quickly moved to use this information against him, and a scandal ensued.

Investigated by a Subcommittee of the Senate Naval Affairs Committee, the two minority members of that committee released their report to *The New York Times* on July 20, 1921. Using enlisted men for such activities, the report claimed, violated "the rights of every American boy who enlisted in the Navy to fight for his country." Indeed, the report claimed that the activities in which these "boy investigators" were engaged was "conduct of such a character at which seasoned veterans . . . would have shuddered." The report also asserted that these activities were "practically thrust upon boys, who, because of their patriotism had responded to the call."[22] The report does not explain that each of the "boy investigators" was given the opportunity to decline the assignment, and that none were forced to engage in sodomy, but often did so on their own initiative.[23]

The report represents one of the earliest and most persistent constructions of the gay man, portraying him as a person of bad character, a person with a defective personality, a sexual pervert. *The New York Times* attributed the "difficulty at Newport" to "a few men of bad character among the many thousands concentrated there under the emergency of war."[24] The Committee report entitled "Alleged Immoral Conditions at Newport" declared that

> to send out into Newport young men, some of them mere boys, to use their own discretion and judgment [as to] whether they should or should not actually permit to be performed upon them immoral acts, is in the opinion of the committee utterly shocking to the American standard of morality and that any civilian or naval officer in charge of young men and boys to be trained for service in the United States Navy should permit such a thing is absolutely indefensible and to be most severely condemned.[25]

In the morality play constructed for the benefit of the "utterly shocked" but titillated Americans, "patriotic boys" became the innocent victims, the defenseless prey of perverted, corrupt men of bad character. These corrupted men lacked the moral decency to resist the temptation of the "boy bounty" presented by the close conditions afforded by military life, and turned this proximity into sexual advantage. The use of the opposition of "innocent boys" versus "corrupt men" is intriguing given that there was little difference in age between the "boy investigators" and the "men of bad character." In fact, often the investigators were older than the "perverted old men" of 19, 20, and 21 that they were entrapping. However, the distinction between boys and men serves well the morality play in which it is used, summoning images of the child molester—the immoralist who cannot, or will not, make the distinctions that polite society requires. Described as a sexual pervert, the homosexual was constructed in opposition to the patriotic, innocent young boys who have left hearth and home to defend their country. In another example of this construction, a military judge allowed the characterization of a suspected homosexual as a "chickenhawk," claiming that "these [comments] were not beyond the bounds of fair comment."[26]

In a third example, the court lectured a victim of a sexual attack for not coming forth sooner. The man testified that "from what I have heard about these homosexual cases I was scared." The victim, a career man in the Air Force, should have come forth, according to the court, based upon his feelings of "outrage and revulsion against the infamous crime against nature, involving as it does a degradation of the virile organ of manhood."[27] Anything short of outrage and revulsion throws suspicion on the victim himself.

Serving as a synonym for "character flaw" or "personality defect," homosexuals are also constructed as individuals who cannot be trusted. The 1982 Defense Department Directive 1332.4 claimed that the presence of homosexuals adversely affected the armed forces' ability to "foster mutual trust and confidence among the members."[28] Many examples exist of doubts concerning the veracity of service personnel once they have been labeled a homosexual. Even in the unfortunate case where a person is a victim of rape or forced sodomy, "evidence of victim's homosexual activity [is] relevant ... to the issue of consent and the victim's credibility."[29] In *Rich v. Secretary of the Army*, Mr. Rich's homosexuality again casts doubt on his veracity. The court rejected his explanation that as he was not gay when he entered the Army; he had therefore not lied on his enlistment questionnaire when answering "no" to the question that asked if he was a homosexual. The use of such a question on an enlistment form is problematic, as many young men and women enter the military before acknowledging or exploring the possibility they may be lesbian or gay. Despite the progress made toward lesbian and gay equality in the last thirty years, the compulsory nature of heterosexuality is so powerful that many men and women reach young adulthood before exploring any possibility other than suburban heterosexuality. This question was removed from the enlistment form in 1993 as part of the Clinton administration's "Don't Ask, Don't Tell" compromise that was written into law.

Prior to this change in policy, James Holobaugh, an Army ROTC man chosen to be a poster boy for recruitment advertisements, was asked to repay his ROTC scholarship after admitting he had discovered he was gay. The Army does not usually seek to recover scholarship money from cadets discharged for homosexuality, unless there is evidence of deceit.[30] Holobaugh's alleged deceit involved his claim that when he entered college in 1984 he was dating women and had no idea he was gay. By 1990 he was sure he was gay, and the Army attempted to bring suit against him. When lawyers for Holobaugh insisted that he would be willing to fulfill his contractual obligation and serve in the Army, the Army dropped the lawsuit against him. In 1992 the Navy ROTC sought to avoid similar dilemmas by instituting a policy under which all recruits would be asked to sign an agreement requiring repayment of scholarships if a midshipman was found to be gay. When many colleges and universities threatened to ban their ROTC programs, the Navy dropped their plans to change the policy.[31]

Any hint of homosexual desire is enough to constitute a threat to the military, and it matters little how long ago one might have felt such desire. In *U.S. v. Kindler*, Airman Kindler was discharged although he vehemently denied the charges of homosexuality made against him, and claimed he was as "normal as anyone." In upholding the Air Force's discharge for homosexuality, the court relied on "acts of sodomy committed between [the] accused and his twin brother at the ages of twelve, thirteen, and fourteen," to establish that he was, and had always been, a homosexual and was therefore subject to discharge.[32] Fannie Mae Clackum ultimately fared better in the outcome of her 1960 case against the United States. She was reinstated for duty, but the circumstances recorded in the court's decision again reveal that despite her denial of lesbianism, and with absolutely no evidence, the Air Force discharged her, totally dismissing the possibility that she could be telling the truth.[33]

Suspicion of homosexual activity by a member of the military has become an automatic reason to question the veracity of the person accused. As each of these examples demonstrates, in the military a homosexual cannot be believed about his past or trusted in the future, and any acts, no matter how distant in the past they may be, remain evidence of one's homosexuality. From the military's point of view, the trusted associate—no matter what her past performance reviews and contributions to the military—must be completely reevaluated in light of this newly uncovered character flaw. In this reevaluation, "it may often take corroboration—or strong evidence of good character—to overcome the repelling nature of the testimony" for the "heinous" and "revolting" crime.[34]

Indeed, it is more than just one's truthfulness that is in question when accusations of homosexuality are made. In *U.S. v. Marcey* the court writes, "certainly a person who practices homosexuality is likely to assault for the purpose of satisfying his perverted sexual cravings."[35] The court believes that all homosexuals are potentially guilty of assault:

> The accused asserts that his motivations were toward consensual homosexuality which would have no probative value with regard to offenses involving violent acts. That is a specious argument when consideration is given to the homosexual who misjudges his prospective partner. If it turns out that his perverted advances are unwanted and the hoped for consent is lacking, the prospect has been victimized by an assault with sodomitical intent.[36]

Following this logic, a man who asks a woman out who does not desire to go out with him is guilty of assault with intent to rape. But as many servicewomen will attest, servicemen are allowed to go a good deal further without consequence in their consensually motivated overtures directed toward women.

Not only behavioral characteristics would be added to the list of corroborating characteristics that could lead to the identification of homosexuals, but physical, psychological, and biological difference as well. Physicians and scientists believed that gays could be detected in preinductive screening exams due to a host of physical and biological irregularities. Everything from low levels of testicular radioactivity,[37] "sloping shoulders, broad hips, excessive pectoral and pubic adipose tissue"[38] and "feminine bodily characteristics," or "effeminacy in manner"[39] were believed to be constitutional deformities that would give the homosexual away to the trained observer. Other guidelines suggested physicians at pre-induction screenings look for "patulous [expanded] rectums" and effeminacy in dress among potential soldiers, and when found, have these soldiers sent for a psychiatric evaluation.[40] Psychiatrists too would try to make the task of discovering homosexuals easier through state-of-the-art "scientific" personality tests that would serve as short cuts to those physicians working in military induction centers. One such shortcut was the 1943 Cornell Selectee Index. It would identify homosexuals by their reported interest in certain "occupational choices." Men who checked off interest in occupations such as interior decorator, dancer, or window dresser were excluded, as they were believed to have problems with "acceptance of the male pattern."[41]

Given the medical community's overwhelming role in the invention, definition, and regulation of homosexuality in the late nineteenth and early twentieth centuries, it is not surprising that they would also play a role in the military's attempts to describe/inscribe the homosexual. After all, it was in the intersection between the medical bureaucracy and military policy—the link between "truth" and power, "expert" and administrator—that the homosexual becomes a public concern, and therefore a state concern. Armed with the medical community's expert assessments of homosexuality's debilitating and degenerative effects, those interested in the maintenance of an effective military force would recognize the "danger" of having gays in the military, and the utility of a scientifically sound means of detecting them for separation. But often these objective scientists' research was informed by the very stereotypes that military courts have used to construct the military's understanding of the homosexual.

BEHAVIOR OR IDENTITY: ESSENTIALISM AND THE MILITARY'S "IDENTIFICATION" OF HOMOSEXUALS

One of the most interesting manifestations revealed in the representations of lesbians and gays in public policy texts and debates about military service has been how little agreement exists over what homosexuals and homosexuality *are*. In public policy debates, those claiming that homosexuality is innate—a product of genetics, biology, or some other deep and immutable property—have been pitted against those who emphasize that homosexuality is an activity—a verb, rather than a noun. The former group includes most members of the gay community, and this understanding of identity is generally seen as the strategy most likely to end discrimination directed at lesbians and gay men. It is one of the first questions courts ask in equal protection law cases to determine whether a group constitutes a "suspect" or "quasi-suspect" class requiring the government to make a more compelling case that their policy is rational and legitimate.[42]

But essentialists have not been found only among supporters of lesbian and gay equality. Retired Colonel David Hackworth described homosexuality as a "biological impulse." Because the sexual impulse itself "is the strongest thing going among 20-year-olds," Hackworth concluded that lesbians and gays should be excluded from the military.[43] Massachusetts Senator Edward Kennedy, explaining why he believed the military's ban against homosexuals should be overturned, said "It's time for the Armed Forces to stop discriminating against anyone because of who they are. . . ."[44]

For example, General Colin Powell's response to the suggested similarity in treatment of gays and lesbians today and the segregation of African Americans in the armed forces in earlier decades was one of dismissal, claiming that skin color was a "benign nonbehavioral characteristic, while sexual orientation is perhaps the most profound of human behavioral characteristics."[45]

The court in *Rich v. Secretary of the Army* reached a similar conclusion when it disagreed with the claim that homosexuality was a "fundamental matter at the core of one's personality, self image, and sexual identity." The court decided instead that there was no difference between acts of sodomy and a person's homosexual orientation: "a statement that a person is homosexual or gay . . . refers not to physical characteristics, but . . . to conduct."[46]

The confusion is present too in the current policy of Don't Ask, Don't Tell, under which members of the service can be expelled for simple declarations of sexual identity even if no homosexual acts have been proven. Although many people accept that *homosexual* is now a noun signifying a type of person, an interesting evolution can be witnessed within the military texts and policy debates. As sexual acts of sodomy and the medical condition of homosexuality were transformed into the noun *homosexual*, this transformation did not rescue the homosexual from state regulation and public abomination as those who led the way in this transformation had hoped. Rather, *homosexual* came to describe one who *chose* to engage in those sexual acts that our culture had anathematized. Described as vice, constitutional degeneration, and mental imbalance, descriptions of homosexual acts and behaviors have been inscribed onto the body and soul, the very personhood of the homosexual, transforming acts and behaviors into identities and orientation. *Orientation* has become a short-cut way of excluding those who might engage in behavior of which our culture does not generally approve. Rather than liberating the homosexual from these anathematized behaviors, in the next torturous turn of the epistemological screw, orientation *reduces individuals to their anathematized sexual acts*, producing a litany of devices that can help "detect" those who might have this problematized orientation. From the examination of one's levels of testicular radioactivity to the search for "patulous rectums" and "effeminacy in manner and dress" in the military's directions for preinductive screening exams, from "inappropriate" interest in occupations such as "dancer" and "interior decorator" listed in the Cornell Selectee Index, homosexuals have been made more detectable, making more rigorous scrutiny and greater conformity to gender stereotypes the general rule.[47]

For example, the intent of the 1982 Department of Defense directive that claimed "homosexuality is incompatible with military service" was to create a category of exclusion based upon homosexual *identity*, not merely homosexual *acts*. Section C of the Department of Defense Directive 1332.14 states that:

C. The basis for separation may include preservice, prior to service or current service conduct or statements. A member shall be separated under this section if one or more of the following approved findings is made:

(1) The member has engaged in, attempted to engage in, or solicited another to engage in a homosexual act or acts unless there are approved further findings that:

(a) Such conduct is a departure from the member's usual and customary behavior;

(b) Such conduct under all circumstances is unlikely to recur;

(c) Such conduct was not accompanied by use of force, coercion or intimidation by the member during a period of military service;

(d) Under the particular circumstances of the case, the member's continued presence in the service is consistent with the interest of the service in proper discipline, good order and morale; and

(e) The member does not desire to engage in or intend to engage in homosexual acts.[48]

While heterosexual servicemembers could engage in homosexual sodomy and be retained for service as long as they have no future *desire* to do so, it is the persistence of homosexual desire that constitutes the real threat to military morale, discipline, and good order, as all homosexuals are *potential* sodomites—potential criminal violators of moral and civil strictures as well as of military law. Apparently heterosexual sodomy contains no similar potential threat, despite the fact that Article 125 of the Uniform Code of Military Justice (UCMJ) proscribes that *all* acts of sodomy, not simply homosexual acts of sodomy, constitute grounds for removal from the military.

Seen in this light, the 1982 Department of Defense Directive 1332.14 that declared that "homosexuality is incompatible with military service" is less a radical departure in which the military cracked down on homosexuals than it is a formal codification of existing practices. It makes explicit what has always been implicit in the gap between the strict reading of Article 125 (makes no mention of homosexuals or homosexual identity) and the interservice regulations issued by each branch of the armed services that do: all homosexuals are sodomites, and by definition guilty of a criminal violation of Article 125. In the military today, suspicion of *being* homosexual remains enough to begin an investigation into a servicemember's background, and *declarations of identity*—not sexual activities—are grounds for removal from service.

DON'T KISS AND TELL IN THE MILITARY

Clinton's compromise with the military, the now infamous "Don't Ask, Don't Tell, Don't Pursue" policy, did little to revise the 1982 Department of Defense Directive. The only real change in policy was the removal from enlistment and reenlistment forms questions that directly ask whether one was homosexual. The investigations into servicemembers' private lives continue today whenever there is a doubt about a servicemember's sexuality. While Don't Ask, Don't Tell may appear to be progress—the best a president could do under such tremendous political resistance—in reality the policy changed very little. Lesbians and gay men have always been allowed to serve as long as they were closeted. The policy did nothing to reduce the hundreds and hundreds of military and civilian investigators in the military's employ who conduct investigations into any allegations of a servicemember's homosexuality. It also did nothing to curtail the routine military police visits to lesbian and gay bars near military bases. In fact, recent reports suggest that nothing at all has changed, and that lesbians and gays are still being discharged at the same rate as before. By June of 1994, there were already 130 cases of lesbians and gay men being discharged from the military, despite their apparent compliance with the new guidelines set forth in Don't Ask, Don't Tell. In the previous year, the year the new policy took affect, there were 797 servicemembers discharged, compared with 708 in the previous year. Dixon Osburn, spokesperson for the Servicemembers Legal Defense Network in Washington, D.C., reports that "military commanders are finding it very easy to get around the new policy."[49] Indeed, if anything, the witch-hunts and persecutions against lesbians and gays have intensified, as investigators want to ensure that they have all of the necessary evidence to prove that a member of the service has committed homosexual acts before proceeding to remove him or her.[50] With all the machinery of the previous policy in place and still functioning, it is extremely likely that once Clinton is no longer President, Don't Ask, Don't Tell will be quickly reversed, ending even the symbolism of the President's actions.

The events surrounding Clinton's attempt to lift the military ban provided political drama for weeks. Pressure groups both pro and con organized White House and Congressional telephone and letter writing campaigns. Even the Joint Chiefs of Staff, in efforts that bordered on insubordination and the subversion of civilian authority over the military, lobbied members of Congress behind the scenes and opened up their phone lines to invite public comment, entering the political process unabashedly.[51] The organized opposition came from conservative religious groups and others on the political right. The Reverend Louis Sheldon of the Traditional Values Coalition boasted that his group shut down the telephone lines at the Capitol with its many calls, and Oliver North made public pleas for money to stop the Clinton plan.[52]

Clinton had underestimated the depth of homophobia, which delighted conservative and evangelical Christian organizations, who claimed they could not have "scripted" a scenario more to their liking for Clinton's first weeks in office.[53] "It's a bonanza for building organizations and raising money; the fundraising letters are already in the mail," claimed one expert on the Christian right.[54] Emotions ran high on both sides of this debate. In an attempt to depict the Democratic party as the "party of queers," Haley Barbour, the new Republican Party Chairman, claimed that Clinton, in moving to lift the ban, acted "not because of principle but as a political payoff to a very powerful special interest group of the Democratic Party."[55]

It is obvious that allowing lesbians and gays in the military would not have been the issue most people in the gay community would have had at the top of their list of wishes to be granted by a new administration in Washington. Greater funding and awareness for AIDS, or a federal civil rights law for lesbians, gays, and other sexual minorities, were issues that could have potentially generated more excitement at the grassroots level of the lesbian and gay movement. While it is true that the National Gay and Lesbian Task Force has had a military project as part of its organization structure for years, it was not the decision of the gay community that this should be the issue on which Clinton gave something back for its support in the 1992 election. Indeed it was not even made by the leaders of the lesbian and gay political organizations, most of whom realized that support in the gay community for lifting the ban might be a mile wide, but an inch thin. Instead, the decision was determined "by gay people inside the Democratic Party and businessmen who came out only recently and positioned themselves as powerbrokers for a community they do not know and cannot represent. But, as 'Friends of Bill' they have access to the White House and an inordinate influence on policy."[56] These political insiders, called "homocrats" by lesbian activist Sarah Schulman, were like many others in the early days of the Clinton Administration: virtual political newcomers to Washington. In an interview following the publication of his book *Conduct Unbecoming*, journalist Randy Shilts recounted a conversation with some of these homocrats:

> I talked to people who were involved in the Clinton Campaign—and these are relatively sophisticated people—and I remember right after he got elected in November, I said, "Well, of course this is going to be a very big deal," and they said, "What he's going to do is to come in January and issue his five or six executive orders and slip this in the middle of the pile and nobody will notice." And I just thought, *My God, what planet are you people living on? It's such an archetypal conflict, of course it's going to be a huge deal!*[57]

Although they did not control the political agenda, the lesbian and gay political organizations also share the responsibility for the failure that became Don't Ask, Don't Tell. Their enthusiasm for candidate Clinton seemed undeserved given his lackluster support of lesbian and gay issues prior to coming to Washington, and that enthusiasm translated into greater trust and a greater benefit of the doubt than Clinton deserved. For example, Human Rights Campaign Fund Executive Director Tim McFeeley, in his November 1992 letter to HRCF's members, explained his organization's decision to support Bill Clinton for President. Marking the first time HRCF had ever endorsed a candidate for President, McFeeley wrote:

> Bill Clinton and Bill Clinton alone, has clearly and unequivocally articulated positive stands on the issues. . . . In the past several months, Bill Clinton has met with lesbian and gay groups and AIDS activists. He has incorporated our agenda and our goals into his own. . . .[58]

The letter continued to suggest that if elected Bill Clinton would be a President who would use "whatever means necessary" to eradicate AIDS, a President who would be an advocate for the National Lesbian and Gay Civil Rights Law, and a President who "with the stroke of a pen" would "end the exclusion of gays and lesbians from the U.S. military and [would] end discrimination in federal employment based on sexual orientation." Having naively built Clinton up as the President who would lead lesbians and gays to the promised land, McFeeley and other political leaders of the lesbian and gay community were swept along in a political drama for which they were ill prepared. Placing almost idealistic hope in Clinton, they were slow to warm to the task of countering the massive grassroots lobbying campaign initiated by those who supported the ban. As late as March 26, 1993, only days after Clinton suggested he would be willing to accept restrictions on the kind of duty lesbian and gay service persons could perform, Tom Stoddard, Director of the Campaign for Military Service (CMS), made excuses for the President's comments, still steadfastly clinging to his belief that Clinton would lift the ban. Stoddard said, "In the end, the motivation for and circumstances of Clinton's comments don't matter. What does matter is that the president reaffirmed his commitment."[59] Stoddard's organization was formed specifically to help overturn the ban, but as a fledgling organization, CMS was long on flash and short on grassroots expertise. The CMS helped transform the 1993 March on Washington into the "khaki siege" of D.C.; their posters, volunteers, and petitions could be found throughout the city during the weekend of the March on Washington. But the signatures of marchers did not translate into real political heat in the form of letters and calls to members of Congress. In May, Congressman Barney Frank, who had been lecturing the gay community for weeks that their activist efforts were falling short on Capitol Hill, infuriated the Washington gay rights organizations when he proposed his own compromise, which he called "Don't Ask, Don't Tell, Don't Investigate." Frank explained that "with less than two months to go before Congressional committees begin voting on this, I believe we have to face a stark fact: if the choice before the Congress is instant equality or a statute which enacts the complete ban into permanent law, Congress will choose the latter." Frank's proposal suggested that the military not ask people their sexual orientation, not investigate them for their sexual orientation, and pay no attention to things that happen when servicemen and women were off base, off duty, and out of uniform.[60]

Frank's compromise drew sharp criticism from the National Gay and Lesbian Task Force, the Human Rights Campaign Fund, and the Campaign for Military Service, as his announcement came without consultation with any of them. Stoddard was especially displeased, claiming that Frank's proposal undermined the CMS's fundraising and lobbying efforts: "[Frank] has created the impression on the part of gay people that we can't possibly get what we want on this issue anymore, and that leads to a sense of despair. The danger is that people will stop giving money and lobbying their members of Congress because they will think we can't possibly get any more out of Capitol Hill."[61]

Although Frank's methods left much to be desired—splitting the gay community away from the political organizations responsible for the bulk of the lobbying on this issue—his sentiments were probably correct. The national lesbian and gay organizations are incapable of creating the kind of constituent pressure required to counter their better organized opposition. A spokesperson for the Human Rights Campaign Fund admitted that while they are able to generate a maximum of 35,000 letters, Pat Robertson's Christian Coalition regularly generates over 100,000.[62]

Even if the Washington political organizations had been better organized and better prepared, and had they had a role in setting the agenda and been able to keep the squabbling among themselves to a minimum, they could have accomplished little more on this issue. After pledging his support, Clinton dropped out of sight, leaving the lesbian and gay community to lobby both Congress and the American people simultaneously, a task that proved too difficult for a still young and underfunded lesbian and gay political movement. Even a more powerful and sophisticated movement would face severe obstacles in attempting to bring change to the military industrial complex and its Congressional allies, as taken together they represent one of the most powerful iron triangles in the national government. Without the committed and active support of the President there was never much chance that lesbians and gay men alone could bring about this change.[63] Clinton's refusal to expend presidential energy on this issue aside, the truth of the matter is that although many in the lesbian and gay community would have fought hard and long had Clinton proposed the passage of a gay federal civil rights law, most lesbians and gay men did not think military inclusion was the best issue on which to expend valuable political and financial capital. Many in the community grumbled quietly when the March on Washington for Lesbian, Gay, and Bisexual Equality was transformed overnight into a demonstration over the military's ban against homosexuals. This was not the march many people had planned to attend, and it was certainly not the march that had been in the works for months before gays in the military was the national circus it would become.

More importantly, the gay political leadership, and especially the homocrats, had misunderstood the depth of the ambivalence of many in the community they purport to represent. Lesbians and gay men on the political left, many of whom had only recently protested against the Persian Gulf War, wanted no part of an effort that had at its heart support for military efforts they abhor. Barbara Smith articulated what many leftists felt:

Given the U.S. military's role as the world's police force, which implements imperialist foreign policies and murders those who stand in their way (e.g., the estimated quarter of a million people, mostly civilian, who died in Iraq as a result of the Gulf War), a progressive lesbian and gay [effort] would at least consider the political implications of frantically organizing to get into the mercenary wing of the military industrial complex. A radical lesbian and gay movement would of course be working to dismantle the military completely. . . .
Thankfully, there were some pockets of dissent at the April march, expressed in slogans like: "Lift the Ban—Ban the Military" and "Homosexual, not Homicidal—Fuck the Military." Yet it seemingly had not occurred to movement leaders that there are lesbians and gays who actively opposed the Gulf War, the Vietnam War, military intervention in Central American, and apartheid in South Africa.[64]

Many more moderates—gay and straight alike, who believe passionately in equality for lesbians and gay men—were uncomfortable with the idea that the military should be the organization that determines and defines notions of citizenship and equality. Hence, many in the lesbian and gay community were indifferent, although reluctantly so. With a divided gay community, and a critically detached progressive straight community on one side and a well-organized, well financed coalition of antigay conservatives, religious right organizations, and military careerists on the other, the battle was lost before it had even begun. But this battle is a microcosm of the difficulties faced by the lesbian and gay political movement today. Far too easily co-opted by political insiders, the movement's real goals of equality for all sexual minorities and ending homophobia and discrimination often take a back seat to the desires of political insiders who want the movement to be clean-cut, respectable, and moderate.

THE POLITICS OF GAY IDENTITY

Explaining why she was contesting her discharge from the military, Colonel Margarethe Cammermeyer had the following to say to a reporter from *The New York Times*:

> What I hope to represent is a part of the normality of being homosexual, of not being in leather or shaving my hair, but rather showing how much we are all alike. If people can see the sameness of me to you, then perhaps they won't have the walls that make it so that they have to hate us.[65]

As Colonel Cammermeyer's statement makes clear, embedded in the gays in the military debate, never far from the surface, were competing notions of who and what lesbian and gay men are. Questions of gay identity were as much a part of the debate as was anything else. Having their justifications for excluding homosexuals challenged and defeated one by one, the military succeeded in making one charge stick: homosexuals as a group will interfere with morale, discipline, and good order because of the hatred and bigotry manifested by straight soldiers who are forced to share intimate quarters and bathroom facilities with them. The tautological reasoning here is not to be missed, as the military has spent the better part of the last century officially constructing lesbians and gay men in ways that make others fear and loathe them. Now that these official constructions have been challenged and defeated, and there exist no tenable justifications for exclusion related to the performance of lesbians and gay servicemen themselves, the military now uses the vestiges of homophobia and bigotry among straights—homophobia the military itself has nurtured and fostered for many decades—as an explanation for keeping lesbians and gay men out of the service, or at least, in the closet.

But Colonel Cammermeyer's claim that lesbians and gay men are just like everyone else seems part plaintiff wish, part self-fulfilling prophecy. When the sexologists of the nineteenth century created the category of "homosexual person" it was done to alleviate the same bigotry and hatred that Cammermeyer seeks to overcome. The sexologists of the day believed that social tolerance would be achieved if it were demonstrated that sodomites did what they did not out of vice or sin, but because it was an expression of who they are. In short, bigotry would end because homosexuals could not help being born homosexuals. The result of course was not greater tolerance, but rather the birth of a new form of life—the homosexual, a category of being that quickly dichotomized into polarizing categories of identity: gay/straight, homosexual/heterosexual, deviant/normal. From these categories of identity the gay political movement was born, and although it is demonstrably correct that lesbians and gay men live more openly and freely than in the past, with that hard-won freedom has come greater levels of regulation, scrutinization, and state control. The history of the treatment of gays in the military is witness to this. As the category of gay identity developed, so too did the greater attention to the personal habits, mannerisms, and personalities of those seeking to enlist. Today, one will scarcely find among military men what the regulations advised physicians to watch for among the recruits for World War II. Any hint of effeminacy in manner and dress has disappeared among the nation's fighting men, so successfully do all men, straight and gay, police their own gender conformity to acceptable models of masculinity. The same can be said of lesbians, and indeed all women in the military who walk an even narrower line between appearing feminine and therefore weak, and appearing tough, "hardworking and among the command's top professionals," and therefore a lesbian.

In 1951, writing in the *Origins of Totalitarianism*, political theorist Hannah Arendt documented the rise of "racism" directed at Jews in nineteenth-century Europe. Integral to this racism was the identification of Jews as a "race," as those *born* to a certain inescapable identity. She writes,

As far as the Jews were concerned, the transformation of the "crime" of Judaism into the fashionable "vice" of Jewishness was dangerous in the extreme. Jews had been able to escape from Judaism into conversion; from Jewishness there was no escape. A crime, moreover, is met with punishment; a vice can only be exterminated. The interpretation given by society to the fact of Jewish birth and the role played by Jews in the framework of social life are intimately connected with the catastrophic thoroughness with which anti-Semitism had its roots in these social conditions. . . .[66]

Arendt was one who realized the same transformation was taking place in the arena of sexuality, arguing that "the 'vice' of Jewishness and the 'vice' of homosexuality . . . became very much alike indeed."[67] The medical transformation of criminal *acts* of sodomy into sexual *vice* and *identities* parallels the transformation described above by Arendt. By replacing the terms "Judaism" and "Jewishness" with "sodomy" and "homosexual" in the quote above, the danger of this parallel transformation to lesbians and gays today becomes clear.

The path toward tolerance does not come in proving to straights that lesbians and gays are kinder and gentler versions of themselves. The acceptance of lesbians and gay men will not occur because we are "born this way," nor because we demonstrate we can be just like the rest of America. Have movement leaders failed to notice what seems so obvious, that life in the rest of America could stand to change a bit itself? Homophobia, racism, and sexism are all the products of the same set of cultural practices that posit straight white men as the standard bearers of culture and mark everyone else as decidedly "other." Putting an end to this enforced conformity to an oppressive cultural ideal of gender, racial, and sexual normalcy will require a political agenda very different from one that seeks simple and unquestioning integration with the values of institutions like heterosexuality and the United States military.

Lesbians and gay men are a long way from building the kind of movement I have in mind. We are a long way from developing needed coalitions with other oppressed groups and articulating a shared agenda. This course, veering away from a simple equal rights agenda, seems difficult; its chances for success slim. But the potential rewards for success are greater. In this political movement freedom will not be bought with conformity, and equality will not require assimilation. In this political movement Colonel Margarethe Cammermeyer can wear leather, shave off her hair, and still receive the acknowledgment, recognition, and respect she deserves as a Colonel in the military service of her nation.

NOTES

1. Hatter's remarks came in response to the Navy's refusal to reinstate Petty Officer Keith Meinhold as had been ordered by the court only two days earlier. The court order was issued on November 11, 1992. See Seth Mydans, "Navy is Ordered to Return Job to a Gay Sailor," *New York Times* (November 11, 1992): A14.

2. For an interesting discussion about sterilization of the poor and mentally handicapped in the United States, see Michael Katz, *In the Shadow of the Poorhouse: A Social History of Welfare in America* (New York: Basic Books, 1986). In 1927, the Supreme Court upheld the constitutionality of sterilization in *Buck v. Bell*, and according to Katz, by 1958 almost 61,000 sterilizations had been recorded across the United States.

3. Jeffrey Weeks, *Coming Out: Homosexual Politics in Britain from the Nineteenth Century to the Present* (London: Quartet Books Limited, 1977), 5.

4. Raphael Sealey, *Women and Law in Classical Athens* (Chapel Hill: The University of North Carolina Press, 1990).

5. Allan Bérubé, *Coming Out Under Fire: The History of Gay Men and Women in World War Two* (New York: The Free Press, 1990); Bérubé and John D'Emilio, "The Military and Lesbians During the McCarthy Years," in

D'Emilio, ed. *Making Trouble: Essays on Gay History, Politics, and the University* (New York: Routledge, 1992).

6. United States Navy, *Report of the Board Appointed to Prepare and Submit Recommendations to the Secretary of the Navy for the Revision of Policies, Procedures, and Directives Dealing with Homosexuality*, Chairman S. H. Crittenden (Washington, D.C.: Government Printing Office, 1957).

7. E. L. Gibson's *Get Off My Ship* (New York: Avon, 1978) contains the history of the suppression and subsequent release of the Crittenden Report.

8. Department of Defense Directive 1332.14, "Enlisted Administrative Separations," dated January 28, 1982.

9. Timothy Egan, "Dismissed From Army as Lesbian, Colonel Will Fight Homosexual Ban," *New York Times* (May 31, 1992): 18.

10. Jeffrey Schmalz, "Difficult First Step: Promises and Reality Clash as Clinton is Moving to end Military's Gay Ban," *New York Times* (November 15, 1992): 22.

11. Defense Personnel Security Research and Education Center, *Nonconforming Sexual Orientation and Military Suitability*, prepared by Theodore R. Sarbin, Ph.D. and Kenneth E. Karols, M.D., Ph.D., December 1988, p. 33.

12. The PERSEREC report, and the Pentagon memos with an introduction to the politics surrounding the release of the report (written by Gerry Studds) has been published by Alyson Press in Kate Dyer, ed., *Gays in Uniform: The Pentagon's Secret Report* (Boston: Alyson Publications, 1990).

13. Defense Personnel Security Research and Education Center, "Preservice Adjustment of Homosexual and Heterosexual Accessions: Implications for Security Clearance Suitability," prepared by Michael A. McDaniel, PERS-TR-89-004, January 1989, p. 19.

14. "Sexual Orientation and U.S. Military Personnel Policy: Options and Assessments," National Defense Research Institute (RAND) MR-323-OSD.

15. John Gallagher, "Terrible Timing," *The Advocate* (October 5, 1993): 28.

16. Ibid., 21.

17. Jane Gross, "Navy is Urged to Root Out Lesbians Despite Abilities," *New York Times* (November 2, 1990): A11.

18. United States General Accounting Office, "Defense Force Management: DOD's Policy on Homosexuality: A Report to Congressional Requesters," GAO/NSIAD-92-98, June 12, 1992.

19. Ibid.

20. For example, Miriam Ben Shalom, President of Gay, Lesbian, and Bisexual Veterans of America, makes this claim. See John Gallagher, "GAO: Military Spent $500 Million Discharging Gays," *The Advocate* (July 30, 1992): 19-20.

21. *Glidden v. U.S.* (185 CT. CL. 515), 1968.

22. "Lay Navy Scandal to F. D. Roosevelt: Senate Naval Sub-Committee Accuses Him and Daniels in Newport Inquiry," *New York Times* (July 20, 1921): Section 4, 7.

23. The investigation of the "boy investigators" and of those allegedly identified as homosexual seamen at Newport Station by a Naval Court of Inquiry filled six thousand pages of testimony and fifteen volumes. Lawrence R. Murphy's *Perverts by Official Order: The Campaign Against Homosexuals by the United States Navy* (New York: Haworth Press, 1988) examines the Navy's 1921 activities and the subsequent scandal and makes use of testimony from this investigation.

It is also of interest that Ervin Arnold, who actually headed the military vice squad, hand picked the "boy investigators" because of their youth and good looks, saying in an ungrammatical way: "a good looking man from the average of 19 to 24 will be the best people." The question "how might Arnold know who would make the best objects of homosexual desire?" remains unasked, and sadly, unanswered. See Murphy, 22.

24. "Alleged Immoral Conditions at Newport," *New York Times* (July 20, 1921): Section 4, 7.

25. U.S. Senate, 67th Congress, First Session, Committee on Naval Affairs, "Alleged Immoral Conditions at Newport (R.I.) Naval Training Station, Report of the Committee on Naval Affairs," (Washington, D.C.: Government Printing Office, 1921; reprinted in *Government Versus Homosexuals* (New York: Arno Press, 1975), 22.

26. *U.S. v. Napoleon Viches* (17 MJ 851), 1984. "Chickenhawk" is slang within the gay community for an older man who finds younger men (chicken) attractive.

27. *U.S. v. Miller* (3 MJ 292), 1977.

28. Department of Defense Directive 1332.4. All seven reasons that the military listed for why they believe "homosexuality is incompatible with military service" are contained in this directive.

29. *U.S. v. Miller* (3 MJ 292), 1977. In this case the victim is constructed as both liar and as promiscuous. The court seems to suggest that consent is not an issue. Once one is a homosexual he/she loses the right to say no to unwanted sexual advances.

30. Tamar Lewin, "Gay Cadet is Asked to Repay R.O.T.C. Scholarship," *New York Times* (March 4, 1990): A7.

31. Ibid.

32. *U.S. v. Kindler* (14 USCMA 394), 1964. In both this case and the 1990 example of James Holobaugh, the armed services will not accept the word of the accused, as if homosexuality affects their veracity. The armed services will not entertain the possibility that sexual identity could solidify later in some people than in others.

33. *Clackum v. U.S.* (296 F.2d 226), 1966.

34. *U.S. v. Phillips* (3 USCMA 137), 1953.

35. *U.S. v. Marcey* (9 USCMA 137), 1958.

36. *U.S. v. Marcey* (9 USCMA 137), 1958.

37. Dr. Albert Abrams, "Homosexuality—A Military Menace," *Medical Review of Reviews* Vol. 24, (1918): 528-29, San Francisco. I am indebted to Jonathan Katz's *Gay/Lesbian Almanac* for first bringing this to my attention.

38. Army Regulation No. 40-105, 1921.

39. These guidelines were established in 1942. See William C. Menninger, *Psychiatry in a Troubled War: Yesterday's War and Today's Challenge* (New York: MacMillan, 1948), 228.

40. Ibid.

41. Arthur Weider et al., "The Cornell Selectee Index: A Method for Quick Testing of Selectees for the Armed Forces," *Journal of the American Medical Association* 124 (January 22, 1944): 224-28. Bérubé also discusses this form. See *Coming Out Under Fire*, 20.

42. Equal protection law requires that when such distinctions between groups of people are made that these distinctions be "rational" and legitimate. When distinctions made by government actions are "suspect" or "quasi-suspect," and when certain characteristics that bear no apparent relationship to the subject in question are employed as the basis of differentiation, courts are asked to apply a more rigorous standard of scrutiny in reviewing the government's actions. The onus is on the government to demonstrate a compelling state interest if the group in question is determined to be a suspect class. If a quasi-suspect class is involved, the government must show that their justification for discriminating is substantially related to a legitimate state interest. In all equal protection cases, whatever the status of the group involved is determined to be, the government must demonstrate a legitimate and rational basis for its policy. As Ken Sherrill has noted in his book about *Steffan v. Cheney*, in their determination of whether or not a group constitutes a suspect or quasi-suspect class, courts have focused on five questions:

1. Has the group suffered a history of purposeful discrimination?

2. Is the group defined by a trait that frequently bears no relation to ability to perform or contribute to society?

3. Is the trait defining the class "immutable" or, in other words, is the trait a product of an accident of birth?

4. Has the group been saddled with unique disabilities because of prejudice or absurd stereotypes?

5. Does the group burdened by discrimination lack the political power to obtain redress through the political process?

Marc Wolinsky and Kenneth Sherrill, eds., *Gays and the Military: Joseph Steffan versus the United States Military* (Princeton, NJ: Princeton University Press, 1993), xvi.

43. Craig Stoltz, "Gays in the Military," *USA Weekend* (August 7-9, 1992): 4-5.

44. Eric Schmitt, "Calm Analysis Dominates Panel Hearings on Gay Ban," *New York Times* (April 1, 1993): A1.

45. Craig Stoltz, "Gays in the Military," *USA Weekend* (August 7-9, 1992): 4-5.

46. *Rich v. Secretary of the Army* (516 F. Supp. 621), 1981.

47. Even one's choice of reading material can be regarded as symptom and threat by signaling your sexual orientation to others. During the Senate Armed Services Committee hearings Senator Levin asked General Norman Schwarzkopf if reading a magazine that catered to homosexuals constituted homosexual activity. The General replied "no," but then added that if a soldier was reading the magazine "in the barracks on a continuous basis to the point where it causes all around you to be concerned about your sexual orientation and it started to cause polarization within your outfit," then the offending servicemember should be removed. See Eric Schmitt, "Compromise on Military Gay Ban Gaining Support Among Senators," *New York Times* (May 12, 1993): A1.

48. Department of Defense Directive 1332.145, January 16, 1981.

49. Neff Hudson, "Is 'Don't Ask, Don't Tell' Working? Depends on Who You Ask," *The Army Times* (June 13, 1994).

50. John Gallagher, "Some Things Never Change," *The Advocate* (May 17, 1994): 46.

51. "Ego and Error on the Gay Issue," *New York Times*, (January 29, 1993): A26.

52. Anthony Lewis, "The Issue is Bigotry," *New York Times* (January 29, 1993): A23.

53. "Gay Issue Mobilizes Conservatives Against Clinton," by Peter Applebome, *New York Times* (February 1, 1993): A14.

54. Professor John Green, at the University of Akron, made these comments to the *New York Times*. See Peter Applebome, "Gay Issue Mobilizes Conservatives Against Clinton," *New York Times* (February 1, 1993): A14.

55. Ibid.

56. Sarah Schulman, *My American History: Lesbian and Gay Life During the Reagan/Bush Years* (New York: Routledge, 1994), 13.

57. Jeff Yarbrough, "The Life and Times of Randy Shilts," *The Advocate* (June 15, 1993): 36.

58. Tim McFeeley, Human Rights Campaign Fund, Letter to Members dated June 25, 1992.

59. John Gallagher, "Half a Loaf," *The Advocate* (May 4, 1993): 25.

60. Barney Frank, member of Congress, Letter Explaining his Decision to Offer a Compromise dated May 20, 1993.

61. Chris Bull, "No Frankness," *The Advocate* (June 29, 1993): 27.

62. Ibid., 29.

63. Ken Sherrill has argued that this represents the Clinton Administration's greatest sin. Thrusting upon the lesbian and gay community the total responsibility for breaking this iron triangle while remaining silent himself doomed the proposed changes to failure. Sherrill writes, "A new President, with much undistributed patronage at his disposal and with a reservoir of good will, might have had a chance against the complex. To assign the responsibility was to throw us to the lions." (Personal communication, Nov. 4, 1995.) I

believe Sherrill is largely right, but as a President without a mandate, without even the support of a majority of voters, and who had faced serious issues surrounding his own military service during the campaign, Clinton's reservoir of good will—especially with those in the military industrial complex he hoped to influence—was never very substantial.

64. Barbara Smith, "Where's the Revolution?" *The Nation* (July 5, 1993): 14.

65. Timothy Egan, "Dismissed From Army as Lesbian, Colonel Will Fight Homosexual Ban," *New York Times* (May 31, 1992): 18.

66. Hannah Arendt, *The Origins of Totalitarianism* (New York: Harcourt Brace Jovanovich, 1973), 87.

67. Ibid., 80.

Selected Bibliography

Anderson, Clinton W., and H. Ron Smith. "Stigma and Honor: Gay, Lesbian, and Bisexual People in the U.S. Military," in *Homosexual Issues in the Workplace*. Louis Diamant (ed.). Washington, D.C.: Taylor and Francis, 1993: 65-89.

Bérubé, Allan. *Coming Out Under Fire: The History of Gay Men and Women in World War Two*. New York: Free Press, 1990.

Binkin, Martin and Mark J. Eitelberg. *Blacks and the Military*. With the collaboration of Alvin J. Schexnider and Marvin M. Smith. Washington, D.C.: Brookings, 1982.

Burk, James. "Power, Morals, and Military Uniqueness." *Society* Vol. 31, #1 (November/December 1993): 29-36.

Cammermeyer, Margarethe, with Chris Fisher. *Serving in Silence*. New York: Viking, 1994.

Card, Claudia. "The Military Ban and the ROTC: A Study in Closeting." *Journal of Homosexuality* 27:3/4 (1994): 117-146.

Carey, John J., ed. *The Christian Argument for Gays and Lesbians in the Military: Essays by Mainline Church Leaders*. Lewiston, NY: Edwin Mellen Press, 1993.

Cathcart, Kevin M., and Evan Wolfson. "Lesbian and Gay Rights in the 1990s: At the Barricades." *Trial* 29 (July 1993): 56-59+.

Davis, Jeffrey S. "Military Policy Toward Homosexuals: Scientific, Historical, and Legal Perspectives." *Military Law Review*, 131 (Winter 1991): 55-109.

Dyer, Kate, ed. *Gays in Uniform: The Pentagon's Secret Reports*. Boston, MA: Alyson, 1990.

Holm, Jeanne. *Women in the Military: An Unfinished Revolution*. 2nd ed. Novato, CA: Presidio, 1993.

Holobaugh, Jim, with Keith Hale. *Torn Allegiances: The Story of a Gay Cadet* (Army ROTC, Washington University). Boston: Alyson, 1993.

Humphrey, Mary Ann. *My Country, My Right to Serve: Experiences of Gay Men and Women in the Military, World War II to the Present*. New York: Harper Collins, 1990.

Jackson, Donna. *Honorable Discharge—Memoirs of an Army Dyke: The Donna Jackson Story*. Elizabeth Brave (ed.) Christie and Steffin, 1994.

RAND. *Sexual Orientation and U.S. Military Personnel Policy: Options and Assessment*. Santa Monica, CA: RAND/National Defense Research Institute, MR-323-OSD, 1993.

Rubenstein, William B. *Lesbians, Gay Men, and the Law*. New York: New Press/W.W. Norton, 1993.

Schmalz, Jeffrey. "Gay Politics Goes Mainstream." *New York Times Magazine*, 11 October 1992, 18.

Scott, Wilbur and Sandra Carson Stanley, eds. *Gays and Lesbians in the Military: Issues, Concerns, and Contrasts*. New York: Aldine de Gruyter, 1994.

Shilts, Randy. *Conduct Unbecoming: Lesbians and Gays in the U.S. Military, Vietnam to the Persian Gulf*. New York: St. Martin's, 1993.

Snyder, William P., and Kenneth L. Nyberg. "Gays and the Military: An Emerging Policy Issue." *Journal of Political and Military Sociology* 8 (Spring 1980): 71-84.

Steffan, Joseph. *Honor Bound: A Gay American Fights for the Right to Serve His Country*. New York: Villard Books, 1992.

Stiehm, Judith Hicks. *Arms and the Enlisted Woman*. Philadelphia: Temple University Press, 1989.

Vaid, Urvashi. *Virtual Equality: The Mainstreaming of Gay and Lesbian Liberation*. New York: Anchor Books, 1995.

Williams, Colin J. and Martin S. Weinberg. *Homosexuals and the Military: A Study of Less Than Honorable Discharge*. New York: Harper and Row, 1971.

Wilson, Donna L. "Women and Homophobia in the Armed Services: An Annotated Bibliography." *Minerva* 7:1 (Spring 1989): 63-80.

Wolinsky, Marc and Kenneth Sherrill, eds. *Gays and the Military: Joseph Steffan versus the United States*. Princeton, NJ: Princeton University Press, 1993.

Zeeland, Steven. *Barracks Buddies and Soldier Lovers: Dialogues with Gay Men in the U.S. Military (Army)*. New York: Harrington Park/Haworth, 1993.

Zeeland, Steven. *Sailors and Sexual Identity: Crossing the Line Between 'Straight' and 'Gay' in the U.S. Navy*. New York: Haworth, 1995.

Zuniga, Jose. *Soldier of the Year*. New York: Pocket, 1994.

Margarethe Cammermeyer v. Les Aspin

UNITED STATES DISTRICT COURT
WESTERN DISTRICT OF WASHINGTON
AT SEATTLE

MARGARETHE CAMMERMEYER, Plaintiff, v. LES ASPIN, Secretary of Defense,[1] et al., Defendants	No. C92-9422 ORDER

Margarethe Cammermeyer brings this declaratory judgment action against the Government claiming that her discharge from military service under Army Regulation 135-175, based solely on her admission that she is a lesbian, violated her rights to equal protection of the laws guaranteed under the Fifth Amendment to the United States Constitution. She also claims her discharge violated her right to privacy under the First, Fourth, Fifth and Ninth Amendments to the Constitution, her substantive due process rights under the Fifth Amendment and her right to freedom of speech under the First Amendment. Cammermeyer further claims that Army Regulation 135-175 is an invalid exercise of executive power violative of the constitutional separation of powers, and that the regulation violates principles of federalism.

The parties have now filed cross-motions for summary judgment. Plaintiff moves for summary judgment on her equal protection claim (docket no. 50). Defendants move for judgment on the pleadings or, in the alternative, summary judgment on all of plaintiff's claims (docket no. 59). The Court heard oral argument on these cross-motions on April 20, 1994, and took the matter under advisement. The Court has reviewed all of the materials submitted by the parties and now GRANTS plaintiff's motion for summary judgment as to her equal protection and substantive due process claims under the Fifth Amendment, and GRANTS defendants' motion for summary judgment as to the remainder of plaintiff's claims.

I. BACKGROUND

Margarethe Cammermeyer is a former Colonel of the Washington State National Guard. She entered the Army Student Nurse Corps in 1961, and with the exception of a four-year period when she was ineligible for service,[2] Cammermeyer served in the Army until 1986. In that year, Cammermeyer transferred to the Washington State National Guard where she continued to serve until she was discharged on June 11, 1992.

Cammermeyer's expertise as an Army Nurse is remarkable. She has earned bachelor's, master's and doctorate degrees in Nursing. She was a member of the Clinical Faculty of the University of San Francisco School of Nursing where she coauthored four research articles published in the *Journal of Military Medicine*. Cammermeyer Decl. at ¶¶ 3, 8, 12, 19. In addition, she has received numerous awards and distinctions, including the Bronze Star for distinguished service in Vietnam.[3] *Id.* at ¶ 6. She volunteered and served in Vietnam for fifteen months with distinction. *Id.* at ¶¶ 5-6. Cammermeyer has served in numerous other capacities in the Army and Washington State National Guard, including medical-surgical supervisor and Assistant Chief Nurse of the 50th General Hospital in Fort Lawton, Washington, Chief Nurse of the 352nd Evacuation Hospital in Oakland, California, and State Chief Nurse and consultant to the State Chief Surgeon at Camp Murray, Washington. *Id.* at ¶¶ 8, 11, 15.

In April, 1989, Cammermeyer applied for admission to the Army War College to receive training she considered essential to her goal of becoming Chief Nurse of the National Guard Bureau ("NGB"). *Id.* at ¶ 16. During a top secret security check required for admission to the Army War College, Cammermeyer was asked about her sexual orientation and answered that she is a lesbian.[4] Notwithstanding this admission, Cammermeyer was told by the Washington State National Guard that she could continue to serve as Chief Nurse, and that the Guard would not pursue her discharge "unless forced to do so" by the Department of the Army. *Id.* at ¶ 18. Alternatively, she was told she could resign. Cammermeyer chose to continue to serve. Six months later, pursuant to service-wide federal regulations barring homosexuals from the military, the United States Army commenced proceedings to withdraw Cammermeyer's "federal recognition" and thus render her ineligible to serve in the Washington State National Guard or any other branch of the military.[5]

Cammermeyer continued to serve in her position as Chief Nurse for more than three years after she admitted that she is a lesbian. During this period, a military retention board was convened to review whether Cammermeyer's federal recognition should be withdrawn because of her lesbian status. On July

14, 1991, after a two-day hearing, the Board recommended withdrawal of Cammermeyer's federal recognition. In presiding over the Board, former Chief Nurse, NGB, Colonel Patsy Thompson openly regretted her "sad duty" of reading the Board's adverse recommendation to "one of the great Americans." Tr. of Hearing before Federal Recognition Board, Vol. 2, at 131-33. Colonel Thompson stated that Cammermeyer "has consistently provided superb leadership and has many outstanding accomplishments to her credit." *Id.* at 132.

On June 11, 1992, Cammermeyer was discharged based upon the Board's recommendation and received an honorable discharge.[6] Cammermeyer's final evaluation, dated July 31, 1992, describing her contributions to the Army and noting her discharge, concluded that "[t]his officer has the potential to serve as Chief Nurse, NGB; and to represent her profession in major research projects in military medicine anywhere in the world." Cammermeyer Decl., Exhibit D, Officer Evaluation Report (OER) dated July 31, 1992. Prior to her discharge, Washington Governor Booth Gardner, Commander-in-Chief of the Washington State National Guard, wrote a letter to then-Secretary of Defense Richard Cheney requesting that Cammermeyer be retained. Cammermeyer Decl. Exhibit H. That letter states, in part, that "if Colonel Cammermeyer's discharge becomes final, this would be both a significant loss to the State of Washington and a senseless end to the career of a distinguished, long-time member of the armed services." *Id.*

II. DISCUSSION

A. Summary Judgment Standard

Summary judgment is appropriate if the record shows "'that there is no genuine issue as to any material fact and that the moving party is entitled to a judgment as a matter of law.'" *Williams v. I.B. Fischer Nev.*, 999 F.2d 445, 447 (9th Cit. 1993) (quoting Fed. R. Civ. P. 56(c)). In determining whether there are any genuine issues of material fact for trial, the court must view all of the evidence in the light most favorable to the nonmoving party. *Abuan v. General Electric Co.*, 3 F.3d 329, 332 (9th Cir. 1993), cert. denied, 114 S.Ct. 1064, 127 L.Ed.2d 383 (1994). This is true even when the court is presented with cross-motions for summary judgment. *High Tech Gays v. Defense Indus. Sec. Clearance Office*, 895 F.2d 563, 574 (9th Cir. 1990). "Summary judgment must be entered 'against a party who fails to make a showing sufficient to establish the existence of an element essential to that party's case, and on which that party will bear the burden of proof at trial.'" *Abuan*, 3 F.3d at 331 (quoting *Celotex v. Catrett*, 477 U.S. 317, 322, 106 S.Ct. 2548, 2552, 91 L.Ed.2d 265, (1986)). Once a summary judgment motion is made and properly supported, the adverse party may not rest on the mere allegations of his or her pleadings, but must set forth specific facts showing that there is a genuine issue for trial. Fed. R. Civ. P. 56(e). If there is any need to *weigh* the evidence at issue, summary judgment is inappropriate. *Anderson v. Liberty Lobby, Inc.*, 477 U.S. 242, 249, 106 S.Ct. 2505, 2510, 91 L.Ed.2d 202 (1986).

B. Equal Protection Challenge

Both parties move for summary judgment on plaintiff's claim that her discharge from the Washington State National Guard violated her equal protection rights under the Fifth Amendment to the United States Constitution.

1. Equal Protection Standard

"The Equal Protection Clause of the Fourteenth Amendment commands that no State shall 'deny to any person within its jurisdiction the equal protection of the laws,' which is essentially a direction that all persons similarly situated should be treated alike." *City of Cleburne v. Cleburne Living Center, Inc.*, 473 U.S. 432, 439, 105 S.Ct. 3249, 3254, 87 L.Ed.2d 313, 320 (1985)(quoting *Plyler v. Doe*, 457 U.S. 202, 216 (1982)). While the Fifth Amendment does not contain an equal protection clause, the due process clause of the Fifth Amendment has an equal protection component that applies to the federal government. *Bolling v. Sharpe*, 347 U.S. 497, 74 S.Ct. 693, 98 L.Ed. 884 (1954).

There are three standards of review applicable to equal protection challenges to governmental regulations: strict scrutiny, heightened scrutiny, and rational basis review. *High Tech Gays*, 895 F.2d at 571 (citing *Cleburne*, 473 U.S. at 440-41, 105 S.Ct. at 3254-55, 87 L.Ed.2d 320-21). Legislative classifications based on race, alienage, or national origin require strict scrutiny. The classification will be upheld only if it is "suitably tailored to serve a compelling state interest." *Cleburne*, 473 U.S. at 440, 105 S.Ct. at 3254, 87 L.Ed.2d at 320. Strict scrutiny is also required when laws impinge upon constitutionally protected "fundamental" rights. *Id.* Legislative classifications based on gender call for a heightened standard of review; the classification survives only if it is "substantially related to a sufficiently important governmental interest." *Id.* at 441, 105 S.Ct. at 3255, 87 L.Ed.2d at 321. Certain restrictions beyond a person's control, such as illegitimacy, are also subject to heightened review. These restrictions "will survive equal protection scrutiny to the extent they are substantially related to a legitimate state interest." *Mills v. Habluetzel*, 456 U.S. 91, 99, 102 S.Ct. 1549, 1554, 71 L.Ed.2d 770, 777-78 (1982). Finally, equal protection challenges that do not involve suspect classifications or fundamental rights are subject to "rational basis" review. *Heller v. Doe*, 509 U.S. ___, 113 S.Ct. 2637, 125 L.Ed.2d 257, 270 (1993). Under this standard, a discriminatory classification is presumed valid and will be sustained "if there is a rational relationship between the disparity of treatment and some legitimate governmental purpose." *Id.*

The Ninth Circuit has previously held that homosexuals are not a suspect or quasi-suspect class for equal protection purposes, and that classifications based on homosexuality are entitled only to rational basis review. *High Tech Gays*, 895 F.2d at 571. In this case, the parties agree that the rational basis standard of review applies to plaintiff's equal protection challenge.

2. Rational Basis Review

Rational basis review is a two-step process. *Jackson Water Works, Inc. v. Public Utilities Comm'n*, 793 F.2d 1090, 1094 (9th Cir. 1986), cert. denied, 479 U.S. 1102, 107 S.Ct. 1334, 94 L.Ed.2d 184 (1987). Initially, the court must determine whether the challenged classification serves a legitimate governmental purpose. If the court answers this question in the affirmative, the court must then determine whether the discriminatory classification is rationally related to the achievement of that legitimate purpose. A discriminatory classification that is based on prejudice or bias is not rational as a matter of law. See *Palmore v. Sidoti*, 466 U.S. 429, 104 S.Ct. 1879, 80 L.Ed.2d 421, 426 (1984)(mother could not be denied custody of her child based on social disapproval of her interracial marriage); *Cleburne*, 473 U.S. at 448, 105 S.Ct. at 3259, 87 L.Ed.2d at 326 (city could not require a special use permit for group home for the mentally retarded where the requirement was based on prejudice).

The defendants contend that Army Regulation 135-175 serves the government's legitimate interest in maintaining the readiness and combat effectiveness of its military forces. Plaintiff does not dispute that this is a legitimate governmental purpose. Thus, the Court can proceed to the second step of its rational basis analysis and determine whether the government's exclusion of homosexuals from military service is rationally related to this legitimate governmental purpose.

Before proceeding with this analysis, however, the Court must resolve three preliminary issues: (a) the appropriate level of deference to accord to military decisions; (b) the viability of the standard of review applied in *Pruitt v. Cheney*, 963 F.2d. 1160 (9th Cir.), cert. denied, 113 S.Ct. 655, 121 L.Ed.2d 581 (1992), following *Heller v. Doe*, 509 U.S. ___, 113 S.Ct. 2637, 125 L.Ed.2d. 257, 270 (1993); and (c) whether, for purposes of equal protection analysis, there is a meaningful distinction between homosexual orientation and homosexual conduct.

a. DEFERENCE TO THE MILITARY. The Constitution confers broad powers on the President and Congress to raise and support armies, provide and maintain a naval force, and promulgate rules governing and regulating both land and naval forces. Traditionally, courts have recognized the Constitution's mandate by according significant deference to the "considered professional judgment" of military officials regarding the composition of the armed forces. *Goldman v. Weinberger*, 475 U.S. 503, 508, 106 S.Ct. 1310, 1313, 89 L.Ed.2d 478 (1986). "While it is clear that one does not surrender his or her constitutional rights upon entering the military, the Supreme Court has repeatedly held that constitutional rights must be viewed in light of the special circumstances and needs of the armed forces." *Beller v. Middendorf*, 632 F.2d 788, 810 (9th Cir. 1980). As the Supreme Court has reflected:

> "[It] is difficult to conceive of an area of governmental activity in which the courts have less competence. The complex, subtle, and professional decisions as to the composition, training, equipping, and

control of a military force are essentially professional military judgments, subject *always* to civilian control of the Legislative and Executive Branches."

Rostker v. Goldberg, 453 U.S. 57, 65-66, 101 S.Ct. 2646, 2652, 69 L.Ed.2d 478, 487 (1981)(quoting *Gilligan v. Morgan*, 413 U.S. 1, 10 (1973)). Furthermore, "[r]egulations which might infringe constitutional rights in other contexts may survive scrutiny because of military necessities." *Beller*, 632 F.2d at 811.

In view of this standard, the Court must be particularly careful not to substitute its own judgment as to what is "desirable" or its own evaluation of what the executive branch may have intended by a given policy. The Court is also mindful, however, that there is not and must never be a "military exception" to the Constitution. Indeed, courts have been willing to defer to the military only within the confines of ordinary constitutional analysis. See *Rostker*, 453 U.S. at 67, 69 L.Ed.2d at 488 (deference to the judgment of other branches in the area of military affairs does not require abdication of "ultimate responsibility to decide constitutional question"). This principle applies with even greater force to equal protection claims since it has traditionally been the domain of the federal courts to scrutinize classifications challenged on equal protection grounds.

This Circuit, in *Pruitt*, 963 F.2d at 1166-67, recognized that deference to the military does not preclude judicial review of military decisions. In *Pruitt*, the plaintiff, a former Army Reserve officer who was discharged because she acknowledged her homosexual orientation, sued to be reinstated. The trial court dismissed the claim, holding that the Army's determination that homosexuality is incompatible with the military mission was entitled to substantial deference. The Ninth Circuit reversed and remanded, holding that the plaintiff had stated an equal protection claim. The court rejected the Army's contention that the court should defer to military judgment and uphold its regulation "without a record to support its rational basis." *Id.* at 1167. The court reasoned that:

> We readily acknowledge, as we must, that military decisions by the Army are not lightly to be overruled by the judiciary. That admonition, however, is best applied inthe process of judging whether the reasons put forth on the record for the Army's discrimination against Pruitt are rationally related to any of the Army's permissible goals.

Id. at 1166 (citations omitted). The *Pruitt* court further stated that if it were to defer to military judgment by affirming the district court's dismissal of Pruitt's complaint, without any supporting factual record, it would "come close to denying reviewability at all." *Id.* at 1167. Thus, simply labelling the government's decision as "military" does not prevent a meaningful review of the decision to discharge the plaintiff because she is a homosexual.

Although this Court must give appropriate deference to the military decisionmaking process, the Court must also review the reasons provided by the defendants to determine whether the classification is "rationally related to any of the Army's permissible goals." *Id.* at 1166.

b. SCOPE OF RATIONAL BASIS REVIEW. The parties in this case dispute the proper standard for review of government policy under the rational basis test. Plaintiff relies on *Pruitt*, and asserts that the defendants have the burden to demonstrate with facts on the record that the challenged policy is rational and legitimate. The *Pruitt* Court, in rejecting the Army's argument that it could discharge Pruitt "without any justification in the record" for the policy, stated that "[a]ssuming that Pruitt supports her allegations with evidence, we will not spare the Army the task . . . of offering a rational basis for its regulation, nor will we deprive Pruitt of the opportunity to contest that basis." *Id.* The court then remanded the case for development of a factual record and a determination of whether the Army's discriminatory regulation was "rationally related to a permissible governmental purpose." *Id.* at 1167.

The defendants argue that "the continuing validity of *Pruitt* is undercut" by *Heller*. Defendants' Memorandum of Points and Authorities (docket no. 59) at 13. At oral argument, the Government further contended that *Pruitt* was "superseded" and "rendered moot" by *Heller*. Tr. April 20, 1994 Hearing (docket no. 93) at 25. Defendants contend that under *Heller*, they have no burden to submit evidence justifying the challenged policy and this Court may reject plaintiff's equal protection claim as a matter of law, without considering any such evidence.

In *Heller*, 509 U.S. ___, 113 S.Ct. 2637, 125 L.Ed.2d 257 (1993), plaintiffs challenged a Kentucky statute that mandated a higher burden of proof in involuntary commitment proceedings for mentally ill persons than for mentally retarded persons. Plaintiffs claimed that this distinction lacked a rational basis.[7] The Supreme Court rejected plaintiffs' argument that the statutory distinctions were irrational, finding that the State had "rationally advance[d] a reasonable and identifiable governmental objective." *Id.*, 125 L.Ed.2d at 277. The Court further found that the State's proffered rationales provided a rational basis for the statutory classification. *Id.*, 125 L.Ed.2d at 276. In so finding, the Court stated that a challenged discriminatory classification:

"must be upheld against equal protection challenge if there is any reasonable conceivable state of facts that could provide a rational basis for the classification." A State, moreover, has no obligation to produce evidence to sustain the rationality of a statutory classification. "[A] legislative choice is not subject to courtroom factfinding and may be based on rational speculation unsupported by evidence or empirical data." A statute is presumed constitutional . . . and "[t]he burden is on the one attacking the legislative arrangement to negative every conceivable basis which might support it" . . . whether or not the basis has a foundation in the record.

Id., 125 L.Ed.2d at 270-71 (citation omitted).

The defendants' contention that *Pruitt*'s vitality has been extinguished by *Heller* is without merit.[8] While it is true that, under *Heller*, the government policymaker is not *required* to submit evidence to justify its policy, and may offer only "rational speculation" to explain the discriminating classification, the Court remains obligated to determine whether there is a rational basis for the policy. Otherwise, it would not have been necessary for the *Heller* court to examine the assumptions underlying the Kentucky statute. If the Government's position were correct, the *Heller* Court could have simply upheld the statute as a matter of law, without any inquiry into its rationality. In fact, the *Heller* Court closely examined the State's asserted bases for the differential treatment of the two classes and found that there were plausible rationales for each of the statutory distinctions challenged in the case. The Court concluded that, "even the standard of rationality as we so often have defined it must find some footing in the realities of the subject addressed by the legislation." *Heller*, 125 L.Ed.2d at 271.

The continued vitality of *Pruitt*, following *Heller*, is further demonstrated by *Jackson v. Brigle*, 17 F.3d 280 (9th Cir. 1994), a sovereign immunity case, where the Ninth Circuit stated in dicta at the end of its opinion:

> The *Pruitt* and *High Tech Gays* cases, upon which the district court relied, do stand for the proposition that if the Government discriminates against an individual on the basis of homosexuality and does not demonstrate a rational basis for doing so, it will have violated that individual's constitutional rights.

Id. at 284.

Heller did not address the proper scope of a court's rational basis review where, as here, the plaintiff alleges the government policy at issue is based solely on prejudice. If the policy is shown to be based solely on prejudice, it cannot survive rational basis review. *Cleburne*, 473 U.S. at 450, 105 S.Ct. at 3259, 87 L.Ed.2d at 327.

In a recent district court case in this circuit, *Dahl v. Secretary of the United States Navy*, 830 F.Supp. 1319 (E.D. Cal. 1993),[9] the court rejected the same arguments made by the government here. Dahl was discharged from the Navy because he admitted during an official interview that he was a homosexual. The *Dahl* court concluded that:

> In sum, there is no support for defendants' argument that the court must accept without question defendants' proffered bases for the homosexual exclusion policy without analyzing the relevant evidence and

determining whether the policy is motivated by prejudice against homosexuals.

Id. at 1327.

In *Dahl*, as in this case, each party moved for summary judgment on the plaintiff's equal protection claim and both offered evidence in support of their respective motions. The *Dahl* court considered the parties' respective burdens of production under Rule 56 as to the policy's rationality or irrationality under the *Heller* standard, and concluded:

> If the evidence, construed in the light most favorable to defendants, shows that there is *no* reasonably conceivable rational basis for the homosexual exclusion policy, and the court cannot conceive of a rational basis (i.e. because it is based solely on illegitimate prejudice), then plaintiff is entitled to summary judgment. Alternatively, if the evidence, construed in the light most favorable to plaintiff, shows that there is *any* reasonably conceivable rational basis for the policy, then defendants are entitled to summary judgment. Finally, if the evidence creates a disputed issue of material fact as to the policy's rationality, then neither party is entitled to summary judgment.

Dahl, 830 F.Supp. at 1327. This Court agrees that this is the proper standard to be applied in evaluating the parties' cross-motions for summary judgment on plaintiff's equal protection claim.

c. ORIENTATION V. CONDUCT. The undisputed evidence in the record establishes that Cammermeyer was discharged from military service *solely* because she admitted her homosexual orientation. The Government argues, nevertheless, that Cammermeyer's admission that she is a lesbian is reliable evidence of her propensity to engage in homosexual conduct. The Government's position, in sum, is that homosexual "orientation" is equivalent to homosexual "conduct." This is a critical issue for plaintiff because the parties acknowledge for purposes of this litigation that, under *Bowers v. Hardwick*, 478 U.S. 186, 106 S.Ct. 2841, 92 L.Ed.2d 140 (1986),[10] and *Pruitt*, 963 F.2d at 1165, the government may exclude individuals from military service on the basis of homosexual conduct.

The Government cites *Ben-Shalom v. Marsh*, 881 F.2d 454, 464 (7th Cir. 1989), cert. denied, 494 U.S. 1004, 110 S.Ct. 1296, 108 L.Ed.2d 473 (1990), as support for its position that acknowledgment of homosexual orientation can "rationally and reasonably be viewed as reliable evidence of a desire and propensity to engage in homosexual conduct." In *Ben-Shalom*, plaintiff Miriam Ben-Shalom, a sergeant in the Army Reserve, admitted that she was a lesbian. As a result of this admission, she was discharged from the Army Reserve pursuant to Army Regulation 135-178,[11] which provided for the discharge of any servicemember who "evidenced homosexual tendencies, desire or interest, but is without overt homosexual acts." The trial court found no reason to believe that the plaintiff's admission that she was a lesbian meant the plaintiff was likely to commit homosexual acts, and ordered injunctive relief in plaintiff's favor. The Seventh Circuit reversed, holding that Ben-Shalom's "lesbian acknowledgment, if not an admission of its practice, at least can rationally and reasonably be viewed as reliable evidence" of a desire or propensity to engage in homosexual conduct. *Id.* at 464. The *Ben-Shalom* court, relying on *Bowers*, denied relief, holding that the Army regulation promoted a legitimate governmental interest sufficient to survive rational basis scrutiny. The Government's reliance on *Ben-Shalom*, and other cases cited in the defendants' Opposition to Plaintiff's Motion for Summary Judgment (docket no. 75) at 5, is misplaced.

The Ninth Circuit has recognized a distinction between homosexual status or orientation and conduct. In *Pruitt*, the plaintiff was discharged from the Army because of her public acknowledgment in a newspaper interview that she is a homosexual. She subsequently brought an action to challenge the same Army regulation at issue in this case. The Government argued, citing several cases, that its right to discharge homosexual servicemembers was so firmly supported in the law that any equal protection claim asserted by Pruitt was legally insufficient on its face. In rejecting this argument, the Ninth Circuit distinguished these prior cases, including *Bowers* and other cases relying on *Bowers*, as cases "relating to conduct, not orientation." *Pruitt*, 963 F.2d at 1165-66 n. 4 and 5.[12]

Supreme Court precedents have also recognized a status-conduct distinction in other contexts. In *Robinson v. California*, 370 U.S. 660, 82 S.Ct. 1417, 8 L.Ed.2d 758 (1962), the Court struck down a statute criminalizing "status" as a drug addict, absent evidence of drug use, as a violation of the Eighth Amendment prohibition against cruel and unusual punishment. Similarly, in *Powell v. Texas*, 392 U.S. 514, 532, 88 S.Ct. 2145, 20 L.Ed.2d 1254 (1968), the Court upheld a conviction for drinking in public but disapproved of arrests based solely on status as a chronic alcoholic. Furthermore, Supreme Court precedents prohibit presumptions of criminal conduct based on orientation. See *Jacobson v. United States*, 503 U.S. ___, 112 S.Ct. 1535, 118 L.Ed.2d 174 (1992) (prior conduct does not demonstrate a propensity to engage in identical conduct later made illegal); *Aptheker v. Secretary of State*, 378 U.S. 500, 501-2, 84 S.Ct. 1659, 12 L.Ed.2d 992, 995 (1964)(government may not deny member of Communist Party right to travel based on statutory presumption the individual will compromise national security). These cases stand for the proposition that status and conduct are distinct, and that it is inherently unreasonable to presume that a certain class of person will violate the law solely because of their orientation or status.

The status-conduct distinction is particularly relevant in the military context, where homosexual conduct by servicemembers is not just discouraged, but is grounds for discipline and, if the conduct is sodomy, criminal charges. The Court notes that the military does not make similar presumptions with regard to other groups.[13]

Plaintiff has also provided the Court with substantial uncontroverted evidence that a distinction between homosexual orientation and homosexual conduct is well grounded in fact. According to Dr. Herek,[14] "no data exist to indicate that lesbians and gay men are less capable than heterosexuals of controlling their sexual or romantic urges, refraining from the abuse of power, or exercising good judgment in handling authority." Herek Decl., ¶ 14. Dr. Herek also states that a person's public identification of his or her sexual orientation does not necessarily imply sexual conduct, past or present, or a future desire for sexual behavior. *Id.* ¶ 8. The plaintiff also relies on the testimony of Dr. Laura S. Brown,[15] who testified that "[t]here is almost no relationship between an individual's orientation and his or her sexual conduct." Brown Decl., ¶ 21. Brown also testified that homosexuals are more likely to control their sexual urges than heterosexuals because they have less opportunity to express their sexuality and have to exercise great discretion in choosing settings and persons who are likely to be receptive, and circumstances that are not likely to result in career problems. Brown Decl., ¶ 22.

Significantly, the very policy challenged by plaintiff in this case recognizes a distinction between orientation and conduct. Dr. Lawrence J. Korb, the former Assistant Secretary of Defense (Manpower, Reserve Affairs, Installation and Logistics) who was responsible for implementing the policy at issue in this case, testified by declaration that:

> As the policy clearly states, the purpose was to authorize the military to discharge gay servicemembers who demonstrate a propensity to engage in homosexual conduct. The policy was never intended to authorize the military to discharge someone simply based on his or her status—absent any evidence of conduct. To the contrary, conduct was the real focus of the policy.
>
> A servicemember's own admission of being gay—absent any indication of her propensity to engage in homosexual conduct—is simply not sufficient grounds for discharging her under the existing policy. Discharging someone based on his or her status is irrational and has no basis in furthering the military mission. The policy I authorized should not be construed as authorizing such an irrational outcome.

Korb, Decl., ¶ 5.

The Court concludes that plaintiff's acknowledgment of her lesbian orientation itself is not reliable evidence of her desire or propensity to engage in homosexual conduct. The Court therefore concludes that there is no rational basis for the Government's underlying contention that homosexual orientation equals "desire or propensity to engage" in homosexual conduct.

3. Rational Review Analysis of the Equal Protection Claim

Plaintiff was discharged from service in the Washington State National Guard pursuant to Army Regulation 135-175 and Department of Defense ("DOD") Directives 1332.14 and 1332.30, 32 C.F.R. Part 41, Appendix A, 46 Fed.

Reg. 9571 (Jan. 29, 1981). Army Regulation 135-175 defines homosexual as "a person, regardless of sex, who engages in, desires to engage in, or intends to engage in homosexual acts." 32 C.F.R. Part 41, Appendix A, 46 Fed. Reg. 9571, 9577 (January 29, 1981). The regulation requires the discharge of any member of the service who has: (1) "engaged in, attempted to engage in, or solicited another to engage in a homosexual act;"[16] or (2) "stated that he or she is a homosexual or bisexual unless there is a further finding that the member is not a homosexual or bisexual." *Id.*, 46 Fed. Reg. 9571, 9577-78. The plain language of the regulation makes clear that the policy targets not only individuals who engage in homosexual conduct but also individuals who merely acknowledge their homosexual orientation. This litigation does not challenge the classification of persons who engage in homosexual conduct, and the constitutionality of laws forbidding such conduct is not at issue here. Rather, this litigation concerns the exclusion of homosexual status or orientation.

The Government contends that the rational basis for the Army's policy of excluding homosexuals is evident from the policy itself and from legislative findings made in connection with the military's new "don't ask, don't tell" policy, effective November 1993. Because the policy is rational on its face, the Government argues, no further judicial inquiry into the policy's rationality is necessary or appropriate.

The regulation, at 32 C.F.R. Part 41.13, provides that homosexuality is incompatible with military service. The regulation provides that the presence of homosexuals in the military environment: (1) seriously impairs the accomplishment of the military mission; (2) adversely affects the ability of the armed forces to maintain discipline, good order and morale; (3) seriously impairs the military's ability to foster mutual trust and confidence among servicemembers; (4) adversely affects the military's ability to insure the integrity of the system of rank and command; (5) impairs the military's ability to facilitate assignment and worldwide deployment of servicemembers who frequently must live and work under close conditions affording minimal privacy; (6) adversely affects the military's ability to recruit and retain members of the armed forces; (7) adversely affects the ability of the armed forces to maintain the public acceptability of military service; and (8) seriously impairs the military's ability to prevent breaches of security. 46 Fed. Reg. 9571, 9577 (January 29, 1981).

Recently, Congress made fifteen express findings in support of its new policy concerning homosexuals in the armed forces. See 10 U.S.C. § 654(a)(1)-(15). The Government argues that these findings also support the exclusion from military service of "persons who demonstrate a propensity or intent to engage in homosexual acts" under the policy at issue in this case.[17] One such finding, cited by the Government, is that the presence of such persons in the military "would create an unacceptable risk to the high standards of morale, good order and discipline, and unit cohesion that are the essence of military capability." 10 U.S.C. § 654(a)(15).

Notwithstanding the Government's arguments to the contrary, this Court is not required to accept the justification in the regulation or the legislative findings at face value. Rather, the Court must determine if these justifications provide a rational basis for the challenged policy. Both parties have submitted substantial evidence concerning the rationality or irrationality of the military's policy. Under these circumstances, the Court should review the entire record to determine whether the proffered bases for the Government's policy are rational or motivated solely by prejudice against homosexuals.

The Government relies heavily upon the professional military judgment of this country's military leaders that the presence of homosexuals in the military will adversely affect the morale, good order and discipline of the military. The Government cites the testimony of General Colin Powell in hearings before the Senate Armed Service Committee in July 1993 that:

> Open homosexuality in units is not just the acceptance of benign characteristics such as race or color or background. It involves matters of privacy and human sexuality that, in our judgment, if allowed to exist in the force would affect the cohesion and well-being of the force.

Hearing to Receive Testimony on DOD Policy on Service of Gay Men and Lesbians in the Armed Forces: Hearing Before the Senate Armed Services Comm., 103d Cong., 1st Sess.(July 20, 1993)(hereinafter *"Senate Hearing"*), Glass Decl., Ex. T, at 25. The Government also relies on the testimony of various military officials who testified before the Armed Services Committee, including Generals Mundy, Sullivan, and McPeak, Admiral Kelso, and former Secretary of Defense Les Aspin. See Glass Decl., Ex. T, at 29-37, 86, and 94. The Court concludes, however, that the testimony of these officials merely restates the justifications listed in the Army regulation.

Most notably, the defendants offer the Rule 30(b)(6) deposition testimony of Major General John P. Otjen and former Assistant Secretary of Defense Edwin Dorn. General Otjen was a member of the Military Working Group ("MWG") that studied the issue of homosexuals in the military and reported its findings to the Secretary of Defense in June, 1993.[18] See Summary Report of Military Working Group (hereinafter "MWG Report"), at 5-7, Otjen Dep., Ex. 10. General Otjen testified that allowing homosexuals in the military would adversely affect unit cohesion[19] and morale. Otjen Dep. 188:5-190:4, 192:19-201:1, 263:10-265:3. Assistant Secretary Dorn testified similarly. General Otjen testified, based on his experience, the experience of members of the MWG, and the experiences of servicemembers who spoke to the MWG, that when a unit is "confronted with a homosexual situation—for lack of a better description—that there is a casting out, if you will, of the individual." See Otjen Dep., 194:4-9. Otjen testified that this "casting out," which can destroy unit cohesion, occurs because the persons doing the casting out are afraid of or prejudiced against the homosexual person or feel "let down," "out of surprise." See Otjen Dep., 196:14-197:4.

The Government's evidence offers justifications for the policy of excluding homosexuals from military service. Under *Heller*, 125 L.Ed.2d at 271, the burden is on the plaintiff "to negative every conceivable basis which might support" the government's policy. To meet this burden, plaintiff offers evidence to the effect that the rationale, as stated in the Army Regulation and advanced by the Government, has no factual foundation, is contradicted by the government's own studies and evidence, and is based solely on prejudice against homosexuals.

a. INCOMPATIBILITY WITH MILITARY SERVICE AND INTERFERENCE WITH MILITARY MISSION. Plaintiff offers evidence that homosexuality is compatible with military service, and in fact, a large number of homosexuals have served and continue to serve in the military with distinction. Plaintiff cites the statements of President Clinton that, "there have been and are homosexuals in the military who serve with distinction" and "there is no study showing them to be less capable or more prone to misconduct." Himes Dec., Ex. 4. Plaintiff also offers the statement of Vice Admiral Joseph S. Donnell, the Commander of the Navy's surface Atlantic Fleet, describing his experience with lesbian servicemembers as follows: "Experience has . . . shown that the stereotypical female homosexual in the Navy is hardworking, career-oriented, willing to put in long hours on the job and among the command's top professionals." Foote Decl., Ex. A.

Plaintiff also relies upon numerous military and government studies, such as the 1957 study popularly known as the "Crittenden Report," and a more recent study, commissioned by the military and performed by the Defense Personnel Security Research and Education Center (PERSEREC), known as the PERSEREC Report. These studies establish that gays and lesbians not only serve in the military, but also that the majority of them do so without incident and receive honorable discharges at the conclusion of their service. See *Report of the Board Appointed to Prepare and Submit Recommendations to the Secretary of the Navy for the Revision of Policies, Procedures and Directives Dealing with Homosexuals in the Military*, Himes Decl., Ex. 5 (hereinafter "Crittenden Report"); and Sarbin & Karols, *Nonconforming Sexual Orientations and Military Suitability* (1988), Himes Decl., Ex. 6 (hereinafter PERSEREC Report).

Plaintiff also offers evidence concerning the experience of foreign countries, such as Canada, Australia, France, Israel, Spain, Sweden, the Netherlands, Denmark, Finland, Norway, and Japan, all of which allow homosexuals to serve in their armed forces. It is undisputed that the United States Government has commissioned studies of these militaries, and those studies have concluded that "the presence of homosexuals in the military is not an issue and has not created problems in the functioning of military units." See *Homosexuals in the Military: Policies and Practice of Foreign Countries* (1993), Himes Decl., Ex. 8, at 3 (hereinafter "GAO Report"). See also the "RAND Report," *Sexual Orientation and U.S. Military Personnel Policy: Options and Assessment*. Himes Decl., Ex. 9, at 65-104 (hereinafter "RAND Report")(homosexuals pose no special problems in foreign militaries).

b. EFFECT ON DISCIPLINE, GOOD ORDER, AND MORALE. Plaintiff offers evidence demonstrating that this justification is based solely on prejudice.

President Clinton has stated that "most military people [are] opposed to lifting the ban because of the feared impact on unit cohesion, rooted in disapproval of homosexual lifestyles," and "those who oppose lifting the ban are clearly focused not on the conduct of individual gay servicemembers, but on how nongay servicemembers feel about gays in general and, in particular, those in the military service." Himes Decl., Ex. 4. Plaintiff also notes that this rationale, as well as virtually every other justification used today to exclude homosexuals from military service, was also used to justify the military's discrimination against African Americans in World War II. Herek Decl. at ¶¶ 19-22, Ex. I. There is no dispute that the exclusion of African Americans from military service was based solely on prejudice.

c. UNIT COHESION. Plaintiff relies on the comprehensive analysis of the impact of homosexual servicemembers on unit cohesion contained in the RAND Report. The RAND Report concludes:

> At present, there is no scientific evidence regarding the effects of acknowledged homosexuals on a unit's cohesion and combat effectiveness. Thus, any attempt to predict the consequences of allowing them to serve in the U.S. military is necessarily speculative.

RAND Report, Himes Decl., Ex. 9, at 283.

d. RANK AND COMMAND. Plaintiff argues that there is no evidence supporting the defendants' contention that the presence of homosexuals in the military will be detrimental to the military's rank and command structure. Plaintiff offers a statement by the Chief of Naval Personnel in a 1976 memorandum to the Judge Advocate General that, "no empirical proof exists at this time [to support the Navy's contention that] homosexuality has an adverse effect upon the completion of the [military] mission." See *Meinhold v. United States Dep't of Defense*, 808 F. Supp. 1455, 1457 (C.D. Cal. 1993). Plaintiff also cites the Crittenden Report, which found that there is no "visible supporting data [to support the conclusion that gays and lesbians] cannot acceptably serve in the military." Crittenden Report, Himes Decl., Ex. 5, at 5. Finally, plaintiff offers government-commissioned reports on foreign militaries. These reports have concluded, "in all cases where a decision has been made to include homosexuals in the [foreign military] force, the organization's leaders believe that the force's organizational performance is unaffected by that presence." RAND Report, Himes Decl., Ex. 9, at 15; Korb Decl. at 9-10; GAO Report, Himes Decl., Ex. 8, at 3.

e. PRIVACY. Plaintiff has submitted substantial evidence refuting the privacy rationale. Plaintiff offers, for example, the PERSEREC Report which concludes that concerns regarding homosexuals invading the privacy of heterosexuals are unfounded because homosexuals, like heterosexuals, are "selective in their choice of intimate partners and in their expression of sexual behavior" and are selective "in observing rules of privacy, in considering appropriateness of time and place, in connecting sexuality with the tender sentiments, and so on." Himes Decl., Ex. 6, at 31.

f. RECRUITMENT AND RETENTION OF MILITARY PERSONNEL. According to plaintiff's expert, Dr. Lawrence Korb, the Assistant Secretary of Defense who was directly responsible for military personnel matters between 1981 and 1985, there is no evidence supporting the defendants' assertion that allowing homosexuals to serve in the military will adversely affect recruitment and retention of military personnel. Korb Decl. at 7. The RAND Report similarly concludes that lifting the ban would likely have no effect on recruitment and only nominal effect on reenlistment. Himes Decl., Ex. 9, at 397-407.

g. PUBLIC DISAPPROVAL OF HOMOSEXUALS IN THE MILITARY. Plaintiff submits the RAND Report, which found that depending upon how the question is phrased, approximately 40-79% of the public favors allowing homosexuals to serve in the military. Himes Decl., Ex. 9, at 201-02. Public polls have yielded similar results. Herek Decl. at ¶ 16; Korb Decl. at 6-7. In any event, to the extent public disapproval of homosexual service in the military is based on prejudice, such disapproval would not be a legitimate basis for the government's policy. See *Cleburne*, 473 U.S. at 448, 87 L.Ed.2d at 326.

h. SECURITY RISK. Plaintiff argues that there is no factual support for the security risk rationale.[20] Former Defense Secretary Cheney has essentially admitted this by acknowledging that the military's argument that homosexuals are greater security risks than heterosexuals is a "bit of an old chestnut." Himes Decl., Ex. 14; *Meinhold*, 808 F. Supp. at 1457. See also the Crittenden Report, Himes Decl., Ex. 5, at 6; PERSEREC Report, Himes Decl., Ex. 6; Korb Decl., at 6; Brigadier General Evelyn Foote Decl., ¶ 34.

Plaintiff has successfully met her burden of negating the proffered justifications for the government's policy of excluding homosexuals from service by offering uncontroverted evidence that the individual justifications either have no basis in fact or are based solely on prejudice. The Government, for its part, has failed to offer any evidence showing that its justifications are based on anything but prejudice.

An examination of the record demonstrates that the sole motivation for the exclusion of acknowledged homosexuals from military service is prejudice. President Clinton has admitted that opposition to lifting the ban on homosexual service is "rooted in disapproval of homosexual lifestyles," and based on "the fear of invasion of privacy of heterosexual soldiers" and "how nongay servicemembers feel about gays in general and, in particular, those in the military service." Himes Decl., Ex. 4.[21] General Colin Powell has also admitted in testimony before Congress that the policy was originally implemented more than ten years ago "[i]n simple language, to keep homosexuals out of the service." Glass Decl., Ex. T, at 111. Dr. Lawrence Korb, the former Assistant Secretary of Defense who was responsible for implementing the policy at issue in this case, testified that:

> Based on my experience in the Pentagon, as a long-time student of national defense policy, and as a retired Navy Captain, I am of the

opinion that there is no longer any justification for the armed services' current ban on homosexuals serving in the military. As detailed below, each of the justifications offered in support of this policy is without factual foundation. Moreover, there is substantial evidence that gays and lesbians have served and continue to serve their country as ably as heterosexuals. Sexual orientation simply does not provide a rational basis upon which to exclude a person from military service. On the other hand, to the extent that sexual *misconduct* threatens to undermine the discipline, good order, and morale that is critical to the accomplishment of the military mission, such misconduct can be and is adequately addressed through existing regulations which prohibit such misconduct whether committed by homosexuals or heterosexuals.

Korb Decl. ¶ 6. The uncontroverted evidence establishes that many homosexuals have served, and currently serve, in the military, and that the majority of them do so without incident and receive honorable discharges at the conclusion of their service. See Crittenden Report, Himes Decl., Ex. 5; PERSEREC Report, Himes Decl., Ex. 6; Remarks by President Clinton at National Defense University, Himes Decl., Ex. 4; Testimony of General Colin Powell, *Senate Hearing*, Glass Decl., Ex. T, at 23.

The testimony of defendants' own witnesses further demonstrates that the policy is rooted solely in prejudice. Both General Otjen and former Assistant Secretary of Defense Dorn admitted in their depositions that the defendants have *no facts* supporting any of the stated rationales.[22] See Otjen Dep., at 54, 68-79, 287-91, 307-14; Dorn Dep., at 190-92 (as to new policy), 199-200 (as to old policy). In addition, and more compelling, both witnesses testified to the effect that the government's objection to homosexual service is based solely on the fears and prejudices of heterosexual servicemembers.

General Otjen was asked hypothetically whether, if everyone in the military had no fear or prejudice against homosexuals and did not morally disapprove of the homosexual lifestyle, there would be any problem with unit cohesion in the military as a result of permitting open homosexuals to serve. See Otjen Dep., at 226:2-10. While General Otjen had difficulty accepting this assumption, he agreed that if that assumption were true, there would be no problem with unit cohesion. See Otjen Dep., at 226:4-233:13; see also Otjen Dep., at 192:3-15, 234:8-237:14, 262, 263-264:14, 264:15-266:3 (testifying to the same effect regarding the rank and command, privacy, morale, and retention rationales). General Otjen also admitted during his deposition that he had no facts to support the finding in the MWG's Report that "the presence of open homosexuals would in general polarize and fragment the unit and destroy the bonding and singleness of purpose required for effective military operation." See Otjen Dep., at 192:19-193:5.

Former Assistant Secretary of Defense Dorn testified similarly. For example, Dorn admitted that he was accurately quoted as saying, "[a]s with the racial desegregation of the military, much of the resistance to gays is grounded in fear and in prejudice." See Dorn Dep., at 133:3-9, Ex. 7, at 3. Secretary Dorn also testified that the problems with unit cohesion and rank and command cited in the policy were based on anticipated negative reactions of heterosexual servicemembers to homosexuals and a "general spirit of ill ease within the unit." See Dorn Dep., at 197:1-4; 221:12-17; 225:3-12. Although Dorn emphasized that the policy excluding homosexuals from service was based on the personal experiences of military professionals with open homosexuals in their units, he admitted that the sum of these personal experiences was that "many individual soldiers don't want to be around gays." Dorn Dep., at 194:14-18. Other problems with homosexual service cited by Dorn, such as lovers' quarrels, involve matters of homosexual conduct, rather than homosexual orientation or status. Dorn Dep., at 196:10-14. See also Dorn Dep., at 159:7-14; 186:12-21.

Defendants' argument that the Army regulation banning homosexuals from service is based on rational, nonprejudicial reasons is unpersuasive. Defendants' military experts have conceded that their justifications for the policy are based on heterosexual servicemembers' fear and dislike of homosexuals. Mere negative attitudes, or fear, are constitutionally impermissible bases for discriminatory governmental policies. *Cleburne*, 473 U.S. at 448, 87 L.Ed.2d at 326. Unsubstantiated presumptions concerning a particular group also constitute prejudice and cannot serve as the rational basis for a discriminatory governmental policy. Thus, to the extent the Government's policy is based on the unfounded presumption that servicemembers with a homosexual orientation will engage in proscribed homosexual conduct,[23] the policy is not rationally based. This Court cannot defer to military decisions based solely on prejudice against a particular group. *Id.* The defendants have not submitted any evidence that supports any other basis for the policy.

Certainly, the undisputed evidence in this case relating to Colonel Cammermeyer's service strongly supports the conclusion that acknowledged homosexuality is not incompatible with military service. Cammermeyer served in the Army and the Washington State National Guard with distinction. She was a highly trained, decorated and dedicated officer in the military. The events that gave rise to her discharge involved her quest to achieve the position of Chief Nurse of the National Guard Bureau. After she disclosed her lesbian status in April 1989, she continued to perform her military duties for over three years until her discharge. Her final evaluation, dated July 31, 1992, provides in part that, "[t]his officer is exemplary in her dedication," that she "has clearly demonstrated outstanding administrative and technical skills" and that "Colonel Cammermeyer's strong leadership has been a key element in improving WAARNG medical readiness." Cammermeyer Decl., Ex. D, at 1-3. The rating officer described Cammermeyer in the professionalism section of her final evaluation as "the most knowledgeable military nurse with whom I have had the pleasure to work," and the senior rater described her as having continued to serve the Washington Army National Guard "with dedicated professionalism." It is ironic that after over three years as an acknowledged homosexual servicemember, Cammermeyer was evaluated as having "the potential to assume responsibility at NGB level as Chief Nurse," yet she was discharged because of the alleged incompatibility of her sexual orientation with military service. *Id.*

In conclusion, viewing all the evidence in the light most favorable to the Government, the Court must conclude that the rationales offered by the Government to justify its exclusion of homosexual servicemembers are grounded solely in prejudice. Under *Palmore* and *Cleburne*, this is impermissible. A cardinal principle of equal protection law is that the federal government cannot discriminate against a class in order to give effect to the prejudice of others. The government has discriminated against Colonel Cammermeyer solely on the basis of her status as a homosexual and has failed to demonstrate a rational basis for doing so. The Court holds that plaintiff's discharge pursuant to the regulation banning homosexuals who merely acknowledge their orientation violates plaintiff's equal protection rights under the Fifth Amendment, and the Court grants summary judgment in favor of plaintiff and against defendants on this claim.

B. Substantive Due Process Claim

Defendants also move for summary judgment on plaintiff's claim that Army Regulation 135-175 violates the due process clause of the Fifth Amendment. Plaintiff claims that the regulation "mandates discharge solely upon an admission of homosexuality, without any nexus between homosexual status and the ability to perform the work duties and responsibilities of the Armed Forces." Complaint at ¶ 6.3. Plaintiff did not move for summary judgment on this issue; however, the parties have briefed and argued the issue. The Court concludes that the issue has been fully and fairly addressed by the parties, and thus the Court may consider the issue as if cross-motions for summary judgment were presented. See *Cool Fuel, Inc. v. Connett*, 685 F.2d 309, 311 (9th Cir. 1982).

1. Standard of Review

The due process clause of the Fifth Amendment provides that no person shall "be deprived of life, liberty, or property, without due process of law." U.S. Const. amend. V. The due process clause contains both substantive and procedural components. The procedural component requires the government to follow appropriate procedures whenever its agents decide to deprive any person of life, liberty or property. *Daniels v. Williams*, 474 U.S. 327, 106 S.Ct. 662, 665, 88 L.Ed.2d 662 (1986)(discussing due process clause of Fourteenth Amendment). The due process clause also "contains a substantive component, sometimes referred to as 'substantive due process,' which bars certain arbitrary government actions 'regardless of the fairness of the procedures used to implement them.'" *Id.* at 337, 106 S.Ct. at 678, 88 L.Ed.2d at 672 (Stevens, J., concurring). The substantive due process clause "serves to prevent governmental power from being 'used for purposes of oppression.'" *Id.* at 331, 106 S.Ct. at 665, 88 L.Ed.2d at 668 (quoting *Murray's Lessee v. Hoboken*

Land & Improvement Co., 18 How. 272, 277, 15 L.Ed. 372 (1856)). Plaintiff's challenge to Army Regulation 135-175 is based on the substantive component of the due process clause.

Federal regulations that infringe upon personal rights may be challenged on either substantive due process or equal protection grounds. Although courts approach equal protection and due process analyses differently, there are similarities in the doctrines:

> When conduct, either by virtue of its inadequate foundation in the continuing traditions of our society or for some other reason, such as lack of connection with interests recognized as private and protected, is subject to some government regulation, then analysis under the substantive due process clause proceeds in much the same way as analysis under the lowest tier of equal protection scrutiny. A rational relation to a legitimate government interest will normally suffice to uphold the regulation. At the other extreme, where the government seriously intrudes into matters which lie at the core of interests which deserve due process protection, then the compelling state interest test employed in equal protection cases may be used by the Court to describe the appropriate due process analysis.

Beller, 632 F.2d at 808 (citing *Roe v. Wade*, 410 U.S. 113, 155, 93 S.Ct. 705, 727, 35 L.Ed.2d 147 (1973); *Griswold v. Connecticut*, 381 U.S. 479, 497, 85 S.Ct. 1678, 1688, 14 L.Ed.2d 510 (1965)(Goldberg, J., concurring); *Skinner v. Oklahoma*, 316 U.S. 535, 541, 62 S.Ct. 1110, 1113, 86 L.Ed. 1655 (1942)). Thus, when a classification penalizes the exercise of a fundamental constitutional right, heightened scrutiny is required. *Reno v. Flores*, 507 U.S. ___, 113 S.Ct. 1439; 123 L.Ed.2d 1, 16 (1993); *High Tech Gays*, 895 F.2d at 572. On the other hand, where a regulation impairs a lesser interest, there need only be a rational relationship between the challenged regulation and a legitimate governmental purpose. *Flores*, 123 L.Ed.2d at 18.

2. Due Process Analysis

Plaintiff asks this Court to hold that the Constitution confers a fundamental right of privacy upon a person to be a homosexual.[24] The United States Constitution does not explicitly mention any right of privacy. The Supreme Court has previously recognized, however, that one aspect of "liberty" protected by the due process clause is "a right of personal privacy, or a guarantee of certain areas or zones of privacy." *Roe*, 410 U.S. at 152. See also *Carey v. Population Services International*, 431 U.S. 678, 97 S.Ct. 2010, 52 L.Ed.2d 675 (1977). The Court has recognized, for example, a right of privacy in personal decisions relating to marriage, contraception, procreation, family relationships and child rearing, education and abortion. *Carey*, 431 U.S. at 685, 52 L.Ed.2d at 684. The Supreme Court has refused, however, to find a fundamental right of privacy to engage in homosexual sodomy. *Bowers*, 478 U.S. at 192, 92 L.Ed.2d at 146-47.

In seeking to identify constitutional rights entitled to heightened judicial scrutiny, the Supreme Court has limited these rights to rights that are "deeply rooted in this Nation's history and traditions," *Moore v. East Cleveland*, 431 U.S. 494, 503, 97 S.Ct. 1932, 1938, 52 L.Ed.2d 531 (1977), or liberties that are "implicit in the concept of ordered liberty" such that "neither liberty nor justice would exist if they were sacrificed." *Palko v. Connecticut*, 302 U.S. 319, 325-26, 58 S.Ct. 149, 152, 82 L.Ed. 288 (1937). Although plaintiff raises an important issue, it is not clear that either of these formulations would confer a fundamental right of privacy to be a homosexual. Moreover, plaintiff concedes that no court has ever found a fundamental right to be, and to identify oneself as, a homosexual.[25]

The Court need not decide whether plaintiff has a fundamental right to be a homosexual in order to resolve her substantive due process claim. The Court has already held that the Army regulation challenged here is based solely on prejudice. As such, it cannot withstand even rational basis review. Regulations based solely on prejudice are irrational as a matter of law and serve no legitimate governmental purpose.

The Government argues that plaintiff's substantive due process claim is foreclosed by *Woodward v. United States*, 871 F.2d 1068 (Fed. Cir. 1989), cert. denied, 494 U.S. 1003, 110 S.Ct. 1295, 108 L.Ed.2d 473 (1990). The Government contends that *Woodward*, like the present case, is a homosexual status case, and thus the *Woodward* court's rejection of the plaintiff's substantive due process claim in that case applies here. In *Woodward*, a Naval Reserve officer contended that homosexuality was protected under the constitutional right of privacy, and thus the Navy could not, consistent with the Fifth Amendment, discharge him on the basis of his homosexuality. In analyzing plaintiff's privacy claim, the Court noted that although Woodward had not admitted to homosexual conduct, he had stated that "he was attracted sexually to, or desired sexual activity with, members of his own sex." *Id.* at 1074 n. 6. In view of these admissions, the *Woodward* court distinguished plaintiff's case from cases involving discharge solely on the basis of status.[26] Thus, *Woodward* is not solely a homosexual status case, and the case is distinguishable on those grounds.[27]

The Court holds that plaintiff's Fifth Amendment substantive due process rights were violated by her discharge under Army Regulation 135-175. The Army's discharge of Cammermeyer based solely on her admission of homosexual orientation was not rationally related to the Government's legitimate interest in maintaining the readiness and combat effectiveness of its military forces. The defendants' motion for summary judgment on this claim is denied and the plaintiff is granted summary judgment on this claim.

C. First Amendment Claim

Defendants move for summary judgment on plaintiff's claim that the policy banning homosexuals from military service violates her right to freedom of speech and association. The Court concludes that this claim is foreclosed by controlling Ninth Circuit precedent. The Ninth Circuit has held that servicemembers' challenges to military regulations requiring discharge of homosexuals based on the individual's statement that he or she is a homosexual do not implicate First Amendment concerns; the servicemember is not being discharged for his or her speech, but rather for his or her status as a homosexual. See *Pruitt*, 963 F.2d at 1163-64; *Schowengerdt v. United States*, 944 F.2d 483, 489 (9th Cir. 1991), cert. denied, 112 S.Ct. 1514, 117 L.Ed.2d 650 (1992).

In *Pruitt*, an Army Reserve officer challenged on First Amendment grounds the Army Regulations mandating her involuntary discharge for admitting she was a lesbian. Plaintiff contended that her discharge was based on public statements to a newspaper reporter that she was a lesbian, which she argued was protected expression. *Pruitt*, 963 F.2d at 1163. The court rejected plaintiff's First Amendment arguments, holding that Pruitt was not discharged under Army regulations for her speech, but rather for her status as a homosexual. The court noted that "Pruitt's admission, like most admissions, was made in speech, but that does not mean that the First Amendment precludes the use of the admission as evidence of the facts admitted." *Id.* at 1164.

Similarly, in *Schowengerdt*, a Naval Reserve officer who was also a civilian employee of the Navy, challenged on First Amendment grounds his discharge from the Navy. Schowengerdt's discharge was based on his admission of bisexuality, and certain written materials describing his bisexual activities discovered during a search of his office. *Schowengerdt*, 944 F.2d at 485. The court held that Schowengerdt's discharge did not violate the First Amendment because "he was not discharged for writing about bisexuality but rather for *being* a bisexual, of which his purely private correspondence was evidence." *Id.* at 489.

Plaintiff cites no precedent in support of her claim under the First Amendment. Further, every court that has addressed this issue has refused to grant relief on First Amendment grounds. See, e.g., *Ben-Shalom*, 881 F.2d at 462; *Dahl*, 830 F.Supp. at 1338. The Court therefore grants defendants' motion for summary judgment on this claim.

D. Other Claims

Plaintiff's complaint asserts two additional claims: first, that Army Regulation 135-175 is an invalid exercise of executive power, in violation of the doctrine of separation of powers; second, that Army Regulation 135-175 violates the principles of federalism because the United States Constitution reserves to the State of Washington the power to appoint officers in the Washington State National Guard. The Court construes plaintiff's failure to respond to defendants' motion for summary judgment on these claims as a concession that these claims are without merit and therefore grants defendants' motion as to these claims.

E. Conclusions

All who had the opportunity to serve with Margarethe Cammermeyer agree that she was an outstanding officer and Army Nurse. Her care and professionalism in performing her duties earned her numerous awards and distinctions, including the Bronze Star Medal for distinguished service in Vietnam. Undoubtedly, Colonel Cammermeyer would have continued to serve in the Washington State National Guard, earning the continued respect and admiration of her peers, had she not applied for a top secret clearance to gain admission to the Army War College, and admitted in response to a direct question during her clearance interview that she is a lesbian. That admission led to her discharge from military service.

Colonel Cammermeyer was discharged from the National Guard pursuant to a governmental policy that is based solely on prejudice. Prejudice, whether founded on unsubstantiated fears, cultural myths, stereotypes or erroneous assumptions, cannot be the basis for a discriminatory classification. *Cleburne*, 473 U.S. at 448. As the Supreme Court stated in *Palmore*, 466 U.S. at 433, "[p]rivate biases may be outside the reach of the law, but the law cannot, directly or indirectly, give them effect." Plaintiff is therefore entitled to judgment as a matter of law on her equal protection and substantive due process claims under the Fifth Amendment. Plaintiff is entitled to summary judgment against defendants on her first and third claims and for judgment as follows:

a. For an order requiring defendants to reinstate her to her former position in the Washington State National Guard and to restore to her all rights, honors and privileges of that status;

b. For an order requiring defendants to expunge all record of plaintiff's sexual orientation and her statements, if any, regarding same from any and all records in defendants' possession;

c. For an order enjoining defendants from taking any adverse action against plaintiff by reason of her homosexual status or on account of statements of her homosexual orientation;

d. For an order enjoining defendants from taking any action against plaintiff based on the purported authority of directives or regulations mandating separation from military service by reason of homosexual status or on account of statements of homosexual orientation;

e. For a declaration that defendants' action in separating plaintiff from military service based solely on her declaration of homosexual orientation was unconstitutional;

f. For a declaration that defendants' regulation mandating separation from service by reason of homosexual status or on account of statements of homosexual orientation is unconstitutional; and

g. Costs of suit.

Defendants are entitled to judgment dismissing plaintiff's second, fourth, fifth and sixth claims.

The Clerk of the Court is directed to enter judgment in accordance with this Order.

IT IS SO ORDERED.

DATED this 1st day of June, 1994.

THOMAS S. ZILLY

UNITED STATES DISTRICT JUDGE

NOTES

1. Although William J. Perry is now the Secretary of Defense, he has not yet been formally substituted as a named defendant.

2. Cammermeyer was married from 1966 until 1980 and she and her husband had four sons. She was forced to resign upon her first pregnancy in 1968 following more than seven years of active duty as a result of then-applicable Army regulations. Due to a change in Army regulations, she was able to reenlist in the Army Reserve in 1972.

3. The recommendation for her Bronze Star provided, in part, that "[h]er professional and personal conduct merit the highest praise and reflect great credit upon herself and the United States Army Medical Service. . . ." Complaint (docket no. 1) at ¶ 4.6.

4. Her formal statement, written by the DIS Investigator based upon their conversation but edited and initialed by Col. Cammermeyer, states: "I am a Lesbian. Lesbianism is an orientation I have, emotional in nature, towards women. It does not imply sexual activity. . . ." Cammermeyer Decl., Ex. G.

5. The Army National Guard is comprised of two separate but overlapping organizations, the National Guards of the various states and the National Guard of the United States ("NGUS"). Under the dual system, a servicemember may not become an officer in the NGUS until he or she has been promoted to the same grade in the State National Guard and been "federally recognized." 10 U.S.C. § 591(a). A board of officers may be convened at any time to investigate an officer's "capacity and general fitness" to retain his or her federal recognition. 32 U.S.C. § 323(b). On the board's recommendation, an officer's federal recognition may be withdrawn, requiring discharge from the State National Guard. 32 U.S.C. §§ 323(b), 324(a)(2).

6. Cammermeyer is believed to be the highest ranking officer in any service of the U.S. Armed Forces to have been discharged because of homosexual status.

7. The Kentucky statute allowed close relatives and guardians to participate as parties in proceedings to commit the mentally retarded but not the mentally ill. The Court noted that mental retardation has its onset during a person's development, in contrast to mental illness, which may arise or manifest itself after minority when family members have far less knowledge of the medical condition. *Heller*, 125 L.Ed.2d at 272.

8. The Government contended at oral argument that under *Heller* no review of the rational basis for the Army regulation is necessary because "we are completely free to rely on rational speculation unsupported by empirical data or evidence." Tr. April 20, 1994 Hearing (docket no. 93) at 26.

9. *Dahl* is currently on appeal.

10. *Hardwick* involved a due process challenge to a Georgia statute which criminalized sodomy. Hardwick challenged the statute after being discovered engaging in sodomy with another consenting adult while in the privacy of his own home. The Supreme Court held that the Constitution confers no fundamental right upon homosexuals to engage in sodomy.

11. This is substantially the same Army regulation challenged by Cammermeyer.

12. In the present case, the Government also relies on *Dronenburg v. Zech*, 741 F.2d 1388 (D.C. Cir. 1984), to support its argument that homosexual orientation equals homosexual conduct. However, whether any agency of the federal government can discriminate against individuals merely because of sexual orientation remains an open question in the D.C. Circuit. See *Doe v. Casey*, 796 F.2d 1508, 1522 (D.C. Cir. 1986), aff'd in part and rev'd in part sub. nom.; *Webster v. Doe*, 486 U.S. 592 (1988); *Steffan v. Aspin*, 8 F.3d 57, 62 (D.C. Cir. 1993), vacated for reh'g en banc, 1994 U.S. App. LEXIS 9977 (D.C. Cir. January 7, 1994). Moreover, the Ninth Circuit distinguished *Dronenburg* in *Pruitt*, 963 F.2d at 1165 n. 4.

13. The military does not discharge servicemembers who identify themselves as alcoholics or drug addicts. See OPNAVINST 5350.4B (titled "Alcohol and Drug Abuse Prevention and Control"), Himes Decl., Ex. 7. Rather, the military requires actual evidence of substance abuse or that the individual's status impairs his or her ability to function in the military. *Id.*

14. Dr. M. Herek is an Associate Research Psychologist at the University of California at Davis.

15. Dr. Laura S. Brown is a clinical professor of psychology at the University of Washington.

16. Discharge is not required under these circumstances, however, if there are findings that: (i) such conduct is a departure from the member's usual and customary behavior; (ii) such conduct under all the circumstances is unlikely to recur; (iii) such conduct was not accomplished by use of force, coercion, or intimidation by the member during a period of military service; (iv) under the particular circumstances of the case, the member's continued presence in the Service is consistent with the interest of the Service in proper discipline, good order, and morale; and (v) the member does not desire to engage in or intend to engage in homosexual acts. 46 Fed. Reg. 9571, 9478 (January 29, 1981).

17. The Court may consider relevant factfinding by Congress as evidence in determining whether the Army's regulations possess a rational basis. See generally *EEOC v. Boeing Co.*, 843 F.2d 1213, 1217 (9th Cir.), cert. denied, 488 U.S. 889, 109 S.Ct. 222, 102 L.Ed.2d 212 (1988). Both parties rely on

the Congressional findings in the new policy, and neither party has filed a formal objection to the other party's use of this factfinding as evidence.

18. The MWG Report made findings as to each of the rationales stated in the Army regulation, with the exception of the security risk rationale, for the purpose of recommending to the President a new policy on homosexuals in the military that would "compl[y] with the President's direction to end discrimination while maintaining high standards of combat effectiveness and unit cohesion." See Memorandum for the Secretary of Defense, Attached to MWG Report, Otjen Dep., at Ex. 10.

19. The Congressional findings define unit cohesion as "the bonds of trust among individual service members that make the combat effectiveness of a military unit greater than the sum of the combat effectiveness of the individual unit members." 10 U.S.C. § 654(a)(7).

20. Defendants would appear to concede this, as the new "don't ask, don't tell" policy, as codified in 10 U.S.C. ¶ 654(a), does not include this rationale.

21. Assistant Secretary of Defense Dorn testified that President Clinton's statements reflect the views of the Department of Defense. Dorn Dep. at 31:1-9.

22. Defining "facts" as statistics, scientific studies, and reports rather than opinions and anecdotes.

23. This Court has already concluded that the Government's presumption has no foundation in law or fact.

24. This issue necessarily encompasses the basic question of whether individuals have a fundamental right under the constitution to their sexual orientation, whether heterosexual, homosexual, or bisexual.

25. Because no authority exists for plaintiff's proposition that homosexual orientation is a fundamental right, she analogizes to Supreme Court precedents that distinguish between "status" and "conduct" in the criminal context. See *Robinson v. California*, 370 U.S. 660, 82 S.Ct. 1417, 8 L.Ed.2d 758 (1962)(striking down California statute criminalizing status of narcotics addiction as violative of Eighth Amendment), and *Powell v. Texas*, 392 U.S. 514, 88 S.Ct. 2145, 20 L.Ed.2d 1254 (1968)(upholding conviction for public drunkenness, as distinguished from arrests based on status of being a chronic alcoholic).

26. The *Woodward* court stated: "While acts of sodomy have not been expressly admitted by Woodward, in view of [his statements, his known association with gays, and his failure to claim celibacy] we need not address the factual situation where there is action based *solely* on 'status as a person with a homosexual orientation.'" *Woodward*, 871 F.2d at 1074 n. 6.

27. The Court notes also that the Ninth Circuit, in *Pruitt*, 963 F.2d at 1165 n. 4, has questioned the *Woodward* court's analysis.

Margarethe Cammermeyer v. William J. Perry

Opinion of *Judge Zilly*

UNITED STATES DISTRICT COURT
WESTERN DISTRICT OF WASHINGTON

MARGARETHE CAMMERMEYER,
Plaintiff

v.

WILLIAM J. PERRY, Secretary of Defense,
et al.,

Defendants

Civil
Action
No. C92-942Z

DEFENDANTS' REPLY MEMORANDUM IN SUPPORT OF
THEIR MOTION FOR JUDGMENT ON THE PLEADINGS
OR, IN THE ALTERNATIVE, FOR SUMMARY JUDGMENT

STATEMENT

Plaintiff has responded to Defendants' motion for judgment on the pleadings or, in the alternative, for summary judgment[1] by reiterating her argument that the policy of the military on homosexual conduct violates the equal-protection component of the Fifth Amendment because it is "impermissibly based upon prejudice." Pl.'s Mem. Opp'n Defs.' Mot. J. Pleadings ("Pl.'s Opp'n") at 12. In addition, Plaintiff argues that the military's policy violates her right to privacy.[2] Because both of Plaintiff's arguments lack merit—and because Plaintiff has not shown that a trial is appropriate in this case—the Court should grant Defendants' motion for judgment on the pleadings or, in the alternative, for summary judgment, deny Plaintiff's motion for summary judgment, and dismiss this case.

ARGUMENT

I. PLAINTIFF HAS NOT SHOWN THAT THE MILITARY'S POLICY ON HOMOSEXUAL CONDUCT VIOLATES HER RIGHT TO EQUAL PROTECTION.

The standard for determining whether the military's policy on homosexual conduct in the military context satisfies the requirements of equal protection is whether the policy is rationally related to a permissible government interest. E.g., Pruitt v. Cheney, 963 F.2d 1160, 1165 (9th Cir, 1991), cert. denied, 113 S. Ct. 655 (1992); Ben-Shalom v. Marsh, 881 F.2d 454, 464 (7th Cir. 1989), cert. denied, 494 U.S. 1004 (1990); Woodward v. United States, 871 F.2d 1068, 1976 (Fed. Cir. 1989), cert. denied, 494 U.S. 1003 (1990). In Heller v. Doe, 113 S. Ct. 2637 (1993), the Supreme Court recently said:

> [R]ational basis review in equal protection analysis "is not a license for the courts to judge the wisdom of legislative choices." Nor does it authorize "the judiciary [to] sit as a superlegislature to judge the wisdom or desirability of legislative policy determinations made in areas that neither affect fundamental rights nor proceed along suspect lines." For these reasons, a classification neither involving fundamental rights nor proceeding along suspect lines is accorded a strong presumption of validity.

113 S. Ct. at 2642 (citations omitted). Accord FCC v. Beach Communications, 113 S. Ct. 2096, 2101-02 (1993).

In this case, the starting point for analysis is that homosexual acts are forbidden by the policy that Plaintiff challenges. It is well established that the military may constitutionally discharge servicemembers who engage in such acts. Dronenburg v. Zech, 741 F.2d 1388, 1397-98 (D.C. Cir. 1984); Rich v. Secretary of the Army, 735 F.2d 1220, 1229 (10th Cir. 1984); Beller v. Middendorf, 632 F.2d 788 (9th Cir. 1980), cert. denied, 452 U.S. 905 & 454 U.S. 855 (1981); see Ben-Shalom, 881 F.2d at 460-61 (upholding discharge based on servicemember's statement that she was a homosexual because military's policy targets those who are likely to engage in homosexual acts); Woodward, 871 F.2d at 1076 (same).

Consistent with the prohibition on acts, the military's policy also provides for the separation of persons who demonstrate a propensity or intent to engage in homosexual acts. This policy is grounded in the judgment that service "in the military environment of persons who engage in homosexual conduct or who, by their statements, demonstrate a propensity to engage in homosexual conduct, seriously impairs the accomplishment of the military mission." Army Regulation ("AR") 135-175 §§ 2-37(a), 2-38(a).

The principle that underlies the military's policy is the common sense notion that people act in accordance with their sexuality. *Ben-Shalom*, 881 F.2d at 464; see also *Woodward*, 871 F.2d at 1076; Nat'l Defense Research Inst., *Sexual Orientation & U.S. Military Personnel Policy: Options & Assessment*, 51, 64 (Rand 1993) (Otjen Dep. ex. 22)(a "strong correlation" exists between persons who identify themselves as homosexuals and homosexual conduct). Thus, the policy presumes that someone who states that he or she is a homosexual engages in, or has a propensity to engage in, homosexual acts. See AR 135-175 §§ 2-38(a), 2-39(b); see also *id.* § 2-37(a)(making the policy applicable to persons who, "by their statements, demonstrate a propensity to engage in homosexual conduct").

However, the presumption upon which the policy is based is not conclusive. Rather, the policy gives servicemembers the opportunity to rebut the presumption by showing that, in fact, they do not engage in homosexual acts and do not have a propensity or intent to do so. See AR 135-175 § 2-39(b)(requiring the discharge of servicemembers who come within the purview thereof "unless there is a further finding" that the servicemembers are not homosexuals, i.e., that they do not engage in, desire to engage in, or intend to engage in homosexual acts). The existence of the opportunity to rebut proves that the policy is directed at preventing homosexual acts, and is not concerned with a person's thoughts or status. The military is permitted to use the above presumption because the military need not take the risk of waiting for disruptive acts to occur. See *Ben-Shalom*, 881 F.2d at 460-61 ("In determining the composition of the Armed Forces, the Army does not have to take the risk that an admitted homosexual will not commit homosexual acts which may be detrimental to its assigned mission"); see also *Greer v. Spock*, 424 U.S. 828, 840 (1976)("nothing in the Constitution . . . disables a military commander from acting to avert what he perceives to be a clear danger to the loyalty, discipline or morale of troops . . . under his command").

Thus, leaders of the military have concluded that service in the armed forces by persons who engage in homosexual acts or demonstrate a propensity or intent to do so creates an unacceptable risk to the morale, good order and discipline, and unit cohesion that are the essence of military capability. Accordingly, the military's policy on homosexual conduct is rationally related to the legitimate governmental purpose of maintaining military readiness and combat effectiveness. See *Heller*, 113 S. Ct. at 2642; *Goldman v. Weinberger*, 475 U.S. 503, 507 (1986).

The fundamental expression of the military's judgment is found in the text of the policy itself. There, the military states that service in the armed forces by individuals who engage in homosexual acts or who, by their statements, demonstrate a propensity or intent to do so, would seriously impair the accomplishment of the military mission by adversely affecting the ability of the military to maintain discipline, good order, and morale; foster mutual trust and confidence among servicemembers; ensure the integrity of the system of rank and command; recruit and retain personnel; and facilitate the assignment and worldwide deployment of servicemembers, particularly in view of the close conditions affording minimal privacy under which servicemembers frequently must live and work. AR 135-175 § 2-37(a).

In enacting the current version of the military's policy in November 1993, Congress stressed the same concerns. Thus, Congress expressly found that the ban on homosexual conduct is a long standing element of military law that continues to be necessary in the unique circumstances of military service and that the presence in the armed forces of individuals who demonstrate a propensity or intent to engage in homosexual acts creates an unacceptable risk to the "high standards of morale, good order and discipline, and unit cohesion that are the essence of military capability." 10 U.S.C. § 654(a) (13), (15), *added by* National Defense Authorization Act for Fiscal Year 1994, Pub. L. No. 103-160, § 571(a), 107 Stat. 1547, 1670 (1993).

Further expressions of the professional judgment of military authorities that underlies the military's policy appear in the deposition testimony of Lieutenant General John P. Otjen, the chairman of the Military Working Group ("MWG") that the Secretary of Defense established in April 1993 to develop and assess alternative policy options with respect to military service by homosexuals. General Otjen testified about the tangible nature of unit cohesion; he described, on the basis of his own experience,[3] the adverse effects on unit cohesion that occur when an individual reveals that he or she is a homosexual; and he discussed the adverse effects on morale and retention that would result, in his judgment, from the abrogation of the military's policy. Otjen Dep. 188:5-190:3, 192:19-201:1, 263:17-265:3. In the report that the MWG issued in July 1993, the adverse effects on unit cohesion and readiness that, in the judgment of the group, would result from the abrogation of the military's policy were likewise discussed.[4] Summary Report of MWG at 5-7 (Otjen Dep. ex. 10).

To Plaintiff, none of the foregoing is sufficient because—according to Plaintiff—"prejudice against gay men and lesbians is the basis for defendants' military judgment." Pl.'s Opp'n at 22. However, Plaintiff's argument ignores the fact that the military's policy on homosexual conduct is grounded in professional military judgment, not prejudice, and that the military's judgment fully meets the requirements of equal protection. See *Goldman*, 475 U.S. at 507. In addition, the prevailing weight of judicial authority rejects the notion that the military's policy is based improperly on prejudice. In *Ben-Shalom*, for example, the court rejected the contention that the "asserted justifications" for the military's policy on homosexual conduct "illegitimately cater[ed] to private bias." The court said: "We do not believe that the concerns set forth in the military policy can be so easily dismissed as mere prejudice, though individual prejudice no doubt exists in the military and elsewhere. The new regulation, we find, clearly promotes a legitimate government interest sufficient to survive rational basis scrutiny." 881 F.2d at 465. *Accord Steffan v. Cheney*, 780 F. Supp. 1, 13 (D.D.C. 1991), rev'd, 8 F3d 57 (D.C. Cir. 1993), vacated & reh. en banc ordered, 1994 WL 6618 (D.C. Cir. Jan. 7, 1994) (en banc). *Contra Dahl v. Secretary of the U.S. Navy*, 830 F. Supp. 1319 (E.D. Cal. 1993).

Congress' codification of the new version of the military's policy bolsters the conclusion that the military's policy is not based on prejudice. Thus, the Senate Armed Services Committee emphasized that the military's policy is not based upon stereotypes but upon the "impact in the military setting of the conduct that is an integral element of homosexuality." S. Rep. No. 112, 103d Cong., 1st Sess. 282 (1993) (Glass Decl. (Feb. 25, 1994) ex. A). In doing so, the committee expressed its agreement with General Powell's distinction between race and sexuality: that skin color is a "benign, nonbehavioral characteristic" while sexuality is "perhaps the most profound of human characteristics" and is expressed by conduct. *Id.*

Even if the prejudice argument that Plaintiff makes had not been rejected by *Ben-Shalom* and Congress, no cause would exist for this Court to accept it. The proper inquiry here, as in other cases, is whether "there is a rational relationship between the disparity of treatment and some legitimate governmental purpose." *Heller*, 113 S. Ct. at 2642. In this case, the military's policy clearly promotes a government interest sufficient to survive rational basis scrutiny, i.e., the maintenance of combat effectiveness.

Nor does *City of Cleburne v. Cleburne Living Center*, 473 U.S. 432 (1985), the case that forms the principal basis for Plaintiff's prejudice argument, require a different result. *See* Pl.'s Opp'n at 3, 30; Mem. Supp. Pl.'s Mot. S.J. ("Pl.'s J. Mem.") at 1. First, *Cleburne* did not arise in the special context of the military. See *Rostker v. Goldberg*, 453 U.S. 57, 67 (1981)(Congress is not free to disregard the Constitution when it acts in the area of military affairs, "but the tests and limitations to be applied may differ because of the military context"). Second, the Court's holding in *Cleburne* was that "mere negative attitudes, or fear, *unsubstantiated by factors which are properly cognizable in a zoning proceeding*, are not permissible bases for treating a home for the mentally retarded differently from apartment houses, multiple dwellings, and the like." 473 U.S. at 448 (emphasis added). Thus, the negative societal attitudes toward retarded people in *Cleburne* were not "properly cognizable" or relevant to legitimate governmental interests in the zoning proceeding, because it was not the responsibility of the city zoning board to make sure that neighbors could get along and live in harmony. Quite the opposite is true in this case, where the military's policy is based on the properly cognizable—indeed, fundamental—interest in maintaining unit cohesion and military readiness.

The military's policy on homosexual conduct does not embody "a bare. . . desire to harm" homosexuals—a plainly "[il]legitimate" objective. See *Cleburne*, 473 U.S. at 447. Moreover, the policy does not represent "unthinking[]" or "reflexive[]" government action, nor is it an "accidental byproduct of a traditional way of thinking about [homosexuals]." *Rostker*, 453 U.S. at 72, 74. Rather, it reflects the considered professional judgment of military authorities, which was recently subjected to careful, thorough, and open-minded review as to "what is best for military effectiveness." S. Rep. No. 112, 103d Cong., 1st Sess. 279 (1993). Because "the policy is based on prudence, not prejudice," see *id.*, the equal-protection challenge to the policy that Plaintiff makes should be rejected.[5]

II. PLAINTIFF HAS NOT SHOWN THAT THE MILITARY'S POLICY VIOLATES HER RIGHT TO PRIVACY.

In a series of cases challenging the military's policy on homosexual conduct, servicemembers who have engaged in homosexual acts or made statements giving rise to a presumption that they engaged or had a propensity to engage in homosexual acts have argued that the right to privacy precluded their separation from the military. In each such case, the argument has been flatly rejected. The courts rejecting the argument include the Ninth Circuit. E.g., *Schowengerdt v. United States*, 944 F.2d 483, 490 (9th Cir. 1991), cert. denied, 112 S. Ct. 1514 (1992); *Ben-Shalom*, 881 F.2d at 465; *Woodward*, 871 F.2d at 1074; *Dronenburg*, 741 F.2d at 1391-97; *Rich*, 735 F.2d at 1228. See also *Hatheway v. Secretary of the Army*, 641 F.2d 1376, 1384 (9th Cir.), cert. denied, 454 U.S. 864 (1981)(holding that the provision of the Uniform Code of Military Justice criminalizing sodomy did not violate the plaintiff's right to "personal autonomy").

Notwithstanding this clear line of authority, Plaintiff argues that her discharge under the military's policy was a violation of her right to privacy because it was based exclusively on her having stated that she is a homosexual. Pl.'s Opp'n at 31-33. On this ground, Plaintiff attempts to distinguish *Schowengerdt v. United States*, 944 F.2d 483 (9th Cir. 1991), cert. denied, 112 S. Ct. 1514 (1992). Pl.'s Opp'n at 30-31. In *Schowengerdt*, the Ninth Circuit rejected the right to privacy claim of a servicemember who was discharged from the military after it came to light that he had written a letter in which he described his sexual activities. See 944 F.2d at 486. The Ninth Circuit said: "Schowengerdt's substantive due process argument, based on a right to privacy, is . . . meritless. We have rejected such a challenge to regulations nearly identical to those requiring Schowengerdt's discharge here, and we did so under a higher level of scrutiny than is currently required." 944 F.2d at 490 (citing *High Tech Gays, Bowers V. Hardwick*, 478 U.S. 186 (1986), and *Beller v. Middendorf*, 632 F.2d 788, 793, 794 (9th Cir. 1980), cert. denied, 452 U.S. 905 & 454 U.S. 855 (1981)).

The distinction that Plaintiff attempts to draw between homosexual acts and statements indicating a propensity or intent to engage in such acts is without merit. Neither the Supreme Court nor the Ninth Circuit has ever suggested that a servicemember has a "fundamental right" to remain in the military after making statements demonstrating a propensity or intent to engage in homosexual acts. In addition, the "privacy expectations" that one might enjoy in civilian life "cannot be compared to the substantially more limited privacy expectations accompanying military life." *Ben-Shalom*, 881 F.2d at 465.

Nor is there any merit to Plaintiff's claim that her discharge under the military's policy violated her right to privacy because the discharge was "precisely for [her] most private integral thought—the nature of [her] sexual orientation." Pl.'s Opp'n at 33. As the text of the policy makes clear, individuals who are discharged for stating that they are homosexuals are not discharged for *thinking* about their sexual orientation; they are discharged for making statements indicating that they either engage in homosexual acts or have a propensity or intent to do so.[6] AR 135-175, § 2-37(a). The distinction is a proper one. In *Ben-Shalom*, for example, a case in which a servicemember was discharged from the military after stating that she was a homosexual, the court ruled that the plaintiff's "lesbian acknowledgment" could "rationally and reasonably be viewed" as reliable evidence of her "propensity to engage in homosexual conduct." 881 F.2d at 464. The court said:

> Such an assumption cannot be said to be without individual exceptions, but it is compelling evidence that plaintiff has in the past and is likely to again engage in such conduct. To this extent, therefore, the regulation does not classify plaintiff based merely upon her status as a lesbian, but upon reasonable inferences about her probable conduct in the past and in the future. *The Army need not shut its eyes to the practical realities of this situation, nor be compelled to engage in the sleuthing of soldier's personal relationships for evidence of homosexual conduct in order to enforce its ban on homosexual acts. . . .*

Id.(emphasis supplied). See also S. Rep. No. 112, 103d Cong., 1st Sess. 282 (1993) (similarly).

In view of the foregoing, Plaintiff's right to privacy claim should be dismissed.

III. PLAINTIFF HAS NOT SHOWN THAT A TRIAL IS NECESSARY IN THIS CASE.

Cases challenging the constitutionality of the military's policy on homosexual conduct have typically been decided on the basis of dispositive motions, not trials. E.g., *Pruitt*, 963 F.2d at 1162; *Schowengerdt*, 944 F.2d at 484; *Woodward*, 871 F.2d at 1069; *Dronenburg*, 741 F.2d at 1389; *Hatheway*, 641 F.2d at 1379; *Beller*, 632 F.2d at 793, 794; *Dahl*, 830 F. Supp. at 1320; *Meinhold v. United States Dep't of Defense*, 808 F. Supp. 1455, 1456 (C.D. Cal. 1993) (app. pend'g); *Steffan*, 780 F. Supp. at 2; *Ben-Shalom v. Marsh*, 703 F. Supp. 1372, 1373 (W.D. Wis.), rev'd, 881 F.2d 454 (7th Cir. 1989), cert. denied, 494 U.S. 1004 (1990). But see *Rich*, 735 F.2d at 1223-24 (three-day trial). The fact that so many other challenges to the military's policy have been resolved on the basis of dispositive motions suggests that the issues presented by this case are issues of law, not issues of fact, and that a trial is neither necessary nor appropriate.

In addition, Plaintiff's principal claim in this case is that the policy of the military on homosexual conduct violates the equal-protection component of the Fifth Amendment. A trial is not necessary to resolve this claim because the government need not present evidence to prove the rational basis of the policy.

As the Supreme Court said in *Heller*: "A State . . . has no obligation to produce evidence to sustain the rationality of a statutory classification. '*[A] legislative choice is not the subject of courtroom factfinding* and may be based on rational speculation unsupported by evidence or empirical data.'" 113 S. Ct. at 2643 (quoting *Beach Communications*, 113 S. Ct. at 2098) (emphasis supplied).

At the recent status conference, Plaintiff suggested that she might require an evidentiary hearing of up to a week's duration in order to attempt to show that the military's policy is based on prejudice. However, Plaintiff has already filed a motion for summary judgment, thereby representing to the Court that "there is no genuine issue as to any material fact." Fed. R. Civ. P. 56(c); see *Anderson v. Liberty Lobby*, 477 U.S. 242, 247-48 (1986). In addition, in moving for summary judgment, Plaintiff has filed 55 pages of briefs and hundreds of pages of exhibits and deposition transcripts on the prejudice issue. See Pl.'s J. Mem. at 1-2, 15-47; Pl.'s Opp'n at 9-30. In doing so, Plaintiff has made no showing that any live testimony is necessary to supplement the record. As a result, Plaintiff has not shown why this case should not be resolved on the basis on the parties' dispositive motions.

CONCLUSION

For the foregoing reasons, Defendants' motion for judgment on the pleadings or, in the alternative, for summary judgment should be granted and Plaintiff's motion for summary judgment should be denied.

Respectfully submitted,

FRANK W. HUNGER
Assistant Attorney General

KATRINA C. PFLAUMER
United States Attorney

VINCENT M. GARVEY
DAVID M. GLASS
Attorneys, Dep't of Justice
901 E Street N.W., Room 1080
Washington, D.C. 20530
Tel: (202) 514-4469
Fax: (202) 616-8470

Attorneys for Defendants

OF COUNSEL:

CAPTAIN TARA O. HAWK
Department of the Army
Office of the Judge Advocate General

NOTES

1. A motion for judgment on the pleadings is appropriate where, as here, the moving party has already filed an answer. See Fed. R. Civ. P. 12(c). In this case, the alternative motion for judgment on the pleadings that Defendants have filed is tantamount to a motion to dismiss under Fed. R. Civ. P. 12(b)(6) for failure to state a cliam upon which relief can be granted. See *Aldabe v. Aldabe*, 616 F.2d 1089, 1093 (9th Cir. 1980).

2. In the Complaint, Plaintiff claims that the military's policy on homosexual conduct violates her right to equal protection, freedom of speech, substantive due process, and privacy; that the policy violates the doctrine of separation of powers; and that the policy violates the right of the State of Washington to select the officers of the state militia. Compl. ¶¶ 6.1-6.6. In moving for judgment on the pleadings or, in the alternative, for summary judgment, Defendants have responded to and refuted each of these claims. Mem. P. & A. Supp. Defs.' Mot. J. Pleadings or, in the Alt., Summ. J. at 9-27. In responding to Defendants' motion, Plaintiff has limited her discussion to the equal-protection and privacy claims that she raises. Pl.'s Opp'n at 1-40. As a result, Defendants' motion for judgment on the pleadings or, in the alternative summary judgment should be viewed as unopposed as to all of Plaintiff's other claims.

3. General Otjen is a graduate of West Point and a decorated combat veteran of the Vietnam War who has served in the Army for the last 29 years. Otjen Resume (Otjen Dep. ex. 20) at 102; Otjen Dep. 19:15-22:8, 23:21-24:15. In the course of his career, he has commanded troops at the company, battalion, brigade, division, and army levels. Otjen Resume at 102; Otjen Dep. 10:8-17.

4. In her recent brief, Plaintiff spends much of her time attempting to show that General Otjen and the other members of the MWG were ideologues whose efforts to consider the need for continuation of the military's policy on homosexual conduct were conclusory and pro forma. See Pl.'s Opp'n at 14-29. The record shows, however, that the members of the MWG "did an incredible amount of reading" in order to "get a comprehensive spread of literature . . . representing all facets of the issue"; that the materials reviewed by the members of the MWG ranged from a videotape known as "The Gay Agenda," "a widely circulated, church produced video that focuses on lewd behavior in gay pride parades," to writings by the late Randy Shilts, "the best selling author and San Francisco Chronicle reporter whose ground-breaking work helped frame the national debate about the gay rights movement and AIDS"; that the materials reviewed by the members of the MWG also included a collection of literature provided to the MWG by the Campaign for Military

Service ("CMS"), "a coalition lobbying to end the military ban on gays"; that the members of the MWG received a briefing from leaders of CMS, including Thomas Stoddard, the former executive director of the Lambda Legal Defense and Education Fund, Plaintiff's cocounsel in this action; and that the members of the MWG heard the views of panels of servicemembers chosen by each of the military services and intended to represent a cross section of the armed forces in terms of rank, branch of service, gender, and ethnic group. Otjen Dep. 151:21-153:12, 173:21-174:14, 255:17-258:1; Bettina Boxall, *Gays, Foes Seek Spin That Sells; Both Sides Have Escalated Propaganda Battle*, L.A. Times, Oct. 12, 1993, pt. A at 1 (Glass Decl. (Mar. 22, 1994) ex. A); Lori Olszewski & David Tuller, *Writer Randy Shilts Dies at 42—Pioneer Coverage of AIDS*, S.F. Chron., Feb. 14, 1994, at A1 (Glass Decl. (Mar. 22, 1994) ex. B); Ron Alexander, "*Chronicle*," N.Y. Times, Nov. 27, 1993, § 1 at 20 (Glass Decl. (Mar. 22, 1994) ex. C).

5. The reliance that Plaintiff places on *Palmore v. Sidoti*, 466 U.S. 429 (1984), see Pl.'s Opp'n at 3, is misplaced because the challenged policy in that case occurred in the civilian context and involved a racial classification. Unlike race, which occupies a unique position in our legal system and in our history, homosexual conduct, or the propensity to engage in homosexual conduct, is not per se an illegitimate consideration for the military to take into account when establishing military regulations. See *High Tech Gays v. Defense Indus. Sec Clearance Office*, 895 F.2d 563, 571-74 (9th Cir.), reh'g & reh'g en banc denied, 909 F.2d 375 (9th Cir. 1990) (for purposes of equal-protection analysis, homosexuals constitute neither a "suspect" nor a "quasi-suspect class").

6. Relying on *Robinson v. California*, 370 U.S. 660 (1962), *Powell v. Texas*, 392 U.S. 514 (1968), and *Jacobson v. United States*, 112 S. Ct. 1535 (1992), Plaintiff notes that the criminal law makes distinctions between a person's status and his or her conduct. See Pl.'s Opp'n at 34-36. However, *Robinson*, *Powell*, and *Jacobson* are inapposite because those cases involve criminal punishment, not discharge from military service. Given its unique mission of remaining prepared for deployment at a moment's notice to conditions of extreme danger around the world, the military must be entitled to take preventive measure against acts that would undermine military readiness and effectiveness.

Index

community to publicize, 238-39

opposition to the ban and role of legal framework, 167-68

right to privacy issues, 122, 195, 202, 213-14, 217

sex discrimination issues, 240-41

substantive due process, 217

success of, 240, 249

support for lesbian/gay efforts, 122-23, 199-203

treatment of cases involving homosexuals in the military, 209-14

use of, by lesbian/gay community, 195-220, 238-39

Credible information standard, misapplication of, 252, 257

Crime, associated with homosexuals, 50

Crittenden, S. H., Jr., 272

Crittenden Report (1957), 18, 272-73, 310

Cuba, 19

Dahl v. Secretary of the United States Navy, 304-5, 318, 326, 329

D'Amato, Al, 231, 232

Daniels v. Williams, 315

Dannemeyer, William, 64

Daschle, Tom, 112

Death threats, 257, 264, 265

Defense Advisory Committee on Women in the Services (DACOWITS), 240

Defense Authorization Act (1994), 5, 235

Dellums, Ronald, 74, 158-59, 164

Denmark, 7, 8, 12

Discharge proceedings, against women, 77, 79-80

Discharge rates

after the compromise, 249, 258-59, 282

in the 1950s, 73

related to homosexuality, comparison by race, gender, and rank, 27-35

under lesbian/gay exclusion policy, statistics on, 7

Discipline, affects of homosexuals on, 57

Discipline and Punish (Foucault), 234

Disease, associated with homosexuals, 51-52

Dodge, Kirstin, 34

DOD's Policy on Homosexuality, 8

Doe v. Commonwealth's Attorney of Richmond, 207-8, 214, 218

Dole, Robert, 154

Domi, Tanya, 178, 238-39

Donnel, Joseph S., 274

Don't Ask, Don't Tell, Don't Pursue policy

Barney Frank compromise, 159-63

Clinton's reasons for, 232-33

creation of, 5, 128, 157

details in, 117-18

"Don't Ask" defined, 251

"Don't Ask" violations, 251, 254-55

"Don't Ask" violations, analysis of, 261

"Don't Harass" defined, 252

"Don't Harass" violations, 252, 257-58

"Don't Harass" violations, analysis of, 263-64

"Don't Pursue" defined, 251-52

"Don't Pursue" violations, 252, 256-57

"Don't Pursue" violations, analysis of, 253-64

"Don't Tell" defined, 251

General Accounting Office
(GAO), 4, 7-15, 28, 31, 231,
233, 274, 310
Gergen, David, 118, 120
Germany, 7, 15
Gesell, Gerhard, 209-10
Gingrich, Newt, 5, 154
Glenn, John, 163
Goldberg, Arthur, 208, 217
Goldman v. Weinberger, 301,
325
Goldwater, Barry, 36
Gomulka, Eugene, 59, 64
Gossett, Ed, 60
Grant De Pauw, Linda, 82-83
Grapple, USS, 76
Greece, 12
Greer v. Spock, 325
Griswold v. Connecticut, 202,
208, 217

Hackworth, David H., 53, 55,
57, 60, 64, 279
Harassment
lesbian baiting and sexual, 75,
84, 87-88
physical and verbal abuse, 257,
264-65
Hardwick, Michael, 212
Harmon v. Brucker, 199-200
Harrison, Mary Beth, 76, 84, 91
Harvard Women's Law Journal,
72
*Hatheway v. Secretary of the
Army*, 328, 329
Hattoy, Bob, 178, 233
Heller v. Doe, 300, 301, 303,
304, 309-10, 324, 325, 327,
330
*High Tech Gays v. Defense
Indus. Sec. Clearance Office*,
299, 300, 304, 316, 328
Hobbs, Michael, 213
Hoffman, Clare E., 61, 66
Holcomb, Thomas, 54

Hollow Hope, The (Rosenberg),
220
Holm, Jeanne, 81-82, 236
Holobaugh, James, 277
Homocrats, 283, 285
Homo/heterosexual segregation
proposal, 35-36
Homophobia, compared to
racism, 49-62
Homosexual act, definition of,
77, 128
Homosexuality exclusion policies
Department of Defense
directives on, 6-7
discharge rates related to
homosexuality, comparison by
race, gender, and rank, 27-35
exclusion policies of other
countries, 7, 8-15
General Accounting Office
reports on, 4, 7-15
lessons from the exclusion
policies of other countries,
19-23
policy proposals and revisions
regarding, 35-38
race and gender issues, 23-27
RAND report on, 4, 7-8, 15-
18, 28, 115, 273
Homosexuality exclusion
policies, reasons for
aversion to social
experimentation, 62-66
discipline would be affected by
homosexuals, 57
homosexuals and heterosexuals
cannot serve together, 53-58
homosexuals are not fit to
serve, 50-53
homosexuals would encounter
violence, 58
military uniqueness, 64
morale would be harmed by
homosexuals, 53-55
performance/efficiency would

be affected by homosexuals, 60-61

recruitment and retention rates would be affected by homosexuals, 55-56

rights of heterosexuals would be compromised, 58-60

role models/command would be affected by homosexuals, 56-57

worldwide and home views of U.S. would be compromised, 61-62

Homosexuals, identifying, 278-81, 286-88

Homosexuals, views toward changing, 237

crime associated with homosexuals, 50

disease associated with homosexuals, 51-52

history of treatment/reactions toward, 5-7, 270-71, 275-79

lack of performance associated with homosexuals, 52-53

Homosexuals in the Military: Policies and Practices of Foreign Countries, 8, 12, 14

Human Rights Campaign Fund (HRCF), 175, 283, 284

Humphrey, Mary Ann, 33

Hungary, 12

Hunter, Nan, 215, 218

Hurley v. Irish-American Gay Group, 218

Immigration and Naturalization Service (INS), 206, 208, 211

Interest groups concerned with lesbian and gay rights, 199-203

Ireland, 7

Israel, 4, 7, 15, 19, 21-22

Jackson, Charles R., 48, 53, 61, 62, 65

Jackson v. Brigle, 304

Jackson Water Works, Inc. v. Public Utilities Commn, 301

Jacobson v. United States, 306

Japan, 12

Johnson, Magic, 237

Joint Chiefs of Staff, reaction to ban, 119, 169-70, 282

Katzenstein, Mary Fainsod, 175

Kelso, Frank, 74

Kennedy, Edward, 152, 157, 163, 279

Kennelly, Barbara, 112

Knight, Robert H., 48, 63

Knox, Frank, 58

Korb, Lawrence J., 36, 238, 260-61, 307, 312-13

Korea, Republic of, 7

Krosnick, Jon, 135

Lambda Legal Defense and Education Fund (LLDEF), 205, 207, 209, 210, 213

Legal decision/strategies. *See* Courts and legal decisions

Lesbian baiting, 71, 72

See also Women in the military

effects of, 85-87

recommendations for handling, 87-92

sexual accessibility and, 84-85

sexual harassment and, 75, 84

women in nontraditional jobs seen as a threat to men, 81-84

Lesbian/gay community

development of gay liberation movement and emergence of a legal strategy, 203-9

gay identity politics, 286-88

public spectacles used by, 233-35, 237-40

reactions to ban, 117, 119-20, 121-23, 124-25

weaknesses and disadvantages

88
as a threat to men, 81-84
Women's Army Auxiliary Corps
(WAAC), 73
Women's Auxiliaries, 72, 73
Woodard, Isaac, 241
Woodlawn, Holly, 237
Wood v. Davison, 218
Woodward v. Moore, 214
Woodward v. United States, 317,
324, 325, 328, 329
Woodyard, John H., 26
Worker's Defense League, 200
World War I, 5
World War II, 5-6, 73

Zeeland, Steven, 28
Zilly, Thomas, 122